Change and Continuity in the 2020 Elections

Change and Continuity in the 2020 Elections

John H. Aldrich, Jamie L. Carson,
Brad T. Gomez, and Jennifer L. Merolla

ROWMAN & LITTLEFIELD
Lanham • Boulder • New York • London

Published by Rowman & Littlefield
An imprint of The Rowman & Littlefield Publishing Group, Inc.
4501 Forbes Boulevard, Suite 200, Lanham, Maryland 20706
www.rowman.com

86–90 Paul Street, London EC2A 4NE

British Library Cataloguing in Publication Information Available

Library of Congress Cataloging-in-Publication Data

Names: Aldrich, John H., 1947- author. | Carson, Jamie L., author. | Gomez, Brad T., 1970- author. | Merolla, Jennifer Lee, 1975- author.
Title: Change and continuity in the 2020 elections / John H. Aldrich; Jamie L. Carson; Brad T. Gomez and Jennifer L. Merolla.
Description: Lanham, Maryland : Rowman & Littlefield, [2022] | Includes bibliographical references and index.
Identifiers: LCCN 2021055179 (print) | LCCN 2021055180 (ebook) | ISBN 9781538164815 (Cloth : acid-free paper) | ISBN 9781538164822 (Paperback : acid-free paper) | ISBN 9781538164839 (eBook)
Subjects: LCSH: Presidents—United States—Election—2020. | United States. Congress—Elections—2020. | Voting—United States. | Elections—United States.
Classification: LCC JK526 2020 .A54 2022 (print) | LCC JK526 2020 (ebook) | DDC 324.973--dc23/eng/20220111
LC record available at https://lccn.loc.gov/2021055179
LC ebook record available at https://lccn.loc.gov/2021055180

♾️™ The paper used in this publication meets the minimum requirements of American National Standard for Information Sciences—Permanence of Paper for Printed Library Materials, ANSI/NISO Z39.48-1992.

To David W. Rohde

Contents

Preface

In the days following the 2020 presidential election, it became clear that Republican Donald Trump was defeated in his bid for reelection despite winning approximately 10 million more votes than he had received in 2016. On the night of the election, many states were too close to call despite the fact that Trump maintained a slim lead in most. Over the course of the next few days, several of these states shifted to Biden as the large number of mail-in ballots cast as a result of the COVID-19 pandemic were counted. Trump proclaimed this shifting tally to be evidence of election irregularity and railed against the late state returns as they came in. Trump had repeatedly claimed throughout the fall that the only way he would lose was if the Democrats cheated, and he encouraged his supporters to eschew mail-in ballots in favor of voting in person. In the end, in virtually every state, voters divided along party lines in their preferred method of voting, with Democrats being more likely to vote by mail and Republicans choosing more traditional modes of voting, which is why many state outcomes shifted as the mail-in ballots were counted.

In the House of Representatives, Republicans picked up a net of 10 seats in the 2020 elections, but the Democrats managed to maintain control of the chamber with a narrow majority for the 117th Congress. Prior to the election, Republicans controlled 53 seats in the Senate, whereas the Democrats held 47. Following the November 2020 elections, along with two Georgia runoff elections held on January 5, 2021, the Democrats and Republicans effectively hold an equal number of seats in the Senate, but Democrats control the chamber since they also control the vice presidency—the vice president serves as the president of the Senate and holds a tie-breaking vote. This is the first time since 2000 that the Senate is so narrowly controlled by one party, a circumstance that has created numerous headaches for the Democrats

ix

throughout 2021 as they have sought to deal with the ongoing pandemic and economic reform, adopt legislation enhancing the nation's infrastructure, deal with immigration issues, and pass a multi-trillion-dollar budget among many other legislative initiatives.

Is America in the midst of an electoral transformation? What were the sources of Biden's victory in 2020, and how do they differ from Democratic coalitions of the past? Does his victory signal a long-term positive trajectory for Democrats' chances in presidential elections? And are the electoral forces at play in presidential elections similar to those that structure congressional elections? These are the sorts of questions that we seek to answer here.

OUR ANALYSIS

In our study of the 2020 elections, we rely on a wide variety of evidence. Because the bulk of our analysis focuses on individuals' voting decisions, we rely extensively on survey evidence—four surveys in particular. In studying voter turnout, we employ the Current Population Survey (CPS) conducted by the US Census Bureau. The CPS provides information on the registration and voting behavior of more than 131,000 individuals from more than 80,000 households. In examining voting patterns, we rely heavily on a survey of more than 24,500 voters interviewed as they exited the voting booths; this survey, conducted by Edison Research for a consortium of news organizations, is commonly referred to as the "pool poll." We employ pool poll data in our analyses of congressional midterm elections as well. In studying the party loyalties of the American electorate, we also analyze data from the General Social Survey (GSS) conducted by the National Opinion Research Center at the University of Chicago, which measured party identification twenty-seven times from 1972 through 2008, usually relying on about 1,500 respondents.

Our main source of survey data is the 2020 American National Election Studies (ANES) survey based on 8,280 pre-election and 7,499 post election interviews. Because of the COVID-19 pandemic, and for the first time in the history of the study, the ANES did not conduct face-to-face interviews with respondents. Instead, respondents in the 2020 ANES were randomly assigned to one of three sequential mode groups: web only, mixed web (i.e., web and phone), and mixed video (i.e., video, web, and phone). In this volume, our analyses utilize the July 19, 2021 release of the ANES data, which is downloadable at https://electionstudies.org/data-center/2020-time-series -study/. The 2020 ANES is part of an ongoing series funded mainly by the National Science Foundation. These surveys, carried out originally by a team of scholars at the University of Michigan, began with a small study of the 1948 election; the first major study was in 1952. The ANES investigative team has studied every subsequent presidential election, as well as all thirteen midterm elections from 1954 to 2002. The 2020 ANES was conducted jointly by Stanford University and the University of Michigan. In the course of our book, we use data from all thirty-two surveys conducted between 1948 and 2020.

The ANES data are available to scholars throughout the world. Although we are not responsible for the data collection, we are responsible for our analyses. The scholars and staff at the ANES are responsible for neither our analyses nor our interpretation of these data. Similarly, the organizers and researchers of the CPS, GSS, and national pool poll bear no responsibility for our analyses or interpretation.

Acknowledgments

Many people assisted us with this study. We deeply appreciate the hard work of our research assistants, Aaron Hitefield and Spencer Hardin at the University of Georgia, Joseph Bommarito at Florida State University, and Stephanie DeMora at the University of California, Riverside. Aaron assisted with the data analyses for chapters 2, 9, and 10; Spencer read over drafts of chapters 2 and 9 and provided valuable feedback; Joseph assisted with the creation of our maps, and Stephanie assisted with the data analyses for chapters 5, 6, and 7.

In our study of turnout, we were greatly assisted by Michael P. McDonald of the University of Florida, who for several years has provided scholars with a valuable resource on voter turnout. McDonald's website, the United States Elections Project (http://www.electproject.org), presents detailed national- and state-level estimates of voter turnout based on both voting-age and voting-eligible population estimates.

Several years ago, Russell J. Dalton of the University of California at Irvine and the late Robert W. Jackman of the University of California at Davis helped us locate information about cross-national estimates of voter turnout. And we thank Gary C. Jacobson of the University of California, San Diego, for sharing his data on 2020 House and Senate race types.

We are grateful for support from the Department of Political Science at the University of Georgia, the Department of Political Science at Florida State University, and the Department of Political Science at the University of California, Riverside.

For the first time in forty years, we have a new publisher of this long-standing text and are pleased to have the chance to work with Jonathan Sisk at Rowman & Littlefield on this latest edition. His encouragement and support along the way has been invaluable. We are grateful to Sarah Sichina, our assistant editor, and Crystal Branson, our production editor, for their diligent work on our behalf. We also thank Kim Lyons, Higher Education Marketing Manager, for her efforts in marketing the book and Nivethitha Tamilselvan, who did an excellent job copyediting the manuscript.

This book continues a series of books that began with a study of the 1980 elections. In many places we refer to earlier editions of this book, all of which were published by CQ Press. Some of this material is available online through the CQ Voting and Elections Collection, which can be accessed through many academic and public libraries.

Similar to our earlier books, this one was a collective enterprise in which we divided the labor. Like the volume preceding this one, however, membership in the collective changed. With John Aldrich's retirement from the writing and data analysis, Jennifer Merolla was invited to join the authorship team. Brad Gomez had primary responsibility for the introduction and chapters 3, 4, and 8; Jennifer Merolla for chapters 1, 5, 6, and 7; and Jamie Carson for chapters 2, 9, and 10. Carson, Gomez, and Merolla collaborated on chapter 11.

Finally, we dedicate this book to our friend and colleague, David W. Rohde, who recently retired from Duke University. Dave coauthored eighteen volumes in the *Change and Continuity* series, beginning with the first volume in 1980. Though he retired from writing on this series, Dave's influence remains. We are indebted to him for his contributions to this project.

We appreciate feedback from our readers. Please contact us if you disagree with our interpretations, find factual errors, or want further clarification about our methods or our conclusions.

John H. Aldrich
Duke University
aldrich@duke.edu

Jamie L. Carson
University of Georgia
carson@uga.edu

Brad T. Gomez
Florida State University
bgomez@fsu.edu

Jennifer L. Merolla
University of California-Riverside
merolla@ucr.edu

Introduction

Presidential elections in the United States are partly ritual, a reaffirmation of our Democratic values. But they are also far more than ceremony. The presidency confers a great deal of power, and those powers expanded during most of the twentieth and into the twenty-first centuries. It is precisely because of these immense powers that presidential elections have at times played a major role in determining public policy and altered the course of American history.

The 1860 election, which brought Abraham Lincoln and the Republicans to power and ousted a divided Democratic Party, focused on whether slavery should be extended to the western territories. After Lincoln's election, eleven southern states attempted to secede from the Union, the Civil War broke out, and, ultimately, the US government abolished slavery. Thus, an antislavery plurality—Lincoln received only 40 percent of the popular vote—set in motion a chain of events that freed some four million black Americans.

In the 1896 election, Republican William McKinley defeated the Democrat and Populist William Jennings Bryan, thereby beating back the challenge of western and agricultural interests to the prevailing financial and industrial power of the East. Although Bryan mounted a strong campaign, winning 47 percent of the popular vote to McKinley's 51 percent, the election set a clear course for a policy of high tariffs and the continuation of the gold standard for American money.

Lyndon B. Johnson's 1964 landslide over Republican Barry Goldwater provided the clearest set of policy alternatives of any election in the twentieth century.[1] Goldwater offered "a choice, not an echo," advocating far more conservative social and economic policies than Johnson. When Johnson received 61 percent of the popular vote to Goldwater's 38 percent, he saw his victory as a mandate for his Great Society programs, the most far-reaching social legislation since World War II. The election also seemed to offer

1

a clear choice between escalating American involvement in Vietnam and restraint. But America's involvement in Vietnam expanded after Johnson's election, leading to growing opposition to Johnson within the Democratic Party, and four years later, he did not seek reelection.

Only the future can determine the ultimate importance of the 2020 election. Some scholars argue that American elections have become less important with time, and there is some truth to their arguments.[2] Yet elections do offer important choices on public policy, choices that may affect the course of governance—even if only in the short term.

Despite the continued, nearly twenty-year-long presence of American combat forces in Afghanistan, the 2020 presidential election focused mainly on the COVID-19 pandemic and its economic fallout, as well as issues of racial injustice. In the spring of 2020, during the early stages of the presidential campaign, America was enjoying the longest economic expansion in the nation's history. The country had experienced unfettered economic growth since Barack Obama's first year in office over a decade earlier, and the rate of growth had accelerated during Donald Trump's first term. The country's unemployment rate was at a fifty-year low. Median household income had grown, and the percentage of Americans below the poverty line declined. Then the pandemic struck.

The COVID-19 pandemic was the most impactful since the influenza pandemic of 1918.[3] By April 2020, about half of the world's population was under some form of lockdown, observing curfews, quarantines, or stay-at-home orders. Social distancing and mask wearing became commonplace, if not required by law. There were widespread food shortages, and panic buying made basic goods, such as toilet paper, in short supply. Businesses—large and small—closed their doors. About 16 million jobs were lost in the United States between the beginning of March and the end of April, and unemployment reached its highest level since 1941. The Standard and Poor's 500 stock-market index dropped 34 percent in a month, wiping out about three years of gains. Consumer spending ground to a halt, and the United States gross domestic product fell 38 percent in the second quarter.[4]

All presidents face crises, and how they respond to these events can shape their electoral fates and historical legacies. Trump's handling of the COVID crisis was on public display. In mid-March, the administration's Coronavirus Task Force began to deliver daily briefings on the status of the pandemic. Public health officials, including Dr. Deborah Birx, the US Global AIDS Coordinator and White House Coronavirus Response Coordinator, Dr. Anthony Fauci, Director of the National Institute of Allergy and Infection Diseases, and the Surgeon General, Vice Admiral Jerome Adams, informed Americans about the spread of the virus and provided the latest information about how to contain its spread. Within days, the president began to appear alongside his medical team, and he regularly commandeered the proceedings.[5] After the medical officials warned of the severity and contagiousness of the virus, Trump downplayed its seriousness, comparing it to the flu.[6] He touted unproven remedies, such as the anti-malaria drug, hydroxychloroquine, and he asked Dr. Birx to investigate whether ultraviolet light or injecting household disinfectants might kill the coronavirus.[7] The president, a former reality TV star, also bragged about the high ratings his press conferences were receiving, stating that they were as high as the season finale of *The Bachelor* and *Monday Night Football*.[8] The ratings eventually declined. A national poll conducted by the Associated Press-National Opinion Research Center (NORC) showed that a majority of Americans trusted the information they received from Trump about coronavirus "a little" or "not at all."[9] And the percentage of Americans in the Gallup Poll who said they "disapproved" of Trump's handling of his job increased by 13 points.[10]

Trump, who rarely wore a mask in public and would later contract the virus, argued that lockdowns were making Americans worse off, tweeting, "We cannot let the cure be worse than the problem itself."[11] In late April, Trump urged governors to reopen their states' economies and schools, even as COVID cases and deaths continued to rise. When right-wing protesters in Michigan and Minnesota rallied against strict social-distancing restrictions, the president tweeted his support, urging the activists to "LIBERATE" their respective states.[12]

Joseph Biden, the presumptive Democratic nominee, who made limited public appearances and primarily campaigned by video from the basement of his Delaware home, criticized the Trump administration's handling of the coronavirus pandemic. The former vice president stated that Trump had left America vulnerable in 2019 when he ended a pandemic early-warning program that began during the Obama administration.[13] Biden charged that Trump had no clear plan and criticized the president's calls to open up the economy and schools against the advice of public health officials. Remember back in March when he called himself a wartime president? Remember when he exhorted the nation to "sacrifice together" to face an "invisible enemy"? What happened? Now it seems the wartime president has surrendered—has waved the white flag and left the field of battle against the coronavirus pandemic.[14] Throughout the late spring and early summer, most polls showed Biden with a comfortable lead over Trump.[15]

In late May of 2020, a wave of racial unrest seized the country following the murder of George Floyd while in police custody. Floyd, a forty-six-year-old black man, was arrested in Minneapolis, Minnesota, on suspicion of using a counterfeit $20 bill at a convenience store. When police attempted to place Floyd in a squad car, he complained of having claustrophobia and became agitated. To subdue him, three police officers placed Floyd face down on the street in handcuffs. Officer Derek Chauvin, a white, nineteen-year veteran of the Minneapolis Police Department and the senior officer at the scene, kneeled on the side of Floyd's neck. As onlookers recorded the events, Floyd repeatedly told the officers, "I can't breathe." He called out for his dead mother and said, "Tell my kids I love them." After six minutes, he became unresponsive. The bystanders urged the officers to check Floyd's pulse as he lay motionless; they did not.[16] Chauvin, who would later be convicted of murder charges, remained on Floyd's neck for nine and a half minutes.

In the weeks that followed, over 7,000 protests against racial injustice and police brutality, many organized by the Black Lives Matter movement, took place across the United States. Protesters called for criminal justice reform with some making calls to "defund the police." Although the vast majority of the protests were peaceful, it was estimated that roughly 7 percent became violent and/or destructive.[17] In several cities, most notably, Portland, Oregon, Seattle, Washington, and Kansas City, Missouri, the protests became prolonged and devolved into riots.[18] At least 200 cities across 27 states imposed curfews or mobilized the National Guard in order to control the crowds.

Joe Biden responded to the racial unrest by saying, the words "'I can't breathe' are a wake-up call for our nation." Although he disagreed with calls to "defund" the police, Biden was largely sympathetic to the Black Lives Matter movement's calls for reform.[19] Referring to a history of police abuse and economic inequality, Biden stated that black communities "have had a knee on their neck for a long time. . . . The moment has come for our nation to deal with systemic racism." He charged that the president had stoked racial resentments and that the 2020 election was a "battle for the soul of America."[20]

Trump was decidedly less sympathetic to the Black Lives Matter movement. When New York City allowed protesters to paint the "Black Lives Matter" logo on the street outside of Trump Tower, the president castigated city officials for "denigrating this luxury Avenue" (Fifth Avenue) and calling the logo a "symbol of hate."[21] Echoing the 1968 campaign of Richard Nixon, Trump declared himself "the law and order candidate."[22] In a conference call with all fifty governors, the president admonished that when dealing with the protesters "you have to dominate. If you don't dominate you're wasting your time. They're going to run over you. You're going to look like a bunch of jerks. You have to dominate."[23]

In Washington DC, thousands of protesters gathered in Lafayette Square across from the White House. Over several days, the demonstrations had turned unruly and violent after nightfall, sparking confrontations with law enforcement. At the historic St. John's Episcopal Church, often called the "Church of the Presidents," a fire was set in the basement nursery, windows were smashed, and graffiti lined the exterior saying, "The Devil is across

[the] street."[24] On June 1, as the city's evening curfew loomed, Park Police, Metropolitan Police, and Secret Service agents cleared Lafayette Square, using tear gas and flash bangs to create a perimeter. Within minutes, President Trump emerged from the White House and walked to the boarded-up church, where he posed for photographers with a Bible held high in the air. "We have a great country," the president said. "Greatest country in the world."[25]

The contrast between the two candidates who squared off in the 2020 presidential election could not have been sharper, both in style and substance. On the Republican side was a highly confrontational and controversial incumbent, who came to politics as an outsider and often engaged on the political trail in both bombast and profanity, pledging to "make America great again." On the Democratic side was the ultimate establishment candidate, who had served thirty-six years in the US Senate and eight years as vice president, promising to "restore American leadership" and have "a presidency for all Americans." But like most presidential elections featuring the sitting president on the ballot, the 2020 election was cast as a referendum on the policies and performance of the incumbent. Against the backdrop of a global pandemic and recession and domestic racial unrest, more Americans cast a ballot in 2020 than in any presidential election in the nation's history, and the turnout rate reached its highest level since 1900. And the judgment was not favorable for Donald Trump. On November 3, 2020, Joseph R. Biden was elected president of the United States, winning a comfortable 306 to 232 Electoral College victory and winning the popular vote with 51.3 percent to Trump's 46.9 percent.

The 2020 presidential election was unusual, to say the least. Because of the public health crisis, the campaigns either abandoned or scaled back their ground game. The traditional party nominating convention activities were scuttled, and both nominees delivered their acceptance speeches remotely. Americans voted by mail in record numbers. And, perhaps most consequential for the health of American democracy, the losing candidate, Donald Trump, refused to concede defeat, claiming that his victory had been stolen amid widespread election fraud.[26] The Trump campaign and its allies filed over sixty lawsuits contesting the election, and most were dismissed as being "frivolous."[27] Trump was undeterred and continued to press his claims of election fraud. On January 6, 2021, following the president's "Save America" rally on the Washington Mall, a crowd of Trump supporters stormed the United States Capitol, interrupting a joint session of the Congress that had gathered to certify the official Electoral College ballots. The 2020 presidential election was indeed unusual.

But none of this means that voting behavior during the 2020 elections was unusual. Indeed, as we hope to show, the 2020 presidential and congressional elections were, in many ways, the product of electoral continuity. Although

American parties have become more ideologically disparate over the past few decades, no party holds a clear advantage. At the presidential level, Democrats have won the popular vote in all but one election since 1992—George W. Bush's reelection in 2004. But the popular-vote balance has been so close that it became feasible for the second-place finisher in the popular vote to capture the Electoral College and the White House in two of these cases—Bush in 2000 and Trump in 2016. With the election of Democratic majorities in both the House and Senate, along with Biden's victory, 2020 brought unified partisan control of government. It is important to note, however, that the Democratic majorities in both the House and Senate are quite small. The Republicans actually gained seats in the House of Representatives in 2020, reducing the Democrat's majority to a narrow nine votes. In the Senate, the partisan divide is evenly split, 50–50, but the Democrats enjoy majority status because the vice president, who serves as the president of the Senate and can vote to break ties, is a Democrat.[28]

Is America in the midst of an electoral transformation? What were the sources of Biden's victory in 2020, and how does his electoral coalition differ from coalitions of the past? Does his victory signal a long-term positive trajectory for Democrats' chances in presidential elections? And are these electoral forces similar to those that structure congressional elections? These are the sorts of questions that we seek to answer here.

This book continues a series of nineteen books that we began with a study of the 1980 elections. Our focus has always been both contemporary and historical. Thus, we offer an extensive examination of the 2020 presidential and congressional campaigns and present a detailed analysis of individual-level voting behavior, examining those factors that lead citizens to vote as well as those that affect how they vote. We also aim to place the 2020 elections in proper historical and analytical contexts.

CHANGE AND CONTINUITY

Elections are at once both judgments on the issues of the day and the product of long-term changes in the relationship between the political parties and voters. For example, Democrats' aspirations for an emerging electoral majority following their 2012 presidential victory were not unfounded. The projections of the US Census Bureau at the time suggested that many of the social groups that supported Democrats in their recent elections, particularly Latinos, were growing as a percentage of the overall US population (these projections remain in place today). Turnout among these groups had also increased in the prior decades. So, for some Democrats, their party's future success in presidential elections over the next few decades seemed all but assured. Then Donald Trump won, and the questions became: Was 2016 the dawn of an emergent Republican majority? Had Trump realigned the American Party system?[29] Was Biden's victory in 2020 a realignment in favor of Democrats?[30]

It is not uncommon for winning parties to make hyperbolic claims about the "historic" nature of their victories or to assert that their win was a sign of impending electoral dominance. Indeed, in 2008, Democrats were exuberant over Obama's sizable victory over John McCain and were even more pronounced in their claims of a bright Democratic future. Some observers saw the election as restoring Democrats to their status as the majority party, which they had enjoyed between 1932 and 1968. Lanny J. Davis, a former special counsel to President Clinton, wrote following the 2008 election, "Tuesday's substantial victory by Barack Obama, together with Democratic gains in the Senate and House, appear to have accomplished a fundamental political realignment. The election is likely to create a new governing majority coalition that could dominate American politics for a generation or more."[31] Two years later, the Democrats lost sixty-three seats, and their majority status in the House of Representatives—the largest seat change since 1946—and six seats in the Senate, where they maintained a slim majority.[32]

In 2004, following incumbent President George W. Bush's victory over Democrat nominee, John Kerry, scholars speculated about a pro-Republican realignment. Indeed, speculation about Republican dominance can be traced back to the late 1960s, when Kevin P. Phillips, in his widely read book, *The Emerging Republican Majority*, argued that the Republicans could become the majority party, mainly by winning support in the South.[33] Between 1969, when his book was published, and 1984, the Republicans won three of the four presidential elections, winning by massive landslides in 1972, when Richard M. Nixon triumphed over George S. McGovern, and in 1984, when Ronald Reagan defeated Walter F. Mondale. In 1985, Reagan himself proclaimed that a Republican realignment was at hand. "The other side would like to believe that our victory last November was due to something other than our philosophy," he asserted. "I just hope that they keep believing that. Realignment is real."[34] Democratic victories in the 1992 and 1996 presidential elections called into question the claims of a pro-Republican realignment.

Obviously not all elections are transformative. So how is electoral change—not simply the ebbs and flows from election to election but changes in the fundamental factors that link parties and voters—to be understood?

For generations of political scientists, theories of electoral change have centered on the concept of political realignment.[35] Political scientists define *realignment* in different ways, but they are all influenced by V. O. Key, Jr., who developed a theory of "critical elections" in which "new and durable electoral groupings are formed."[36] Elections like that in 1860 in which Lincoln's victory brought the Republicans to power, in 1896 in which McKinley's victory solidified Republican dominance, and in 1932 in which the Democrats came to power under FDR are obvious candidates for such a label.

But later, Key argued that partisan shifts could also take place over a series of elections—a pattern he called "secular realignment." During these periods, "shifts in the partisan balance of power" occur.[37] In this view, the realignment that first brought the Republicans to power might have begun in 1856, when the Republicans displaced the Whigs as the major competitor to the Democrats and might have been consolidated by Lincoln's reelection in 1864 and Ulysses S. Grant's election in 1868. The realignment that consolidated Republican dominance in the late nineteenth century may well have begun in 1892, when Democrat Grover Cleveland won the election, but the Populist Party, headed by James D. Weaver, attracted 8.5 percent of the popular vote, winning four states and electoral votes in two others. In 1896, the Populists supported William Jennings Bryan and were co-opted by the Democrats, but the electorate shifted to the Republican Party. The pro-Republican realignment might have been consolidated by McKinley's win over Bryan in 1900 and by Theodore Roosevelt's victory in 1904.

Though the term *New Deal* was not coined until Franklin Roosevelt's campaign of 1932, the New Deal realignment may have begun with Herbert C. Hoover's triumph over Democrat Al Smith, the first Roman Catholic to be nominated by a major political party. Although badly defeated, Smith carried two New England states, Massachusetts and Rhode Island, which later became the most Democratic states in the nation.[38] As Key points out, the beginnings of a shift toward the Democrats was detectable in Smith's defeat.[39] However, the "New Deal coalition" was not created by the 1932 election but after it, and it was consolidated by Roosevelt's 1936 landslide over Alfred M. Landon and his 1940 defeat of Wendell Willkie. The New Deal coalition structured the distribution of party support within the electorate during the earliest decades of the post–World War II period, and its decline and eventual replacement are important to understanding the changes and continuities of modern electoral politics.

Past partisan realignments in the United States have had five basic characteristics. First, realignments have traditionally involved changes in the regional bases of party support. Consider, for instance, the decline of the Whig Party and rise of the Republicans. Between 1836 and 1852, the Whigs drew at least some of their electoral support from the South.[40] The last Whig candidate to be elected, Zachary Taylor in 1848, won sixty-six of his electoral votes from the fifteen slave states. In his 1860 victory, Lincoln did not win a single electoral vote from the fifteen slave states. Regionalism may be less important to future electoral changes, however. Today television and other media have weakened regionalism in the United States, and politics is much more nationalized. Two-party competition has diffused throughout the country, and the issues on which the parties compete tend to be more national in scope.[41]

Second, past party realignments have involved changes in the social bases of party support. Even during a period when one party is becoming dominant, some social groups may be moving to the losing party. During the 1930s, for example, Roosevelt gained the support of industrial workers, but at the same time, he lost support among business owners and professionals.

Third, past realignments have been characterized by the mobilization of new groups into the electorate. Indeed the mobilization of new voters into the electorate can result in significant electoral volatility.[42] Between Calvin Coolidge's Republican landslide in 1924 and Roosevelt's third-term victory in 1940, turnout among the voting-age population rose from 44 percent to 59 percent. Although some long-term forces were pushing turnout upward, the sharp increase between 1924 and 1928 and again between 1932 and 1936 resulted at least in part from the mobilization of new social groups into the electorate. Ethnic groups that were predominantly Catholic were mobilized to support Al Smith in 1928, and industrial workers were mobilized to support Franklin Roosevelt in 1936.

Fourth, past realignments have occurred when new issues have divided the electorate. In the 1850s, the Republican Party reformulated the controversy over slavery to form a winning coalition. By opposing the expansion of slavery into the territories, the Republicans contributed to divisions within the Democratic Party. Of course, no issue since slavery has divided America as deeply, and subsequent realignments have never brought a new political party to power. But those realignments have always been based on the division of the electorate over new issues.

Last, most political scientists argue that partisan realignments occur when voters change not just their voting patterns but also the way they think about the political parties, thus creating an erosion of partisan loyalties. During the Great Depression in 1932, for example, many voters who thought of themselves as Republicans voted against Hoover. Later, many of these voters returned to the Republican side, but others began to think of themselves as Democrats. Likewise, in 1936, some voters who thought of themselves as Democrats disliked FDR's policies and voted against him. Some of these defectors may have returned to the Democratic fold in subsequent elections, but others began to think of themselves as Republicans.

Not all scholars believe that the concept of realignment is useful. In 1991, Byron E. Shafer edited a volume in which several chapters questioned its utility.[43] A decade later, David R. Mayhew published a monograph critiquing scholarship on realignment.[44] Mayhew cites fifteen claims made by scholars of realignment and then tests each. He argues that many of these claims do not stand up to empirical scrutiny, questions the classification of several elections as "realigning," and suggests that the concept of realignment should be abandoned.

Although we agree with some of the claims made by Mayhew, we see no reason to abandon the concept completely. Some electoral changes may correspond to the critical election-realignment dynamic—a long period of stability in the party system is altered by a rapid and dramatic change, which leads to a new, long-term partisan equilibrium. Using biological evolution as a theoretical analogue, Edward G. Carmines and James A. Stimson argue that partisan realignments of this type are similar in form to the evolutionary dynamic known as cataclysmic adaptation.[45] But the authors note that biological examples of the cataclysmic adaptation dynamic are extraordinarily rare and suggest that critical election realignments are likely to be rare also.

Carmines and Stimson articulate two additional evolutionary models of partisan change. The authors argue that Key's secular realignment dynamic is consistent with the model of Darwinian gradualism. In this view, electoral change does not result from a critical moment but instead is "slow, gradual, [and] incremental."[46] As noted in Key's original work, the secular realignment dynamic "operate[s] inexorably, and almost imperceptibly, election after election, to form new party alignments and to build new party groups."[47]

The third model of partisan change espoused by Carmines and Stimson is consistent with the "punctuated equilibrium" model of evolution.[48] In this dynamic process,

> the system moves from a fairly stationary steady state to a fairly dramatic rapid change; the change is manifested by a "critical moment" in the time series—a point where change is large enough to be visible and, perhaps the origin of a dynamic process. Significantly, however, the change—the dynamic growth—does not end with the critical moment; instead it continues over an extended period, albeit at [a] much slower pace.[49]

In our view, the punctuated equilibrium model best captures the dynamic nature of electoral change in the United States since the 1960s. The 1960s were a critical moment in American politics. The events of the decade were the catalysts for fundamental changes in the rules that govern political parties and the partisan sentiments that would govern voters for years to come.[50] Of particular interest is the transformative power of the issue of race. By 1960, the national Democratic Party's sponsorship of civil rights for African Americans had created a schism between the more-liberal elements of the party and white southern Democrats. But it had also allowed the party to chip away at black voters' allegiance to the Republican Party, "the party of Lincoln." The partisan loyalties of African Americans had been shaped by the Civil War, and black loyalties to the Republican Party—where and when allowed to vote—lasted through the 1932 election. By 1960, a majority of African Americans identified with the Democratic Party, but there was still a substantial minority of Republican identifiers. Between 1960 and 1964, however, African American loyalties moved sharply toward the Democrats. The civil rights demonstrations of the early 1960s and the eventual passage of the 1964 Civil Rights Act solidified the position of the Democratic Party as the party of civil rights. By late 1964, more than 70 percent of African Americans identified as Democrats, a level of loyalty that persists today. The change in partisanship among blacks and the subsequent mobilization of black voters following the passage of the 1965 Voting Rights Act provided the rapid, critical moment that disrupted the stable equilibrium created by the New Deal Coalition. And, as the punctuated equilibrium dynamic suggests, the electorate continued to change in a direction set forth by the critical era of the 1960s, but it did so at slower rate, and it continues to have ramifications for politics today.

The political events of the 1960s also had an effect on white partisanship, but the change was neither immediate nor decisive. From the mid-1960s to the mid-1970s, there was a substantial erosion in party loyalties among whites. The proportion of the white electorate who considered themselves "independent" increased noticeably. By 1978, nearly 40 percent of whites said they were either pure independents or independents who "leaned" toward one of the two parties, nearly double that found in the late 1950s and early 1960s.[51] These changes led some scholars to use the term *dealignment* to characterize American politics during the period.[52] The term was first used by Ronald Inglehart and Avram Hochstein in 1972.[53] A dealignment is a condition in which old voting patterns break down without being replaced by newer ones. Yet, beginning in the 1980s, the proportion of whites claiming to be pure independents declined as whites nationally began to lean toward the Republican Party. In the once "solid Democratic South," whites have become decidedly Republican. Voters appear to be aligned.

Despite these changes, the Republicans have never emerged as the majority party among the electorate. Democrats, however, saw a growth in political loyalties between 2004 and 2016, and in 2020, the party once again emerged as the majority party among two-party identifiers, albeit a small majority.[54] This is not to say that Republicans cannot win, of course; it simply means that the GOP has entered recent elections at a numerical disadvantage. Democrats' electoral gains have largely been the product of the critical events of the 1960s, which established them as the party of civil rights. As America's nonwhite population has increased—more than half of the growth in the US population between 2000 and 2020 was due to an increase in the nonwhite population—Democrats have been the beneficiaries. For instance, roughly two out of every three Latino voters in the United States identify with the Democratic Party.[55] America's racial and ethnic minorities continue to view the Democrats' adherence to the civil rights agenda of the 1960s as providing them with a natural political home, and America's whites are increasingly more likely to side with the Republicans. In our view, the 2020 elections do not represent a fundamental change in America's electoral politics. Instead, the 2020 elections continue to reflect electoral alignments set in motion by a critical era that occurred nearly a half century ago.

VOTERS AND THE ACT OF VOTING

Voting is an individual act. Indeed the national decision made on (or before) November 3, 2020, was the product of more than 239 million individual decisions.[56] Two questions faced Americans eighteen years and older: whether to vote and, if they did, how to cast their ballots. These decisions, of course, are not made in isolation. Voters' decisions are influenced by the social, economic, and information contexts in which they live; they are influenced by the political attitudes that they have acquired throughout their lifetime; and they are influenced by the voting decisions they have made in the past.[57] Voters' decisions are also constrained by America's electoral rules and two-party system—these are the primary sources of continuity in our political system.

How voters make up their minds is one of the most thoroughly studied subjects in political science—and one of the most controversial.[58] Voting decisions can be studied from at least three theoretical perspectives.[59] The first approach is *sociological* in character and views voters primarily as members of social groups. Voters belong to primary groups of family members and peers; secondary groups such as private clubs, trade unions, and voluntary associations; and broader reference groups such as social classes and religious and ethnic groups. Understanding the political behavior of these groups is central to understanding voters, according to Paul F. Lazarsfeld, Bernard R. Berelson, and their colleagues. Social characteristics determine political preferences.[60] This perspective is still popular, although more so among sociologists than political scientists.[61]

A second approach places greater emphasis on the *psychological* (or, more aptly, attitudinal) variables that affect voting. The "socio-psychological model" of voting behavior was developed by Angus Campbell, Philip E. Converse, Warren E. Miller, and Donald E. Stokes, scholars at the University of Michigan Survey Research Center, in their classic book *The American Voter*.[62] The Michigan scholars focused on attitudes most likely to have the greatest effect on the vote just before the moment of decision, particularly attitudes toward the candidates, the parties, and the issues. An individual's party identification emerged as the most important social-psychological variable that influences voting behavior. The Michigan approach is the most prevalent among political scientists, and party identification continues to be emphasized as one of the most influential factors affecting individual vote choice, although some deemphasize its psychological underpinnings.[63]

A third approach draws heavily from the work of economists. According to this perspective, citizens weigh the costs of voting against the expected benefits when deciding whether to vote. And when deciding for whom to vote, they calculate which candidate favors policies closest to their own policy preferences. Citizens are thus viewed as rational actors who attempt to maximize their expected utility. Anthony Downs and William H. Riker helped to found this *rational choice* approach.[64]

Taken separately, none of these approaches adequately explain voting behavior; taken together, the approaches are largely complementary.[65] Therefore, we have chosen an eclectic approach that draws on insights from each viewpoint. Where appropriate we employ sociological variables, but we also employ social-psychological variables such as party identification and feelings of political efficacy. The rational choice approach guides our study of the way issues influence voting behavior.

SURVEY RESEARCH SAMPLING

Because of our interest in individual-level voting behavior, our book relies heavily on surveys of the American electorate. It draws on a massive exit poll conducted by Edison Research for the National Election Pool, a consortium of four news organizations, as well as surveys conducted in-person or by phone by the US Census Bureau, and online surveys conducted by the Pew Research Center. But our main data source for 2020 is the 8,280 pre-election and 7,449 postelection recontact interviews conducted after the election as part of the ANES Time Series Survey.[66] Originally conducted by the Survey Research Center (SRC) and Center for Political Studies at the University of Michigan, the ANES surveys have been conducted using national samples in every presidential election since 1948 and in every midterm election between 1954 and 2002. The 2020 ANES was conducted jointly by Stanford University and the University of Michigan, with funding by the National Science Foundation. Since 1952, the ANES surveys have measured party identification and feelings of political effectiveness. The Center for Political Studies, founded in 1970, has developed valuable questions for measuring issue preferences. The ANES surveys are the best and most comprehensive for studying the issue preferences and party loyalties of the American electorate.

Readers may question our reliance on the ANES surveys of just over 8,200 people when some 239 million Americans are eligible to vote. Would we have similar results if all adults eligible to vote had been surveyed?[67] The ANES uses a procedure called multistage probability sampling to select the particular individuals to be interviewed. This procedure ensures that the final sample is likely to represent the entire population of US citizens of voting age, except for Americans living on military bases, in institutions, or abroad.[68]

Because of the probability procedures used to conduct the ANES surveys, we are able to estimate the likelihood that the results represent the entire population of noninstitutionalized citizens living in the United States. Although the 2020 ANES survey sampled only about one in every 29,000 voting-eligible Americans, the representativeness of a sample depends far more on the size of the sample than the size of the population being studied, provided the sample is drawn properly. With samples of this size, we can be fairly confident (to a level of 0.95) that the results we get will fall within three percentage points of that obtained if the entire population had been surveyed. For example, when we find that 52 percent of respondents approved of the job Donald Trump was doing as president, we can be reasonably confident that between 50.9 percent (52 − 1.1) and 53.1 percent (52 + 1.1) approved of his performance. The actual results could be less than 50.9 percent or more than 53.1 percent, but a confidence level of 0.95 means that the odds are 19 to one that the entire electorate falls within this range. The range of confidence becomes somewhat larger when we look at subgroups of the electorate. For example, with subsets of about 500 (and the results in the 50 percent range) the confidence error rises to plus or minus 4.4 percentage points. Because the likelihood of sampling error grows as our subsamples become smaller, we sometimes supplement our analysis with reports of other surveys.

Somewhat more complicated procedures are needed to determine whether the difference between two groups is likely to reflect the relationship found if the entire population were surveyed. The probability that such differences reflect real differences in the population is largely a function of the size of the groups being compared.[69] Generally speaking, when we compare the results of the 2020 sample with an earlier ANES survey, which typically used smaller samples, a difference of three percentage points is sufficient to be reasonably confident that the difference is real. For example, in 2008 during the final year of the George W. Bush presidency and during the onset of the "great recession," only 2 percent of respondents said that the economy had improved in the last year; in 2020, 19 percent did. Because this difference is greater than three percentage points, we can be reasonably confident that the electorate was more likely to think the national economy had improved in 2020 than they had back in 2008.

When we compare subgroups of the electorate sampled in 2020 (or compare those subgroups with subgroups sampled in earlier years), a larger percentage is usually necessary to conclude that differences are meaningful. For example, in 2016, 35 percent of whites who did not complete high school favored Hillary Clinton; among those who graduated high school but did not continue their education, 33 percent favored Clinton. We cannot be confident this is real, however, because the subsample sizes are quite small—only seventy-seven people are in the first category, whereas there are 463 people in the latter. With subsamples of this size, we would need to see a difference of thirteen points to be confident in the results. Thankfully, the unusually large sample size that we obtained in the 2020 sample means that statistical confidence in our subgroup comparisons is much easier to achieve. For instance, among voters, we have 3,557 men and 3,892 women.[70] With subsamples of this size, a two-point difference is large enough to conclude that a gender difference is likely real. However, it is important to recognize that in previous years, our sample sizes were much smaller. Generally speaking, comparisons of men and women using data from previous ANES studies require a difference of five percentage points. Similarly, it is important to be mindful of racial differences in the sample. In 2020, our sample contains 4,853 whites (65.7 percent) and 834 blacks (11.3 percent). Thus, to be confident in racial difference, we require a spread of roughly 3.4 percentage points. When using data from previous years with smaller sample sizes, a difference of at least eight percentage points is needed to conclude that differences between whites and blacks are meaningful.

This discussion represents only a ballpark guide to judging whether reported results are likely to represent the total population. Better estimates can be obtained using the formulas presented in many statistics textbooks. To make such calculations or even a rough estimate of the chances of error, the reader must know the size of the groups being compared. For that reason, we always report in our tables and figures either the number of cases on which our percentages are based or the information needed to approximate the number of cases.

PLAN OF THE BOOK

We begin by following the chronology of the campaign itself. Chapter 1 examines the battle for the Democratic and Republican Party presidential nominations. Fifteen major Democratic candidates and three major Republican candidates campaigned for the chance to square off in the general election. As is typical when an incumbent president stands for reelection, President Trump received no significant opposition for the Republican

Party nomination. In chapter 1, we discuss the regularities in the nomination process that explain why some candidates run and others do not. We then examine the rules governing the nomination contests, and we also assess the importance of campaign finance. The dynamics of multicandidate contests and the concept of momentum to discuss nomination contests are covered in chapter 1 as well.

Chapter 2 moves to the general election campaign. Because of the rules set forth by the US Constitution for winning presidential elections, candidates must think about how to win enough states to gain a majority (270) of the electoral vote (538 since 1964). We examine the Electoral College strategies adopted by the campaigns. There were two presidential debates (a third was scheduled but was canceled when the president contracted COVID) and one vice-presidential debate, and we discuss their impact. Last, we turn to the endgame of the campaign, the battle over turnout. Because of the pandemic, each campaign had a limited "ground game" and took different approaches to get out the vote—we will examine how these strategies differ from previous presidential campaigns.

Chapter 3 turns to the actual election results, relying largely on the official election statistics. Our look at the electoral vote is followed by a discussion of the election rules, noting that the US plurality-vote system supports "Duverger's law." We examine the pattern of results during the eighteen postwar elections as well as those in all forty-eight elections between 1832 and 2020. We then analyze the state-by-state results, paying particular attention to regional shifts in the elections between 1980 and 2020. We focus special attention on electoral change in the postwar South because this region has been the scene of the most dramatic changes in postwar US politics. Finally, we study the results of the last five presidential elections to assess the electoral vote balance.

Chapter 4 analyzes what is perhaps the most important decision of all: whether to vote. We examine the dynamics of electoral participation in US politics, particularly changes in turnout during the postwar period. Although turnout grew fairly consistently between 1920 (the year women were enfranchised throughout the United States) and 1960, it fell in 1964 and in each of the next four elections. We show that the decline in turnout during this period coincides with steep declines in partisan attachment and political efficacy in the electorate. As partisan attachments have increased in recent decades, turnout has risen. Turnout in the 2020 election was 6.8 percentage points higher than in 2016. Yet turnout is low in the United States compared with other advanced democracies, although it is not equally low among all social groups. In chapter 4 we examine social differences in turnout in detail, using both the 2020 ANES survey and the CPS conducted by the US Census Bureau.

In chapter 5, we examine how social forces influence the vote. The ANES surveys enable us to analyze the vote for Biden and Trump by race, gender, region, age, education, income, union membership, and religion. The impact of these social factors has changed considerably in the postwar period as the New Deal coalition broke down and new partisan alignments emerged after the critical era of the 1960s. We show that minorities—specifically blacks and Latinos—are now central to the modern Democratic coalition.

Chapter 6 explores the impact of party loyalties on voting using the ANES data. Since the 1980s, there has been a substantial shift in whites' partisan loyalties—particularly in the South—toward the Republican Party. The clear advantage Democrats once held among whites dissipated. Although the 2008 election that initially brought Obama to office saw a resurgence in whites' Democratic identification, that advantage proved temporary as whites' party loyalties reverted to near parity in 2012. In 2016 and 2020, the Democrats held a slight advantage. We examine partisanship among whites and blacks separately, tracking changes from 1952 to 2020. This analysis reveals that the patterns of change among whites and blacks have been markedly different. We also compare Latino partisanship in recent elections. Finally, we take a close look at the role of party loyalties in shaping voting preferences, retrospective evaluations, and voting preferences. We find that the relationship between party identification and the vote was very strong in every US election since 2000, including 2020.

Chapter 7 examines attitudes toward both the candidates and the issues. We begin by examining voters' feelings toward the candidates before turning our attention to their appraisals of the candidates' personal traits. We then attempt to assess the extent to which voters based their votes on issue preferences. We conclude that voters' prospective issue concerns were important in determining their vote choices in 2020.

We then examine how "retrospective evaluations" influence voting decisions. Existing research suggests that many voters decide how to vote on the basis of past performance. In other words, voters decide mainly on the basis of what the candidates or their parties have done in office, not what they promise to do if elected. In chapter 8, we show that retrospective evaluations of Donald Trump's performance, particularly with regard to the pandemic and international affairs, were a powerful reason underlying citizens' vote decisions. Perhaps most interesting, we find that just one in four American voters in 2020 thought that the country was on the right track.

In chapters 9 and 10, we are reminded that election day 2020 featured many elections. In addition to the presidential election, there were eleven gubernatorial elections, elections for thousands of state and local offices, as well as thirty-five elections for the US Senate and elections for all 435 seats in the US House of Representatives.[71] We focus our analysis on the 2020 House and Senate elections, which are by far the most consequential for national public policy.

Chapter 9 examines the pattern of congressional outcomes for 2020 and brings to light those factors that affect competition in congressional elections. We review the pattern of incumbent success in House and Senate races between 1954, the first Democratic victory in their forty-year winning streak, and 2020. Despite citizens' low levels of trust in government and the large portion of voters who believed the country was heading in the wrong direction, congressional incumbents were returned to office in droves. In the House, about 95 percent of incumbents were reelected in 2020, whereas the success rate for Senate incumbents was 85 percent. We examine the interplay of national and regional factors in structuring congressional election outcomes. And, of course, we give particular attention to the critical factors of candidate recruitment, incumbency, and campaign finance. Finally, we speculate on the future of congressional elections and party polarization in Congress in 2022 and beyond.

Chapter 10 explores how voters make congressional voting decisions. Using the same ANES surveys we employed to study presidential voting, we examine how social factors, issues, partisan loyalties, incumbency, and retrospective evaluations of congressional and presidential performance influence voters' choices for the House and Senate. We also try to determine the existence and extent of presidential "coattails," that is, whether Democrats were more likely to be elected to Congress because of Biden's presidential victory.

Finally, in chapter 11, we attempt to place the 2020 elections in the proper historical context. Although we examine changes and continuities in American elections over the course of the nation's history, the great advantage of our analysis is its use of high-quality surveys of the electorate over the last sixty years. This wealth of data provides extraordinary insights regarding the political preferences of the America people, how those preferences have varied with time, and how they relate to voting behavior. Thus, we explore the long-term changes and continuities in the politics of American national elections.

Part I

THE 2020 PRESIDENTIAL ELECTION

Chapter 1

The Nomination Struggle

Presidential nomination campaigns are the contests through which the two major political parties in the United States select their presidential nominees. As they have done since 1832 (Democrats) and 1856 (Republicans), the delegates who are chosen to be seated at the national party conventions do the actual selecting. However, since about 1972, both parties have used public campaigns for popular support as a way of selecting and/or instructing most delegates to the convention on how they should vote. Many people think of these primary contests as formal elections, just like those in general elections in the fall. Whereas presidential primary elections are, indeed, run by the government, they are actually designed solely to help each political party select delegates to choose its presidential nominee, and that applies only to states that use primary elections to select or instruct their delegates.[1] States that use the alternative means, caucus or convention procedures, instead of primaries (see what follows) do so without involving the government at all. Presidential nominations are thus a mixture of public and private selections, and they are conducted at the state level only, even though their ultimate outcome is to select the two major parties' nominees for president.

Primaries are nearly unique to America. In almost no other country have the leaders of the major political parties' ceded so much control over candidate selection to the general public. While now and then there are primary elections run by political parties in other nations, they are rare, typically isolated to one or a few parties, and are often used only once or twice before being discarded. American nominations, on the other hand, have run this way for Democrats and Republicans since the 1970s and have become entrenched in the public's and the political leaderships' minds. It would be very difficult for a party to nominate someone the public did not support at near or actual majority levels in the primary season. The leadership has, in that sense, ceded its control over its own party to the general public, though the party still plays a role in shaping outcomes through endorsing candidates in the lead up to the nomination contests.[2] This system has also empowered the media who seek to inform the public and the many activists, supporters, and financial donors of the presidential nomination campaigns who provide the wherewithal for most candidates to have any chance of reaching the public to win their support.

The 2020 campaigns in many respects were like all of those since the 1970s, that is, in the era of the "new nomination system," as we call it. As we shall see there were a number of similarities between the campaigns of 2020 and their predecessors. However, people may also talk with wonder about specific and individual aspects of the campaigns regardless of the similarities to earlier contests. While in 2016, individuals may have asked, "How could someone like Donald J. Trump win the Republican nomination?," in 2020, they may have wondered why he didn't face any serious opposition for the nomination, especially given how controversial his presidency was. On the Democratic side the question more often seemed to be, "In a year with a record number of women and candidates of color running for the nomination, why did Joe Biden emerge as the nominee, especially given that he epito- mizes the 'establishment'?"

However, when people speak of 2020, they may be most likely to remem- ber one additional unique feature, that the country went into lockdown in the midst of the nomination contests to combat a global pandemic on a scale unlike any the country had experienced in over a century. In what ways did the pandemic impact both candidate choices and evaluations of the public? As we will see the answers to these questions are that the two parties' cam- paigns largely unfolded in replication of the many and well-established con- tinuities established since the empowering of the public and consequent loss of party leadership control over nominations. But the unique properties of the two winners, the fallout from the 2016 election, and the fact that the nomi- nation unfolded in the midst of a global pandemic made the two campaigns distinct in some important ways.

In short, reforms in the late 1960s and early 1970s brought about a new form of nomination campaign, one that required public campaigning for resources and votes. The new nomination system has shaped many aspects of all contests from 1972 onward, and we examine the similarities that have endured over its more than forty-year existence. Each contest, of course, dif- fers from all others because of the electoral context at the time and because the contenders themselves are different. And in the new nomination system, the rules change to some degree every four years as well. The changes in rules and the strategies that candidates adopt in light of those rules combine with the context and contenders to make each campaign unique.

WHO RAN

A first important regularity of the nomination campaign is that when incumbents seek renomination, only a very few candidates will challenge them, and perhaps no one will at all. In 1972, although President Richard M. Nixon did face two potentially credible challengers to his renomination, they were so ineffective that he was essentially uncontested. Similarly, in 2020, some Republicans challenged Donald Trump in the primaries, but they generated such little support that they were not viewed as posing a credible challenge to his renomination. Ronald Reagan in 1984, Bill Clinton in 1996, George W. Bush in 2004, and Barack Obama in 2012 were actually unopposed. They were so, in large part, because even a moderately successful president is virtually undefeatable for renomination. Conversely Gerald R. Ford in 1976 and Jimmy Carter in 1980 each faced a serious challenge.[3] Ford had great difficulty defeating Reagan, and Carter likewise was strongly contested by Democratic senator Edward M. Kennedy of Massachusetts.[4]

The second major regularity in the nomination system concerns the contests—such as the Democratic nomination in 2020—in which the party has no incumbent seeking renomination. Only a few incumbents have chosen not to run for reelection even though eligible, such as Harry S. Truman in 1952 and Lyndon B. Johnson in 1968. Most often, this happens when a party is out of power or an incumbent is ineligible to run for a third term. In such cases a relatively large number of candidates run for the nomination. For our purposes we count candidates as "running" if they were actively campaigning on January 1, 2020 (or entered even later). That definition means that there were fifteen major candidates who sought the Democratic Party's nomination in 2020. There were actually quite a few more in 2019—by most counts twenty-four—although that means that nine were sufficiently "defeated" (or at least believed their chances of winning were too remote) so that they dropped out before January 1, 2020.[5] By our counting procedure there were three Republican candidates in 2020.[6] Thus, in this section, we will be considering eighteen major-party contenders.

Since 1980 there have been fourteen campaigns in which there was no incumbent seeking a major party's nomination, and the number of major candidates that were in the race as the year began varied remarkably little: seven in 1980 (R); eight in 1984 (D); eight (D) and six (R) in 1988; eight in 1992 (D); eight in 1996 (R); six (R) and two (D) in 2000; nine in 2004 (D); eight in both parties' contests in 2008; eight in 2012 (R); twelve Republicans and three Democrats in 2016; in addition to the fifteen Democrats in 2020. Therefore most contests featured at least six candidates, with only 2000 (D) and 2016 (D) having noticeably fewer, and 2016 (R) and 2020 (D) having over ten candidates.

The three candidates on the Republican side in 2020 were incumbent President Donald Trump; Bill Weld, former governor of Massachusetts; and Joe Walsh, former US representative of Illinois. The large number of Democrats was somewhat unusual in that the list included three candidates who had held no previous political office experience, though such candidates (Tom Steyer, Marianne Williamson, and Andrew Yang) fared poorly. There was one former vice president (Joe Biden) and one former housing secretary (Julián Castro). There were also five incumbent senators (Michael Bennet, CO; Corey Booker, NJ; Amy Klobuchar, MN; Bernie Sanders, VT; and Elizabeth Warren, MA), one former governor (Deval Patrick, MA), one incumbent and one former US House representative (Tulsi Gabbard, HI; John Delaney, MD), and two former mayors (Michael Bloomberg, NY; Pete Buttigieg, IN). See table 1.1 for these, and other details we will discuss shortly. We have so far illustrated two regularities: few or no candidates will challenge incumbents, but in most cases, many candidates will seek the nomination when no incumbent is running. In this, 2020 is not particularly exceptional. However, 2020 was exceptional in that a record number of women (Gabbard, Klobuchar, Warren, and Williamson)[7] and candidates of color (Booker, Castro, Patrick, Gabbard, Yang) ran for the Democratic nomination, as did the first openly gay candidate (Buttigieg).

A third regularity is that among the candidates who are politicians, most hold or have recently held one of the highest political offices. This regularity follows from "ambition theory," developed originally by Joseph A. Schlesinger to explain how personal ambition and the pattern and prestige of various elected offices lead candidates to emerge from those political offices that have the strongest electoral bases.[8] This base for the presidential candidates includes the offices of vice president, senator, governor, and of course, the presidency itself. One surprising thing from 2020 is that about half of the candidates running for the Democratic nomination did not hold one of these offices. It could be that candidates were looking to Trump's surprising win in 2016 as an example of someone without any political experience winning the nomination as a model.

Table 1.2 presents data on the highest office held by those who ran for the presidential nomination in 2020 and for all campaigns from 1972 to 2020 combined. More than two-thirds of the presidential candidates had already served as president, vice president, senator, or governor; another one in eight was a member of the US House. In 2020 those ratios were largely true again, though only half of the candidates had already served as president, vice president, senator, or governor. Many of the presidents in the early years of the nation were chosen from the outgoing president's cabinet (especially the sitting secretary of state) and other high-level presidential appointees, but the cabinet is no longer a common source of presidential candidates, and

Table 1.1   Candidates for Nomination to the Presidency by the Democratic and Republican Parties, 2020, with Various Aspects Pertinent to Their Candidacy

	Name	Last Political Office	Withdrawal Date[a]	Campaign Expenditures (in Millions of Dollars)[b]	Independent Expenditures[c]
Democrats	Bennet	Sen (current)	11-Feb	$ 7.5	$0
	Biden	Vice President (former)	None	$169.9	$24,697,835
	Bloomberg	Mayor (former)	4-Mar	$1,111.8	$0
	Booker	Sen (current)	13-Jan	$26.0	$0
	Buttigieg	Mayor (former)	1-Mar	$96.7	$3,699,751
	Castro	Secretary (former)	2-Jan	$9.7	$0
	Delaney	Rep (former)	31-Jan	$23.5	$0
	Gabbard	Rep (current)	19-Mar	$15.0	$2,339
	Klobuchar	Sen (current)	2-Mar	$53.8	$0
	Patrick	Gov (former)	12-Feb	$0	$2,367,169
	Sanders	Sen (current)	8-Apr	$216.2	$0
	Steyer	None	29-Feb	$351.6	$0
	Warren	Sen (current)	5-Mar	$129.5	$0
	Williamson	None	10-Jan	$8.2	$0
	Yang	None	11-Feb	$41.8	$719,394
Republicans	Trump	Pres (current)	None	$181.4	$26,789.013
	Walsh	Rep (former)	7-Feb	$0.5	$0
	Weld	Gov (former)	18-Mar	$2.1	$84,784

Source: Compiled by authors.
[a]Information obtained from the *New York Times*, https://www.nytimes.com/interactive/2019/us/politics/2020-presidential-candidates.html; accessed July 9, 2021
[b]Information obtained from the Federal Election Commission, http://www.fec.gov/disclosurep/pna tional .do—and various subpages from there; accessed July 9, 2021. Includes expenditures from January 1, 2019 to June 30, 2020.
[c]Information obtained from OpenSecrets,org, https://www.opensecrets.org/outsidespending/summ.php ?cycle=2020&disp=C&type=P

the same is true for the nation's many mayors. The percentage from these offices was a bit higher in 2020 compared to prior years, 11 percent, as was the percentage of US Representatives, 17 percent. Historically, about one in seven candidates run for president without ever holding any elective office. That percentage was a little higher in 2020 as one in six of the Democratic candidates in 2020 had not held office previously. While there has been a slight increase in the percentage of candidates emerging from less prestigious political offices, as we will see later in the chapter, most of the candidates from these offices dropped out of the race fairly early on.

A fourth regularity, also consistent with ambition theory, is that of the many who run in nomination contests without incumbents, only a few put their current office at risk to do so. In 2020 only one senator, Booker, and

Table 1.2   Current or Most Recent Office Held by Declared Candidates for President: Two Major Parties, 1972–2020

Office Held	Percentage of All Candidates Who Held That Office	Number, 1972–2020	Number, 2020
President	5	9	1
Vice President	3	5	1
US Senator	35	58	5
US Representative	13	21	3
Governor	23	37	2
US Cabinet	4	6	1
Other	7	11	2
None	10	17	3
Total	100	164	18

Sources: 1972–1992: *Congressional Quarterly's Guide to U.S. Elections,* 4th ed. (Washington, DC: CQ Press, 2001), 522–525, 562. 1996: Paul R. Abramson, John H. Aldrich, and David W. Rohde, *Change and Continuity in the 1996 and 1998 Elections* (Washington, DC: CQ Press, 1999), 13. 2000: *CQ Weekly,* January 1, 2000, 22. 2004: *CQ Weekly,* Fall 2003 Supplement, vol. 61, issue 48. The 2008–2020 results were compiled by the authors.

one US representative, Gabbard, were up for reelection. Booker withdrew on January 13, a few weeks before the Iowa caucuses, and was able to still run for his Senate seat and won reelection. Gabbard withdrew later, on March 19, but had already withdrawn from her US House race.

THE RULES OF THE NOMINATION SYSTEM

The method that the two major parties use for nominating presidential candidates is unique and includes an amazingly complicated set of rules. To add to the complication, the various formal rules, laws, and procedures in use are changed, sometimes in large ways and invariably in numerous small ways, every four years. As variable as the rules are, however, the nomination system of 1972 has one pair of overriding characteristics that define it as a system. The first is that whereas delegates actually choose their party's nominee, it is the general public, at least those who vote in the primaries and attend the caucuses, that chooses the delegates and often instructs them as to how to vote. The second characteristic is that the candidates, as a consequence, campaign in public and to the public for their support, mostly by heavy use of traditional media, such as television and newspapers, and, increasingly, social media, such as Facebook and Twitter. Obama pioneered fund-raising and campaign contact on social media in 2008 and 2012. Trump adroitly used the "free media" of television and newspaper coverage in lieu of buying campaign ads on them, and he pioneered the use of Twitter, especially, in 2016.

The complexity of the nomination contests is a consequence of four major factors. The first of these, federalism, defines the state as the unit of selection for national nominees and has been central to party nominations for nearly two centuries now. The second factor is the specific sets of rules governing primaries and caucus/convention procedures—established at the level of the national party in terms of general guidelines and then more specifically by state parties and/or state laws—these rules are at the heart of the nomination system of 1972. These rules govern delegate selection (and sometimes dictate instructions for delegates' presidential voting at the convention). The third factor is the set of rules about financing the campaign, which are also the oft-revised products of the reform period itself, starting in 1972. The fourth factor is the way in which candidates react to these rules and to their opponents, strategies that grow out of the keen competition for a highly valued goal. These factors are described in more detail in the sections that follow.

Federalism or State-Based Delegate Selection

National conventions to select presidential nominees were first held for the 1832 election, and for every nomination since then, the votes of delegates attending the conventions have determined the nominees. Delegates have always been allocated at the state level; whatever other particulars may apply, each state selects its parties' delegates through procedures adopted by state party organizations whether they choose to use caucuses and conventions, by state law, or the party organization wants to use a primary election, or both. Votes at the convention are cast by a state's delegation, and in general the state is the basic unit of the nomination process. Thus there are really fifty separate delegate selection contests in each party.[9] There is no national primary, nor is there serious contemplation of one.

The fact that there are more than fifty separate contests in each party creates numerous layers of complexity, two of which are especially consequential. First, each state is free to choose delegates using any method consistent with the general rules of the national party. Many states choose to select delegates for the parties' conventions via a primary election. States not holding primaries use a combination of caucuses and conventions, which are designed and run by each political party and not by the state government. Caucuses are simply local meetings of party members. Those attending the caucuses report their preferences for the presidential nomination and choose delegates from their midst to attend higher-level conventions such as at the county, congressional district, state, and eventually national levels.

The second major consequence of federalism is that the states are free (within the bounds described as follows) to choose when to hold their primaries or caucuses. These events are thus spread out over time, although both parties now set a time period—the delegate selection "window"—during which primaries and caucuses can be held. Both parties began delegate selection on February 3, 2020, with the Iowa caucuses, and closed the process on August 11, in Connecticut. This was much later than prior years, in which the process would usually close sometime in June. However, many states shifted the dates of their primaries or caucuses due to the global pandemic. For example, Connecticut was originally slated to hold its primary on April 28. Fourteen other states ended up pushing back their primaries or caucuses.[10]

Over time, many states have shifted their primaries or caucuses to earlier in the nomination calendar, which political scientists have coined with the term front-loading. One reason for this is to have more say in who the party nominee is. There is also an incentive to get the nomination wrapped up on the earlier side. For example, Republicans, concerned about how long the Romney nomination in 2012 took to unfold to victory, not only favored shortening the length of the primary season but also tried to regulate front-loading even further. In particular, starting in 2016, they required that states holding their primaries before March 15 had to use some kind of proportional allocation method so that the delegates awarded to candidates were to some degree proportionate to the votes those candidates received in the primary or caucus. It was not until March 15 that states could use the winner-take-all (WTA) rule, such that the candidate with the most votes wins all that state's delegates. WTA rules are often favored by GOP states, due to the larger impact that state's delegation might have on the race, concentrating their vote on a single candidate. All of the Democratic contests, in contrast, use a proportional allocation method.[11]

The Nomination System: Delegate Selection

Through 1968 presidential nominations were won by appeals to the party leadership. To be sure, public support and even primary election victories could be important in a candidate's campaign, but their importance stemmed from the credibility they would give to the candidacy in the eyes of party leaders. The 1968 Democratic nomination, like so many events that year, was especially tumultuous.[12] The result was that the Democratic Party created a committee, known as the McGovern-Fraser Commission, which recommended a series of reforms that were proposed to the Democratic National Committee between 1969 and early 1972 and then finally adopted by the party convention in 1972. The reforms were sufficiently radical in changing delegate selection procedures that they, in effect, created a new nomination system. Although it was much less aggressive in reforming its delegate selection procedures, the Republican Party did so to a certain degree. However, the most consequential results of the Democratic reforms for our purposes—the proliferation of presidential primaries and the media's treatment of some (notably the Iowa) caucuses as essentially primary-like—spilled over to the Republican side as well.

The two most significant consequences of the reforms were the public's great influence on each state's delegate selection proceedings and the proliferation of presidential primaries. Caucus/convention procedures, however, also became better publicized, and in short, were more primary-like. Today the media treat Iowa's caucuses as critical events, and the coverage of them is similar to the coverage of primaries—how many "votes" were "cast" for each candidate, for example.

Whereas the McGovern-Fraser Commission actually recommended greater use of caucuses, many of the state party officials concluded that the easiest way to conform to the new Democratic rules in 1972 was to hold a primary election. Thus the number of states (including the District of Columbia) holding Democratic primaries increased from fifteen in 1968 to twenty-one in 1972 to twenty-seven in 1976, and the number of Republican primaries increased comparably. The numbers peaked in 2000, when forty-three states conducted Republican primaries, and Democratic primaries were held in forty states. One concern to emerge in the divisive 2016 Democratic contest was that caucuses are not as representative of the electorate, as participation rates are generally much lower than in primaries. One of the reforms implemented by the Democratic National Committee after 2016 was to encourage more states to shift to primaries instead of caucuses. In the 2020 election, only six states held caucuses (IA, NV, KS, KY, ND, WY), and of these Kentucky held a Democratic primary but a Republican caucus. Thus it is fair to say that the parties' new nomination systems have become largely based on primaries or in more primary-like conventions.

The only major exception to this conclusion is that historically about 15 percent of delegates to the Democratic National Convention were chosen because they were elected officeholders or Democratic Party officials. Supporters of this reform of party rules (first used in 1984) wanted to ensure that the Democratic leadership would have a formal role to play at the conventions of the party. These "superdelegates" may have played a decisive role in the 1984 nomination of Walter F. Mondale, in the nomination of Obama over Clinton in 2008, and again for Clinton's nomination in 2016, when she, like Mondale and Obama, at one point had a majority of the non-superdelegates but not a majority of all delegates. Each candidate needed only a relatively small number of additional superdelegates to commit to vote for them to win the nomination. All three received those commitments soon after the regular delegate selection process ended, and with that, they were assured the nomination.[13] However, superdelegates became a point of controversy in the 2016 election, particularly among Sanders supporters. In the reforms implemented by the DNC after that election, one important change was limiting the role of superdelegates, who now cannot vote on the first ballot (unless a candidate already has a majority of pledged delegates heading into the convention).[14] This change further erodes the ability of party elites to affect the nomination, though they can still play a more informal role in influencing the fortunes of candidates during the "invisible primary" period, the year or two before the first caucus in Iowa. According to the authors of *The Party Decides*, party elites can help winnow the field of candidates during this period by coordinating their endorsements for particular candidates.[15]

The delegate selection process has, as noted, become considerably more front-loaded.[16] The rationale for front-loading was clear enough: for much of this time period, the last time California's (actual or near) end-of-season primary had an effect on the nomination process was in the 1964 Republican and the 1972 Democratic nomination contests. Once candidates, the media, and other actors realized, and reacted to, the implications of the reformed nomination system, the action shifted to the earliest events of the season, and nomination contests, especially those involving multiple candidates, were effectively completed well before the end of the primary season. More and more state parties and legislatures (including California's) realized the advantages of front-loading, bringing more attention from the media, more expenditures of time and money by the candidates, and more influence to their states if they held primaries sooner rather than later.

Soon, however, other factors started to affect state decisions. First, the rewards for early primaries were concentrated in a relatively small number of the very earliest primaries. And as we have noted, the national parties regulated which ones could go when and threatened to penalize states that violated the national party decisions. Indeed Michigan and Florida were actually penalized in 2008 and 2012 for holding their contests too early in the season. In addition the very early presidential primaries forced states to make an increasingly difficult choice. If they held their presidential primaries early in the year, they had to decide whether to hold the primary elections for all other offices at the same time, which was proving quite a bit earlier than made sense for candidates for local, state, and even national congressional posts, or to pay the costs of running two primaries, one for the president and one much later for all other offices.[17] Some states like California, for example, which were not able to reap the major benefits of being among the very earliest of events in 2012, chose to return too late in the season in 2016, only to switch back to earlier in the calendar in 2020 (March 5).

If the rationale for front-loading was clear by 1996, when it first became controversial, the consequences were not. Some argued that long-shot candidates could be propelled to the front of the pack by gathering momentum in

Iowa and New Hampshire and could, before the well-known candidates had a chance to react, lock up the nomination early. The alternative argument was that increasing front-loading helps those who begin the campaign with the advantages associated with being a front-runner, such as name recognition, support from state and local party or related organizations, and most of all, money. The dynamic of this adjustment, described in the following paragraphs, can be seen clearly in figure 1.1, which reports the week in which the winning candidate was assured nomination in contested nomination campaigns since 1976.

Indeed as the primary season has become more front-loaded, the well-known, well-established, and well-financed candidates have increasingly dominated the primaries. Senator George S. McGovern of South Dakota and Carter won the Democratic nominations in 1972 and 1976, even though they began as little-known and ill-financed contenders. George H. W. Bush, successful in the 1980 Iowa Republican caucuses, climbed from being, in his words, "an asterisk in the polls" (where the asterisk is commonly used to indicate less than 1 percent support) to become Reagan's major contender and eventual vice-presidential choice and his successor to the presidency. And Colorado senator Gary Hart nearly defeated former Vice President Mondale in 1984. However, by 1988 the two strongest candidates at the start of the

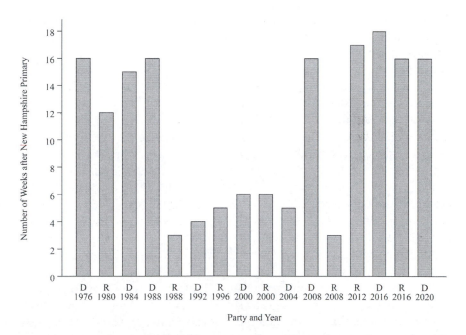

Figure 1.1 Length of Multicandidate Campaigns: Two Major Parties, 1976–2020.
Source: Compiled by authors.

Republican race, George H. W. Bush and Bob Dole, contested vigorously, with Bush winning, while their presence basically locked other lesser-known contenders out. Gov. Michael S. Dukakis of Massachusetts, the best-financed and best-organized (albeit little known) Democrat, won the nomination surprisingly easily. Bill Clinton's victory in 1992 appeared, then, to be the culmination of the trend toward an insuperable advantage for the strongest and best-financed candidates.

Front-loading had simply squeezed too much into too short a post-New Hampshire time frame for a candidate to be able to capitalize on early victories as, say, Carter had done in winning the nomination and election in 1976. The events of 1996 supported the alternative argument—that increased front-loading benefits the front-runner—even though it took nearly all of Dole's resources to achieve his early victory that year.[18]

This lesson was not lost on the candidates for 2000, especially George W. Bush. In particular he began his quest in 1999 (or earlier!) as a reasonably well-regarded governor but one not particularly well-known to the public outside of Texas (although sharing his father's name made him instantly recognizable). He worked hard to receive early endorsements from party leaders and raised a great deal of money well ahead of his competition. When others sought to match Bush's early successes in this invisible primary, they found that he had sewn up a great deal of support. Many, in fact, withdrew before the first vote was cast, suddenly realizing just how Bush's actions had lengthened the odds against them. Bush was therefore able to win the nomination at the very opening of the primary season.

The pre-primary period on the Republican side in 2008 was quite variable, with first McCain, then Giuliani, then Romney surging to the front. McCain's campaign was considered all but dead in the water by that point, but it regathered strength before 2007 ended. There was, then, no strong front-runner in the GOP. On the Democratic side, Hillary Clinton was a clear front-runner, though Obama had developed an impressive organization both by mobilizing support across the nation and by fund-raising, especially through adroit use of the Internet. Thus it was no surprise that he and Clinton easily defeated their rivals. Having boiled down to a two-candidate contest, each had carved out their own bases of support, and neither could decisively defeat the other. Obama led in delegates after the primary season ended, and as heretofore unbound superdelegates determined their choices, they soon favored Obama sufficiently to put him over the top.

The 2012 Republican contest had some similarities to 2008, with Romney moving from his also-ran slot to replace McCain as the candidate who early on seemed strong, lost steam, and then resurged back to victory. One effect of the modest reversal in front-loading was that Romney, even though ahead, was not able to completely shut the door on his opposition until much later in the season. Much the same appeared to happen in 2016 on the Republican side. The unusual nature of someone like Trump emerging as the leading contender led to calls for the remaining candidates (fairly soon into the season, the race reduced effectively to Trump versus Cruz, Kasich, and Rubio) and the "Republican establishment" to figure out a way to stop Trump. When that failed to happen, the divided opposition allowed Trump to build his delegate lead to victory.[19]

The slowed rate of delegate selection also affected the Clinton-Sanders contest on the Democratic side. Clinton, as she had in 2008, began her quest for nomination as a very strong front-runner. Of the remaining actual candidates, Sanders effectively had the liberal wing of the party on his own, and the race narrowed almost immediately to a tight two-person contest. In such races it is typically the case that the nomination takes a longer time to resolve. Even when Clinton had secured an outright majority of delegates, Sanders failed to concede and thus continued to be able to criticize Clinton and to remain a holding place for liberal Democrats who were disenchanted with her.

This pattern of a slowed rate of delegate selection also occurred in the 2020 Democratic nomination contest (as Trump did not face any serious opposition). Biden had been leading in the national polls for much of the invisible primary period, which is not surprising given his name recognition and positive association serving as Obama's vice president. He drew support from the center of the party and was perceived as most likely to beat Trump in the general election. However, in the months leading up to the first caucus, he was closely trailed by other candidates, particularly Sanders and Warren, who drew support from the left-wing of the party. He under-performed in the early states, but his luck started to shift with South Carolina, but that was already into week four of the nomination. He did well the following week on Super Tuesday, though with the system of allocating delegates proportionally, Sanders was still accumulating enough delegates to remain competitive and justify staying in the race, while Warren decided to drop out (on March 5). However, unlike the prior cycle, Sanders dropped out of the race earlier (April 8) as it became clear that Biden's lead in delegates was likely to remain insurmountable, and given the unique crisis the country faced with the pandemic.[20]

These effects can be seen in figure 1.2, which reports the cumulative selection of delegates. As can be seen there, 1976 (the first primary season defined by the rules adopted at the 1972 Democratic Convention) shows a slow, gradual increase in the number of delegates selected. It is not until week thirteen, just over a month before the season ends, that 50 percent of the delegates were selected, and even later that a sufficiently large proportion of the delegates had been selected to make a majority likely to be held by the

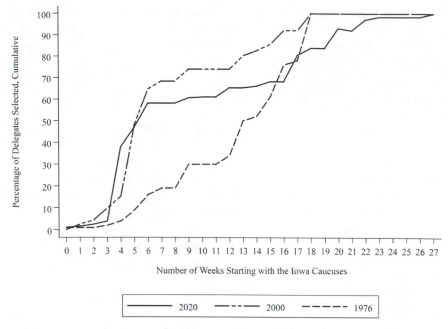

Figure 1.2   Front-Loading: Comparing Democratic Party Delegate Totals Weekly, 1976, 2000, and 2020. *Source*: Compiled by authors.

leading candidate, if he or she faced any opposition at all. The 2000 season was dramatically different, with the 50 percent mark being reached in week six (indeed reaching nearly two-thirds of the delegates selected by that week). The 50 percent mark is also reached by week six in 2020, but we see a slower accumulation of delegates after that point. Part of this is due to the movement away from the heavy front-loading in 2000, but a large part of the trend in 2020 is due to many states pushing their contests back as the country went into lockdown during the global pandemic in mid to late March. However, while the slight retreat from such heavy front-loading in 2020 is visually apparent, it is also apparent that it is rather slight, looking far more like the 2000 apogee than the 1976 perigee.

The final consequence—and possibly the most important for differentiating the nomination system of 1972 from its predecessors—is "momentum," the building of success over time during the extended campaign period, such that every nomination has, so far, always been decided before the convention balloting and always going to the candidate who won the greatest support from the party's electorate.

The most significant feature of the nomination process, from the candidates' perspectives, is its dynamic character. This system was designed to empower the general public, giving it opportunities to participate more fully in the selection of delegates to the national party conventions. The early state delegate selection contests in Iowa and New Hampshire allow largely unknown candidates to work a small state or two using the "retail" politics of door-to-door campaigning to achieve a surprising success that would attract media attention and then money, volunteers, and greater popular support. In practice this was exactly the route Jimmy Carter followed in 1976.

John H. Aldrich developed this account of "momentum" in campaigns, using the 1976 campaigns to illustrate its effect. He first showed that there is no stable balance to this process.[21] In practical terms he predicted that one candidate will increasingly absorb all the money, media attention, and public support and thereby defeat all opponents before the convention. He further showed that the tendency for this process to focus rapidly on a single winner increases the *more* candidates there are. This finding was just the opposite of the original speculation and, indeed, what at the time seemed obvious: the greater the number of candidates, the longer it would take to reach victory. But common sense was not a helpful guide in this case. Like other contests with large numbers of contenders, the Democratic race of 2020 illustrates the power of momentum. Biden did not start off the campaign with a large lead in popular support, and even under-performed in the early states, but he turned that around fairly dramatically in South Carolina and the following two weeks, forcing mostly early exits from most of his opponents.

There is one exception to this pure "momentum" result: the possibility of an unstable but sustainable balance with two candidates locked in a nearly precise tie. Early campaigns offered two illustrations compatible with two candidates in (unstable) equipoise, the 1976 Republican and 1980 Democratic contests. In both the 1984 Democratic and 2008 Democratic contests, the campaigns began with a large number of candidates. Each featured a strong, well-financed, well-known, well-organized candidate (former Vice President Mondale and Hillary Clinton, respectively) who, it turned out, was challenged strongly by a heretofore little-known (to the public) candidate who offered a new direction for the party (Sen. Gary Hart and Sen. Barack Obama, respectively). The multicandidate contest quickly shrank to just two viable candidates. The 2016 Democratic contest fits the pattern of balanced two-party contests very nicely, with neither bloc of voters willing to move from Sanders to Clinton nor from Clinton to Sanders in any great numbers, as inevitably happens in a momentum-driven contest. It is possible that the 2020 Democratic contest would have followed this pattern if Sanders had decided to stay in the race longer.

The Nomination System: Campaign Finance

Campaign finance is the third aspect of the reform of the presidential nomination process. In this case, changes in law (and regulation in light of the law) and in the technology for raising money in nomination contests have made the financial context widely different from one campaign to the next. The 2020 campaign was no exception. Candidates were able to learn some of the lessons from strategies tried in 2012, the first run under a new (de-) regulatory environment in light of the Supreme Court case popularly known as *Citizens United* (2010), as well as earlier elections, where changes in technology made it much easier to raise money. Two major changes were the increased reliance on what are known as independent expenditures by a number of candidates, as well as raising more money from small donors online.

The modern period of campaign finance begins with the Federal Election Campaign Act of 1971 and especially amendments to that act in 1974 and 1976. The Watergate scandal during the Nixon administration included revelations of substantial abuse in raising and spending money in the 1972 presidential election (facts discovered in part due to the implementation of the 1971 act). The resulting regulations limited contributions by individuals and groups, virtually ending the power of individual "fat cats" and requiring presidential candidates to raise money in a broad-based campaign. The federal government would match small donations for the nomination, and candidates who accepted matching funds would be bound by limits on what they could spend.

These provisions, created by the Federal Election Commission to monitor campaign financing and regulate campaign practices, altered the way nomination campaigns were funded. Still, just as candidates learned over time how to contest most effectively under the new delegate selection process, they also learned how to campaign under the new financial regulations. Perhaps most important, presidential candidates learned—although it is not as true for them as for congressional candidates—that "early money is like yeast, because it helps to raise the dough."[22] They also correctly believed that a great deal of money was necessary to compete effectively.

The costs of running presidential nomination campaigns, indeed campaigns for all major offices, have escalated dramatically since 1972. But a special chain of strategic reactions has spurred the cost of campaigning for the presidential nomination. The *Citizens United* case accelerated the chain reaction by creating a much more fully deregulated environment.

When many states complied with the McGovern-Fraser Commission reforms by adopting primaries, media coverage grew, enhancing the effects of momentum, increasing the value of early victories, and raising the costs of early defeat. By 2008 very few candidates were accepting federal matching funds because doing so would bind them to spending limits in individual states and over the campaign as a whole, and these limits were no longer realistic in light of campaign realities. No major candidates accepted matching funds in 2016 or 2020.

Much money was being raised, however. Through May 2008, for example, the fund-raising totals for the three major contenders were $296 million for Obama, $238 million for Clinton, and $122 million for McCain.[23] By the same point in 2012, Romney reported raising $121 million, with Paul having raised $40 million, Gingrich $24 million, and Santorum $22 million. By the end of June 2020, Trump had raised $275 million, Biden had raised $279 million, and Sanders had raised $218 million. And, much money was being spent. See table 1.1 for reports on campaign expenditures in 2020. Note that, for example, Biden and Sanders spent much more than Romney raised in 2012, while Bloomberg spent over a billion dollars.

The 2008 campaign also marked a dramatic expansion in the use of the Internet to raise money, following on the efforts of Democrat Howard Dean, the former governor of Vermont, in 2004 (and, to an extent, McCain in 2000). Obama's success in 2008 served as the model for future campaigns, such as the $55 million he raised in February at a critical moment for the campaign.[24] This has resulted in campaigns raising more money from small donors, a strategy Sanders relied on in 2016, and in 2020, all of the Democratic candidates raised a substantial amount of money from small donors.[25]

The *Citizens United* decision in 2010 changed some of the landscape dramatically. In the narrow it overturned the 2002 Bipartisan Campaign Reform Act and held that corporations and unions could spend unlimited money in support of political objectives and could enjoy First Amendment free-speech rights, just as individuals could. These organizations, however, continued to be banned from direct contribution to candidates and parties. The case, and especially a subsequent one decided by the US Court of Appeals in light of this case, spurred the development of what are known as "super PACs," which are Political Action Committees (PCAs) that can now accept unlimited contributions from individuals, corporations, and unions and spend as much as they like so long as it is not in explicit support of a candidate or party's election campaign or coordinated with their campaign organization.[26]

According to data from the Center for Responsive Politics, expenditures on behalf of the three major nomination contenders were quite large. In 2012 about $14 million was spent on behalf of Romney, $19 million for Gingrich, and $21 million for Santorum. In 2016, expenditures on behalf of many candidates, especially Republicans, had as much, or even more, spent on behalf of their campaigns than they spent themselves.[27] Data from Open Secrets are reported in table 1.1 for the 2020 campaign. Both major-party contenders received a great deal of money from these groups. These organizations altered the terms of the campaign in that their expenditures had to be independent of the candidates and their (and their party's) organizations. It is therefore not necessarily the case that the candidate and, in the fall, the party retain total control over the campaign and its messages. One important consequence of these changes is that what were previously dubbed "fat cats" are once again permitted, though most of the super PACs are funded and led by small numbers of individuals, and we often do not know their names. That said, the majority of candidates for the Democratic nomination pledged not to accept money from outside groups, in part to attract more donations from small donors; thus many of the candidates have zero expenditures from these groups in table 1.1.[28]

The lessons are that money is very helpful, that early money still must be better than that raised late, that candidates are still trying to figure out the best configuration in this largely deregulated campaign finance regime, and that it is not money that is important, but what it will buy. We will discuss campaign strategy in the pages that follow, but this also raises the final lesson for the future, that if candidates come to rely on super PACs, they risk control over their campaign, or they simply agree to adopt the stances of their party or its backers as their own. This concession to the party and its "image" is greatly strengthened due to the dramatic increase in partisan polarization that began around 1980 and continues to increase today, though there were signs of pushback against this on the Democratic side in 2020.

STRATEGY AND THE CANDIDATES' CAMPAIGNS IN 2020: THE ELECTORAL SETTING AND HOW THE CANDIDATES WON THEIR NOMINATIONS

The Strategic Context: One of the most dramatic changes of the last half century has been the increase in partisan polarization among party elites.[29] Although there are debates about the extent to which this holds in the electorate, mounting evidence suggests that partisan polarization also exists and is growing among the electorate, particularly among the more attentive and engaged in politics, who are most likely to participate in primaries and caucuses.[30]

Here we illustrate that the context for the 2020 presidential nomination campaign has become much more deeply polarized along party lines than it was in 1980 in terms of overall affective evaluations of the candidates running for the presidential nomination. The ANES ran nationwide surveys in January 1980 and in April 2020.[31] These years turn out to be especially appropriate ones for this look at partisan polarization of candidate evaluations for two reasons. The 1980 presidential election, as it happens, was the year in which elite partisan polarization began its sharp increase, and thus we have data from the beginning and (current) end points of elite polarization.

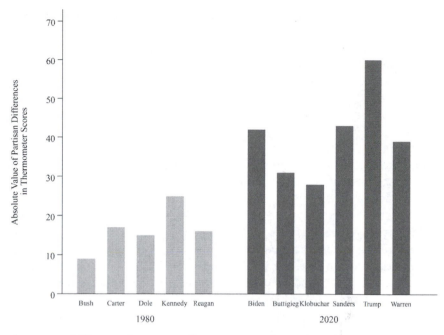

Figure 1.3 Difference in Average Thermometer Rating: Selected Candidates, January 1980 and 2020. *Source*: Authors' analysis of "feeling thermometers" is from the respective ANES surveys. Note: Data are weighted.

Figure 1.3 reports the difference between how the average Democrat and average Republican evaluated that candidate.[32] The figure reports data using candidate thermometers, which ask how "warmly" or "coolly" the respondent feels toward the candidate, where 100 is the warmest possible feeling, 50 is neutral (neither warm nor cool), and 0 is the coldest possible feelings toward that candidate.[33] In 1980, although each party felt more positively toward its own candidates than did those identifying with the other party, the difference between the two parties was fairly muted, with differences typically under 20 degrees on the 100-point scale. Only evaluations of Kennedy were higher, at 27 points. None of these were as large as the smallest partisan gap in 2020, and the partisan polarization between the two eventual nominees was great—more than 40 points for Biden and around 60 for Trump. In 2016, the gap for Trump was just over 40, so there was a dramatic growth in the difference between Democrats and Republicans in those intervening years.

These gaps are important for two reasons. Even at the start of the campaign, that is, the contenders were in a strategic context that rewarded focus on one's own party with no incentive to build toward a cross-party coalition, either in open primary states or for the general election—or thereafter when in office. The public has become deeply divided emotionally over our electoral contests even before they have barely begun in a way that simply was not true a generation ago. Second, the large difference between partisans in feelings toward Trump, more so than any other candidate, meant that Democrats were razor-focused on identifying a candidate that could defeat Trump in the general election. For example, a poll during the invisible primary period (May 2019) found that 65 percent of Democrats and independents said it was more important to them to select a primary candidate who can defeat Trump, while only 35 percent said it was more important to select someone closest to them on issues.[34]

Although it is always true that nomination politics leads candidates to focus on their party to win, this was truer in 2020 than ever before. How, then, did the candidates win? We focus on Democrats, since Trump did not face any serious opposition. Joe Biden started the 2020 campaigns in the enviable position of being an unusually well-known candidate in the public, having served as Barack Obama's vice president, with many areas of support in the Democratic electorate already won. His position was thus well-defined with appeal to moderate Democrats, African Americans, and older voters. If he had a vulnerability in the Democratic primary electorate, it was on the party's left. He entered the nomination contest on the late side (in April 2019); thus, well after a number of candidates had already announced their candidacies. Had he announced his candidacy earlier, others may have strategically decided not to run. Nonetheless, he led in national tracking polls for most of the invisible primary period, though Bernie Sanders and Elizabeth Warren were not far behind.[35]

Sanders was better known in 2020 after his contentious battle for the party's nomination against Clinton in 2016. He clearly fashioned his appeal to the left of the party, given his long-term reputation as a leftist. Indeed his original election as mayor of Burlington, VT, was as a socialist, and he has long served in Congress as an independent who caucuses with the Democrats. While running for the nomination, he signed a pledge with the Democratic National Committee to run and serve as a Democrat if elected president. As in 2016, he drew particular strength from younger voters and was polling behind Biden in national tracking polls leading up to the nomination contests, and often just second to him.

While Sanders did not face any competition from the party's left in 2016, Senator Elizabeth Warren (MA) did decide to run in 2020. Warren was considered a strong alternative to Sanders, with similar credentials on the left, and also membership in the Democratic Party. Like Sanders, she took vocal stances against super PACs and corruption in politics, big corporations taking advantage of workers, and the need for improvements to health care. However, in terms of style, she was distinct from Sanders, coming across as a charismatic policy wonk, with her unofficial campaign slogan being, "I have a plan for that."[36] She also drew support from the left but did better among highly educated voters, particularly women. Warren's support in national polls peaked in the fall, at one point being ahead of Sanders and statistically indistinguishable from Biden, but her support diminished in October and November of 2019.[37] Having both Sanders and Warren in the race helped Biden, since it split support among those on the left.

The remaining candidates to amass delegates positioned themselves as alternatives to Biden among more moderate voters, but were generally well behind Biden, Sanders, and Warren in national tracking polls during the invisible primary period. Senator Amy Klobuchar (MN) touted her credentials as one of the most effective lawmakers, who never lost a race, and as a possible alternative for women who wanted to support a female candidate, but one more moderate than Warren.[38] Pete Buttigieg was one of the more surprising candidates in that the highest office he held prior to running for president was mayor of South Bend, Indiana. However, many voters were impressed with his skills on the debate stage, and he drew support from highly educated white centrists within the party.[39] Michael Bloomberg, the billionaire former mayor of New York City, also positioned himself as a moderate alternative to Biden and self-financed his campaign. Prior to 2001, Bloomberg was a Democrat, but ran as a Republican for mayor of New York, became an independent in 2007, and identified as a Democrat again in 2018. He hoped to draw support given his experience in business and government, and efforts to fight gun violence. Since these candidates were polling well behind Biden, Sanders, and Warren, they set their sights on particular states, with Buttigieg and Klobuchar focusing on IA and NH, and Bloomberg sitting out some of the early contests to try to make a splash during Super Tuesday.

Biden had a disappointing showing in the Iowa caucuses, coming in fourth behind Buttigieg, Sanders, and Warren, though picking up slightly more delegates (see table 1.3 for delegates won by these candidates over the nomination campaign). The biggest surprise of the night was Buttigieg winning the biggest percentage of the vote, 26.2 percent, so his gamble of pouring most of his resources into the first state seemed to pay dividends. Meanwhile, Warren under-performed relative to Sanders, and Klobuchar did better than expected, picking up one delegate. According to exit polls, it was pretty clear that moderate Democrats split their vote between Biden and Buttigieg pretty evenly (25 percent), with Klobuchar close behind (20 percent), and Sanders (28 percent) did slightly better than Warren (21 percent) among liberal Democrats. Support was also higher for Biden and Buttigieg among those who thought Democrats should nominate someone who can beat Trump.[40]

Biden and Warren had another disappointing showing in New Hampshire, where neither picked up any delegates, and instead Sanders carried the state, followed closely by Buttigieg and Klobuchar. According to exit poll

Table 1.3   Democratic Nomination Results, 2020: Bound Delegates Won in State Primaries and Caucuses

Date	State	Biden	Sanders	Bloomberg	Buttigieg	Klobuchar	Warren
3-Feb	IA	14	12	–	9	1	5
11-Feb	NH	0	9	–	9	6	0
22-Feb	NV	9	24	–	3	0	0
29-Feb	SC	39	15	–	0	0	0
3-Mar	AL	44	8	0	–	–	0
	AR	19	9	3	–	–	0
	CA	172	221	9	–	–	12
	CO	26	24	9	–	–	8
	ME	13	9	0	–	–	2
	MA	45	29	0	–	–	17
	MN	43	27	0	–	–	5
	NC	68	37	3	–	–	2
	OK	21	13	2	–	–	1
	TN	38	20	5	–	–	1
	TX	113	99	11	–	–	5
	UT	7	16	3	–	–	3
	VT	5	11	0	–	–	0
	VA	66	31	0	–	–	2
10-Mar	ID	11	9	–	–	–	–
	MI	73	52	–	–	–	–
	MS	34	2	–	–	–	–
	MO	44	24	–	–	–	–
	ND	6	8	–	–	–	–
	WA	46	43	–	–	–	–
17-Mar	AZ	39	28	–	–	–	–
	FL	162	57	–	–	–	–
	IL	94	60	–	–	–	–
7-Apr	WI	56	28	–	–	–	–
10-Apr	AK	11	4	–	–	–	–
17-Apr	WY	10	4	–	–	–	–
28-Apr	OH	115	21	–	–	–	–
2-May	KS	29	10	–	–	–	–
12-May	NE	29	0	–	–	–	–
19-May	OR	46	15	–	–	–	–
22-May	HI	16	8	–	–	–	–
2-Jun	DC	20	0	–	–	–	–
	IN	81	1	–	–	–	–
	MD	96	0	–	–	–	–
	MT	18	1	–	–	–	–
	NM	30	4	–	–	–	–
	PA	151	33	–	–	–	–
	RI	24	0	–	–	–	–
	SD	13	3	–	–	–	–
9-Jun	WV	28	0	–	–	–	–
	GA	105	0	–	–	–	–
	NY	199	18	–	.	–	–
23-Jun	KY	52	0	–	–	–	–

(Continued)

Table 1.3 Democratic Nomination Results, 2020: Bound Delegates Won in State Primaries and Caucuses (Continued)

Date	State	Biden	Sanders	Bloomberg	Buttigieg	Klobuchar	Warren
7-Jul	DE	21	0	–	–	–	–
	NJ	121	3	–	–	–	–
11-Jul	LA	54	0	–	–	–	–
12-Jul	PR	36	5	–	–	–	–
11-Aug	CT	60	0	–	–	–	–
Listed numbers are for bound delegates							

Source: Author compiled from https://www.cnn.com/election/2020/primaries-and-caucuses

data, moderates and conservatives were more likely to support Buttigieg and Klobuchar, and Sanders did better among liberals.[41] Sanders trounced the competition in Nevada, though Biden's standing improved, coming in second, while Buttigieg's support seemed to be running out of steam, and no other candidate received delegates. Biden did better among moderates in NV compared to NH and benefited from his appeal to the more diverse electorate in Nevada, as Buttigieg struggled to expand his base to non-whites.[42]

Heading into South Carolina, Biden was trailing Sanders in pledged delegates. However, a key endorsement from Representative James Clyburn helped turn the tide for Biden.[43] He had a commanding win in South Carolina, demonstrating particular strength with the black community.[44] This put pressure on moderate Democrats still in the race who were not amassing significant delegates to drop out and rally behind Biden. The first to do so was Buttigieg, who withdrew the next day, endorsing Biden, followed closely by Klobuchar the following day. Around the same time, Biden was receiving endorsements from others in the party who had already dropped out, such as Beto O'Rourke. Biden's South Carolina victory became a clear turning point in the nomination contest as party elites began to clearly rally behind Biden. This was a clear effort on the part of the party to help decide who the eventual nominee would be, though it happened much later than earlier nomination contests where elites would endorse candidates earlier in the process.

Biden then won 13 of 18 states the following week during the "Super Tuesday" primaries, most of which were in the South and thus featured two sources of Biden's strength, moderate white Democrats and African Americans, which meant that Sanders fell behind in delegates won, though was still doing well enough to remain competitive. According to exit polls, Biden was preferred by 22 percentage points over Sanders among those who preferred a candidate who can beat Donald Trump, and by 31 percentage points among those who decided in the last few days.[45] Following Super

Tuesday, Warren decided to drop out of the race. Biden continued to have a strong showing the following two weeks, including in key midwestern states like Michigan, and his support in national tracking polls grew dramatically. Because the Democratic rules require some form of proportional selection of delegates (i.e., roughly in proportion to the percentage of votes received), Biden's delegate lead became insurmountable.

At around this same time, the global pandemic worsened and many states began to institute lockdowns, with several moving their primaries to later dates. As it became clear that Sanders had no chance of winning the nomination, and Democratic elites and many in the electorate were rallying behind Biden in response to the crisis, Sanders decided to end his campaign in early April, thus much earlier than he had four years before. At the point that Sanders dropped out of the race, Biden's numbers in tracking polls had jumped to over 60 percent to Sanders's 32 percent.[46]

The Republican side was, of course, rather different in many ways. As a popular incumbent within his own party, Trump did not face any significant opposition. It is therefore not surprising that he won all of the pledged delegates, save one (See table 1.4). Nine states and Puerto Rico did not even hold a Republican caucus or primary, which is fairly typical when an incumbent does not face any serious challengers.

National Party Conventions: As we noted earlier, the purpose of the state primary or caucus convention procedures is to select who will be the delegates from that state to attend their national party convention and/or to instruct those delegates on how to vote for the presidential nomination. The delegates are those entrusted with voting on all the convention's major pieces of business. These include resolving any remaining problems that arose in selecting one state's or another's delegations, adopting rules that will govern the party for the next four years, voting on the proposed party platform, and choosing the presidential and vice-presidential nominees. Thus the delegates are entrusted with essentially all of the party's major decisions. But, as we have already seen with respect to the presidential nomination, they may cast the formal ballots—and it could well be some day that they will in fact play active roles—but their decision-making is so tightly constrained that they almost invariably have no real choices to make. Their choice for presidential nominee is constrained by the vote of the public in their state.[47] The presidential nominee selects a candidate she or he would like to see serve as a running mate, and it has been a very long time since there was any real opposition to that choice.[48]

Party platforms once were regularly contended, as this was the one time when the party leadership could interact and work out just what the party stood for. Although this has not been true in recent years, both parties have had protests over the platform committee's proposals on one issue or another (e.g., the change in the 1980 Republican platform from its long-held stance of endorsing an Equal Rights Amendment to the Constitution for women to opposing it), whereas the last truly contended (nearly violently contended) battle over a platform plank was the debate over the Vietnam War in the 1968 Democratic Convention.

Instead of the traditional role of party conventions serving as the one time the party gathers from around the nation to debate and decide party business, the conventions have changed in recent decades to serve as major public presentations of the party to the nation. This leads the party and its leadership to seek to downplay internal divisions (although when they are really there, they are typically not able to be completely hidden) and present a united front to the public. Their other central role is to serve as the end of the intra-party competition of nominations and the transition to the general election campaign. The acceptance speeches of the nominees (and certainly of the presidential nominee) are generally used to showcase the major themes of the candidates for the general election campaign.

The party conventions were quite different in 2020 due to the global pandemic. The Democratic National Convention was originally scheduled to take place in mid-July in Milwaukee, but was postponed to August in the hopes that conditions with the pandemic would improve. When that did not happen, the Democratic Convention was held from August 17 to August 20 across four stages in New York City, Los Angeles, Milwaukee, and Wilmington. There were no delegates in attendance; instead, votes took place remotely from August 3 to 16. The Republican Party held its national convention from August 24 to 27 in Charlotte, NC. The RNC had some limited in-person events, even further reducing the number of in-person delegates to 336 (after originally planning for 2,500). The executive committee decided to adopt the 2016 party platform, the first time there was no new platform selected at a party convention, in part since the platform committee would not be meeting.[49]

Trump selected Vice President Michael Pence (Indiana) to be his running mate again. Pence is as understated as Trump is flamboyant and had considerable experience in politics to balance Trump's outsider status back in the 2016 campaign. Pence is known for having particularly deep religious beliefs, which guide many of his policy positions and, of course, appeal strongly to the large and important religious right in the party. That he hails from a combined Rust Belt, agricultural midwestern state also helped balance the ticket, as is a common tradition, counterbalancing a New York City, high-rolling businessman with little formal connections to religion. Given the highly scripted nature of the largely virtual convention, there were no moments of contention. During his acceptance speech, Trump touted his accomplishments during his first term, such as trade deals and a strong economy before

Table 1.4 Republican Nomination Results, 2020: Bound Delegates Won in State Primaries and Caucuses—Trump, Walsh, and Weld

Date	State	Trump	Walsh	Weld
3-Feb	IA	39	1	0
11-Feb	NH	22	–	0
3-Mar	AL	50	–	0
	AR	40	–	0
	CA	172	–	0
	CO	37	–	0
	ME	22	–	0
	MA	41	–	0
	MN	39	–	0
	NC	71	–	0
	OK	43	–	0
	TN	58	–	0
	TX	117	–	0
	UT	40	–	0
	VT	17	–	0
10-Mar	ID	32	–	0
	MI	73	–	0
	MS	40	–	0
	MO	54	–	0
	WA	43	–	0
17-Mar	FL	122	–	0
	IL	66	–	0
7-Apr	WI	52	–	–
28-Apr	OH	82	–	–
12-May	NE	36	–	–
19-May	OR	28	–	–
2-Jun	DC	19	–	–
	IN	58	–	–
	MD	38	–	–
	MT	27	–	–
	NM	22	–	–
	PA	34	–	–
	RI	19	–	–
	SD	29	–	–
9-Jun	WV	35	–	–
	GA	76	–	–
23-Jun	KY	46	–	–
7-Jul	DE	16	–	–
	NJ	49	–	–
11-Jul	LA	46	–	–
11-Aug	CT	28	–	–

Listed numbers are for bound delegates.

Source: Author compiled from https://www.cnn.com/election/2020/primaries-and-caucuses
*AZ, AK, KS, SC, ND, NV, NY, Puerto Rico, VA, and WY did not hold a Republican caucus or primary.

the pandemic, warned of the economic collapse and chaos that would ensue with a Biden presidency, and promised a vaccine for Covid-19 before election day.

Biden, for his part, selected Senator Kamala Harris (California) as his running mate, who had dropped out of the presidential nomination race in December. Harris gained acclaim as a prosecutor in California, showcasing those skills in Senate committee hearings for some of Trump's controversial Supreme Court nominees, such as Brett Kavanaugh. The choice of Harris also had an element of ticket balancing, not with respect to uniting the ideological wings of the party, but with respect to recognizing the gender and racial diversity within the party, as Kamala Harris would be the first woman, black, and South Asian person to occupy the vice presidency. This seemed particularly important on the heels of historic protests such as the women's marches following Trump's election in 2016, protests over the killing of George Floyd[50] in the spring and summer of 2020, as well as the record number of women, men of color, and women of color who vied for the Democratic nomination. The party was able to present a united image to the public, especially given the virtual format, and this enabled Biden to focus on the general election campaign in his acceptance speech, with themes centered around a battle for the soul of the nation. He critiqued Trump's presidency, especially his handling of the pandemic, and called for the country to come together, across partisan lines, to develop a more comprehensive approach to combating the pandemic, and building back the economy, with lofty goals for infrastructure, health care, and climate change.

Chapter 2

The General Election Campaign

Once they have been nominated, candidates choose their general election campaign strategies based on their perceptions of what the electorate wants, the relative strengths and weaknesses of their opponents and themselves, and their chances of winning. A candidate who is convinced that he or she has a dependable lead may choose very different strategies from those used by a candidate who believes he or she is seriously behind. A candidate who believes that an opponent has significant weaknesses is more likely to run an aggressive, attacking campaign than one who does not perceive such weaknesses.

After the 2020 conventions, Joe Biden maintained a modest lead over Donald Trump in national polls (although many early polls were within the margin of error). Many political observers thought that Biden would win the election and that the stark differences in campaign messages and styles for the two candidates would make a significant difference in the outcome. Chapters 4 through 8 of this book will consider in detail the impact of particular factors (including issues and evaluations of President Trump's job performance) on the voters' decisions. This chapter will provide an overview of the fall campaign—an account of its course and a description of the context within which strategic decisions were made.

THE STRATEGIC CONTEXT AND CANDIDATES' CHOICES

One aspect of the strategic context that candidates must consider is the track record of the parties in recent elections. In presidential races the past is certainly not a determinant of the future, but it is relevant. From this perspective, the picture was slightly more encouraging for the Republicans than for the Democrats. From 1952 through 2016 there had been eighteen presidential elections, and the Republicans had won eleven of them. On the other hand the Democrats had won three of the last six races since 1996, and in both 2000 and 2016 they secured a narrow popular-vote margin despite falling short in the Electoral College.

The nature of the American system for electing presidents requires that we consider the state-by-state pattern of results. US voters do not directly vote for president or vice president. Rather, they vote for a slate of electors pledged to support a presidential and a vice-presidential candidate. Moreover, in every state except Maine and Nebraska, the entire slate of electors that receives the most popular votes is selected and in no state is a majority of the vote required. Since the 1972 election, Maine has used a system in which the plurality-vote winner for the entire state wins two electoral votes. In addition the plurality-vote winner in each of Maine's two House districts receives that district's single electoral vote. Beginning in 1992, Nebraska allocated its five electoral votes in a similar manner: the statewide plurality-vote winner gained two votes, and each of the state's three congressional districts awarded one vote on a plurality basis.[1]

If larger states used the district plan employed by Maine and Nebraska, the dynamics of the campaign would be quite different. For example, candidates might target specific congressional districts and would probably campaign in all large states, regardless of how well they were doing in the statewide polls. But given the WTA rules employed in forty-eight states and the District of Columbia, candidates cannot safely ignore the pattern of past state results when coordinating their own campaign strategies. Each presidential candidate typically has a base of support in certain states (i.e., Democrats in California and New York and Republicans in states like Kansas and Texas) with only a handful of states up for grabs in a given election year.

Although most observers thought Biden had a distinct advantage over Trump in the election, both campaign organizations viewed the same set of states determining the outcome of the election. These would be the "battleground" states, where both campaign organizations would concentrate the lion's share of their time, money, and effort. Indeed, even before the beginning of 2020, the two parties had already focused their attention on about eight states, and most of the other states would be largely ignored until election day.[2] The larger states in this group—particularly Florida, Georgia, Michigan, and Pennsylvania—would be the main focus of their efforts. Many of the non-battleground states, on the other hand—even large ones like California and New York—would see little evidence that a presidential campaign was in progress. A state perspective through the lens of the Electoral College would influence the strategy of the 2020 campaign.[3]

POLITICAL CONTEXT, OVERALL
STRATEGY, AND OPENING MOVES

The strategic choices of candidates and parties are shaped by the particular context of the election. One feature of that context is whether an incumbent is running. Incumbent races are different from contests without incumbents. They tend to unfold in a regular pattern, and the first stage of the pattern centers on the public's attitude toward the current occupant of the White House. As we will discuss in detail in chapter 8, elections involving incumbents tend to be referenda on presidential performance. From 1956 through 2016 (a time when we have dependable measurements of the public's evaluation of the president's performance), there were eleven elections in which an incumbent president could stand for reelection (in five other elections—1960, 1988, 2000, 2008, and 2016—the incumbent was constitutionally ineligible to run again). In five of those elections, the president had approval ratings above 50 percent during the spring before the vote—that is, before the general election campaign, and even well before the selection of the opposing nominee by his party's convention. In all five instances, the incumbent won comfortably. On the other hand, the incumbent's approval was below 50 percent in five cases. In four of those five instances, he either withdrew from the race or lost—the exception was President Barack Obama in 2012, who won reelection despite his approval averaging between 46 and 48 percent earlier in the year.[4] An additional incumbent race was 2004, when President George W. Bush sought reelection. Between the beginning of March and the end of July 2004, Bush's approval rating measured by the Gallup Poll ranged between 46 and 53 percent.[5] The outcome was a narrow victory for the incumbent.

These data suggest that Trump's approval rating was an important indicator of his prospects for reelection, and in early 2020 the news was decidedly mixed. Using the same window of March 1 to July 31 used for Bush, Trump's approval ratings from Gallup polls ranged from 38 to 49 percent, with an average of 44 percent.[6] Thus the president's standing was right on the historical borderline between victory and defeat, confirming the prospects for a real contest that either major party could potentially win. This moved the race into the pattern of incumbent races in which the public evaluates the opposing candidate and makes a judgment on whether he is a plausible alternative to the incumbent. In years when the incumbent's approval is quite high (e.g., 1956 and 1964), the electorate doesn't seriously consider the challenger and the race is effectively over before it begins. Clearly 2020 was not to be one of those cases, and Joe Biden would have the opportunity to make his case for election.

The Trump campaign's strategic planning started long before 2020. In fact, Donald Trump declared his intent to seek reelection the day he initially took office in 2017. By early 2019, the Trump reelection campaign had already raised $100 million dollars, and the president regularly boasted about this on Twitter. Later that year, that amount had doubled and would continue to increase throughout 2020. By the end of October 2020, the Trump reelection campaign had raised nearly $800 million dollars. This excluded money from outside groups such as super PACs, which added in excess of $300 million dollars. When factoring in funds raised by the Republican National Committee and other contributions, Trump had access to approximately $1.96 billion dollars for his reelection campaign. By comparison, the Biden campaign ended up raising almost $1.7 billion dollars, which included an important late surge of several hundred million dollars in the three months preceding the election.[7]

One factor that loomed over the Trump campaign throughout 2020 was the coronavirus pandemic. Despite receiving warnings from intelligence agencies and various medical experts about the potential seriousness of the coronavirus as early as January, the president largely downplayed the risk of the virus and the threat it posed to Americans out of likely fear that he might be held accountable for it in the general election. One of the main reasons he continued to publicly dismiss the severity of the virus is that he recognized that aggressively addressing the problem would likely require closing down large segments of the economy (which ultimately occurred in the spring). The president also started to shift the blame to the governors in "blue" states where the number of cases were significantly higher, arguing that they were not doing enough to limit citizen exposure. On occasion, he also targeted the World Health Organization, Barack Obama, and even the Democratic nominee, Joe Biden, for various issues associated with the pandemic.[8]

As a result of the enormous attention the coronavirus was receiving in the news media, the Trump campaign did not aggressively criticize former vice president Joe Biden during the early months of 2020. Many of the initial attacks leveled against Biden focused primarily on his mental capacity stemming from his age, but these criticisms proved to be less than effective. Although Trump himself seemed hesitant at times to challenge Biden prior to him receiving the nomination at the Democratic Convention, many Republicans encouraged him to do so since the president was being relentlessly hammered in the news about the pandemic given his inconsistent response to date. Eventually, Trump and his reelection campaign started to get more assertive in their criticism of Biden during the early summer, focusing on his relationship with China, his son's connections and past dealings with Ukraine, and some of his actions related to the 2009 financial crisis oversight. These issues became the central focus of many of Trump's and other campaign ads that tried to paint Biden as someone who has been in politics for over forty years, but was largely out of touch with American interests.[9]

Meanwhile, the Biden campaign sought to consistently portray the upcoming election as a referendum on Donald Trump and his presidency by illustrating how ineffective he had been as a leader. Although the former vice president initially stayed out of the fray during the early days of the coronavirus pandemic since he did not want to politicize the crisis, he quickly switched gears once it became apparent that the president was ineffective at handling the situation.[10] Indeed, over the next few months, Biden repeatedly criticized the president for his inconsistent handling of the virus, not closing the border with China sooner, and failing to provide states with the resources and medical equipment they needed to deal with the virus. During the summer, the Biden campaign also began to emphasize the immediate need for racial justice in light of the brutal killing of George Floyd by a white Minneapolis policeman, which contributed to protests across the country against racially motivated police practices as well as racism more generally.[11]

THE FALL CAMPAIGN

It is often the case that nominating conventions provide a short-term boost in the polls to the candidate of the party holding them. After all, the party and its candidate receive a lot of attention, and they largely control what is seen and heard during the convention. In 2020, with the conventions so close together and given the unique nature of how each was handled in light of the pandemic, it is difficult to be sure of the effects, but data from a Morning Consult poll conducted shortly after the Republican convention gave Trump a bounce of four percentage points. Meanwhile, a similar poll conducted a week earlier showed that Biden received no immediate bump from the Democratic National Convention. By late August, a Yahoo News-YouGov poll showed that Biden's lead over Trump had shrunk to six percentage points following the Republican convention, the smallest lead all year for the former vice president.[12] When combined with the declining number of cases of the coronavirus in late July and August, this was exactly the type of turnaround the Trump campaign was hoping for going into the fall election season.

In light of the growing unrest in cities such as Portland, Oregon, and Kenosha, Wisconsin, regarding racial justice and police reform, President Trump attempted to use the Republican National Convention to reframe the race around the subject of law and order. These latter issues are traditionally viewed more favorably by Republican voters and the Trump campaign sought to use them to win back voters in suburban areas who might defect from the president in the election. Despite their efforts, however, a new series of polls released in early September showed that the president continued to trail the former vice president both nationwide and in key battleground states across the country. Biden had maintained an eight to nine point lead over Trump prior to the Democratic Convention, but these new polls showed less than a one-point gain for the president, including one conducted by Fox News.[13]

Throughout the month of September, Trump continued to hold campaign rallies in person around the country, some of which were held in venues with limited opportunities for social distancing or where Trump supporters congregated in large groups despite potential health risks stemming from COVID-19. Biden, in contrast, limited himself mostly to remote or virtual campaign events in an attempt to limit the spread of the coronavirus. At several of these campaign events, the president continued to offer inconsistent perspectives on the coronavirus, including a rally in Ohio where he claimed that it "affects elderly people, elderly people with heart problems and other problems. If they have other problems, that's what it really affects. That's it." He also suggested that young people are "virtually immune . . . because they have a hell of an immune system" and that "it affects virtually nobody."[14] These comments that sought to downplay the seriousness of the virus came just hours before the US death toll from the total number of COVID-19 cases surpassed 200,000.[15]

On September 18, the narrative of the election profoundly changed when President Trump learned of the death of Supreme Court Justice Ruth Bader Ginsburg as a result of complications stemming from her long battle with pancreatic cancer. Although Ginsburg had initially been diagnosed with pancreatic cancer in 2009, she elected to remain on the Court during President Obama's eight years in office, when she could have been replaced with another like-minded justice. In brief remarks after learning of her death following a campaign rally in Minnesota, the president hailed Ginsburg as a "brilliant mind" and stated that "her opinions, including well-known decisions regarding the legal equality of women and the disabled, have inspired all Americans, and generations of great legal minds."[16] These statements notwithstanding, at least one source close to the president indicated that Trump had been eager to replace Ginsburg on the bench and was "salivating" at the prospects of naming a conservative jurist to fill her seat prior to the election.[17]

Within hours of Ginsburg's death, Senate Majority Leader Mitch McConnell indicated that the Senate would move quickly to confirm whomever the president named to replace Justice Ginsburg on the bench and would endeavor to do so before the election, which was less than two months away. "Americans reelected our majority in 2016 and expanded it in 2018 because we pledged to work with President Trump and support his agenda, particularly his outstanding appointments to the federal judiciary. Once again, we will keep our promise," McConnell noted.[18] Not surprisingly, Democrats were outraged by this declaration since McConnell had refused to act four years earlier on President Obama's nomination of Merrick Garland to fill the seat vacated following

Justice Antonin Scalia's unexpected death in February 2016. Indeed, this seat remained vacant until President Trump nominated Neil Gorsuch in early 2017 to replace Scalia and he was later confirmed on April 7, 2017, by a vote of 54–45, which necessitated the Republicans having to eliminate the use of the filibuster on Supreme Court nominations.[19]

The following day, President Trump attended a campaign rally in Fayetteville, North Carolina and vowed to appoint a woman to fill the vacancy on the Court. "Hoping to shift the public's attention from his handling of the coronavirus pandemic, Trump moved quickly on Saturday to make the new Supreme Court vacancy a central issue in his campaign, announcing that he would name a woman to replace Ginsburg this week."[20] Among the likely contenders that Trump had previously mentioned were Judge Amy Coney Barrett, who was serving on the US Court of Appeals for the Seventh Circuit and had previously clerked for Justice Scalia, as well as Judge Barbara Lagoa, a Hispanic judge who Trump had appointed to the 11th US Circuit Court of Appeals in 2019. Former vice president Biden, in contrast, was very critical of McConnell's announcement made shortly after Ginsburg's death that the Senate would vote on Trump's nominee in light of his refusal to hold a vote on Merrick Garland four years earlier despite his nomination by then-president Obama. Biden also reiterated his intention to nominate an African American woman to the Supreme Court if given the opportunity, but declined to put forward a list of potential nominees as Trump had done when campaigning for the presidency in 2016.[21]

A week later, the president made good on his promise when he announced that he would be naming Judge Barrett to the Court to fill the seat previously held by Ginsburg. He also encouraged the Senate to act quickly on his appointment to ensure that she was seated on the Court prior to the election. This announcement was immediately hailed by conservatives who recognized that if the forty-eight-year-old judge was eventually confirmed by the Senate, it would "solidify the court's conservative majority, shaping the trajectory of health care law, abortion rights and many corners of American life for generations to come."[22] Democrats, in contrast, were highly critical of the announcement and braced for a bitter confirmation battle over the next few weeks. Eventually, and in direct response to the Republicans' hurried efforts to replace Ginsburg prior to the election, Democrats began discussing potentially increasing the size of the Supreme Court by four justices if Biden were to win the presidency and Democrats gain control over both the House and Senate.[23] This became a rallying point for Democratic supporters during the remaining weeks of the campaign, especially when it became apparent that Barrett might indeed be appointed to the Court.

The day after Trump announced Barrett's nomination to the Supreme Court, the *New York Times* released a story indicating that President Trump only paid $750 in federal income taxes the year he won the presidency along with the same amount the following year. The story continued by noting that Trump "paid no income taxes at all in 10 of the previous 15 years—largely because he reported losing much more money than he made."[24] The president's tax returns had been the source of inquiry all throughout his presidency since he had declined to make them available when running for president as is generally the case. He claimed time and again that he was undergoing a decades-long audit by the IRS and would only release his tax returns once the audit was completed and he was ultimately vindicated. Unfortunately, such assurances did little to assuage many critics who felt that the president was attempting to hide the sources of much of his income, including money originating from countries such as Russia that might be adversely affecting his behavior while in office.[25]

The Debates

In the days leading up to the first presidential debate in late September, the former vice president continued to maintain a sizable 7–10 point lead over Trump in the presidential race according to most public opinion polls. In preparation for the first debate, Biden remained at his home in Delaware with a small group of advisers who were helping him gear up for his exchange with an unpredictable president on the national stage. In a year characterized by a deadly pandemic and corresponding recession, considerable social unrest, the recent death of Supreme Court Justice Ginsburg and the pending fight over filling her seat, Biden recognized the enormous stakes associated with his performance in the first debate even though he sought to downplay it publicly. "The former vice president plans to attack Trump's leadership as unsteady, challenge the president's repeated falsehoods, and contrast his own experience in a crisis."[26]

In contrast to Biden, the president seemed to favor a different style of preparing for the first debate. "President Trump publicly insists he doesn't rehearse for debates, claiming recently that he is preparing for his first debate on Tuesday in Cleveland with Democratic nominee Joe Biden 'just by doing what I'm doing.'"[27] In private, however, Trump was reported to have been studying Biden's vice-presidential debate performances from both 2008 and 2012 to gain a better understanding of his debate tactics and to try to identify any weaknesses he can seek to exploit. Advisers close to the president noted that Trump was not holding formal or mock sessions, but instead was trying out potential attack lines with his personal attorney Rudy Giuliani and former New Jersey Governor Chris Christie. Nevertheless, many of those close to the president saw the first debate as a make-or-break opportunity for the president given the trends in recent public opinion polling. When asked whether he was looking forward to the event while campaigning in Ohio the day before the event, Trump responded by grinning and saying, "Yeah, I am. I am looking very forward to the debate."[28]

The first presidential debate was held on September 29 at Case Western Reserve University in Cleveland, OH and was moderated by Fox News anchor Chris Wallace. The debate was divided into six 15-minute segments with a range of topics including COVID-19, racial and social unrest, the US Supreme Court, the economy, the past records of both Trump and Biden, and election integrity. After the first few minutes, however, it became readily apparent that the president had no interest in legitimately debating these issues with the former vice president. Instead of engaging with either the moderator or Biden on the debate topics, the president "interrupted constantly and tried to distract, deflect and interject."[29] Additionally, when asked by Wallace to denounce white supremacists and militia groups such as the right-wing group Proud Boys, the president instead said, "Proud Boys, stand back and stand by," before then criticizing left-wing extremist groups.[30] Later in the debate when discussing the integrity of the election, Trump refused to urge his voters to remain peaceful if there were delays in counting votes, instead stating, "I'm urging my supporters to go into the polls and watch very carefully because that's what has to happen. If it's a fair election, I am 100% on board. If I see tens of thousands of ballots being manipulated, I can't go along with that."[31]

Although Biden's performance was not as crisp as some Democrats might have preferred and he likely missed some opportunities to criticize the president on various issues, he did come off as the more reasonable candidate by almost any metric. He also had some notable one-liners in the debate including "would you just shut up man" and referring to Trump as a "clown" more than once. Biden refused to be baited by the president on numerous occasions and stuck with his criticisms of Trump, especially on matters such as the coronavirus, racial justice, and the economy.[32] Many who watched the debate characterized it as a disaster from the very beginning with the moderator often as flummoxed by Trump's behavior as Biden was. Soon after the debate ended, CNN's Jake Tapper offered a memorable comment when he described the chaotic exchange as "a hot mess, inside a dumpster fire, inside a train wreck." He continued by noting, "That was the worst debate I have ever seen. In fact, it wasn't even a debate. It was a disgrace and it's primarily because of Trump who spent the entire time interrupting not abiding by the rules he agreed to."[33]

Despite its unusual nature, the audience for the first presidential debate was sizable. An estimated 73.1 million viewers tuned into the 16 stations that were carrying the debate live, approximately 10 million fewer viewers than watched the first debate in 2016.[34] In reality, the viewership was potentially even higher because many individuals likely ended up watching the debate online. By the next morning, the media consensus was that Biden was the winner of the first debate. According to a CBS News Survey of individuals who watched the exchange between the two candidates, 48 percent thought Biden had won compared with 40 percent who felt Trump was the winner. At the same time, an overwhelming number of respondents (83 percent) referred to the debate's tone as quite negative while 69 percent indicated they were "annoyed" by the debate. Biden was more effective at convincing fellow partisans he was the winner compared with Trump's supporters. "Ninety-two percent of Democrats who watched say he won, compared to 82% of Republicans who say Mr. Trump won."[35]

Three days after the first presidential debate, a shocking news story broke that may have been the ultimate "October surprise" in the campaign. Shortly after 1:00 a.m. on October 2, President Trump tweeted that he and the first lady had tested positive for the coronavirus. This announcement came less than a week after the Rose Garden ceremony attended by over 100 people where the president had officially nominated Amy Coney Barrett to fill the vacancy on the Supreme Court. In the interim, several other current or past White House advisers including Kellyanne Conway and Hope Hicks, along with Senators Mike Lee and Thom Tillis as well as former New Jersey Governor Chris Christie—all who had attended the ceremony—tested positive for COVID-19. Later that day, the White House announced that the president had received a dose of Regeneron, the experimental drug that had shown promising results when treating patients with the coronavirus. That evening, the president flew to Walter Reed Hospital aboard Marine One where he would undergo additional treatment for COVID-19 and would remain under the care of medical staff for the next few days.[36]

After receiving medical attention and undergoing close observation over the weekend, President Trump was released from Walter Reed Hospital three days later on October 5 and allowed to finish his treatment at the White House. The doctors who had treated the president reported that he had received supplemental doses of oxygen on two separate occasions along with an injection of the steroid dexamethasone and a five-day course of remdesivir, an antiviral drug that makes it difficult for the coronavirus to replicate itself. The president seemed to be responding well to the treatment, according to his personal physician, Dr. Sean Conley, but noted on Monday morning before Trump left the hospital that he was not "entirely out of the woods yet" regarding the potential risks associated with the coronavirus. Nevertheless, Conley believed that Trump could complete the remainder of his treatment over the next couple of days at the White House.[37]

Next in the debate sequence was the vice-presidential debate held on October 7. Not surprisingly, it received far less attention than the first presidential debate and was considerably less chaotic. Trump's vice president, Mike Pence of

Indiana, sought to promote the economic success of the country prior to the pandemic and downplay the behavior of President Trump during the first debate between him and Biden. For Senator and Democratic Vice-Presidential Nominee Kamala Harris, her twin goals were to bolster and defend Biden's record while repeatedly challenging the president on his inconsistent response to the coronavirus. Each side made their case with a few dodges and deflections along the way and both were evaluated more favorably relative to President Trump in his first debate performance. According to a 538.com/Ipsos poll released the following day, those watching the debate "were more impressed with Harris's performance than Pence's, with 69 percent saying her performance was 'very good' or 'somewhat good,' compared to 60 percent who said the same for him." In the end, however, the debate did little to move poll numbers for the two presidential candidates, reflecting the trends from previous vice-presidential debates.[38]

Although the second presidential debate initially had been scheduled for October 15 at the Adrienne Arsht Center for the Performing Arts in Miami, Florida, the president's recent COVID-19 diagnosis complicated the logistics for the debate despite his subsequent release from the hospital. On Thursday, October 8, the Commission on Presidential Debates announced that the second debate would be held virtually, with the two candidates appearing remotely, since the president had previously tested positive for the coronavirus. Despite the backing of the Commission's health advisers in support of this recommendation, Trump immediately rejected the plan indicating that he would not participate in a remote debate. After trying to find a compromise solution, the Commission elected to cancel the debate the following day while each candidate agreed to hold separate town-hall meetings in lieu of the originally scheduled debate.[39] This meant that the debate in Nashville on October 22 would be the final meeting between the candidates prior to the election.

The final presidential debate held less than two weeks prior to the election was a much more dignified exchanged compared to the first meeting of the candidates. "The moderator, NBC News' [*sic*] Kristen Welker, kept a tight lid on the Republican president and the Democratic nominee as she peppered them with questions about the coronavirus pandemic, the economy and foreign interference in the election, as well as the candidates' finances."[40] She was aided by a mute button this time, which allowed either candidate to be cut off if their answers went on too long or they sought to interrupt the other debater while speaking. "Compared with the first debate—which was defined by furious crosstalk and personal insults—the final face-off was an almost staid affair. But despite the clearer delivery, neither candidate pulled punches, and the volume started to rise later in the evening."[41] According to a CNN poll, Biden was the winner of the final debate by a fourteen-point margin, giving him a clean sweep over Trump in both presidential debates.[42]

The consensus among political scientists is that presidential debates usually do not have a significant impact on a race.[43] The most prominent explanation is that by the time the debates occur, the vast majority of voters have made up their minds and are thus unlikely to have their position reversed by the event. There are, however, a few exceptions where some analysts perceive a greater impact. These include 1960 (Kennedy vs. Nixon), 1976 (Ford vs. Carter), 1984 (Reagan vs. Mondale), 2012 (Obama vs. Romney), and potentially 2016 (Clinton vs. Trump).[44] Robert Erikson and Christopher Wlezien took a systematic look at the ten presidential elections with debates (1960 and 1976–2008), comparing the poll standings of candidates before and after the debates. They found that with one exception, the pre-debate polls were closely matched by the post-debate polls (the exception was 1976, when Carter was already in decline before the debates and the decline persisted). They conclude that debates do not have as great an impact as the conventions (the effect of which they find to be substantial) but that they may have as much or more of an effect than other campaign events.[45] Although the 2020 debate cycle was unusual in many respects as noted above, it does not appear to be an exception to the rule.

THE END GAME AND THE STRUGGLE OVER TURNOUT

The Final Weeks of the Campaign

In the days following the final debate, both candidates continued to make their case to the American people, repeating their respective messages about how each of them offered a better alternative for the country than their opponent, but in very different ways. In the final two weeks of the campaign, "Trump is packing his schedule with boisterous in-person events as he works to narrow his polling deficit with Biden—and to make up for the time spent off the trail while he was being treated for the coronavirus."[46] Biden, in contrast, hosted far fewer public events in keeping with public health guidelines regarding the spread of the coronavirus, and none with large crowds like the president's campaign. Nevertheless, the Biden campaign capitalized on the momentum it received following the debates and continued raising large sums of money in the final weeks of the campaign. Indeed, the Biden campaign far outraised Trump during this crucial stage of the election, "allowing him to blanket the airwaves with ads and spend gobs of cash in crucial swing states."[47]

Perhaps because Biden maintained a steady lead in the polls following both debates, the president continued to reiterate that multiple vaccines for the coronavirus were in development and might soon be available to the American people. Although there was little public health evidence to support this assertion, the president often repeated this same rhetoric at each of his campaign rallies around the country.[48] He also repeatedly dismissed any talk of shuttering the country as a result of the potential risk to the slowly recovering economy or pushing for greater social-distancing measures given the economic effects it had on the nation earlier in the year. Meanwhile, Biden continued to criticize the president's handling of the coronavirus and emphasized that Trump was responsible for the over 200,000 deaths attributed to the virus since the start of the year and that things would only get worse with a "dark winter" fast approaching.[49]

In late October, the Trump campaign latched onto a *New York Post* story that had been published earlier in the month claiming to show evidence that Hunter Biden had tried to set up a meeting between his father and an executive at an Ukrainian company that he had worked for while Biden served as vice president. The story alleged that the former vice president pressured governmental officials in the Ukraine to fire a prosecutor who had been investigating the company and that email evidence corroborating the story was available on a laptop that was believed to be owned by the former vice president's son. Among the sources cited in support of the story were former White House adviser Steve Bannon and Trump's lawyer, Rudy Giuliani.[50] The Trump campaign sought to raise awareness of the story after the president brought it up during the second debate and publicly criticized both Facebook and Twitter for seeking to limit the distribution of the story on their respective platforms. In the end, the story only seemed to generate modest interest among Trump supporters despite efforts to the contrary.[51]

In the final few days before the election, Biden maintained a double-digit lead in most national polls, including a final NBC News/*Wall Street Journal* poll reported the Monday preceding the election. In exit polls reported among those voting early, many reported being frustrated with the president's handling of the coronavirus throughout much of 2020 as well as the overall state of the economy. Others stated that the election was a referendum on the Trump presidency and that they were generally dissatisfied with the direction of the country under his leadership. The former vice president was in a stronger position at this point in the campaign than Hillary Clinton had been four years earlier, but some within the Biden team still privately admitted that they were worried how some of the close competitive state races could end up influencing the final Electoral College vote.[52]

Mobilizing the Vote in a Pandemic

In 2004, the Republicans had a distinct advantage with respect to mobilizing and turning out voters on election day. The Democrats significantly reversed this trend in 2008, leading to the highest turnout in a presidential election since 1968.[53] Four years later, the Democrats' voter identification and mobilization efforts took a big leap forward in terms of both technology and effort.[54] When Jim Messina took on the job of Obama's campaign manager, he said: "We are going to measure every single thing in this campaign."[55] Messina "hired an analytics department five times the size that of the 2008 campaign."[56] These analysts believed that the product of their efforts—their data—was the principal advantage President Obama had over his opponent, and they guarded it diligently. In 2016 both Democrats and Republicans continued using new data analytic techniques to mobilize voters, but this strategy was becoming increasingly difficult as the country continued to polarize along partisan lines.

In 2020, both parties faced unique challenges to turnout given the ongoing pandemic that had many voters worried about the risks of standing in long lines and voting in person. Democrats were more likely to be cautious about voting in person and preferred voting by mail or absentee given the added risks associated with the coronavirus. Republicans, in contrast, largely preferred to vote in person and were more skeptical of voting by mail, most likely as a result of President Trump's oft-repeated rhetoric that it would lead to more fraudulent outcomes.[57] This difference was reflected in a survey released by the Pew Research Center in early August indicating that

> Republicans and Democrats will be voting in very different ways. Overall, about 6 in 10 Americans expect to vote in person, and 4 in 10 by mail. But among Republicans, 8 to 10 say they will vote in person, compared to just 40% for Democrats.[58]

The same Pew Research Center survey also suggested that we would see a record turnout in the fall as a result of the enormous stakes associated with the election.

> Prior to the 2000 election between George W. Bush and Al Gore, just 50% of the voters thought that it really mattered who won, versus 44% who thought that things would be pretty much the same, whoever won. This year, a record 83%— including 85% of Democrats, 86% of Republicans—say that it really matters.[59]

Democrats had a significant turnout advantage in 2018 during the midterms, but Republicans seemed especially motivated to vote in 2020. This heightened interest in the election, while encouraging from the perspective of Democratic participation, also signaled that there could be logistical challenges in counting the ballots and reporting the results in a timely manner. "Unless mail-in ballots are counted far more quickly than they were during most primary elections this year, the returns on election night will be dominated by Republicans and will then shift toward Democrats over the next day or two."[60] This is simply a function of electoral rules varying by states and often by individual counties.

The possibility of election returns coming in on Tuesday evening suggesting one outcome and then changing over the next few days directly fed into the president's narrative that the Democrats would use whatever means were available to steal the election. President Trump echoed these misleading concerns repeatedly at campaign stops around the country and his supporters readily embraced them. In reality, the differences in voting behavior by Democrats and Republicans would account for any changes in outcomes, especially in states that were closely divided on election night. "This matter may not alter the results in deep red and deep blue states. But depending on the extent of the 'blue shift' after election night, several swing states could move from President Trump's column to Joe Biden's."[61] Such an occurrence in one or more states contributed to the distinct possibility that the election might be drawn out, preventing us from knowing who the eventual winner would be and further contributing to partisan strife among voters.

DID THE CAMPAIGN MAKE A DIFFERENCE?

It is appropriate to ask whether the general election campaign made any difference, and the answer depends on the yardstick used to measure the campaign's effects. Did it determine the winner? Did it encourage voters to go to the polls? Did it affect the choices of a substantial number of voters? Did it put issues and candidates' positions clearly before the voters? Would a better campaign by one of the major-party candidates have yielded a different result? Did the campaign produce significant events that will have a lasting impact on American politics? We cannot provide firm answers to all of these questions, but we can shed light on some of them.

Regarding the outcome and voters' decisions, it seems clear that the campaign did indeed have an effect, at least with respect to the issues on which the 2020 campaign focused.[62] Early in the year, many economic signs initially pointed to a potential advantage for President Trump until the coronavirus stalled economic growth and contributed to a surge in unemployment in early April. As the number of COVID-19 cases and deaths began to increase, more people looked to the administration for guidance, but they received at best an inconsistent response from a president who did not appear prepared to lead. Although the number of cases declined a bit over the summer, former vice president Biden continued to maintain a steady lead over President Trump that only increased following the national conventions and the fall debates. In the final days of the campaign, a lot fewer undecided voters appeared to move toward Trump compared with 2016, which was key four years earlier with respect to his narrow wins in states like Michigan, Pennsylvania, and Wisconsin in the Rust Belt.[63]

Perhaps the best evidence of the campaign's impact relates to turnout. As noted earlier, many Democrats believed they had an advantage in 2020 in light of the president's divisive actions during the previous four years and his inconsistent messaging regarding the coronavirus that likely contributed to the increased number of deaths. Nevertheless, Republicans were also cautiously optimistic about the president's chances of reelection despite what many of the polls were suggesting in the weeks leading up to election day. Indeed, the record-setting turnout in early voting supported both narratives as more than 101.4 million people voted either in person or by mail prior to the election, which was 2.5 times as many who had voted early in 2016—then a record.[64] Both Democratic and Republican-led states had relaxed absentee voting requirements in the months leading up to the election as a result of the coronavirus and Democrats took advantage of these changes to vote in large numbers by mail. Republicans also increased their likelihood of voting by mail, but also indicated a greater willingness to vote in person on election day.[65]

The success of the Democrats' mobilization effort is indicated by the turnout data compiled for 2016 and 2020 by Michael McDonald of the University of Florida.[66] The data show that the national turnout rate increased by an impressive 6.5 points, from 60.2 percent to 66.7 percent. The increase, however, varied across the battleground states. Table 2.1 lists the thirteen battleground states and their turnout in the two elections. In all thirteen states, turnout increased relative to 2016. Biden ended up winning a majority (9 out of 13) of the battleground states—including key Rust Belt states that had voted for Trump in 2016—which is notable given the nature of Biden's lack of in-person campaign appearances relative to Trump, who campaigned in a more traditional fashion despite the ongoing risks associated with the pandemic where there were large gatherings of people. At the same time it appears that Trump managed to increase his turnout across the country relative to 2016, but not enough to ultimately win the election.[67]

There is also the question of whether a better campaign by a candidate, specifically by the president, would have led to a different result. President Trump repeatedly sought to disparage his Democratic opponent at campaign rallies, especially with respect to his lack of campaigning in person throughout the summer and fall. He also sought to paint the former vice president as out of touch with mainstream America and too beholden to the Washington establishment and the former Obama administration. Even though Biden may not have been the most dynamic candidate and often campaigned from the safety of his home, this is exactly the difference that many voters were looking for compared to the fiery campaign rhetoric employed by President

Table 2.1   Change in Turnout in Battleground States and Nationally, 2016–2020

	Turnout 2016	*Turnout 2020*	*Change 2016–2020*
National	60.2	66.7	+6.5
Colorado	72.1	76.4	+4.3
Florida	65.8	71.7	+5.9
Iowa	69.0	73.2	+4.2
Michigan	65.7	73.9	+8.2
Minnesota	74.8	80.0	+5.2
Nevada	57.3	65.4	+8.1
New Hampshire	72.5	75.5	+3.0
New Mexico	55.2	61.3	+6.1
North Carolina	65.2	71.5	+6.3
Ohio	64.2	67.4	+3.2
Pennsylvania	63.0	71.0	+8.0
Virginia	66.1	73.0	+6.9
Wisconsin	69.4	75.8	+6.4

Source: Data are from the United States Elections Project, http://www.electproject.org/, Accessed March 2, 2021.

Trump. Some voters who ultimately supported Biden maintained that they might have preferred a candidate like Senator Bernie Sanders as the nominee, but in the end they wanted someone who had the best shot possible at defeating Trump in the election.[68]

One can see the differences in the candidates' campaign strategies as reflected by their placement of presidential campaign field offices during 2020 as shown in figure 2.1 (data from 2016 is included for comparison purposes).[69] For instance, Trump had over 300 field offices across the country in twenty-two different states. In most of these twenty-two states, he had multiple field offices, presumably because these states were considered competitive electorally. Nevertheless, he did maintain a limited number of field offices in states like California, Illinois, and New York that were likely never really in play. In contrast, Biden did not have any field offices as a result of the pandemic and stemming from his pledge to conduct his campaign virtually. Overall, the 2020 placements reflect a significant decline for the Democrats from the 2016 campaign—Clinton, for instance, had a total of 500 offices across the country and in every state. In contrast, Trump only had 145 field offices in 2016, about half as many as he had in 2020.

Finally, and perhaps most consequential for the outcome of the election, Trump seemed to be at a strategic disadvantage as a result of his rather inconsistent responses to the pandemic during the election year. With the steadily increasing number of cases and deaths associated with the coronavirus as well as the significant effect it had on the economy (as well as Trump's overall approval ratings), the president was at a disadvantage electorally in

2016 Presidential Campaign

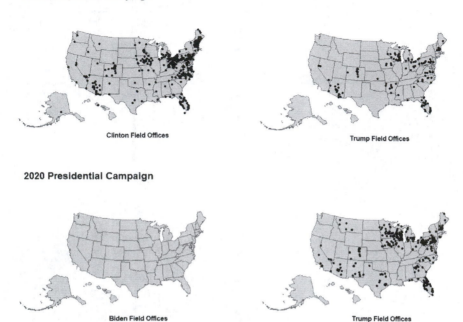

Clinton Field Offices   **Trump Field Offices**

2020 Presidential Campaign

Biden Field Offices   **Trump Field Offices**

Figure 2.1   Location of Presidential Campaign Field Offices, 2016 and 2020. *Source*: Field office information and addresses were collected by Joshua Darr and shared with the authors. Google Maps were used to identify the longitude and latitude coordinates for each office. Data were collected and updated through October 24, 2020.

the months leading up to the election. Although there was a modest decline in cases over the summer, the increase in the number of deaths during the fall campaign most likely had a pronounced impact on turnout, which clearly benefited Biden in the election. Voters who came out in support of both candidates recognized the enormous stakes associated with the election, despite facing the risks associated with voting in person, which likely accounts for the significant increase in mail-in and early voting relative to past elections.

Chapter 3

The Election Results

In the closing days of the 2020 campaign, it appeared that Joe Biden held an electoral advantage. Because of the Covid-19 pandemic, a record number of Americans voted early or by mail, and registered Democrats were turning out—or turning in ballots—at much higher rates than Republicans.[1] But there was reason to treat this partisan advantage cautiously. Although the Biden campaign had urged his supporters to vote early, either in person or by mail, President Donald Trump had spent most of the fall claiming that voting by mail would lead to widespread fraud. Polls showed that Trump voters would wait to cast their ballots in person on election day.[2] The polls also suggested a Biden victory was on the horizon. The average of thirteen national public opinion polls conducted during the final week of the campaign showed Biden with 51.2 percent of the vote and Trump with 44.0 percent, a seemingly comfortable lead for the Democratic nominee.[3] Yet the polls had famously underpredicted Trump's vote share in 2016, leading many in 2020, especially Trump, to discount pollsters' prognostications.[4] A series of academic forecast models also predicted a Biden victory.[5] The median prediction from these models projected that Biden would win 52.5 percent of the two-party vote. Seven of the forecasts predicted the Electoral College winner, and the median prediction for Biden was 308 electoral votes. Of the fifteen models, only three predicted a Trump victory.

Despite over 100 million ballots cast before election, the outcome was still in doubt on election day, November 3, 2020. Biden began his day in prayer, attending Mass with his family at a Catholic church near their home in Wilmington, Delaware.[6] He visited the family burial plot adjacent to the church, stopping at the graves of his parents, his first wife and daughter, who were killed in a car crash in 1972, and his eldest son, Beau, who died of cancer in 2015. Biden had experienced tragic losses in the past, but he spent the rest of the day trying to ensure victory. He traveled to Pennsylvania, hoping to swing the hotly contested state in his favor. He visited his childhood home in Scranton and then campaigned in Philadelphia, before returning to Delaware to watch the election night returns. For his part, President Trump spent most of election day at the White House. In the three days prior, Trump had crisscrossed the nation, holding fourteen large public rallies in battleground states, despite public health concerns. Trump held telephone interviews with "Fox & Friends" and several local media outlets during the morning before visiting his campaign offices in Virginia.[7] Trump told his campaign staff, "I hear we're doing very well in Florida; we're doing very well in Arizona; we're doing incredibly well in Texas. The lines have been amazing, and I think we're gonna have a great night."[8] The president watched the election returns in the private residence at the White House with family, friends, advisers, and his Twitter feed close at hand. Neither Biden nor Trump visited a voting booth on election day; like millions of other Americans, both candidates had voted early.

With a record number of ballots cast early, election officials across the country warned it might take several days to determine a winner and partial results showing which candidate was in the lead might fluctuate systematically.[9] In most states, early votes cast in-person are reported contemporaneously with election-day ballots. But states' rules governing how absentee or vote-by-mail ballots are opened, validated, and counted can differ markedly—sometimes these rules vary at the county level. Some states, such as Arizona, Florida, and Ohio, allow counties to process absentee or mail ballots before election day, and these ballots are among the first to be reported. Other states, such as Pennsylvania, don't allow absentee or mail ballots to be opened until after the polls close on election day, meaning that these ballots are among the last to be reported. Compounding this, twenty states plus the District of Columbia accept absentee or mail ballots several days after election day, so long as the ballots were postmarked by election day. Election officials cautioned voters that the disparate state-level rules would likely make the reporting of initial, partial returns misleading: the margins in states that release absentee and mail ballots first were likely to show an early lead for Democrats (a "blue mirage") before trending toward Republicans, while other states would show an early lead for Republicans (a "red mirage") before shifting toward the Democrats as absentee and mail ballots were counted.[10]

On election night, the vote tallies largely followed the expected trends. In Ohio, for instance, the blue mirage was on full display.[11] With 25 percent of votes reporting, Biden held a nearly 20 percentage-point advantage, and, at 50 percent reporting, Biden's margin was still nearly 10 points. Once all the votes were counted, Trump won Ohio by just over 8 percentage points. In Florida, early returns had Biden leading by as much 5 percentage points, but the lead evaporated, and Trump won by 3.3 percentage points. The red mirage was at work in two states that would prove pivotal (and controversial) during the days to come, Georgia and Pennsylvania. In Georgia, Trump held a sizable lead of around 10 percentage points early in the count, but his edge dissipated as absentee ballots and votes from the heavily populated counties around Atlanta trickled in, making the election too close to call. Similarly, in Pennsylvania, Trump's seemingly sizable lead faded as absentee ballots and votes from Philadelphia entered the count.

As his lead in these states began to shrink, Trump took to Twitter: "We are up BIG, but they are trying to STEAL the Election. We will never let them do it. Votes cannot be cast after the Polls are closed!"[12] Claims of voter fraud were commonplace for Trump. When he lost the 2016 Wisconsin Republican Primary to Texas Senator Ted Cruz, Trump claimed the Republican establishment was trying to "steal the election."[13] In the lead up to the 2016 general election, Trump similarly argued that the election was being "rigged"—he would, of course, win that election.[14] During a 2:30 a.m. speech from the East Room of the White House, the president claimed that "a very sad group of people" were trying to take the election from him, and further exhorted that the election was "a major fraud on our nation." Trump claimed that he had "clearly won" Arizona, Georgia, North Carolina, and Pennsylvania. In fact, millions of votes remained to be counted in those states.[15] On Fox News, anchor Chris Wallace stated, "This is an extremely flammable situation, and the president just threw a match on it. He hasn't won these states. Nobody is saying he's won the states. The states haven't said that he's won."[16] News organizations would not begin calling the election for Biden until four days after election day.[17]

In the weeks following the 2020 presidential election, the Trump campaign and others filed approximately 63 lawsuits in multiple states contesting state and county election procedures, vote counts, and certification processes. Nearly all of the lawsuits were dismissed or dropped due to a lack of evidence with some judges declaring the suits "frivolous."[18] Judge Stephanos Bibas, who was appointed to the US Court of Appeals for the Third Circuit by Trump, declared in one judgment:

> Free, fair elections are the lifeblood of our democracy. Charges of unfairness are serious. But calling an election unfair does not make it so. Charges require specific allegations and then proof. We have neither here.[19]

The United States Supreme Court declined to hear any of the election cases. Trump's claims of electoral fraud were further disputed by some in his own administration. A statement by the Department of Homeland Security declared, "The November 3rd election was the most secure in American history. . . . There is no evidence that any voting system deleted or lost votes, changed votes, or was in any way compromised."[20] And, Attorney General William Barr told the Associated Press that the Department of Justice and the FBI "have not seen fraud on a scale that could have effected a different outcome in the election."[21]

Despite his failed legal efforts, the president continued to press his claims that the election was fraudulent. On December 19, 2020, the president tweeted a call to his supporters: "Big protest in D.C. on January 6th. . . . Be there, will be wild!"[22] January 6, 2021 was the date Congress was scheduled to certify the Electoral College votes submitted by the states and formalize the election of Joe Biden as president of the United States. The typically ceremonial gathering would be presided over by the president of the Senate, Vice President Mike Pence.

At noon on January 6, the president held a "Save America" rally on The Ellipse, the park just south of the White House. He told the gathered crowd, "We will never give up. We will never concede. . . . You don't concede when there's theft involved. . . . We will stop the steal." The president then repeated his false claim that Vice President Pence could stop the congressional certification proceedings and call for a new election:

> I hope Mike is going to do the right thing. . . . I hope so because if Mike Pence does the right thing, we win the election. . . . States want to re-vote, the states got defrauded. They were given false information, then voted on it. Now they want to recertify; they want it back. All Vice President Pence has to do is send it back to the states to recertify, and we become president, and you are the happiest people.[23]

Trump told his supporters to walk down Pennsylvania Avenue to the Capitol and "fight like hell, and if you don't fight like hell you're not going to have a country anymore."

Shortly after 1:00 p.m., the crowd of protesters gathered on the Capitol steps; they began to topple barricades and surge past Capitol Police.[24] Soon the small contingent of officers, some in riot gear, was overwhelmed, and the Capitol perimeter was breached. By 2:00 p.m., the rioters began to scale the scaffolding that had been put in place in preparation for the inauguration as well as the Capitol walls. Within minutes, while House and Senate proceedings were underway, the violent mob gained entry into the Capitol. Representatives, senators, and Vice President Pence were evacuated to safe quarters, as the rioters continued their siege of the House and Senate chambers. Shots were fired outside of the House chamber, and one of the rioters, an Air Force veteran, was killed. The siege continued. By 3:00 p.m., the rioters had taken control of both chambers and the office of Speaker of the House, Nancy Pelosi. An additional three protesters died due to medical emergencies during the siege, 138 officers were injured and 15 were hospitalized, and Capitol Police officer Brian Sicknick, who was pepper-sprayed by rioters, suffered two strokes and died the next day. Police also discovered two pipe bombs that had been placed outside of Democratic and Republican Headquarters. It would take several hours for Capitol and DC Metropolitan Police, with the assistance of the Maryland and Virginia National Guard and state troopers, to secure the Capitol.

After 8:00 p.m., with the building secured, the House and Senate were gaveled back into session. In the House, eighty-three Republicans, including Minority Leader Kevin McCarthy (CA) and Minority Whip Steve Scalise (LA), objected to the Electoral College votes reported from Arizona and Pennsylvania. After a lengthy debate, the chamber voted 303-121 to reject the challenge, and the proceedings moved to the Senate. At 3:32 a.m. on January 7, 2021, Vice President Mike Pence officially affirmed the election results and Joseph Robinette Biden of Delaware was declared the winner of the 2020 presidential election.[25]

Table 3.1 presents the official 2020 election results by state and includes those for Maine's two congressional districts and Nebraska's three districts.[26] Biden won a record 81.3 million votes, a total easily eclipsing the 65.8 million votes won four years earlier by Hillary Clinton, the popular-vote winner in 2016. Yet, given the increased level of turnout in 2020, the total vote differential tells us little about Biden's performance compared to the previous Democratic nominee. If we examine Biden's two-party vote share in each state, however, we see the strength of his performance. Biden's state-level vote shares in 2020 surpassed Clinton's 2016 vote shares in all 50 states and the District of Columbia by an average of 3.92 percentage points.[27] Trump won roughly 74.2 million votes nationally. Compared to his 2016 performance, Trump was able to increase his two-party vote share in 35 states and Washington DC by an average of 1.6 percentage points, but those gains did not allow Trump to secure reelection.

As shown in figure 3.1, Biden won 306 electoral votes to Trump's 232.[28] Biden's 306 electoral votes easily surpassed the 270 needed for election. Biden carried twenty-five states, Washington DC, and Nebraska's second congressional district. Biden was able to match Clinton's Electoral College performance in 2016, holding twenty states and DC. His average two-party vote margin in those areas was 21.9 percentage points—only Nevada was within a five-point margin. Biden was able to add five states to his electoral coalition that Trump won in the previous election: Arizona, Georgia, Michigan, Pennsylvania, and Wisconsin, states comprising a total of 73 electoral votes. Biden's margin in these five states was extraordinarily thin. The average margin of victory in these five states was 1.02 points. Only 10,457

Table 3.1   Presidential Election Results by State, 2020

State	Total Vote	Biden (Dem.)	Trump (Rep.)	Other	Two-Party Differential		Total Vote (%) Dem.	Rep.
Alabama	2,323,282	849,624	1,441,170	32,488	591,546	R	36.6	62.0
Alaska	359,530	153,778	189,951	15,801	36,173	R	42.8	53.8
Arizona	3,387,326	1,672,143	1,661,686	53,497	10,457	D	49.4	49.1
Arkansas	1,219,069	423,932	760,647	34,490	336,715	R	34.8	62.4
California	17,500,881	11,110,250	6,006,429	384,202	5,103,821	D	63.5	34.3
Colorado	3,256,980	1,804,352	1,364,604	88,021	439,745	D	55.4	41.9
Connecticut	1,823,857	1,080,831	714,717	28,309	366,114	D	59.3	39.2
Delaware	504,346	296,268	200,603	7,475	95,665	D	58.7	39.8
Florida	11,067,456	5,297,045	5,668,731	101,680	371,686	R	47.9	51.2
Georgia	4,999,960	2,473,633	2,461,854	64,473	11,779	D	49.5	49.2
Hawaii	574,469	366,130	196,864	11,475	169,266	D	63.7	34.3
Idaho	868,014	287,021	554,119	26,874	267,098	R	33.1	63.8
Illinois	6,033,744	3,471,915	2,446,891	114,938	1,025,024	D	57.5	40.6
Indiana	3,033,121	1,242,416	1,729,519	61,186	487,103	R	41.0	57.0
Iowa	1,690,871	759,061	897,672	34,138	138,611	R	44.9	53.1
Kansas	1,372,303	570,323	771,406	30,574	201,083	R	41.6	56.2
Kentucky	2,136,768	772,474	1,326,646	37,648	554,172	R	36.2	62.1
Louisiana	2,148,062	856,034	1,255,776	36,252	399,742	R	39.9	58.5
Maine[a]	819,461	435,072	360,737	23,652	74,335	D	53.1	44.0
Maryland	3,037,030	1,985,023	976,414	75,593	1,008,609	D	65.4	32.2
Massachusetts	3,631,402	2,382,202	1,167,202	81,998	1,215,000	D	65.6	32.1
Michigan	5,539,302	2,804,040	2,649,852	85,410	154,188	D	50.6	47.8
Minnesota	3,277,171	1,717,077	1,484,065	76,029	233,012	D	52.4	45.3
Mississippi	1,313,759	539,398	756,764	17,597	217,366	R	41.1	57.6
Missouri	3,025,962	1,253,014	1,718,736	54,212	465,722	R	41.4	56.8
Montana	603,674	244,786	343,602	15,286	98,816	R	40.6	56.9
Nebraska[b]	956,383	374,583	556,846	24,954	182,263	R	39.2	58.2
Nevada	1,405,376	703,486	669,890	32,000	33,596	D	50.1	47.7
New Hampshire	806,205	424,937	365,660	15,608	59,277	D	52.7	45.4
New Jersey	4,549,353	2,608,335	1,883,274	57,744	725,061	D	57.3	41.4
New Mexico	923,965	501,614	401,894	20,457	99,720	D	54.3	43.5
New York	8,594,826	5,230,985	3,244,798	119,043	1,986,187	D	60.9	37.8
North Carolina	5,524,804	2,684,292	2,758,775	81,737	74,483	R	48.6	49.9
North Dakota	361,819	114,902	235,595	11,322	120,693	R	31.8	65.1
Ohio	5,922,202	2,679,165	3,154,834	88,203	475,669	R	45.2	53.3
Oklahoma	1,560,699	503,890	1,020,280	36,529	516,390	R	32.3	65.4
Oregon	2,374,321	1,340,383	958,448	75,490	381,935	D	56.5	40.4
Pennsylvania	6,915,283	3,458,229	3,377,674	79,380	80,555	D	50.0	48.8
Rhode Island	517,757	307,486	199,922	10,349	107,564	D	59.4	38.6
South Carolina	2,513,329	1,091,541	1,385,103	36,685	293,562	R	43.4	55.1
South Dakota	422,609	150,471	261,043	11,095	110,572	R	35.6	61.8
Tennessee	3,053,851	1,143,711	1,852,475	57,665	708,764	R	37.5	60.7
Texas	11,315,056	5,259,126	5,890,347	165,583	631,221	R	46.5	52.1
Utah	1,488,289	560,282	865,140	62,867	304,858	R	37.7	58.1
Vermont	367,428	242,820	112,704	11,904	130,116	D	66.1	30.7
Virginia	4,460,524	2,413,568	1,962,430	84,526	451,138	D	54.1	44.0
Washington	4,087,631	2,369,612	1,584,651	133,368	784,961	D	58.0	38.8

(*Continued*)

Table 3.1   Presidential Election Results by State, 2020 (Continued)

State	Total Vote	Biden (Dem.)	Trump (Rep.)	Other	Two-Party Differential		Total Vote (%) Dem.	Rep.
West Virginia	794,731	235,984	545,382	13,365	309,398	R	29.7	68.6
Wisconsin	3,298,041	1,630,866	1,610,184	56,991	20,682	D	49.5	48.8
Wyoming	276,765	73,491	193,559	9,715	120,068	R	26.6	69.9
District of Columbia	344,356	317,323	18,586	8,447	298,737	D	92.2	5.4
United States	158,383,403	81,268,924	74,216,154	2,898,325	7,052,770	D	51.3	46.9

[a]In Maine the statewide plurality-vote winner gained two votes, and each of the state's two congressional districts was awarded one vote on a plurality basis (the official results reported by congressional district do not match the official statewide totals reported):

Maine								
	819,461	435,072	360,737	23,652	74,335	D	53.1	44.0
1st District	447,981	266,376	164,045	17,560	102,331	D	59.5	36.6
2nd District	380,324	168,696	196,692	14,936	27,996	R	44.4	51.7

[b]In Nebraska the statewide plurality-vote winner gained two votes, and each of the state's three congressional districts was awarded one vote on a plurality basis (the official results reported by congressional district do not match the official statewide totals reported): Nebraska

	956,383	374,583	556,846	24,954	182,263	R	39.2	58.2
1st District	320,046	132,261	180,290	7,495	48,029	R	41.3	56.3
2nd District	337,754	176,468	154,377	6,909	22,091	D	52.3	45.7
3rd District	293,912	65,854	222,179	5,879	156,325	R	22.4	75.6

Source: Federal Election Commission, "Official 2020 Presidential General Election Results," January 28, 2021, https://www.fec.gov/documents/2840/2020presgeresults.pdf. Based on reports of the secretaries of state of the fifty states and the District of Columbia.

votes separated Biden and Trump in Arizona, and Biden won Georgia by 11,779 votes. Biden's victory in these two states, slim as it might have been, was still very impressive. Arizona had only voted Democratic once since 1948, and Georgia had only voted Democratic once since 1980, when its native son, Jimmy Carter, was on the ballot.

THE ELECTION RULES

Rules matter. And this is certainly the case in US presidential elections.[29] Electoral rules, specifically those pertaining to the Electoral College, structure the nature of party competition and voter behavior, they influence the strategic actions of candidates (as we saw in both chapters 1 and 2), and they sometimes dictate who wins and who loses. In 2016, for instance, Hillary Clinton won the popular vote, but Donald Trump won the Electoral College and was elected president. Simply put, the rules governing US presidential elections do not guarantee that the candidate who receives the most votes wins. In addition to the 2016 election, on four other occasions in American

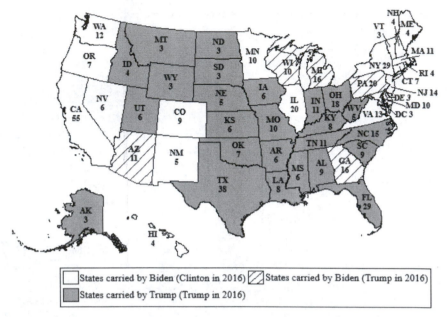

States carried by Biden (Clinton in 2016) States carried by Biden (Trump in 2016)
States carried by Trump (Trump in 2016)

Figure 3.1   Electoral Votes, by State, 2020. *Source*: Federal Election Commission, "Official 2020 Presidential General Election Results," January 28, 2021, https://www.fec .gov/documents/2840/2020presgeresults.pdf. Based on reports of the secretaries of state of the fifty states and the District of Columbia. Note: Joseph R. Biden won 306 electoral votes; Donald J. Trump, 232. *Biden was awarded one electoral vote from Nebraska for winning the state's second congressional district. Trump was awarded one electoral vote from Maine for winning its second congressional district."

history—the elections of John Quincy Adams in 1824, Rutherford B. Hayes in 1876, Benjamin Harrison in 1888, and George W. Bush in 2000—the plurality winner of the popular vote failed to achieve a majority in the Electoral College and lost the presidency.[30] Confusion or a lack of knowledge about the electoral rules that govern the United States can cause consternation among voters, and calls for Electoral College reform (or its elimination) resound when the outcome of the electoral process does not seem to coincide with the general wishes of the electorate, but the rules are well-defined.[31]

As we saw in chapter 2, voters do not vote directly for president. Rather they vote for a slate of electors pledged to support certain presidential and vice-presidential candidates.[32] In every state except Maine and Nebraska, the slate that receives the most popular votes (a plurality) is awarded all of the state's electoral votes. In no state is a majority required to win. In 2020 Biden won majorities in twenty-two of the twenty-five states he carried, plus the District of Columbia; Trump won majorities in twenty-four of the twenty-five states in which he led voting. Plurality winners are most likely to occur when a prominent independent or third-party candidate (or candidates) is on the ballot. In 2020 only 1.8 percent of the national popular vote went to candidates outside of the two main parties, resulting in plurality winners in four of the fifty states. Compare this to 2016, when 5.7 percent of the national popular vote went to candidates outside of the two main parties.

The plurality rule, WTA system usually transforms a plurality of the popular vote into a majority of the electoral vote. And it takes a majority of the electoral vote (currently 270 votes) to produce a winner. If no candidate wins a majority of the electoral vote, the US House of Representatives, voting by state delegations, chooses among the three candidates with the highest number of electoral votes. The House has not chosen a winner since 1825, but it is noteworthy that if the three closest states in 2020—Arizona, Georgia, and Wisconsin—had voted for Trump, there would have been an electoral vote tie of 269 electors each, throwing the election into the House of Representatives where Trump held an advantage. In forty-five of the forty-nine elections from 1828 to 2020, the candidate with the most popular votes has won a majority of the electoral vote. During this period there were fourteen elections in which a candidate won a plurality of the national vote—but not a majority—and won a majority of the electoral vote.[33] So why does the plurality rule, WTA system typically produce a majority winner? The answer lies in the tendency for plurality rule voting systems to yield a two-party system.

The US plurality-vote system is a confirmation of Duverger's Law, a proposition advanced by French jurist and political scientist Maurice Duverger in the 1950s.[34] According to Duverger, "the simple-majority single-ballot system favours the two-party system."[35] Indeed Duverger argued that "the American procedure corresponds to the usual machinery of the simple-majority single-ballot system. The absence of a second ballot and of further polls, particularly in the presidential election, constitutes in fact one of the historical reasons for the emergence and the maintenance of the two-party system."[36]

According to Duverger, this principle applies for two reasons. First, a plurality-vote system produces a "mechanical factor": third parties may earn a large number of votes nationally but fail to gain a plurality of the votes in many electoral units. Scholars agree that this effect is important, except in countries where smaller parties have a geographic base. Second, some voters who prefer a candidate or party they think cannot win will cast their votes for their first choice between the major-party candidates, which Duverger labels the "psychological factor." This behavior is called "sophisticated" or "strategic" voting and in Britain is referred to as "tactical" voting. William H. Riker defines strategic voting as "voting contrary to one's immediate tastes in order to obtain an advantage in the long run."[37] Whether strategic voting occurs to any significant extent is controversial, yet evidence suggests that a substantial number of voters who preferred a third-party or independent

candidate in the 1968, 1980, 1992, 1996, and 2000 elections wound up voting for one of the major-party candidates instead of voting their "sincere"
preferences.[38]

The plurality rule system thus places a heavy burden on third-party or independent candidates. Even a relatively successful third-party candidate typically receives a far smaller share of the electoral vote than of the popular vote.[39]
Here it is useful to review the fates of the four most successful third-party
and independent candidacies (in popular-vote results) since World War II:
George C. Wallace won 13.5 percent of the popular vote in 1968, John B.
Anderson won 6.6 percent in 1980, and H. Ross Perot won 18.9 percent in
1992 and 8.4 percent in 1996. Despite relatively high levels of popular support among these candidates, only Wallace was able to win enough votes in
a state to obtain electoral votes. Wallace came in first in five states (winning
majorities in Alabama and Mississippi) and gained forty-six electoral votes
(including one from a faithless elector from North Carolina). Yet Wallace
won only 8.5 percent of the electoral vote, significantly less than his popular-
vote share.[40]

In America, the electoral rules create the conditions that have led to major-
party dominance; they help shape the strategies that campaigns employ, and
they also constrain the choices that voters make. Choosing the president
by presidential electors is a central part of these rules, and a strong case
can be made for eliminating the Electoral College.[41] Some critics, such as
presidential scholar George C. Edwards III, argue in favor of direct election
of the president. Direct election would force candidates to campaign nationally (although candidates would likely concentrate their efforts in densely
populated, urban areas) and would promote equality by making every vote
in every state count. Moreover, direct election would eliminate questions
of fairness that arise when popular-vote winners do not win the presidency.
The main obstacle to adopting a direct election system is that it requires a
constitutional amendment, which is unlikely because gaining approval of
three-fourths of the states would be difficult in a system that overrepresents
the smaller states.[42]

An alternative reform would retain the Electoral College but would
diminish its importance by establishing a compact among states that would
guarantee that electors would vote for the national popular-vote winner
regardless of the outcome within their own state. This compact would come
into effect only after it is enacted by states collectively possessing a majority
of the electoral votes. As of June 2021, fifteen states and Washington, DC
with a total of 195 electoral votes (roughly 72 percent of the 270 electoral
votes needed) had agreed to the National Popular Vote Interstate Compact.[43]
Because an interstate compact requires congressional approval, there would
still be an additional hurdle, but only a majority of both chambers is required

to approve an interstate compact, not the two-thirds supermajority to initiate a constitutional amendment.

As described earlier Maine and Nebraska both have district systems for choosing electors, and widespread state-level adoption of this method is often put forward as a way of reforming the Electoral College. The district system does away with the WTA rule for assigning electors and makes it possible for candidates to split a state's electoral vote. However, this method does not guarantee that electors will be divided in proportion to candidates' popular-vote shares. Indeed, because partisan majorities in state legislatures typically gerrymander congressional district lines to make the districts uncompetitive and unbalanced in their favor, the adoption of the district method would likely bias Electoral College outcomes relative to the popular vote.[44] Had there been a uniform application of the district method in 2020, Joe Biden still would have been elected.[45] Biden won more congressional districts than Trump (225 of 435) while carrying 25 states (two votes each) and the District of Columbia for a total of 278 electoral votes. Trump would have received 260 electoral votes based on 210 congressional district wins and twenty-five state popular-vote wins. Obviously this result is in line with the real Electoral College outcome and the national popular vote, but this is not always the case. In 2016, the district method would have given Trump 290 electoral votes to Clinton's 248. This outcome was in line with the true Electoral College outcome, but like the Electoral College it was also out of step with the national popular vote. The district method is not always in line with the Electoral College, however. In 2012 Barack Obama won the popular vote (51.1 percent) and the Electoral College (332 electoral votes to Mitt Romney's 206), yet the district method would have resulted in a Romney victory because he carried 226 of 425 districts and twenty-four states, a total of 274 electoral votes.[46] Widespread adoption of the district system is unlikely, however, because most states do not want to diminish their potential influence by making it likely that their electoral votes will be split.

THE PATTERN OF RESULTS

The 2020 election can be placed in perspective by comparing it with previous presidential elections. Three conclusions emerge. First, the election further demonstrates the competitive nature of postwar elections in the United States, which exhibits a relatively even balance between the two major parties. Second, postwar elections continue to display a pattern of volatility. Third, although incumbent presidents seem to have an electoral advantage, it is clearly not a behavior rule.

The competitive balance between the two parties over the postwar period is rather remarkable. In the nineteen elections held since World War II, the Republicans have been victorious in ten, whereas the Democrats have won nine. If one considers popular-vote winners, the Democrats have had slightly more success, winning eleven of the nineteen contests. The Republicans have been slightly more successful in establishing electoral majorities, winning a majority of the popular vote in seven of these elections (1952, 1956, 1972, 1980, 1984, 1988, and 2004). With Biden's 2020 victory, the Democrats have now won a popular-vote majority five times, including both of Obama's victories (1964, 1976, 2008, 2012, and 2020). The mean level of popular support shows the competitive balance: the Republicans have won 48.6 percent of the popular vote, and the Democrats have won 47.2 percent. This division of popular support also demonstrates the dominance of the two major parties in presidential elections. During the postwar period, third-party and independent candidates have only garnered an average of 4.2 percent of the popular vote.

Examining electoral history is like looking at clouds: if you look hard enough, you'll find something that looks like a pattern. Yet, with a few important historical exceptions, American electoral history is best described as volatile. This is especially true in the postwar period, where competitive balance would appear to place a party's chances at winning the presidency at 50-50.[47] Evidence of electoral volatility should give pause to pundits and partisans alike who are too quick to label the most recent election as the dawn of a new era of electoral dominance.

Table 3.2 presents presidential election results since 1832, the first election in which political parties used national nominating conventions to select their candidates. From 1832 to 1948 there are four instances in which the same party won three elections or more in a row. Scholars often associate these episodes with partisan realignments. Walter Dean Burnham, for instance, identifies the elections of 1860, 1896, and 1932 as realigning elections during this period.[48] However, across the nineteen elections since World War II, the incumbent party has been able to retain the presidency only eight times; voters have voted out the incumbent party nine times. There is only one example of a party winning three straight presidential elections during this period—the Republican victories of 1980, 1984, and 1988. After Ronald Reagan's landslide reelection in 1984 and George H. W. Bush's election in 1988, some may have wondered whether America was entering into a period of GOP dominance.[49] But the Democrats recaptured the White House with Bill Clinton's victory in 1992, and he was reelected—with a larger popular-vote margin—in 1996. Indeed, the Democrats have won the popular-vote in seven of the eight elections since 1992, but they have failed to capture Electoral College majorities in two of those. Yet the Democrats' popular-vote success over the

Table 3.2 Presidential Election Results, 1832–2016

Election	Winning Candidate	Party of Winning Candidate	Success of Incumbent Political Party
1832	Andrew Jackson	Democrat	Won
1836	Martin Van Buren	Democrat	Won
1840	William H. Harrison	Whig	Lost
1844	James K. Polk	Democrat	Lost[a]
1848	Zachary Taylor	Whig	Lost
1852	Franklin Pierce	Democrat	Lost
1856	James Buchanan	Democrat	Won
1860	Abraham Lincoln	Republican	Lost
1864	Abraham Lincoln	Republican	Won
1868	Ulysses S. Grant	Republican	Won[b]
1872	Ulysses S. Grant	Republican	Won
1876	Rutherford B. Hayes	Republican	Won
1880	James A. Garfield	Republican	Won
1884	Grover Cleveland	Democrat	Lost
1888	Benjamin Harrison	Republican	Lost
1892	Grover Cleveland	Democrat	Lost
1896	William McKinley	Republican	Lost
1900	William McKinley	Republican	Won
1904	Theodore Roosevelt	Republican	Won
1908	William H. Taft	Republican	Won
1912	Woodrow Wilson	Democrat	Lost
1916	Woodrow Wilson	Democrat	Won
1920	Warren G. Harding	Republican	Lost
1924	Calvin Coolidge	Republican	Won
1928	Herbert C. Hoover	Republican	Won
1932	Franklin D. Roosevelt	Democrat	Lost
1936	Franklin D. Roosevelt	Democrat	Won
1940	Franklin D. Roosevelt	Democrat	Won
1944	Franklin D. Roosevelt	Democrat	Won
1948	Harry S. Truman	Democrat	Won
1952	Dwight D. Eisenhower	Republican	Lost
1956	Dwight D. Eisenhower	Republican	Won
1960	John F. Kennedy	Democrat	Lost
1964	Lyndon B. Johnson	Democrat	Won
1968	Richard M. Nixon	Republican	Lost
1972	Richard M. Nixon	Republican	Won
1976	Jimmy Carter	Democrat	Lost
1980	Ronald Reagan	Republican	Lost
1984	Ronald Reagan	Republican	Won
1988	George H. W. Bush	Republican	Won
1992	Bill Clinton	Democrat	Lost
1996	Bill Clinton	Democrat	Won
2000	George W. Bush	Republican	Lost
2004	George W. Bush	Republican	Won
2008	Barack Obama	Democrat	Lost
2012	Barack Obama	Democrat	Won

(Continued)

Table 3.2 Presidential Election Results, 1832–2016 (Continued)

Election	Winning Candidate	Party of Winning Candidate	Success of Incumbent Political Party
2016	Donald J. Trump	Republican	Lost
2020	Joseph Biden	Democrat	Lost

Source: *Presidential Elections, 1789–2008* (Washington, DC: CQ Press, 2009); 2012–2020, compiled by authors.

[a]Whigs are classified as the incumbent party because they won the 1840 election. In fact, their presidential candidate, William Henry Harrison, died a month after taking office and his vice president, John Tyler, was expelled from the party in 1841.

[b]Republicans are classified as the incumbent party because they won the 1864 election. (Technically Lincoln had been elected on a Union ticket.) After Lincoln's assassination in 1865, his vice president, Andrew Johnson, a war Democrat, became president.

past thirty years hardly seems like a strong predictor of future success. The postwar period has been an era of sustained electoral volatility.

The electoral volatility of the postwar period is not without precedent. In fact, two periods in the nineteenth century were more volatile. From 1840 to 1852 the incumbent party lost four consecutive elections—a period of volatility between the Democrats and the Whigs. This occurred again from 1884 to 1896, when the Republicans and the Democrats alternated elections. Both of these periods, however, were followed by party realignments. In 1854, just two years after the decisive defeat of the Whigs, the Republican Party was founded, and by the 1856 election the party's nominee, John C. Fremont, came in second behind James Buchanan, the Democratic winner.[50] By 1860 the Republicans had captured the presidency, and the Whigs were extinct.[51] Although many Whigs, including Abraham Lincoln himself, became Republicans, the Republican Party was not just the Whig Party renamed. The Republicans had transformed the political agenda by capitalizing on opposition to slavery in the territories.[52]

The 1896 contest, the last of four incumbent party losses, is usually considered a critical election because it solidified Republican dominance.[53] Although the Republicans had won five of the seven elections since the end of the Civil War, after Ulysses S. Grant's reelection in 1872, all their victories had been by narrow margins. In 1896 the Republicans emerged as the clearly dominant party, gaining a solid hold in Connecticut, Indiana, New Jersey, and New York, states that they had frequently lost between 1876 and 1892. After William McKinley's defeat of William Jennings Bryan in 1896, the Republicans established a firmer base in the Midwest, New England, and the Mid-Atlantic states. They lost the presidency only in 1912, when the GOP was split, and in 1916, when the incumbent, Woodrow Wilson, ran for reelection.[54] The Republicans would win again in 1920, 1924, and 1928.

The Great Depression ended Republican dominance. The emergence of the Democrats as the majority party was not preceded by a series of incumbent losses. As the emergence of the New Deal coalition demonstrates, a period of electoral volatility is not a necessary condition for a partisan realignment. Nor perhaps is it a sufficient condition. No party currently dominates American politics. Volatility persists, and that volatility does not presage a period of stability or an electoral realignment.

One clear pattern that does emerge when one examines presidential elections across history is that incumbent candidates appear to have an advantage. Between 1792 and 2020, in-office parties retained the White House about two-thirds of the time when they ran the incumbent president but only won half the time—a coin flip—when they did not run an incumbent.[55] Of those presidents who were able to secure renomination by their party, twenty-two won reelection. In 2020, Donald Trump was unable to capitalize on his incumbent status and became the eleventh president to lose his reelection bid. The last incumbent to be denied a second term was George H. W. Bush in 1992. If Trump were to run again in 2024, he would seek to follow in the footsteps of Grover Cleveland, the only president to serve nonconsecutive terms.[56] In chapter 8, we examine voters' evaluations of presidential performance and how it relates to voting.

STATE-BY-STATE RESULTS

The modern electoral map is a conglomeration of Republican "red states" and Democratic "blue states." Yet this color pairing has no real historical meaning and, in fact, has only become convention in recent decades.[57] In 1976, for instance, election-night news coverage on NBC classified Republican (Ford) wins in blue and Democratic (Carter) victories in red. ABC News featured an electoral map that colored Democratic states in blue and Republican states in yellow.

Although the colors on the electoral map may be meaningless, the political geography of presidential elections most certainly is not. Because states deliver the electoral votes necessary to win the presidency, the election is effectively fifty-one separate contests, one for each state and one for Washington DC. With the exception of Maine and Nebraska, the candidate who wins the most votes in a state wins all of the state's electors. Regardless of how a state decides to allocate its electors, its number of electors is the sum of its senators (two), plus the number of its representatives in the US House.[58] Since 1964 there have been 538 electors and a majority, 270, is required to win. In 2020 the distribution of electoral votes ranged from a low of three in Alaska, Delaware, Montana, North Dakota, South Dakota, Vermont, Wyoming, and DC to a high of fifty-five in California.

Because each state, regardless of population, has two electoral votes for its senators, the smaller states are overrepresented in the Electoral College and the larger states are underrepresented. The twenty least-populated states and DC were home to roughly 10.4 percent of the US population according to the 2020 Census, but these states had 16.5 percent of the electoral votes. The nine most-populated states had 51.1 percent of the population, but only 44.8 percent of the electoral vote.

Even though smaller states are overrepresented in the Electoral College, presidential campaigns tend to focus their resources on larger states unless pre-election polls suggest that a state is unwinnable. Consider the two most populous states, California and Texas. California's fifty-five electoral votes represent one-fifth of the votes needed to win the Electoral College. Texas has thirty-eight electoral votes, one-seventh of the votes necessary to win. Clearly both are vital for building an Electoral College victory. Yet pre-election polls suggested landslide wins for Biden in California and Trump in Texas, and neither campaign spent significant resources in either state. For example, between April 9 and October 25, the two campaigns aired a total of 6,050 ads in media markets in California and Texas combined, only 0.006 percent of the estimated 1,065,176 campaign ads broadcast across all states during that time.[59] Florida, Pennsylvania, Wisconsin, Michigan, and North Carolina, on the other hand, were competitive, large states with a total of ninety electoral votes at stake, and both campaigns littered the airwaves with campaign ads. Each of these states was subjected to over 100,000 campaign ads, and over 225,000 ads were broadcast in Florida alone. The five states combined for 71 percent of all campaign ad broadcasts.[60]

States are the building blocks of winning presidential coalitions, but state-by-state results can be overemphasized and may sometimes be misleading for three reasons. First, although much attention is given to battleground states, the nature of broadcast and social media coverage means that candidates must develop national campaign messages. Candidates can make appeals to specific states and regions, but those messages are likely to be reported across geographic boundaries. Thus, whereas battleground contests and regional bases of support may color a campaign's message and strategy, most campaigns seek to form a broad-based coalition throughout the nation.

Second, comparing state-level election results over time can be misleading and may even conceal change. To illustrate this point, we compare the results of two close Democratic victories—John Kennedy's defeat of Richard Nixon in 1960 and Jimmy Carter's defeat of Gerald Ford in 1976—that have many similarities. In both 1960 and 1976, the Republicans did very well in the West, and both Kennedy and Carter needed southern support to win. Kennedy carried six of the eleven southern states—Arkansas, Georgia, Louisiana, North Carolina, South Carolina, and Texas—and gained five of Alabama's eleven electoral votes, for a total of eighty-one electoral votes. Carter carried ten of the eleven southern states (all but Virginia) for a total of 118 electoral votes. Yet the demographic basis of Carter's support was quite different from Kennedy's. In 1960, only twenty-nine percent of African Americans in the South were registered to vote compared with 61 percent of whites. According to our analysis of the ANES, only about one in fifteen of the Kennedy voters in the South was black. In 1976, 63 percent of African Americans in the South were registered to vote compared with 68 percent of whites.[61] We estimate that about one in three southerners who voted for Carter was black. A simple state-by-state comparison would conceal this massive change in the social composition of the Democratic presidential coalition.

Third, state-by-state comparisons do not tell us why a presidential candidate received support. Of course such comparisons can lead to interesting speculation, especially when the dominant issues are related to regional differences. Following the 2016 election, for example, some observers speculated that Trump's victory, particularly in states such as Michigan, North Carolina, Ohio, and Pennsylvania, could be attributed to manufacturing job losses in those states.[62] Yet exit polls from these states show that voters who reported that the economy was the "most important issue facing the economy" were actually more likely to vote for Clinton than Trump.[63] Inferences based solely on who won the state may be fallacious and lead to mischaracterizations of the electorate. Indeed similarly constructed inferences often lead to hyperbolic comparisons of "red states" versus "blue states," creating an illusion of a deeply divided electorate.[64] State-level election results should not be used to infer voters' preferences; for this we must examine individual-level survey responses—as we do in later chapters.

With these qualifications in mind, we now turn to the state-by-state results. Figure 3.2 shows Biden's margin of victory over Trump in all states. As noted earlier both of the parties maintain regional bases of strong support, whereas relatively few states are competitive and truly in play. A continuing base of strength for the Democrats was the Northeast, sweeping all nine states in the region (by an average popular-vote margin of 18.5 points).[65] The Democrats have dominated the Northeast in presidential elections since Bill Clinton's election in 1992.[66] But Hillary Clinton was unable to hold the region's second-largest electoral prize, Pennsylvania, which Trump won by a slim 0.72 points. Despite the party's electoral strength in the Northeast, the region is proving to be a precarious base of electoral support for the Democrats. Whereas comparison of vote shares across the last seven elections suggests that the region has not waned in its support of the Democratic

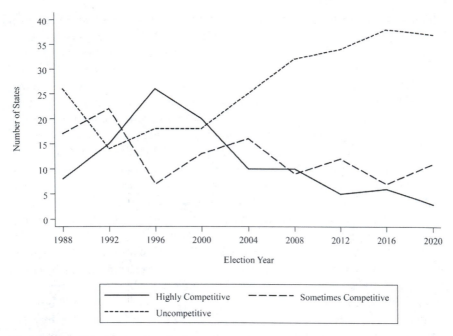

Figure 3.2 Biden's Margin of Victory over Trump, 2020. *Source*: Federal Election Commission, "Official 2020 Presidential General Election Results," January 28, 2021, https://www.fec.gov/documents/2840/2020presgeresults.pdf. Based on reports of the secretaries of state of the fifty states and the District of Columbia. Note: We classify Maine as being carried by Biden and Nebraska as being carried by Trump in 2020. Biden actually won the statewide race and one of Maine's two congressional districts, thus winning three of the state's four Electoral College votes. Trump won the statewide race in Nebraska plus two of its three congressional districts, thus winning four of the state's five Electoral College votes.

Party—only Pennsylvania and New Hampshire have been competitive—the region is declining in population and thus carries less weight in the Electoral College. In 1992, the region offered 106 electoral votes. In 2020 that number was only ninety-six, and Pennsylvania and New York will each lose electoral votes in 2024 following the 2020 Census. Whether the region continues to vote consistently for the Democratic Party remains to be seen.

Biden's coalition was not restricted to one region. Outside of the Northeast he carried ten other states, as well as Washington DC, by ten percentage points or more, including the electorally rich states of California and Illinois. Biden's sizable victories in Oregon and Washington continue the Democrat's dominance in those states, which have voted Democratic in each of the last nine presidential elections. Biden also won electoral majorities in Nevada, Colorado, and New Mexico, matching the majority victories of Barack Obama in 2008 and 2016—Hillary Clinton won pluralities in the three states.

Biden's ability to keep these states in the Democratic column is notable because between 1968 and 1988 the states were Republican strongholds. Biden also won a majority in Virginia. This is the fourth straight victory for the Democrats in the commonwealth. Until Obama's victory there in 2008, Virginia had voted Democratic only once (1964) since Eisenhower's election in 1952.

Biden's victories in Michigan, Pennsylvania, and Wisconsin brought three once-reliable Democratic states back into the party's win column. Each of the states had provided Trump with narrow victories—all by less than one percentage point—in 2016 and were central to his Electoral College victory that year. These states represented a substantial haul for Biden, totaling 46 electoral votes (17 percent of the 270 needed for victory). But it was Biden's ability to capture two traditionally Republican states, Arizona and Georgia, that was perhaps most impressive—both had provided Trump with decisive victories in 2016. Before Biden's victory, the Democrats had won Arizona only once since 1948; Bill Clinton won a plurality in the state in 1996. Population growth and diversification in the Phoenix area (Maricopa County) in recent years has weakened the GOP's hold on the area and made Democrats more competitive in statewide elections.[67] Population growth and diversification in the Atlanta area (Cobb, Gwinnett, and Henry counties) has also made Georgia more competitive for the Democrats. The Peach State had only voted Democrat three times since 1960. Native son and former Georgia governor, Jimmy Carter, won the state in 1976 and 1980, and Clinton, a southerner, captured the state in 1992. Biden's margin of victory in Arizona (0.31 percentage points) and Georgia (0.24 percentage points) was razor-thin.[68] It remains to be seen whether these states will continue to be in play for the Democrats or whether Biden's victories were aberrations.

Trump's victories in Florida and Ohio were critical to his electoral coalition. The states, which offer 47 electoral votes combined, have been highly competitive in recent decades and are often viewed as critical to victory in presidential elections. (In fact, Ohio, which had voted for the Electoral College winner in every election since 1960, had been considered a bellwether for the nation.) Trump was able to win both in 2016, and, in 2020, Trump was able to increase his electoral support in both states by roughly two percentage points.

The remaining states captured by Trump in 2020 are at the core of the Republican electoral coalition. These twenty-three states, which Trump won by an amazing average margin of 21 percentage points, all voted Republican in the last six presidential elections with the exception of Indiana (Obama in 2008), Iowa (Obama in 2008 and 2012), and North Carolina (Obama in 2008).[69] Thirteen of these states (Alabama, Alaska, Idaho, Kansas, Mississippi, Nebraska, North Dakota, Oklahoma, South Carolina, South Dakota, Texas,

Utah, and Wyoming) have voted Republican in every election dating back to 1980. The problem for Republicans, generally, is that the twenty-three solidly Republican states tend to be smaller in population and result in only 185 of the needed 270 electoral votes. Texas, with its thirty-eight electoral votes, is the largest state in this coalition, followed by North Carolina with fifteen electoral votes, but five of these states have only three electoral votes each. To make the point clearer, consider the subset of thirteen states that have voted Republican since 1980. These 13 states cumulatively represent 102 electoral votes. If we exclude Texas, the remaining 12 states combine for a total of 64 electoral votes, slightly more than the 55 votes held by California alone, which has been solidly in the Democratic column since 1988.

The region that offered Trump his greatest electoral rewards was the South. One hundred thirty-one of Trump's electoral votes were from the South, over half of his total (56.5 percent). In the last half century, the South has been transformed into the base of the Republican Party, and this transformation is the most dramatic change in postwar American politics. Biden's only victories in the South were in Georgia and Virginia. In 2016, Hillary Clinton captured only Virginia. In 2008 and 2012 Obama cut into the Republican's southern base by winning both Florida and Virginia, and in 2008, he also carried North Carolina. In each of those elections, however, Obama would have won the Electoral College without winning a single southern state. The same is true of Bill Clinton's victories in 1992 and 1996. Yet it is infeasible for the Republicans to win the presidency without southern electoral votes.

Republican strength in the South and Democratic advantage in the Northeast does not mean that sectionalism has beset the country. Indeed, regional differences in presidential voting have declined in the postwar period and are currently low by historical standards. This can be demonstrated by statistical analysis. Joseph A. Schlesinger has analyzed state-by-state variation in presidential elections from 1832 through 1988, and we have updated his analyses through 2020.[70] Schlesinger measures the extent to which party competition in presidential elections is divided along geographic lines by calculating the standard deviation in the percentage of the Democratic vote among the states.[71] The state-by-state standard deviation was 10.43 in 2020, slightly higher than the 10.35 estimated in 2016. In 2012, the standard deviation was 10.29 deviation, and it was 9.54 in 2008. This suggests that states have been slightly more divided during the recent Trump elections.[72] Schlesinger's analysis clearly reveals the relatively low level of state-by-state variation in the postwar US elections.[73] According to his analysis (as updated), all fifteen of the presidential elections from 1888 to 1944 displayed more state-by-state variation than any of the seventeen postwar elections. To a large extent, the decline in state-by-state variation has been a result of (1) the transformation of the South and the demise of local party machines, which has allowed partisan cleavages to become more consistent across states and allowed party competition to increase across the country, and (2) the advent of television, which has nationalized partisan agendas.[74]

ELECTORAL CHANGE IN THE POSTWAR SOUTH

The South is a growing region that has undergone dramatic political change. Even though five of the eleven southern states have lost congressional representation since World War II, Florida and Texas have made spectacular gains. In the 1944 and 1948 elections, Florida had only eight electoral votes, but in the 2020 election, it had twenty-nine. In 1944 and 1948, Texas had twenty-three electoral votes; in 2020 it had thirty-eight. Since the end of World War II, the South's electoral vote total has grown from 127 to 160. The South gained seven electoral votes following the 2010 Census and is set to gain an extra four in 2024 based on the 2020 Census.[75]

The political transformation of the South was a complex process, but the major reason for the change was simple. As V. O. Key, Jr., brilliantly demonstrated in *Southern Politics in State and Nation* in 1949, the main factor in southern politics is race. "In its grand outlines the politics of the South revolves around the position of the Negro. . . . Whatever phase of the southern political process one seeks to understand, sooner or later the trail of inquiry leads to the Negro."[76] And it was the national Democratic Party's sponsorship of African American civil rights that shattered the party's dominance in the South.[77]

Between the end of Reconstruction in 1877 and the end of World War II, the South was functionally a one-party system. Unified in its support of racial segregation and in its opposition to Republican social and economic policies, the South was a Democratic stronghold—the "Solid South." Indeed, in fifteen of the seventeen elections from 1880 to 1944, all eleven southern states voted Democratic. Between 1896 (the first election after many southern states adopted the "white primary") and 1944, the average Democratic Party vote share in presidential elections was 71.6 percent.[78] The only major defections were in 1928, when the Democrats ran Alfred E. Smith, a Roman Catholic. As a result, the Republican candidate, Herbert Hoover, won five southern states.

After Reconstruction ended in 1877, many southern blacks were prevented from voting, and in the late nineteenth and early twentieth centuries, several southern states changed their voting laws to further disenfranchise blacks. The Republicans effectively ceded those states to the Democrats. Although the Republicans garnered black support in the North, they did not attempt to enforce the Fifteenth Amendment, which bans restrictions on voting on the basis of "race, color, or previous condition of servitude."

In 1932, a majority of African Americans in the North remained loyal to the Republicans; although by 1936, Franklin D. Roosevelt had won the support of northern blacks. But Roosevelt made no effort to win the support of southern blacks, most of whom remained disenfranchised. Even as late as 1940, about 70 percent of the nation's blacks lived in the states of the old Confederacy. Roosevelt carried all eleven of these states in each of his four victories. His 1944 reelection, however, was the last contest in which Democrats carried all eleven southern states.

World War I led to massive migration of African Americans from the agrarian South and into the industrial North, where—given the absence of laws restricting their suffrage—many would enjoy the franchise for the first time. The influx of African Americans alarmed some Democratic politicians in the North, who would likely see their electoral prospects decline unless they were able to siphon a share of African American voters who were loyal to the party of Lincoln. In 1932, African American voters in most major cities in the North voted for Herbert Hoover by a roughly two-to-one margin.[79] To appeal to black voters, many northern Democrats encouraged their party to adopt a supportive position toward civil rights. By 1948 President Harry Truman was making explicit appeals to blacks through his Fair Employment Practices Commission, and in July 1948 he issued an executive order ending segregation in the armed services.[80] These policies led to defections from the "Dixiecrats" and cost Truman four southern states in the 1948 election; he still won the seven remaining southern states by an average margin of 26.2 points. In 1952 and 1956 the Democratic candidate, Adlai E. Stevenson, de-emphasized appeals to blacks, although his opponent, Dwight Eisenhower, still made inroads in the South. In 1960 Kennedy also played down appeals to African Americans, and southern electoral votes were crucial to his win over Nixon.[81] Kennedy strengthened his campaign in the South by selecting a Texan, Lyndon Johnson, as his running mate. Johnson helped Kennedy win Texas, which he carried by two percentage points.

If Johnson as running mate aided the Democrats in the South, Johnson as president played a different role. His explicit appeals to African Americans, including leading the Civil Rights Act into law in 1964, helped end Democratic dominance in the South. As a senator, Barry Goldwater, the Republican candidate, had voted against the Civil Rights Act, creating a sharp difference between the two candidates. Goldwater carried all five states in the Deep South.[82] The only other state he won was his native Arizona. In 1968 Hubert Humphrey, who had long championed black equality, carried only one southern state, Texas, which he won with only 41 percent of the vote. He was aided by George Wallace's third-party candidacy because Wallace, a segregationist, won 19 percent of the Texas vote. Wallace carried Alabama, Arkansas, Georgia, Louisiana, and Mississippi; Nixon carried the remaining five southern states. Nixon won every southern state in 1972, and his margin of victory was greater in the South than in the rest of the nation. Although Carter won ten of the eleven southern states in 1976 (all but Virginia), he carried a minority of the vote among white southerners.

In 1980, Reagan won every southern state except Georgia, Carter's home state. In his 1984 reelection victory, Reagan carried the South, and his margin of victory in the region was greater than his margin outside it. In 1988 George H. W. Bush was victorious in all eleven southern states, and the South was his strongest region. Four years later, in 1992, Clinton, a native of Arkansas, made some inroads in the South and somewhat greater inroads in 1996. All the same the South was the only predominantly Republican region in 1992, and in 1996 Bob Dole won a majority of the electoral vote only in the South and mountain states. In 2000 the South was the only region in which Bush carried every state, and more than half of his electoral votes came from that region. Bush again carried every southern state in 2004, along with all of the states in the Mountain West. As was the case four years earlier, more than half of his electoral votes came from the states of the old Confederacy. Despite slippage in 2008 and 2012, Republicans have won every southern state in five of the thirteen elections (1972, 1984, 1988, 2000, and 2004) between 1972 and 2020.

Although the transformation of the South is clearly the most dramatic change in postwar American politics, the 2020 election underscores that the Republicans do not hold the same level of dominance in the region that the Democrats once enjoyed. The average Republican vote share in the South between 1972 and 2016 was 54.2 points—much smaller than the 71.6 vote share that we reported earlier for the Democrats from 1896 to 1944. Florida, for instance, is highly competitive. Bill Clinton won the Sunshine State in 1996, and in 2000 George W. Bush carried the disputed contest by a negligible margin. Obama narrowly won Florida in both 2008 and 2012, and Trump won the state in the last two elections. Trump also won pluralities in North Carolina in 2016 and 2020. The state has only voted Democratic once since 1980—giving Obama a 0.3 percentage-point victory in 2008—but the two-party vote margins were much closer in the past four elections than they had been previously, leading Democrats to believe that the state is up for grabs. Although Virginia did not vote Democratic between 1968 and 2004, the growing number of suburbanites in northern Virginia has made the state more competitive, and the Democrats have now captured the state in four straight elections. And, as we saw earlier, in Georgia, Democrats see Atlanta and its suburbs as fertile ground to keep the state competitive. Republicans have an advantage in the South, to be sure, but Democrats are competitive in few southern states, thus allowing the South to keep its place of prominence in modern presidential politics.

Some scholars predict that the South will play a part in the next major transformation in American politics, one they argue could make the Electoral College less competitive. John Judis and Ruy Teixeira contend that shifting demographics, specifically a growing professional class and an increase in America's nonwhite population, are setting the stage for an "emerging Democratic majority."[83] Central to this argument is that in the next two decades, the proportion of Latinos in the electorate is likely to double.[84] Latino growth in the South, where African Americans already compose a large share of the electorate, could greatly benefit the Democrats. Three southern states—Arkansas, North Carolina, and South Carolina—were among the top five states in Hispanic population growth between 2000 and 2010 according to the US Census.[85] And Texas (39.3 percent) and Florida (26.5 percent) already have the second- and third-largest Hispanic populations, respectively. Judis and Teixeira predict that further growth in the Latino population could make Texas a Democratic-leaning state and Florida a safe Democratic state within the next several election cycles, giving Democrats, who already hold advantages in the electorally rich states of California and New York, an easier path to victory in the Electoral College.[86]

We have heard predictions of impending electoral realignment before, and as in the past, we encourage caution when evaluating these claims.[87] After his reelection in 1984, Ronald Reagan proclaimed that his victory represented a Republican realignment. Indeed some scholars went so far as to argue that the Republicans held an electoral vote "lock."[88] But the Democrats won two consecutive elections in the 1990s. The scenario outlined by Judis and Teixeira offers reason for optimism for the Democrats and pessimism for the Republicans. Yet there are two major assumptions undergirding this scenario that complicate things for the Democrats. First, it should not be assumed that Latino voting participation will increase proportionately with Latino population growth; it has not thus far. Although Latino voter participation surged in 2010, the "number of Latino eligible voters is increasing faster than the number of Latin voters in presidential election years."[89] Second, it should not be assumed that Latinos will continue to support Democrats at the same levels. The Latino vote is not monolithic and has changed somewhat over time (we will have more to say about Latino political preferences in chapter 5). For instance, Cuban Americans in Florida, many of whom fled their homeland to escape Fidel Castro's dictatorship, have long been a reliable voting bloc for Republicans. "In Florida, Cubans were about twice as likely as non-Cuban Latinos to vote for Donald Trump" in 2016.[90] And, in 2020, Trump was able to make significant gains among Hispanic voters in South Florida.[91] All this serves to remind both parties that old loyalties are not easily maintained and that voters respond to changing issues and interests, not simply on the basis of ethnicity. However, this battle for Latino votes plays out, it appears the South will be the focus of both parties' attention for many elections to come.

THE ELECTORAL VOTE BALANCE

Recent electoral history suggests that Democrats are currently advantaged in US presidential elections. Since 1988, the Democrats have won the presidency in five of eight elections and the popular vote in seven out of the eight. But the recent past is not always a guide to the future. Consider the fact that in the six elections between 1968 and 1988, the Republicans held the advantage, winning five of the six and several by significant margins.[92] Republican strength in the 1980s was soon replaced by Democratic victories in the 1990s. Yet because competition for the presidency has always rested upon some assessment of a candidate's relative strength in each of the states, recent election results often guide how parties develop future electoral strategies, helping to determine where the competition for electoral votes will occur and, in some cases, the issues that will be debated.[93]

Figure 3.3 illustrates over-time changes in the electoral balance of the Electoral College. We calculated how each of the states voted in the prior

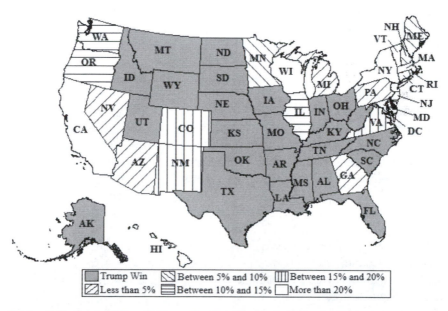

Figure 3.3 Competitive Balance in the Electoral College, 1988–2020. *Source:* Calculated by the authors.

five elections, doing so for each election from 1988 to 2020.[94] We categorized
states that voted for the same party in three of the five previous elections as
"highly competitive." States that voted for the same party in four of the five
elections were labeled "sometimes competitive," and those that voted for the
same party in each of the five were labeled "uncompetitive."[95]

The figure shows that the number of uncompetitive states has more than
doubled since the 2000 election. Thirty-seven of the fifty states currently
appear to be uncompetitive, having voted for one of the two parties consistently over each of the last five elections. This rise coincides with a decline
in the number of highly competitive states, which is now down to three—in
1996 the number of highly competitive states was twenty-six! While we have
seen in this chapter that American presidential elections in recent decades
are on the whole highly variable and competitive, figure 3.3 suggests that the
geographic scope of that competition is limited. Most state electorates are
strongholds of one party or the other, and few states are currently "in play."
But the figure also conveys another clear message: the current electoral vote
balance is subject to change . . . indeed, perhaps rapid change. The competitive balance in 1988 was somewhat similar to that seen today, relatively few
highly competitive states and a large number of uncompetitive states. Yet the
challenge confronting Democrats following the 1988 elections, having lost
three presidential elections in a row, was arguably more daunting than that
confronting Republicans today. Whereas there are thirty-seven uncompetitive
states following the 2020 elections, sixteen (plus the District of Columbia)
are Democratic and twenty are Republican states. In 1988, however, twenty-
five of the twenty-six uncompetitive states were in the Republican ledger.
Based on the electoral vote balance alone, no one could have reasonably
predicted Democratic victories in 1992 and 1996.

To assess the future prospects of the major parties, we must go beyond
analyzing official election statistics. Although these statistics are useful for
understanding competitive outcomes and future party strategies, they tell us
little about why Americans vote the way they do or whether they vote at all.
To understand how social coalitions have changed over time, as well as the
issue preferences of the electorate, we must turn to surveys. These surveys
help reveal how Biden was able to win election and why Trump wasn't
able to retain the presidency. Furthermore, to determine the extent to which
Americans really are polarized along party lines, we must study surveys to
examine the way in which the basic party loyalties of the American electorate
have changed during the postwar period. Thus, in the next five chapters, our
study turns to survey data to examine the prospects for continuity and change
in American electoral politics.

Part II

VOTING BEHAVIOR IN THE 2020 PRESIDENTIAL ELECTION

Chapter 4

Who Voted?

More than 158 million Americans cast ballots in the 2020 presidential election—more than any prior election in US history. Yet this number is less impressive when one considers that some 80 million Americans who were eligible to vote did not.[1] Overall the turnout rate in 2020 was 61.5 percent of the population (66.2 percent if we count only those eligible to vote). This figure represented a remarkable 6.8 percent point increase from turnout in the 2016 election and marks the highest turnout in a US presidential election since John F. Kennedy was elected in 1960.

Despite these gains in voter participation, turnout in the United States is lower than in any other Western industrialized democracy. In table 4.1, we present average turnout rates during the postwar period for twenty-five democracies, including the United States.[2] Clearly there is much variation in turnout among these democracies. And although it is not our goal to provide a full accounting of these differences, several points are worth noting.[3] Australia and Belgium, which have the highest turnout rates shown in table 4.1, are among several democracies with laws that enforce some form of compulsory voting. Although the penalties for not voting are relatively mild, compulsory voting obviously increases turnout.[4] A country's electoral system has also been shown to affect voter turnout rates. In democracies that use some form of proportional representation (PR) system, political parties have an incentive to mobilize the electorate broadly because every vote contributes to a party's proportional share. In plurality rule, WTA systems, such as the United States and Britain, many electoral units are uncompetitive, and get-out-the-vote efforts are likely to be of little value.[5] Differences among party systems may also encourage the lower social classes to vote in some societies and do little to encourage them to vote in others.

Table 4.1   Voter Turnout in National Elections, 1945–2021 (Percent)

Country	National Parliamentary	Presidential
Australia (29)	94.7	
Belgium (23)	92.0	
Luxembourg (16)	90.0	
Malta (18)	89.4	
Austria (23)	88.0	(13) 85.2
Iceland (22)	87.9	(9) 77.6
Italy (19)	87.3	
New Zealand (26)	86.9	
Denmark (27)	86.1	
Sweden (22)	85.5	
Netherlands (23)	84.8	
Germany (19)	82.7	
Norway (20)	79.7	
Greece (21)	76.2	
Israel (24)	75.5	
Finland (21)	73.8	(12) 72.9
Spain (14)	73.1	
United Kingdom (20)	72.7	
Ireland (20)	71.3	(8) 55.3
Canada (24)	71.3	
France (19)	71.3	(10) 81.1
Portugal (16)	70.0	(10) 61.2
Japan (28)	67.6	
Switzerland (19)	54.1	
United States (37)	44.8	(19) 55.7

Source: All countries except United States: mean level of turnout computed from results in International Voter Turnout Database, http://www.idea.int/data-tools/data/voter-turnout. US turnout results: 1946–2010: US Census Bureau, *Statistical Abstract of the United States, 2012* (Washington, DC: Government Printing Office, 2012), Table 397, 244, https://www.census.gov/prod/2011pubs/12statab/election.pdf. US results for 2012, 2014, 2016, and 2020 were calculated by authors; total votes cast in US House elections obtained from Clerk of the House of Representatives, "Statistics of the Presidential and Congressional Election," http://history.house.gov/Institution/Election-Statistics/Election-Statistics/; voting-age population estimates obtained from Michael P. McDonald, United States Elections Project, http://www.electproject.org/home/voter-turnout/voter-turnout-data.

Note: For all countries except the United States, turnout is computed by dividing the number of votes cast by the number of people registered to vote. For the United States, turnout is computed by dividing the number of votes cast for the US House of Representatives (or for president) by the voting-age population. Numbers in parentheses are the number of parliamentary or presidential elections. For all countries with bicameral legislatures, we report turnout for the lower house.

No matter whether one is examining turnout in legislative or presidential elections, the United States lags well behind other industrialized democracies in voter participation. To be fair, US congressional elections, especially midterm elections, are not wholly comparable to parliamentary elections in these other democracies. In the United States, the head of government is elected separately from the legislature. The president, for instance, remains in office regardless of the outcomes of the congressional midterms. In parliamentary systems, the head of government, typically a prime minister, is dependent upon the performance of his/her legislative party in parliamentary elections. Even in a semipresidential system such as France, the president may be forced to replace his prime minister and cabinet as a result of a National Assembly election. Yet, even when the president is on the ballot, turnout for US House elections during the nineteen presidential elections since World War II was only 55.7 percent, which is substantially lower than that of any democracy except for Switzerland. Indeed, turnout for US presidential elections ranks well below voting rates in Austria, Finland, France, Iceland, and Portugal. Voter participation in US presidential elections is roughly equivalent to presidential turnout in Ireland, where the presidency is essentially a ceremonial position.

Although not evident in table 4.1, it is important to note that voter turnout in most democracies has declined significantly over the postwar period. Indeed, by our analysis, eighteen of the twenty-five democracies have experienced a statistically significant decline in voter participation, by an average of roughly 2.3 percentage points per decade.[6] In our sample of democracies, average parliamentary turnout during the 1990s was 75.7 percent ($N = 72$); average turnout since then has dropped roughly 4 percentage points to 71.8 percent ($N = 151$). This average remains substantially higher than turnout in US national elections.

In comparative perspective, the low-turnout rate of the United States can be explained in part by institutional differences. But this does little to explain the tremendous amount of individual-level variation in voter turnout that occurs within the United States. If roughly 56 percent of Americans participate in presidential elections, that means 44 percent *do not*. Thus, before discovering how people voted in the 2020 election, we must answer a more basic question: Who voted? The answer to this question is partly institutional because federal and state laws in the United States—both historically and still today—often serve to inhibit (and sometimes facilitate) individuals' ability to vote. These state-level differences were perhaps never so obvious to the American public as they were in 2020, when the COVID-19 pandemic shined a spotlight on states' alternative rules regarding early voting and vote-by-mail. Political parties also play a role in affecting individuals' turnout decisions because parties' electoral strategies help define which voters are mobilized. And, of course, personal characteristics, such as an individual's socioeconomic status, political predispositions, and feelings of efficacy, contribute to someone's decision to go to the polls. Using survey data from the 2020 ANES, we will consider how each of these factors affected who voted in the most recent presidential election. Before doing so, however, it is important to place the study of voter turnout in the United States in a broader historical context.[7]

VOTER TURNOUT, 1789–1916

As noted by the historian Alexander Keyssar, "At its birth, the United States was not a Democratic nation—far from it. The very word democracy had pejorative overtones, summoning up images of disorder, government by the unfit, even mob rule."[8] Between 1789 and 1828 popular elections were not the norm in the United States. The Constitution did not require the Electoral College to be selected by popular vote, so many state legislatures simply appointed their presidential electors. Indeed, as late as the election of 1824, six of the twenty-four states appointed their slate of electors. Because US senators were also appointed by state legislatures, voting in national elections was essentially limited to casting ballots for members of the House of Representatives.[9] Even then voter participation was strictly limited. Race exclusions and property requirements, combined with the lack of female suffrage, effectively narrowed the eligible electorate during this period to white male landowners.[10] As a result of this limited electoral competition and restricted suffrage, voter turnout rates during this period are the lowest in American history.

The presidential election of 1828 is the first election in which the vast majority of states chose their presidential electors by popular vote, thus making it the first for which meaningful measures of voter turnout can be calculated.[11] Historical records can be used to determine how many people voted in presidential elections, but constructing a measure of the turnout rate requires us to choose an appropriate denominator. Turnout in presidential elections is typically determined by dividing the total number of votes cast for president by the voting-age population.[12] But, given limited voting rights, should the turnout denominator be all people who are old enough to vote? Or should it include only those who were eligible to vote? The answer greatly affects our estimates of turnout in presidential elections through 1916. Women, for instance, were eligible to vote in a handful of states before the ratification of the Nineteenth Amendment in 1920.[13] Clearly women should be included in the turnout denominator in states where they had the right to vote, but including them in the states where they could not vote would grossly deflate our estimates of turnout.

In figure 4.1, we present two sets of estimates of turnout in presidential elections from 1828 through 1916. The alternative estimates reflect the difference in the choice of denominator used to measure the turnout rate. The first set was compiled by Charles E. Johnson, Jr., who calculated turnout by dividing the number of votes cast for president by the voting-age population. The second set is based on calculations by Walter Dean Burnham, who measured turnout by dividing the total number of votes cast for president by the number of Americans eligible to vote. Burnham excludes African Americans

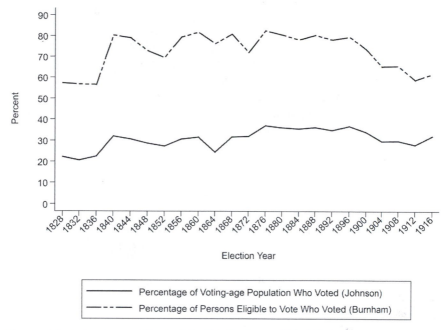

Figure 4.1 Voter Turnout in Presidential Elections, 1828–1916. *Source:* Estimates of turnout among the voting-age population based on Charles E. Johnson, Jr., *Nonvoting Americans*, series P-23, no. 2, US Department of the Census (Washington, DC: Government Printing Office, 1980), 2; estimates of turnout among the population eligible to vote based on calculations by Walter Dean Burnham, "The Turnout Problem," in *Elections American Style*, ed. A. James Reichley (Washington, DC: Brookings, 1987), 113–114. Note: Johnson's estimate for 1864 is based on the entire US adult population. Burnham's estimate for that year excludes the eleven Confederate states that did not take part in the election.

before the Civil War, and from 1870 on, he excludes aliens where they were not allowed to vote, basing his estimates on what he calls the "politically eligible" population. But the main difference between Burnham's estimates and Johnson's estimates is that Burnham excludes women from the turnout denominator in states where they could not vote.

Most political scientists would consider Burnham's calculations more meaningful than Johnson's. But whichever set of estimates one employs, the pattern of change is very similar. One clearly sees the effect of the advent of mass political parties and reemergence of two-party competition on voter participation. There is a large increase in turnout after 1836, when both the Democrats and Whigs began to employ popular appeals to mobilize the electorate. Turnout jumped markedly in 1840, during the "Log Cabin and Hard Cider" campaign in which William Henry Harrison, the hero of the Battle of Tippecanoe (1811), defeated the incumbent Democrat, Martin Van Buren.

Turnout waned somewhat after 1840, only to increase by roughly 10 percentage points in 1856 after the Republican Party, founded in 1854, polarized the
nation by taking a clear stand against slavery in the territories. In Abraham
Lincoln's election in 1860, four out of five eligible white men went to the polls.

Turnout vacillated during the Civil War and Reconstruction era. The
presidential election of 1864, held just weeks after General Sherman's Union
troops seized Atlanta, saw a decline in turnout. Voter participation increased
in 1868, but the turnout rate declined sharply in the 1872 election, the first to
take place after African Americans were granted suffrage by the ratification
of the Fifteenth Amendment.[14] Voter participation peaked in the 1876 contest
between Republican Rutherford B. Hayes and Democrat Samuel J. Tilden.
Although Tilden won a plurality of the popular vote, he did not win an electoral majority, and twenty electoral votes were disputed. To end the ensuing
controversy, an informal compromise was made where the Democrats conceded the presidency to the Republican, Hayes, and the Republicans agreed
to end Reconstruction.

Once the protection of federal troops was lost, many African Americans
were prevented from voting. Although some southern blacks could still
vote in 1880, their overall turnout dropped sharply, which reduced southern
turnout as a whole. Between 1880 and 1896 national turnout levels were
relatively static, but turnout began a long decline in 1900, an election that
featured a rematch of the candidates from 1896, Republican incumbent
William McKinley and William Jennings Bryan (Democrat and Populist).
By the late nineteenth century, African Americans were denied the franchise
throughout the South, and poor whites often found it difficult to vote as
well.[15] Throughout the country, registration requirements, which were in part
designed to reduce fraud, were introduced. Because individuals were responsible for placing their names on the registration rolls before the election, the
procedure created an obstacle that reduced electoral participation.[16]

Introducing the secret ballot also reduced turnout. Before this innovation
most voting in US elections was public. Because the political parties printed
their own ballots, which differed in size and color, any observer could see
how a person voted. The "Australian ballot"—as the secret ballot is often
called—was first used statewide in Massachusetts in 1888.[17] By the 1896
election nine in ten states had followed Massachusetts's lead.[18] Although the
secret ballot was designed to reduce fraud, it also reduced turnout.[19] When
voting was public, men could sell their votes, but candidates were less willing
to pay for a vote if they could not see it delivered. Ballot stuffing was also
more difficult when the state printed and distributed the ballots. Moreover,
the Australian ballot also proved to be an obstacle to participation for many
illiterate voters, although this was remedied in some states by expressly per-
mitting illiterate voters to seek assistance.[20]

As figure 4.1 shows, turnout trailed off rapidly in the early twentieth century. By the time the three-way contest was held in 1912 among Democrat Woodrow Wilson, Republican William Howard Taft, and Theodore Roosevelt, a Progressive, only three in five politically eligible Americans were going to the polls. In 1916 turnout rose slightly, but just over three-fifths of eligible Americans voted, and only one-third of the total adult population went to the polls.

VOTER TURNOUT, 1920–2016

With the extension of suffrage to all women by constitutional amendment in 1920, the rules that governed eligibility for voting became much more uniform across the states. This makes it easier to calculate turnout from 1920 onward, and we provide estimates based on both the voting-age and voting-eligible populations. As suffrage becomes more universal, these two populations grow in similarity (and the large gap between the measures evident in figure 4.1 dissipates). Indeed, these alternative measures of voter turnout produce fairly similar estimates, although differences have increased since 1972. In the modern period, we prefer focusing on turnout among the voting-age population for two reasons. First, it is difficult to estimate the size of the eligible population. Walter Dean Burnham and coauthors Michael P. McDonald and Samuel L. Popkin have made excellent efforts to provide these estimates.[21] Even so Burnham's estimates of turnout differ from McDonald and Popkin's, with the latter reporting somewhat higher levels of turnout in all five elections between 1984 and 2000. One difficulty in determining the eligible population is estimating the number of ineligible felons.[22] Incarceration rates, which have grown markedly during the last four decades, are frequently revised, and the number of permanently disenfranchised is nearly impossible to measure satisfactorily.[23] According to McDonald, in 2020 more than 1.5 million prisoners were ineligible to vote, as were 1.9 million on probation and more than 616,000 on parole.[24]

Second, excluding ineligible adults from the turnout denominator may yield misleading estimates, especially when US turnout is compared with turnout levels in other democracies. For example, about one in thirteen voting-age Americans cannot vote, whereas in Britain only about one in fifty is disenfranchised. In the United States about one in seven black males cannot vote because of a felony conviction. As Thomas E. Patterson writes in a critique of McDonald and Popkin, "To ignore such differences, some analysts say, is to ignore official attempts to control the size and composition of the electorate."[25]

In table 4.2, we show the percentage of the voting-age population who voted for the Democratic, Republican, and minor-party and independent candidates

Table 4.2   Percentage of Adults Who Voted for Each of the Major-Party Candidates, 1920–2020

Election Year	Democratic Candidate	Republican Candidate	Other Candidates	Did Not Vote	Total	Voting-Age Population
1920	14.8 James M. Cox	26.2 Warren G. Harding	2.4	56.6	100	61,639,000
1924	12.7 John W. Davis	23.7 Calvin Coolidge	7.5	56.1	100	66,229,000
1928	21.1 Alfred E. Smith	30.1 Herbert C. Hoover	0.6	48.2	100	71,100,000
1932	30.1 Franklin D. Roosevelt	20.8 Herbert C. Hoover	1.5	47.5	100	75,768,000
1936	34.6 Franklin D. Roosevelt	20.8 Alfred M. Landon	1.5	43.1	100	80,174,000
1940	32.2 Franklin D. Roosevelt	26.4 Wendell Willkie	0.3	41.1	100	84,728,000
1944	29.9 Franklin D. Roosevelt	25.7 Thomas E. Dewey	0.4	44.0	100	85,654,000
1948	25.3 Harry S. Truman	23.0 Thomas E. Dewey	2.7	48.9	100	95,573,000
1952	27.3 Adlai E. Stevenson	34.0 Dwight D. Eisenhower	0.3	38.4	100	99,929,000
1956	24.9 Adlai E. Stevenson	34.1 Dwight D. Eisenhower	0.4	40.7	100	104,515,000
1960	31.2 John F. Kennedy	31.1 Richard M. Nixon	0.5	37.2	100	109,672,000
1964	37.8 Lyndon B. Johnson	23.8 Barry M. Goldwater	0.3	38.1	100	114,090,000
1968	26.0 Hubert H. Humphrey	26.4 Richard M. Nixon	8.4	39.1	100	120,285,000
1972	20.7 George S. McGovern	33.5 Richard M. Nixon	1.0	44.8	100	140,777,000
1976	26.8 Jimmy Carter	25.7 Gerald R. Ford	1.0	46.5	100	152,308,000
1980	21.6 Jimmy Carter	26.8 Ronald Reagan	4.3	47.2	100	163,945,000
1984	21.6 Walter F. Mondale	31.3 Ronald Reagan	0.4	46.7	100	173,995,000
1988	23.0 Michael S. Dukakis	26.9 George H. W. Bush	0.5	49.7	100	181,956,000
1992	23.7 Bill Clinton	20.6 George H. W. Bush	10.8	44.9	100	189,493,000
1996	24.1 Bill Clinton	19.9 Bob Dole	4.9	51.1	100	196,789,000
2000	24.8 Al Gore	24.5 George W. Bush	1.9	48.8	100	205,813,000
2004	26.7 John F. Kerry	28.1 George W. Bush	0.6	44.6	100	220,804,000
2008	30.0 Barack Obama	26.0 John McCain	0.8	43.2	100	230,917,000
2012	27.4 Barack Obama	25.2 Mitt Romney	0.9	46.5	100	240,926,957

(Continued)

Table 4.2 Percentage of Adults Who Voted for Each of the Major-Party Candidates, 1920–2020 (Continued)

Election Year	Democratic Candidate	Republican Candidate	Other Candidates	Did Not Vote	Total	Voting-Age Population
2016	26.3 Hillary Clinton	25.2 *Donald J. Trump*	3.1	45.4	100	250,055,734
2020	31.6 *Joseph R. Biden*	28.8 Donald J. Trump	1.1	38.5	100	257,606,088

Sources: Voting-age population, 1920–1928: US Census Bureau, *Statistical Abstract of the United States, 1972*, 92nd ed. (Washington, DC: Government Printing Office, 1972), Table 597, 373. Voting-age population, 1932–2000: US Census Bureau, *Statistical Abstract of the United States, 2004–2005*, 124th ed. (Washington, DC: Government Printing Office, 2004), Table 409, 257. Voting-age population, 2004–2020: Michael P. McDonald, United States Election Project, http://www.electproject.org/home/voter-turnout/voter-turnout-data. Number of votes cast for each presidential candidate and the total number of votes cast for president: Federal Election Commission, "Official 2020 Presidential General Election Results," January 28, 2021, https://www.fec.gov/documents/2840/2020presgeresults.pdf.
Note: The names of the winning candidates are italicized.

("other candidates") between 1920 and 2020. The table also shows the percentage that did not vote as well as the overall size of the voting-age population.

Joe Biden won 51.3 percent of the popular vote in 2020, a majority, but this number does not mean that his supporters composed a comparable portion of the voting-age population. As table 4.2 shows, it is more likely for American adults to stay away from the polls on election day than support any one candidate. In all the elections between 1920 and 2020, except 1964, the percentage that did not vote easily exceeded the share cast for the winning candidate. In 2020, 31.6 percent of American adults could be counted as a Biden voter; 28.8 percent of the adult population cast ballots for Trump. The proportion of Americans who supported Biden in 2020 was above the average for all winning presidential candidates (29.0 percent). Indeed, Biden's share of support within the population is the highest since 31.1 percent of Americans voted for Ronald Reagan in his 1984 landslide.

Figure 4.2 illustrates the percentage of the voting-age population that voted for president in each of these twenty-six elections as well as the percentage of the politically eligible population between 1920 and 1944 and the voting-eligible population between 1948 and 2020.[26] The extent to which these trend lines diverge depends on the percentage of the voting-age population that is eligible to vote. In eras when few people were ineligible, such as between 1940 and 1980, it makes very little difference which turnout denominator one employs. Today, however, there is a much larger noncitizen population, and incarceration rates are nearly 2.6 times higher than they were in 1980. Back in 1960, when turnout peaked, only 2.2 percent of voting-age Americans were not citizens; in 2020 7.8 percent were not. In 1960, only 0.4 percent of Americans were ineligible to vote because of their felony status; in 2020,

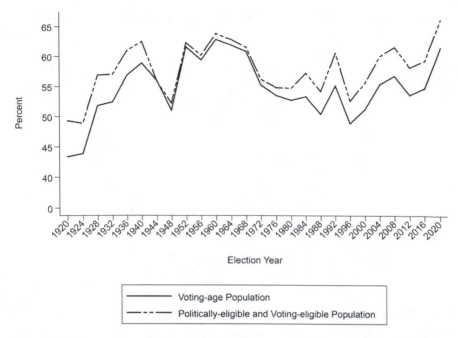

Figure 4.2   Percentage of Voting-Age Population and of the Politically Eligible and Voting-Eligible Population Voting for President, 1920–2020. *Source*: Voting-age population, see table 4.2 in this volume. Politically eligible population, 1920–1944: Walter Dean Burnham, "The Turnout Problem," in Elections American Style, ed. A. James Reichley (Washington, DC: Brookings, 1987), 113–114. Voting-eligible population, 1948–2000: Michael P. McDonald and Samuel L. Popkin, "The Myth of the Vanishing Voter," *American Political Science Review* 95 (December 2001): 966. Voting-eligible population, 2000–2020: Michael P. McDonald, United States Election Project, http://www.electproject.org/home/voter-turnout/voter-turnout-data.

1.3 percent was ineligible. Thus as figure 4.2 shows, in 1960 there was very little difference between turnout among the voting-age population and turnout among the voting-eligible population.

In the 2020 election, 158,383,403 votes were cast for president. Because the voting-age population was 257,605,088, turnout among this population was 61.5 percent. But, according to McDonald, the population eligible to vote was only 239,247,182. Using this total as our denominator, turnout was 66.2 percent. If we use McDonald's measure to calculate turnout in all nineteen postwar presidential elections, turnout would rise from 55.8 percent to 58.6 percent. However, US presidential turnout would still be lower than turnout in parliamentary elections in any country except Switzerland and lower than in presidential elections in any country except Ireland.

Turnout among the voting-age population generally rose between 1920 and 1960. Two exceptions were the elections of 1944 and 1948, when turnout decreased markedly due to social dislocations during and after World War II. Although short-term forces affect turnout in specific elections, long-term forces also contributed to the increase in turnout during this period. Three examples—not an exhaustive list certainly—help illustrate how long-term forces affect turnout. First, women who came of age before the Nineteenth Amendment, perhaps out of habit or long-held social expectations, often failed to exercise their right to vote once suffrage was granted.[27] But women who came of age after 1920 were more likely to turn out, and as this younger generation of women gradually replaced older women in the electorate, turnout levels rose.[28] Second, because all states restrict voting to citizens, immigrants enlarge the voting-age population but do not increase the number of voters until they become citizens. After 1921, however, as a result of restrictive immigration laws, the percentage of the population that was foreign-born declined. Over time this led to an increase in turnout as a percentage of the voting-age population. Finally, levels of education rose markedly throughout the twentieth century, a change that acts as an upward force on turnout. Americans who have attained higher levels of education are much more likely to vote than those with lower levels of education.

From 1960 to 1980 voter turnout in the United States declined with each election, followed by a variable pattern through 2016. Turnout among the voting-age population in 1960 was roughly 8 percentage points higher than it was in 2016. The decline in turnout during this period occurred even though there were several institutional changes that should have increased turnout. Between 1960 and the century's end, the country underwent changes that tended to increase turnout. After passage of the Voting Rights Act of 1965, turnout rose dramatically among African Americans in the South, and their turnout spurred voting among southern whites too. Less restrictive registration laws introduced since the 1990s also have made it easier to vote. The National Voter Registration Act, better known as the "motor voter" law, went into effect in January 1995, and it may have added 9 million additional registrants to the rolls.[29]

One recent institutional innovation that has altered the way many voters cast their ballots in many states is the adoption of convenience voting methods, such as in-person early voting, no-excuse absentee balloting, and vote-by-mail. Indeed, several states altered their voting laws—some only on a temporary basis—to adopt or extend convenience voting during the 2020 election cycle to accommodate voters during the COVID-19 pandemic.[30] Texas was the first state to use in-person early voting in 1988. Since then the number of states adopting in-person early voting laws has increased in every election period. In 2020, thirty-eight states and the District of Columbia had laws allowing voters to cast a ballot in person during a designated period prior to election day. Although all states offer some form of absentee balloting, they differ in whether or not voters need to provide a valid excuse to do so.[31] In about two-thirds of the states, any registered voter may vote absentee without an excuse, and, in the remaining one-third, an excuse is required. In 2020, seven states conducted voting strictly by mail.[32] The state of Oregon became the first to adopt vote-by-mail in 1998 when voters by an over two-to-one margin passed a statewide initiative, and neighboring Washington adopted vote-by-mail elections through legislative statute in 2011.

We analyzed the 2020 CPS conducted by the US Census Bureau to determine the extent to which voters made use of these convenience voting mechanisms in 2020.[33] Figure 4.3 shows that in-person early voting and voting-by-mail (no-excuse or excused) varies greatly among the states. According to the Census estimates, approximately 69 percent of voters nationally cast their ballots either by mail and/or before election day in 2020. This is a remarkable increase over 2016, when an estimated 38.6 percent of Americans reported voting using these nontraditional methods. Some states that used in-person early voting heavily in 2016, such as Texas and Tennessee, continued to favor this method of convenience voting in 2020. While other states, such as New Jersey, which expanded access to vote-by-mail ballots during the pandemic, saw a tremendous increase in convenience voting: less than 10 percent of New Jersey voters used in-person early voting and voting-by-mail in 2016; over 90 percent used these voting methods in 2020. Still, some states, such as Alabama, Mississippi, and Oklahoma, continue to limit in-person early voting and absentee voting in favor of the traditional in-person balloting on election day. In these states, fewer than one in five voters made use of convenience voting mechanisms in 2020, the lowest rates in the country.[34]

Despite all of the institutional changes related to voting since the 1960s, the United States has not seen sustained increases in voter turnout. The midterm elections of 2018 and presidential election of 2020, however, provide reasons for optimism for an increase in political participation. Voter participation rose significantly during the 2018 congressional elections to 50.3 percent, the highest turnout in a midterm election since 1914—the first time senators were directly elected by the people—and a 13.6 percentage-point increase in turnout since the previous midterm in 2014.[35] In 2020, voter turnout was 61.5 percent; it was 54.7 percent in 2016. This represents the largest increase in voter turnout across consecutive presidential elections since 1952. It remains to be seen whether the high turnouts of 2018 and 2020 are aberrations or the start of a new normal. Some of the increase in turnout in 2020 can be attributed to the increased use of convenience voting mechanisms. But this does not tell the whole story as voter turnout in 2020 also increased significantly in jurisdictions that did not adopt new convenience voting rules.[36] Voter enthusiasm in 2020—like 2018—was high among supporters of both parties. Of

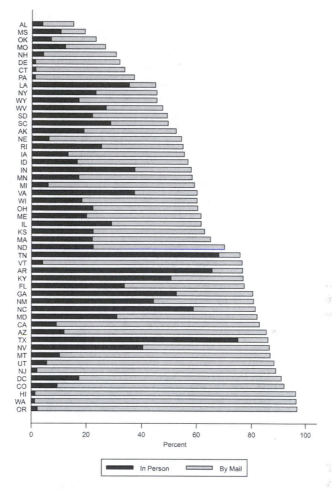

Figure 4.3 Percentage of Voters Who Voted Early (In-Person or By-Mail), by State, 2020. *Source*: US Census Bureau, 2020 Current Population Study, November Supplement. Note: Data are weighted.

course, one common factor that likely mobilized voters on both sides was the public's response—positive and negative—to the Donald Trump presidency.

VOTER TURNOUT AMONG SOCIAL GROUPS

In 2020, turnout increased by 6.8 percentage points, meaning that over 17 million more people voted in the election than four years earlier. Yet aggregate numbers often mask many interesting nuances about the changing composition of the American electorate, nuances that not only inform us about who participates in politics and who does not, but also about the dynamic nature of electoral competition and representation. One of the remarkable features about voter turnout in the 2020 elections—in addition to the unique challenges to voter registration and voting caused by the COVID-19 pandemic—is that voters from virtually every social group turned out in greater numbers. According to the US Census Bureau, turnout rates were higher in 2020 compared to 2016 among whites (6 percentage points), blacks (3 percentage points), Hispanics (6 percentage points), and Asians (10 percentage points).[37] Turnout increased among both women (5 percentage points) and men (6 percentage points), as well as across all age groups, with turnout among voters ages 18–34 increasing the most (8 percentage points). To further compare voter turnout among various social groups, we rely on the 2020 ANES survey.[38]

Roughly 66 percent of the voting-eligible population turned out in 2020, but roughly 84 percent of the respondents interviewed in the postelection survey reported that they voted. The ANES surveys commonly overestimate turnout for three reasons. First, even though the ANES respondents are asked a question that provides reasons for not voting, some voters falsely claim to have voted, perhaps owing to social pressure.[39] In past years, the ANES has undertaken vote validation efforts in which state voting and registration records were checked to authenticate respondents' claims. The vote validation for the 2016 ANES suggests that about 5 percent of the respondents who say that they voted did not do so, whereas only a handful of actual voters claim they did not vote. Importantly, for our purposes, most analyses that compare the results of reported voting with those measured by the validation studies suggest that *relative* levels of turnout among most social groups can be compared using reported turnout.[40] Second, the ANES surveys do not perfectly represent the voting-age population. Lower socioeconomic groups, which have very low turnout, are underrepresented. Discrepancies between the distribution of reported turnout in the ANES and actual turnout are exacerbated by low survey-response rates.[41] When response rates are low, surveys like the ANES tend to overrepresent higher socioeconomic groups and those who are interested in the survey's political subject matter. The overall response rate among eligible respondents for the 2020 ANES was 42.1 percent.[42] Third, during presidential election years, the ANES attempts to interview respondents both before and after the election. Being interviewed before the election may provide a stimulus to survey respondents, thus increasing turnout among the ANES sample.

With these caveats in mind, we examine differences in voter turnout among various social groups. Nearly one hundred years ago, the political scientists Charles Merriam and Harold Gosnell noted in one of the earliest quantitative studies of voter participation that racial and ethnic minorities, women, and young people were among the lowest turnout groups. In the decades that followed, numerous scholars reaffirmed these basic group differences. Nearly fifty years ago, Sidney Verba and Norman Nie articulated the "standard socioeconomic status model" and demonstrated that there is a socioeconomic bias in voter turnout in the United States, where the economic "Haves" in American society are more likely to participate in elections than the "Have Nots."[43] Later, Verba, along with colleagues Henry Brady and Key Lehman Schlozman, put forward the "resource model of political participation," by which they argue that individuals' resources, particularly time, money, and civic skills, facilitate political participation.[44] According to this view, individuals high in socioeconomic status are also more likely to be located in social networks that encourage participatory norms. Today, women are more likely to vote than men, and the gap in voting rates between whites and blacks has largely disappeared, but disparities in participation rates between some groups linger. In the following sections, we examine patterns of voter participation among various social groups.

Race, Gender, Region, and Age

Table 4.3 compares reported turnout among social groups using the 2020 ANES survey. Our analysis begins by comparing turnout differences among America's racial and ethnic groups.

To many observers the 2016 presidential election reflected growing levels of resentment among white Americans toward a political system that in their view, seemed to cater to minorities and immigrants and an economic system that valued global trade and devalued the domestic manufacturing jobs usually held by working-class whites.[45] Donald Trump's populist message seemed tailored to these voters, and during the course of his presidential term questions of racial conflict, social inequality, and identity politics were regularly at the fore. In 2017, Trump was criticized for his response to the violence that ensued between far-right and white nationalist groups and counter-protesters following a "Unite the Right" rally in Charlottesville, Virginia. Trump condemned the violence, neo-Nazis, and white nationalists but stated that there were "very fine people on both sides," leading some to question the legitimacy of his condemnation.[46] In 2020, following the death of George Floyd, an African American man who was murdered by Minneapolis police officer Derek Chauvin, over 450 Black Lives Matter protests erupted throughout the country with calls to "defund the police" and to reform law enforcement.[47] Trump condemned the group's views against law enforcement, and, when the City of New York allowed protesters to paint "Black Lives Matter" on the street outside of Trump Tower, the president tweeted that the sign was a "symbol of hate."[48] In the weeks that

Table 4.3   Percentage of Electorate Who Reported Voting for President, by Social Group, 2020

Social Group	Did Vote	Did Not Vote	Total	(N)[a]
Total electorate	84	16	100	(7,378)
Electorate, by Race				
African American	81	19	100	(828)
White	88	12	100	(4,865)
Other	75	25	100	(1,623)
Latinos (of any race)	72	28	100	(945)
Whites, by Gender				
Female	89	11	100	(2,512)
Male	86	14	100	(2,338)
Whites, by Region				
New England and Mid-Atlantic	90	10	100	(906)
North Central	88	12	100	(1,150)
South	85	15	100	(1,333)
Border	85	15	100	(473)
Mountain and Pacific	90	10	100	(1,003)
Whites, by Birth Cohort				
Before 1950	95	5	100	(807)
1951–1960	92	8	100	(944)
1961–1970	90	10	100	(878)
1971–1980	86	14	100	(696)
1981–1990	82	18	100	(708)
1991–1998	78	22	100	(463)
1999–2002	80	20	100	(229)
Whites, by Level of Education				
Not high-school graduate	63	37	100	(253)
High-school graduate	80	20	100	(1,180)
Some college	90	10	100	(1,409)
College graduate	94	6	100	(1,231)
Advanced degree	95	5	100	(725)
Whites, by Annual Family Income				
Less than $15,000	68	32	100	(232)
$15,000–34,999	75	25	100	(475)
$35,000–49,999	83	17	100	(384)
$50,000–74,999	86	14	100	(773)
$75,000–89,999	91	9	100	(352)
$90,000–124,999	93	7	100	(996)
$125,000–174,999	93	7	100	(615)
$175,000 and over	94	6	100	(725)
Whites, by Union Membership[b]				
Member	89	11	100	(775)
Nonmember	88	12	100	(4,115)
Whites, by Religion				
Jewish	91	9	100	(133)
Catholic	91	9	100	(988)

(Continued)

Table 4.3 Percentage of Electorate Who Reported Voting for President, by Social Group, 2020 (Continued)

Social Group	Did Vote	Did Not Vote	Total	(N)[a]
Protestant	93	7	100	(1,391)
None	83	17	100	(1,372)
White Protestants, by Whether Born Again				
Not born again	93	7	100	(593)
Born again	94	6	100	(779)
White Protestants, by Religious Commitment				
Medium or low	93	7	100	(508)
High	93	7	100	(651)
Very high	96	4	100	(217)
White Protestants, by Religious Tradition				
Mainline	95	5	100	(534)
Evangelical	93	7	100	(467)

Source: Authors' analysis of the 2020 ANES survey.
[a]Sample includes both Internet, video, and phone respondents. Numbers are weighted.
[b]Respondent or family member in union.

followed, Trump would refer to the Confederate flag as a "proud symbol" of the South and said that he would veto any legislation that would require the military to rename military bases in honor of Confederate leaders.[49] He also issued an executive order banning racial diversity training sessions at federal government agencies, saying that these efforts were "divisive, un-American propaganda."[50] With heightened awareness of issues of race and ethnicity, did white voters flock to the polls in disproportionate numbers in 2020? What about turnout among other racial and ethnic groups; what can we say about their levels of voter participation? Was voter turnout in 2020 significantly different than in years past?

Our analysis begins by comparing African Americans and whites.[51] In both 2008 and 2012, with Barack Obama on the ballot, election studies showed that whites and blacks reported voting at equal rates. In 2016, however, white respondents reported voting at a higher rate than that of blacks, a difference of 4 percentage points. Data from the CPS also suggest that whites were more likely to vote in 2016 than blacks, 65.3 percent to 59.6 percent. This gap, it is important to note, was primarily attributable to a decrease in black turnout rather than an upswing in white turnout. The ANES did not detect an increase in white voter participation between 2016 and 2020, estimating turnout in both years at 88 percent. However, the CPS, which features a significantly larger sample and is more precise, suggests that non-Hispanic white turnout in 2020 increased by 5.6 percentage points from 65.3 to 70.9 percent. According to the ANES, reported turnout among blacks decreased from 84 percent in 2016 to 81 percent in 2020, but this is at odds with the more precise estimates of the CPS, which suggest that black turnout increased from 59.4 percent in 2016 to 62.6 percent in 2020. Interestingly, the heightened level of black voter participation in 2020 was still lower than the group's turnout rates during Obama's 2008 and 2012 elections. Black voter participation in 2020 lagged white turnout nationally by just over 8 percentage points—this is the largest racial gap in voting that we have seen since 1992.[52]

Roughly 11 percent of the 2020 ANES sample is composed of self-identified African American respondents, making it possible to make within-group comparisons. As with earlier ANES surveys, blacks with higher levels of education are more likely to vote than those with lower levels of education. Blacks with college degrees were 10 percentage points more likely to vote than those with only a high-school diploma, and turnout among younger blacks continues to lag behind older generations. In 2020 the ANES suggests that black women and black men turned out at roughly the same rate, but the CPS estimates that black women were actually 8 percentage points more likely to vote than black men. Perhaps the most influential variable for predicting voter turnout among blacks is income. By our estimate, using the ANES, blacks in the upper quartile (top 25 percent) of income are roughly 20 percentage points more likely to vote than those in the bottom quartile (lowest 25 percent).[53]

Table 4.3 reveals that turnout among Latinos was lower than turnout among whites and African Americans. This is consistent with the historical record. Low levels of Latino turnout have typically been attributed to lower levels of education, income, and English language skills, and some have demonstrated differences between native- and foreign-born Latinos—although evidence varies on this issue—as well as ethnic group.[54] ANES data reveal the importance of education as a predictor of Latino participation; college graduates were 15.3 percentage points more likely to vote than Latinos with only a high-school degree. The 2020 ANES sample includes roughly 13.5 percent Latinos with approximately half of these identifying as Mexican in origin and 10 percent as Puerto Rican. The data suggest that the groups turned out at roughly the same rates, about 67 percent. The ANES did not distinguish those who were Cuban in origin. This is unfortunate, since Cuban Americans historically turn out at higher rates than other Hispanic groups and tend to have different partisan preferences. To further examine differences among Latinos, we turn to the CPS. The Census Bureau data show that Latinos (53.7 percent turnout) were significantly less likely to vote than blacks (62.6 percent), non-Latino whites (70.9 percent), and Asian Americans (59.7 percent), a group that saw their turnout rise by 10 percentage points in 2020. The data also show that foreign-born, naturalized Latinos were 1 percentage point more likely to vote than native-born Latinos. And ethnicity seems to matter as well, but these differences may be confounded by political geography. Turnout among Mexican Americans (the lowest among Latino groups) was roughly 9.5 percentage points lower than that of Cuban Americans according to the CPS. This difference is likely attributable to Mexican Americans, many of whom live in California and Texas, residing in uncompetitive states, whereas many Cuban Americans live in the battleground state of Florida. Overall, though, Latino turnout, which reached 53.7 percent in 2020, was roughly 6 percentage points higher than in 2016.

The 2020 presidential election was the third to feature a woman on the ticket of one of the major parties, and gender differences in voter turnout might be expected.[55] To be sure, women have voted at higher rates than men for some time now. The 1980 election was the last year in which the ANES surveys show white males to have a clear tendency to report voting more often than white females. Early ANES surveys show a clear decline in the turnout differential that advantaged men. In 1952, 1956, and 1960, the average male advantage was just over 10 points, whereas in the 1964, 1968, 1972, and 1976 elections, the gap narrowed to an average of just over 5 points. This pattern of a long period of male advantage in turnout followed by a long period of female advantage has also been evident in midterm elections. In the 2008 election white women were 7 points more likely than white men to report voting, the largest female advantage in any of the presidential elections we studied prior to that year.[56] But the gender gap in voting declined some in 2012 and all but disappeared in 2016.

The 2020 ANES estimates the gender gap to be about 1.7 percent with the difference largely attributable to gender differences among whites: 89 percent of the study's white female respondents reported voting compared to 86 percent of white men; no discernable difference in turnout is detected between black women and men. The gender differences found in the 2020 CPS, however, tell a different story. Among non-Hispanic whites, the CPS estimates a 2.6 percentage-point gap in turnout, with women (69.6 percent) voting at a higher rate than men (67.0 percent). The difference is similar to that found in the ANES, but the CPS suggests that the gender gap among blacks was actually quite sizable. The Census estimates indicate that black women turned out at a rate of 66.3 percent, while turnout among black males was 58.3 percent, a gender gap of 8 percentage points.

Surveys are not needed to study turnout in the various regions of the country. Because we have estimates of both the voting-age population and the voting-eligible population for each state, we can measure turnout once we know the number of votes cast for president. According to McDonald's data, turnout among the voting-age population ranged from a low of 51.5 percent in Texas to a high of 75.2 percent in Minnesota. But regional differences as a whole were modest. Among the voting-age population in the

South, 59.4 percent voted; outside the South, 63.3 percent did. There are small regional differences among whites. As the data in table 4.3 show, 85 percent of southern whites in the ANES said they voted; this estimate is 3.8 percent lower than the estimated turnout rates for whites outside the South. We used CPS state-level estimates to calculate non-Hispanic white turnout in the eleven southern states. The CPS estimates white voter turnout in the South to be 68.6 percent and 71.9 percent turnout outside the South, a difference of 4.3 percentage points. This difference reflects a fundamental change in postwar voting patterns since the Voting Rights Act of 1965. The one-party South was destroyed, electoral competition increased, and with blacks enfranchised for the first time since the turn of the twentieth century, turnout increased among whites as well. Outside the South, turnout has declined.

Young Americans are more likely to have higher levels of formal education than their elders, and one might thus expect them to have higher levels of turnout. But they do not. Voter participation tends to increase with age, and this is supported by the ANES data presented in table 4.3. This relationship is often attributed to changes in the life cycle; as people get older, settle down, and develop more community ties, they develop a greater appreciation for the role of government and politics in their lives, and they participate more.[57] John B. Holbein and D. Sunshine Hillygus argue that the gap in youth voting is not related to apathy; young people *are* interested in politics and motivated, they argue. Instead, young people tend to lack the noncognitive skills—capabilities related to self-regulation, effortfulness, and interpersonal interactions—that provide the applied knowledge and practical skills needed to follow through on the desire to participate in politics.[58] Whatever the cause, the relationship between age and voter turnout is evident in each of the studies we examined.

Although older voters continue to vote at higher rates than younger voters, the youth vote in 2020 was nothing short of historic. Ratified in July of 1971, the Twenty-sixth Amendment to the United States Constitution extended the right to vote to all citizens over the age of eighteen. Yet Census estimates show that, in every successive election since youth suffrage was granted, voter turnout among 18–24 has been the lowest among all age cohorts. In the twelve presidential elections between 1972 and 2016, the average turnout among 18–24 year olds was 40 percent.[59] In 2016, the CPS estimated youth turnout at 39.4 percent, but youth participation increased by a remarkable 12 percentage points in 2020. Somewhat ironically, given that the campaign featured the oldest candidates to ever run for the presidency, the 2020 election marked the first time that a majority of 18–24 years turned out to vote. A record 51.4 percent of young voters went to the polls, comprising nearly 10 percent of the 2020 electorate.

Income and Union Membership

Jan Leighley and Jonathan Nagler argue that there is no better measure of an individual's social class than income, and income is strongly linked to voter participation.[60] The 2020 ANES shows that respondents' family income is related to reported turnout. White respondents with family incomes less than $50,000 were roughly 15 percentage points less likely to vote than those with higher incomes. Earlier analyses of ANES data also demonstrate a strong relationship between family income and turnout in all the presidential elections between 1952 and 2016 and all the midterm elections between 1958 and 1978.[61] Previous CPS surveys have also shown a strong relationship between income and turnout, and the data for 2020 are no different. The CPS data show that turnout among all respondents with incomes less than $50,000 was 50.7 percent, whereas turnout among those with incomes greater than $50,000 was 73.9 percent, a difference of over 23 percentage points.

Surveys over the years have found a weak and inconsistent relationship between union membership and turnout. Being in a household with a union member may create organizational ties that encourage voting. And unions, historically, were an important mobilizing agent for the Democratic Party, which for a significant portion of the postwar period relied on white working-class support as part of its electoral coalition.[62] Yet Leighley and Nagler argue that the small and sporadic empirical association between union membership and turnout may result from union mobilization efforts increasing turnout among members and nonmembers alike. To support their claim, they provide evidence that the decline in union membership since 1964 has resulted in a decrease in voter turnout among low and middle-class income groups regardless of membership. Exit polls show that voters from union households made up approximately 20 percent of the electorate. The 2020 ANES shows the effect of union membership to be statistically indistinguishable, with members and nonmembers reporting turnout at roughly equal rates. In both 2008 and 2012, we also found no difference in turnout between union members and nonmembers, but in 2016 union members reported turning out at a slightly higher rate (3 percent more) than nonmembers.

Religion

Religion continues to play a powerful role in American public life.[63] A 2019 survey by the Pew Research Center shows that 72 percent of Americans say that religion is an important part of their lives, but less than half say they attend religious services on at least a monthly basis—both of these numbers declined over the prior decade.[64] Religious individuals tend to have strong social networks, which facilitate the transmittal of political information and ease the costs of voting.[65] Churches also serve as direct and indirect vehicles for voter mobilization.[66]

In the earlier postwar years, Catholics were more likely to vote than Protestants, but these differences have declined.[67] The low turnout of Protestants, clearly documented by ANES surveys conducted between 1952 and 1978, resulted largely from two factors.[68] First, Protestants were more likely to live in the South, which was once a low turnout region. And, second, Protestants were more likely to be black, a group that had much lower turnout than whites. We have always compared turnout or reported turnout by comparing white Catholics with white Protestants. Except for the 1980 election, when there were no differences between Catholics and Protestants, Catholics were more likely to vote when vote validation measures were used (1984 and 1988). Catholics were also more likely to report voting in the five elections between 1992 and 2004, but in 2008, 2012, and 2016 Protestants and Catholics were equally likely to turn out. The 2020 ANES inquired about respondents' religious affiliations and practices, and as seen in table 4.3, Protestants and Catholics once again reported turning out in roughly equal rates. Exit polls estimate that Protestants composed about 40 percent of the electorate, whereas Catholics were a quarter of the electorate.[69] Twenty-two percent of voters did not profess a religion.

Between 1952 and 1996 Jews had higher reported turnout than either Protestants or Catholics in six of the seven presidential elections as well as in five of the six midterm elections between 1958 and 1978. We found Jews to have higher levels of turnout or reported turnout in each of the ten elections between 1980 and 2016. In 2016, we found that Jews were nearly 10 percentage points more likely to vote than Protestants or Catholics—the highest turnout level among any religious group. But in 2020 Jewish voter participation was roughly equal to that of white Protestants and Catholics, as the latter two groups experienced higher than normal levels of turnout. Exit polls estimated that Jewish voters represented only 2 percent of the electorate.

For nearly three decades, fundamentalist Protestants have been a pivotal player in American politics. As we will see in chapter 5, fundamentalist Protestants are conservative on social issues, such as abortion and same-sex marriage, and tend to throw their support overwhelmingly toward Republican presidential candidates. Indeed Christian conservative churches and organizations expend considerable resources mobilizing voters through get-out-the-vote efforts and attempt to galvanize supporters through the circulation of voter information guides.[70] In examining turnout among white fundamentalist Protestants since the 1992 election, we have found that the success of these groups in mobilizing their supporters has varied from election to election. In 2016 we found no statistically significant difference in reported turnout between Protestants who say they are born-again Christians and those who say they are not, and the data in 2020 show similar results.[71]

Lyman A. Kellstedt argues that religious commitment is an important factor contributing to voting behavior.[72] Using multiple indicators we were able to construct a measure of religious commitment using the ANES.[73] To score "very high" on this measure, respondents had to report attending church at least once a week. In addition, they had to say that religion provided "a great deal" of guidance in their lives and to believe that the Bible is literally true or the "word of God." In 1992, 1996, 2000, 2004, and 2016, respondents who scored very high on this measure were the most likely to report voting, but in 2008 there was only a weak relationship between religious commitment and whether white Protestants said they voted. We lacked the data necessary to measure religious commitment in 2012. The 2020 ANES shows that white Protestants with very high religious commitment are about 3 percentage points more likely to vote than those with lower levels of commitment.

Most white Protestants can be classified into two categories, mainline and evangelical, which according to Pew Research Center's Religious Landscape Survey, make up more than two-fifths of the total US adult population.[74] As R. Stephen Warner has pointed out, "The root of the [mainline] liberal position is the interpretation of Christ as a moral teacher who told his disciples that they could best honor him by helping those in need." In contrast, says Warner, "the evangelical interpretation sees Jesus (as they prefer to call him) as one who offers salvation to anyone who confesses in his name." Liberal or mainline Protestants stress the importance of sharing their abundance with the needy, whereas evangelicals see the Bible as a source of revelation about Jesus.[75]

In classifying Protestants as mainline or evangelical, we rely on their denomination. For example, Episcopalians, Congregationalists, and most Methodists are classified as mainline, whereas Baptists, Pentecostals, and many small denominations are classified as evangelicals.[76] In each presidential election between 1992 and 2016, white mainline Protestants were more likely than white evangelicals to report voting. In 2020, mainline and evangelicals Protestants reported turning out at roughly equal rates.

Education

Surveys consistently reveal a strong relationship between formal education and electoral participation. The tendency for better-educated citizens to be more likely to vote is one of the most extensively documented facts in the study of politics. Indeed in their classic study, *Who Votes?*, Raymond E. Wolfinger and Steven J. Rosenstone note the "transcendent power of education" as a predictor of voter turnout.[77] Better-educated Americans have higher levels of political knowledge and political awareness; they also are more likely to possess the resources—money, time, and civic skills—that reduce the information costs of voting.[78]

The 2020 ANES reveals a strong relationship between formal education and voter turnout. Whites who did not graduate from high school were nearly 31 percentage points less likely to report voting than those who graduated college. The 2020 CPS also found a strong relationship between education and reported voter turnout. Among all citizens (i.e., regardless of race) with less than a high-school education, only 35.2 percent reported voting, and among those with only a high-school diploma, 51.1 percent said they cast a ballot. Among those citizens with some college-level education, 66.8 percent reported voting, and among college graduates, turnout was 74.2 percent.

Earlier we noted that education was also strongly associated with voter turnout for African Americans and Latinos. According to the 2020 ANES, blacks with less than a high-school education turned out at a reported rate of 61.3 percent, whereas those with a high-school diploma reported turning out at a 80.4 percent rate. Turnout among African Americans with some college education was also around 80 percent, and among those with a college degree the reported rate was about 10 percentage points higher (91.5 percent). Turnout differences among Latinos at varying levels of education were also quite sharp. Latinos with less than a high-school education turned out a reported rate of 48.9 percent; the rate was 69.3 percent among Latinos who are high-school graduates. Turnout among Latinos with some college education was 73.15 percent, and for those with a college degree, turnout was 86.1 percent.

CHANGES IN TURNOUT AFTER 1960

The postwar turnout rate peaked in 1960. According to the US Census Bureau, in that year, only 43.2 percent of whites and 20.1 percent of blacks twenty-five years and older were high-school graduates. By 2010, 87.6 percent of whites and 84.2 percent of blacks were high-school graduates. In 1960, only 8.1 percent of whites and 3.1 percent of blacks were college graduates. By 2010, 30.3 percent of whites and 19.8 percent of blacks had obtained college degrees. The growth in educational attainment is a remarkable change in American society, and this social transformation plays a central role in one of the longest-standing empirical puzzles in the study of political behavior, a puzzle Richard A. Brody labels the "puzzle of political participation."[79] Given that education is a strong predictor of voter turnout at the individual level, why did national turnout levels decline between 1960 and 1980, and why did they stabilize, roughly speaking, thereafter, during a time when education levels rose dramatically?

Political scientists have studied the postwar changes in voter turnout extensively over the past several decades. Given the influence of education on turnout, one would expect increasing levels of education would lead to a substantial increase in turnout over this time, and certainly not a decline in voter participation of any degree, as happened between 1960 and 1980. This suggests that any stimulating effect of education on voter turnout was likely offset by other factors that depressed it. Some scholars argue that the decline in turnout was a function of social forces, such as the changing age distribution of the electorate and a decline in social institutions generally. Others point to institutional changes, such as the expansion of suffrage to eighteen-year-olds or to the ways in which the political parties conduct their campaigns as sources for the decline in voter turnout. Still others argue that the decline in voter turnout reflected changes in political attitudes that are fundamental for encouraging political participation. In a comprehensive study of the decline in turnout between 1960 and 1988, Ruy Teixeira argues that the decline in church attendance, which reduces Americans' ties to their communities, was the most important of these three factors in reducing turnout and suggests that voter participation would have declined even further had education not been a countervailing force.[80]

Steven J. Rosenstone and John Mark Hansen also develop a comprehensive explanation for the decline in turnout. Using data from the ANES, they examine the effect of expanded suffrage (estimating that the inclusion of eighteen-, nineteen-, and twenty-year-olds in the 1972 elections likely caused about a 1 percentage-point decline in turnout) and reduced voter registration requirements on voting. They found that reported turnout declined 11 percentage points from the 1960s to the 1980s. Yet their analysis also demonstrates that the increase in formal education was the most important factor preventing an even greater decline in voter participation. They estimate that turnout would have declined 16 percentage points if it had not been for the combined effect of rising education levels and liberalized election laws.[81]

Most analysts agree that attitudinal changes contributed to the decline in electoral participation. Indeed our own analysis has focused on the effects of attitudinal changes, particularly the influence of changes in party loyalties and the role of what George I. Balch and others have called feelings of "external political efficacy"—that is, the belief that political authorities will respond to attempts to influence them.[82] We found these attitudes contributed to the decline in turnout from 1960 through 1980, and they have remained influential in every presidential election we have studied from 1980 to 2016.[83]

To measure party identification, we use a standard set of questions to gauge individuals' psychological attachment to a partisan reference group.[84] In chapter 6, we examine how party identification contributes to the way people vote. But party loyalties also contribute to *whether* people vote. Strong feelings of party identification contribute to one's psychological involvement in politics.[85] Moreover, party loyalties also reduce the time and effort needed to decide how to vote and thus reduce the costs of voting.[86] In every presidential election since 1952, the ANES studies have shown that strong partisans are more likely to vote than weaker partisans and independents who lean toward one of the parties. And in every election since 1960, independents with no partisan leanings have been the least likely to vote.

Partisanship is an important contributor to voters' decisions to turn out, but the strength of party loyalties in the United States has varied over time. Between 1952 and 1964 the percentage of self-identified "strong partisans" among the white electorate never fell below 25 percent. It then fell to 27 percent in 1966 and continued to fall, reaching its lowest level in 1978, when only 21 percent of voters identified strongly with one of the two major parties. In more recent years, party identification has risen; indeed, by 2004, it had returned to 1952–1964 levels. After a temporary decline in 2008 due to a decrease in Republican loyalties, the percentage of whites who were strong party identifiers rose to just over 30 percent in 2012, 37.4 percent in 2016, and reached 45.9 percent in 2020.[87] Among African Americans, 56.4 percent identify themselves as strong partisans, but partisanship is much lower among Latinos, where 35.8 percent say they are strong partisans.

Feelings of political efficacy also contribute to voter participation. Citizens may expect to derive benefits from voting if they believe that government is responsive to their demands. Conversely, those who believe that political leaders will not or cannot respond to popular demands may see little reason to engage in political participation.[88] From 1960 to 1980 feelings of political efficacy dropped precipitously, and they remain low and in decline today. In 1956 and 1960, 64 percent of whites reported high levels of political efficacy, with only 15 percent scoring low. In 2020, few Americans felt that that government responded to their needs. Indeed, efficacy was at an all-time low. Only 17.7 percent of whites scored "high" on our measure of political efficacy, and 62.3 percent scored "low." Incredibly the portion of respondents with low levels of political efficacy increased roughly 10 percentage points since 2016.

The steepest declines in partisan attachment and political efficacy occurred between 1960 and 1980, contemporaneous with the sharpest decline in voter participation. Our analysis of voter turnout during this two-decade period suggests that the combined impact of the decline in party identification and the decline in beliefs about government responsiveness accounts for roughly 70 percent of the decline of electoral participation. The ANES reports a decline in validated turnout among white voters of 10.3 percentage points between 1960 and 1980. By our estimates, if there had been no decline in either partisan attachments or external political efficacy, the decline in turnout would have been only 2.9 percentage points.[89] In previous volumes, we have noted the persistent role these attitudes play in predicting voter turnout in subsequent election years. Whereas party loyalties have rebounded to high levels, Americans' feelings of efficacy remain anemic, thus preventing a substantial increase in turnout levels. Using a rather simple algebraic procedure, we can estimate the percentage of whites in 2020 who would have reported voting for president had strength of partisanship, and external political efficacy remained at 1960 levels.[90] Our estimate suggests that reported turnout among whites in 2020 would be 3.9 percentage points higher if not for these attitudinal changes.

In table 4.4 we present the joint relationship between strength of party identification, feelings of efficacy, and reported electoral participation in the 2020 presidential election. As we have found in the past, strength of party identification and feelings of political efficacy are weakly related, but both contribute to turnout. Reading across each row reveals that strength of party identification is positively related to reported electoral participation, but the strength of this relationship has been weaker in the past two elections relative to years we have studied. The difference in reported voting among whites with strong partisanship and those describing themselves as independents who lean toward a party is 6 percentage points for those high in efficacy and seven points for those low in efficacy. These differences are similar to those found in 2016, but in 2008, we reported differences of 15 percentage points for those high in efficacy and 34 points for those low in efficacy. Reading down each column, we see a consistent relationship between feelings of political efficacy and reported voting within each partisan group—on the magnitude of 2 to 23 percentage-point differences. This suggests that the record-low level of political efficacy in 2020—63.3 percent of whites report "low" levels of efficacy—was distributed among strong, weak, and nonpartisans alike and that efficacy had a strong relationship with decisions to turn out. This finding is similar to what we found in 2016, when political efficacy was at a then record low (50 percent scored "low"). In 2008, by comparison, we found a strong relationship between feelings of efficacy and reported

Table 4.4 Percentage of Whites Who Reported Voting for President, by Strength of Party Identification and Sense of External Political Efficacy, 2020

Score on External Political Efficacy Index	Strength of Party Identification							
	Strong Partisan		Weak Partisan		Independent Who Leans toward a Party		Independent with No Partisan Leaning	
	%	(N)	%	(N)	%	(N)	%	(N)
High	94	(478)	96	(164)	92	(620)	88	(37)
Medium	94	(404)	90	(177)	96	(172)	57	(43)
Low	92	(1,177)	83	(559)	85	(154)	65	(237)

Source: Authors' analysis of the 2020 ANES survey.
Note: The numbers in parentheses are the totals on which the percentages are based. Numbers are weighted.

turnout in only one partisan group: independents who lean toward a political party. In that year, 43.7 percent of respondents reported low feelings of political efficacy.

A comprehensive analysis of the role of attitudinal factors would have taken into account other factors that might have eroded turnout. For instance, as has been well documented, there has been a substantial decline in trust during the past four decades, a decline that appears to be occurring in a large number of democracies.[91] In 1964, when political trust among whites was highest, 77 percent of whites trusted the government to do what was right just about always or most of the time, and 74 percent of blacks endorsed this view.[92] Political trust reached a very low level in 1980, when only 25 percent of whites and 26 percent of blacks trusted the government. Trust rebounded during the Reagan years, but it fell after that, and by 1992 trust was almost as low as it was in 1980. After that, trust rose in most elections, and by 2004, 50 percent of whites and 34 percent of blacks trusted the government. But trust dropped markedly among whites during the next four years, and it dropped somewhat among blacks. In 2008, 30 percent of whites and 28 percent of blacks trusted the government.[93] In 2012, after the first term of the first black president, 19 percent of whites—a sharp decline—and 40 percent of blacks— a sharp increase—trusted the government in Washington to do what is right. Among Latinos, trust declined by 6 points over the course of Obama's first term from 36 to 30 percent. In 2016 only 8.6 percent of whites professed trust in government, whereas 20.8 percent of blacks and 17.8 of Latinos did. At the end of President Trump's first term in 2020, whites expressed a higher degree of trust than they did four years earlier, reporting a 5.5 percentage-point increase to 14.1 percent. However, trust among African Americans decreased during Trump's time in office, dropping 7.3 points to 13.5 percent. Trust among Latinos rose marginally during this time to 20.2 percent.

Although the decline in trust in government would seem to be an obvious explanation for the decline in turnout since the 1960s, scholarship shows little evidence supporting this. In most years, Americans who distrusted the government were as likely to vote as those who were politically trusting. In the past two elections, the evidence has been mixed. In both 2016 and 2020, trust in government was positively related to voter turnout among white voters but not blacks or Latinos. For blacks and Latinos, we see no statistically significant relationship between trust in government and voter turnout.

ELECTION-SPECIFIC FACTORS

Focusing on long-term stable factors related to voting, such as social demographics and partisan attachments, might give one the impression that election-specific factors may not matter. Yet in any election there will be political and nonpolitical circumstances that affect voting. Among the non-political factors shown to affect voter turnout is election-day weather. Bad weather is likely to increase the physical costs of voting and make it more difficult for potential voters to get to the polls. A study by Brad T. Gomez, Thomas G. Hansford, and George A. Krause, which examined county-level voter turnout in every presidential election from 1944 to 2000, showed that for every inch of rain a county received above its thirty-year average rainfall, turnout declined by nearly 1 percentage point.[94] In close elections, a nonpolitical factor like weather could have real political consequences by keeping voters in some localities away from the polls and potentially changing electoral outcomes.[95]

Of course, in 2020, the nonpolitical factor that had the greatest effect on voter participation was the coronavirus pandemic. In their study of primary voting in the spring of 2020, W. Dana Flanders, William D. Flanders, and Michael Goodman report that localities with high COVID rates experienced lower levels of voter turnout, controlling for a variety of other factors.[96] By the fall, many states and localities either adjusted their voting rules or increased their resources to facilitate convenience voting to offset the effects of the pandemic.

Politics matters, too, of course. Not all elections are competitive, and one factor that stimulates voter turnout is the expected closeness of the outcome.[97] According to the rational choice theory of voting developed by Anthony Downs and refined by William H. Riker and Peter C. Ordeshook, a person's expected benefit from voting increases in close elections because the probability that one's vote will directly affect the outcome is higher.[98] Close elections also make it easier for potential voters to become politically informed as heightened media coverage, television advertising, and interpersonal discussion of politics help create an information-rich environment. And parties and candidates are more likely to engage in get-out-the-vote efforts when election outcomes hang in the balance.

In chapter 2, we identified the thirteen battleground states in the 2020 election.[99] Early predictions suggested these states might have close elections. According to the 2020 CPS, however, average voter turnout (voting-age population) in these thirteen states was 71.5 percent, whereas the average in non-battleground states was 70.6 percent. The lack of a significant difference in turnout between battleground and non-battleground states is rather remarkable and attests to the high level of voter interests and participation across the country.

The most direct way that campaigns attempt to influence turnout is through get-out-the-vote efforts. Modern campaigns expend exorbitant amounts of money and effort trying to bring their voters to the polls. Campaigns employ local phone banks and door-to-door canvassing; they use direct mail and social networking technology and even old-fashioned political rallies all in an effort to stimulate voter interests. But to what effect? Over two decades ago, political scientists Donald Green and Alan Gerber began a research agenda aimed at answering this question. Green and Gerber use field experiments to gauge the effectiveness of voter mobilization tactics.[100] The field experiments typically use voter registration rolls to assign a subset of voters randomly into "treatment" and "control" conditions. Those assigned to the treatment group are exposed to the specific get-out-the-vote tactic being tested, whereas those in the control group are not.[101] After the election the voter rolls are reexamined to determine whether voter turnout was higher among those in the treatment group than those in control group, thus providing evidence that the mobilization tactic *caused* an increase in turnout. Green and Gerber's work, as well as that undertaken subsequently by others, suggests, among other things, that voters tend to respond best to personalized methods and messages, such as door-to-door canvassing, than impersonal techniques, such as "robocalls."[102] Pressure from one's social network is also important in mobilizing voters to the polls. In one of their most well-known experiments to date, Gerber and Green, joined by Christopher Larimer, find that voters are more likely to turn out—by an increased probability of 8.1 percentage points—when they are told prior to election day that their decision to vote will be publicized to their neighbors. This experiment not only demonstrates the effectiveness of social pressure in mobilizing voters; it provides supporting evidence for the argument that the historic decline in turnout could have been caused in part by the concomitant decline in Americans' willingness to join associational groups, such as fraternal organizations and churches.

Unlike these experimental designs, it is difficult to estimate the *causal* effect of mobilization on turnout using surveys. Consider the fact that campaigns often contact voters based on how likely they are to vote. Can we really say that mobilization causes turnout, or does the potential for turnout cause mobilization? Because the survey environment typically measures whether the individual was contacted by a political party and the individual's reported turnout contemporaneously, it is hard to establish for certain which variable came first. Thus an analysis of the relationship between whether an individual was contacted by a political party and their reported turnout using the 2020 ANES is likely to only establish correlation, not causation.[103]

The longitudinal nature of the ANES does offer interesting insights into changes in the mobilization of the electorate, however. Most notably the percentage of Americans who say they have been contacted by a political party increased after the 1960 election. In 1960, 22 percent of the electorate said a political party had contacted them.[104] By 1980, 32 percent said they had been contacted. The upward trend abated in 1992, when only 20 percent said they had been contacted by a political party. The percentage that said they had been contacted by a political party grew in 1996 and in 2000, and it increased slightly between 2000 and 2004. It grew again somewhat in 2008, when 43 percent said they had been contacted, with whites somewhat more likely to claim they were contacted (45 percent) than blacks (38 percent). In 2012, 39 percent of the electorate said a political party had contacted them, a decrease from four years earlier. This number dropped precipitously in 2016, when only 31.8 of respondents reported contact by one of the parties. That party contact went down in 2016 may not be a surprise to close observers of the campaigns. Much was made during the general election season about the limited resources dedicated by the Trump campaign to the mobilization "ground game."[105] As we noted in 2020, the COVID-19 pandemic greatly limited field operations for both campaigns. Nevertheless, roughly 39 percent of ANES respondents reported being contacted directly by one of the two campaigns. Clearly, in the age of social media, direct contact does not require campaigns to go door-to-door.

DOES LOW VOTER TURNOUT MATTER?

Many bemoan the low levels of turnout in US elections—although the increase in turnout in 2020 may offer some reason for optimism. Some claim that low rates of voter participation undermine the legitimacy of elected political leaders. Seymour Martin Lipset, for instance, argues that the existence of a large bloc of nonparticipants in the electorate may be potentially dangerous because it means that many Americans have weak ties to the established parties and political leaders.[106] This may increase the prospects of electoral instability or perhaps political instability generally. Others argue that the low levels of turnout, at minimum, increase the probability that American elections produce "biased" outcomes, reflecting the preferences of an active political class while ignoring those who may be alienated or disenfranchised.

Turnout rates may also increase the electoral fortunes of one party over the other. Conventional wisdom holds that because nonvoters are more likely to come from low socioeconomic-status groups and ethnic minorities—groups that tend to vote Democratic—higher turnout benefits the Democrats. James DeNardo, using aggregate election data from 1932 to 1976, and Thomas Hansford and Brad Gomez, using aggregate data from 1948 to 2000, provide evidence that increases in turnout enlarge the vote share of Democratic candidates, although the nature of the relationship is more complex and weaker than one might assume.[107]

Elected officials appear convinced that their reelection fates depend on the level of turnout.[108] Over the past several decades, at both the national and state level, legislators have debated a number of laws aimed at making it easier (or sometimes harder) for citizens to vote. Bills that make it easier to register to vote, such as the 1993 motor voter law, and bills that promote convenience voting mechanisms, such as early voting or vote-by-mail, have typically divided legislators along strict party lines with Democrats supporting efforts to expand the electorate and Republicans opposing them.

Over the past decade Republicans have led a push to require voter identification at the polls, typically by requiring the presentation of a government-issued identification card, such as a driver's license. At the time of the 2016 election, these bills had passed in thirty-four states.[109] After the 2012 election, North Carolina, which had a Republican legislature and governor, passed a strict voter identification requirement. In addition to requiring people to show photo identification, the North Carolina law condensed the number of early voting days, abolished same-day registration, and eliminated out-of-precinct voting. Supporters of the North Carolina bill argued that the bill attempted to increase the integrity of elections; opponents of the bill argued that the aim of the bill was voter suppression, particularly minority voters.[110] In July 2016 the Fourth Circuit Court of Appeals struck down the North Carolina law, stating that the state legislature had acted with "discriminatory intent" and that the law targeted the state's black voters with "almost surgical precision" to reduce their voter participation.[111] In May 2017, the US Supreme Court rejected the state's appeal of the case.[112] And in the wake of the record increase in turnout in the 2020 elections and amid cries from former President Trump and his allies that the election had been stolen, nineteen states have enacted laws that, among other things, limit early voting hours, narrow eligibility to vote absentee, require stricter identification requirements and generally make it more difficult for Americans to vote.[113]

As argued originally by the authors of *The American Voter*, if nonvoters and occasional voters hold preferences that differ from those of regular (or core) voters, then variation in turnout is likely to have meaningful electoral implications.[114] Thus, in table 4.5, we examine whether respondents reported voting for president in 2020, according to their party identification, their positions on the issues (the "balance-of-issues" measure), and their evaluations of the performance of the incumbent president (Trump), which party is best able to handle the important problems facing the country, and their beliefs about whether the country is going in the right direction (the summary measure of "retrospective" evaluations).

Table 4.5 shows that strong Republicans and strong Democrats voted at roughly equivalent rates. Similarly, independents who felt close to the

Table 4.5   Percentage of Electorate Who Reported Voting for President, by Party Identification, Issue Preferences, and Retrospective Evaluations, 2020

	Voted	Did Not Vote	Total	(N)
Strong Democrat	91	9	100	(1,726)
Weak Democrat	81	19	100	(816)
Independent, Leans Democratic	85	15	100	(849)
Independent, No Partisan Leaning	61	39	100	(884)
Independent, Leans Republican	86	14	100	(760)
Weak Republican	84	16	100	(778)
Strong Republican	90	10	100	(1,547)
Electorate, by Scores on Balance-of-Issues Measure				
Strongly Democratic	92	8	100	(1,193)
Moderately Democratic	82	18	100	(1,024)
Slightly Democratic	78	22	100	(1,147)
Neutral	76	24	100	(747)
Slightly Republican	82	18	100	(1,041)
Moderately Republican	86	14	100	(1,097)
Strongly Republican	95	5	100	(975)
Electorate, by Scores on Summary Measure of Retrospective Evaluations of Incumbent Party				
Strongly opposed	90	10	100	(2,920)
Moderately opposed	68	32	100	(956)
Slightly opposed	73	27	100	(304)
Neutral	78	22	100	(462)
Slightly supportive	88	12	100	(876)
Moderately supportive	77	23	100	(396)
Strongly supportive	90	10	100	(1,252)

Source: Authors' analysis of the 2020 ANES survey.

Note: Sample includes both face-to-face and Internet respondents. Numbers are weighted. Chapter 7 describes how the balance-of-issues measure was constructed, and chapter 8 describes how the summary measure of retrospective evaluations was constructed. Both measures differ slightly from those presented in previous volumes of *Change and Continuity*, so care should be given when comparing to earlier election studies.

Republican Party and those who leaned toward the Democratic Party also turned out at somewhat similar rates. The only noticeable partisan difference is that weak Republican identifiers turned out at a slightly higher rate (3 percentage points) than weak Democrats, but did this result in an advantage? If we assume that each of the low-turnout groups had turnouts as high as each of the comparable high-turnout groups, and assume that the additional voters drawn to the polls voted the same way as actual voters, we estimate that Joe Biden would have gained an extra 0.79 percentage points to his popular-vote total—thus we find little evidence that higher turnout would have produced major gains for one of the parties.

In chapter 7, we examine the issue preferences of the electorate. For every presidential election between 1980 and 2008, we built a measure of overall issue preferences based on the seven-point scales used by the ANES surveys to measure the issue preferences of the electorate.[115] But we have found little or no evidence of issue differences between those who vote and those who do not.

In 2020, our overall measure of issues preferences is based on scales measuring the respondent's position on six issues: (1) reducing or increasing government services, (2) decreasing or increasing defense spending, (3) government health insurance, (4) government job guarantees, (5) government helping blacks, and (6) protecting the environment.[116] As table 4.5 shows that those who agreed with Republican issue position were more likely to vote than those who agreed with Democratic positions. Respondents who are strongly Republican on the issues were 3 percentage points more likely to report voting than those who are strongly Democratic. Respondents who were moderately Republican were 4 points more likely to vote than those who were moderately Democratic on the issues. Those who were slightly Republican on the issues were also about 4 points more likely to vote as those who lean toward the Democrats on the issues. Based on our simulation, we find that if voters had agreed with Democratic policies as much as they agreed with Republican policies, Biden's popular-vote share would have increased by 1.1 percentage points.

In chapter 8, we discuss the retrospective evaluations of the electorate. Voters, some analysts argue, make their decisions based not just on their evaluation of policy promises but also on their evaluation of how well the party in power is doing. In past studies we used a summary measure based on presidential approval, an evaluation of the job the government was doing dealing with the most important problem facing the country, and an assessment of which party would do a better job dealing with this problem. Across each of the elections that we have studied, the relationship between retrospective evaluations and turnout has been weak, at best, and often nonexistent.

In 2020, we employed a summary measure based on the respondent's approval of the president, the respondent's evaluation of how good a job the government had been doing over the last four years, and the respondent's belief about whether things in the country are going in the right direction or are on the wrong track. Only 42 percent of respondents in the ANES survey approved of President Trump, and 73 percent of respondents stated they believed that the nation was headed on the "wrong track." Clearly, evaluations of Trump's performance did not bode well for his case for reelection. On our summary scale a clear majority, 58.4 percent, had negative views of recent governmental performance; 35.2 percent had a positive view. Yet, interestingly, those who were supportive were more likely to vote on balance. Whereas those with the strongest views turned out in roughly equal proportions, those who were moderately supportive of the incumbent's performance were 9.4 percentage points more likely to vote than those who opposed the incumbent moderately. Among those who were slightly supportive of the president's past performance the turnout advantage was 14.7 percentage points. Thus, in our simulation, evening out turnout differences based on retrospective evaluations brings more voters with negative views of the recent past into the equation. Nevertheless, adding more voters to the tally, even those with a pessimistic view of things, would have aided Biden a scant 0.9 percentage points.

In most elections, higher turnout is unlikely to affect the outcome. But in close elections, variation in voter turnout is most likely to have an effect on who wins or loses. In previous studies, the largest and most consistent turnout effects that we observed were associated with differences in voter participation among party identifiers. Consistent with other scholarship we found that higher turnout benefits the Democrats, but in 2020 these effects were relatively small.[117] We also found limited evidence in our analyses to support the argument that low voter turnout biases election outcomes on the basis of issue preferences or retrospective evaluations. Because in most presidential contests increased turnout would not have affected the outcome, some analysts might argue that low turnout does not matter.[118]

Despite this evidence we do not accept the conclusion that low turnout is unimportant. We are especially concerned that turnout is low among the disadvantaged. Low turnout can scarcely be healthy for a democracy. As we have shown, much of the initial decline in US voter turnout following the 1960s could be attributed to decreases in partisan attachment and external political efficacy. Partisan identification has largely returned to 1960s levels, and turnout increased markedly in 2020. Yet it remains to be seen whether the nation will maintain this level of voter participation. Feelings of political efficacy have continued to decline and, as we reported, were at an all-time low in 2020. If turnout remains low because an ever-growing segment of the American public believes that "public officials don't care much what people like me think" and "people like me don't have any say about what the government does," then concern about turnout seems warranted.

Chapter 5

Social Forces and the Vote

Although voting is an individual act, group characteristics influence voting choices because individuals with similar social characteristics may share similar political interests. Group similarities in voting behavior may also reflect past political conditions. The partisan loyalties of African Americans, for example, were shaped by the Civil War. Black loyalties to the Republican Party, the party of Lincoln, lasted through the 1932 election, and the steady Democratic voting of southern whites, the product of those same historical conditions, lasted even longer, at least through 1960.

It is easy to see why group-based loyalties persist over time. Studies of pre-adult political learning suggest that partisan loyalties are often passed on from generation to generation.[1] And because religion, ethnicity, and to a lesser extent, social class are often transmitted across generations as well, social divisions have considerable staying power. The interactions of social-group members also reinforce similarities in political attitudes and behaviors.

Politicians often make group appeals. They recognize that to win an election, they need to mobilize the social groups that supported them in the past while attempting to cut into their opponents' bases of support. These group-based electoral coalitions often become identified at election time with the particular candidate being supported and the nature of the particular campaign, creating what we might think of as "Trump voters" or "Biden voters," for example. Yet group-based electoral coalitions tend to be relatively stable from one election to the next, so it is perhaps best to think of these social-group loyalties as the basis for partisan coalitions, for example, "Republican voters" or "Democratic voters." Indeed political scientists often identify periods of significant electoral change, "realignments," by virtue of observing dramatic and lasting shifts in group-based support from one party to another.

Thus examining the social forces that influence voting behavior is a crucial aspect for understanding change and continuity within an electoral system.

To place the 2020 presidential election within the context of recent electoral history, we examine the evolution of the Democratic Party's broad and diverse electoral coalition from its zenith in the years following the New Deal to its eventual unraveling and how the subsequent shifting of white political loyalties structures the major parties' bases and electoral competition today. It is sometimes said that Democrats tend to think in group terms more than Republicans, but it is most certainly the case that both of the major parties count on the support of core groups as part of their electoral bases. Yet the historical alteration of the Democratic Party's group-based coalition provides an important examination of how partisan allegiances change over time and how this has changed both parties' electoral fortunes. Beginning with the election of Franklin D. Roosevelt in 1932, the Democratic Party brought together sometimes disparate groups, a "coalition of minorities" that included both union and nonunion working-class households, both African Americans and native white southerners, and both Jews and Catholics. Yet by the late twentieth century, the coalition was in decline. African Americans maintained, even strengthened, their loyalty to the Democrats, but southern white conservatives have drifted to their more natural ideological home on the right and are now more likely to identify with the Republican Party. Working-class voters are a cross-pressured group who sometimes side with the Democrats on economic issues but sometimes agree with Republicans on social issues.[2] Union membership in the United States has declined greatly, making it difficult for the party to mobilize working-class voters. Jewish voters remain loyal to the Democrats, but non-white Catholic voters now support the two major parties at roughly the same rate, and churchgoing Catholics now lean toward the Republican Party. And growing Latino and Asian populations appear to be joining the Democratic coalition.

The 1992 and 1996 presidential elections provide an example of the fragile nature of the Democratic coalition. Bill Clinton earned high levels of support from only two of the groups that made up the New Deal coalition formed by Roosevelt—African Americans and Jews. Most of the other New Deal coalition groups gave fewer than half of their votes to Clinton, though Clinton managed to win a plurality of the vote. In 1996, he gained ground among the vast majority of groups analyzed in this chapter, making especially large gains among union members (a traditional component of the New Deal coalition) and Latinos. In many respects, the Democratic losses after 1964 can be attributed to the party's failure to hold the loyalties of the New Deal coalition groups.

In 2008, Barack Obama's victory returned a Democrat to the White House. His victory marked the first time since 1976 that a Democrat won the presidency with a majority of the popular vote. But Obama did not restore the New Deal coalition. Obama gained nearly a fourth of his total vote from black voters. This was possible because black turnout equaled white turnout and because blacks voted overwhelmingly Democratic. Yet, among the groups that we examined, only blacks and Jews gave a clear majority of their vote to Obama. Obama had only a slight edge among white union members, and he split the white Catholic vote with the Republican nominee, John McCain. Among white southerners, a mainstay of the New Deal coalition, Obama won only a third of the vote.[3]

In 2012, the coalitional divisions of 2008 were accentuated slightly. As noted in chapter 4, 2012 marked the first time in the nation's history that turnout among African Americans exceeded that of whites, and they over-whelmingly supported Obama. No other Democratic presidential winner has received as large a share of his vote (between 23.7 to 24.4 percent by our estimates) from the black electorate than Obama. Conversely, Obama lost support from southern whites and non-Latino Catholics, core groups that were once part of his party's electoral coalition. In 2016, without Obama on the ballot, turnout among African Americans declined from the record levels of 2012, which helped Trump win over Clinton, especially in key midwestern states. In 2020, Biden enjoyed high levels of support from African Americans and Jews, two New Deal coalition groups, and also enjoyed high levels of support from groups newer to the Democratic fold, including Asians, Latinos, and those who do not identify with a religion.

HOW SOCIAL GROUPS VOTED IN 2020

Table 5.1 presents the results of our analysis of how social groups voted in the 2020 presidential election.[4] Among the 5,250 respondents who said they voted for president, 53.7 percent said they voted for Joe Biden, 43.8 percent for Donald Trump, and 2.5 percent for other candidates—results that are within roughly 2–3 percentage points of the actual results (see table 3.1). The ANES are the best source of data for analyzing change over time, but the total number of self-reported voters is sometimes small. This can make group-based analysis tenuous if the number of sample respondents within a group is exceedingly small. Therefore, we will often supplement (some-times by necessity) our analysis with the exit polls (pool polls) conducted by Edison Research for a consortium of news organizations.[5] For the 2020 exit polls, 37,000 voters were interviewed. Most were randomly chosen as they left polling places from across the United States on election day. Respondents who voted absentee/by mail or voted early were contacted via telephone. More interviews were conducted via phone in 2020 given the

Table 5.1 How Social Groups Voted for President, 2020 (Percent)

Social Group	Biden	Trump	Other	Total	(N)
Total Electorate	54	44	2	100	(5,251)
Electorate, by Race					
African American	90	7	3	100	(532)
Asian	67	32	1	100	(219)
White	44	54	2	100	(3,693)
Other	70	27	3	100	(995)
Latino (of Any Race)	75	22	4	101	(536)
Whites, by Gender					
Female	46	52	2	100	(1,922)
Male	42	55	2	99	(1,761)
Whites, by Region					
New England and Mid-Atlantic	51	47	2	100	(724)
North Central	43	54	3	100	(859)
South	31	67	1	99	(964)
Border	44	54	2	100	(354)
Mountain and Pacific	56	42	2	100	(792)
Whites, by Birth Cohort					
Before 1950	43	56	1	100	(581)
1951–1960	44	55	1	100	(687)
1961–1970	36	63	1	100	(721)
1971–1980	45	53	3	101	(548)
1981–1990	48	48	4	100	(539)
1991–1998	54	41	5	100	(344)
1999–2002	62	38	0	100	(173)
Whites, by Level of Education					
Not High-School Graduate	25	72	4	101	(132)
High-School Graduate	32	67	1	100	(855)
Some College	37	61	2	100	(1,098)
College Graduate	54	43	3	100	(986)
Advanced Degree	65	33	3	101	(573)
Whites, by Annual Family Income					
Less than $15,000	41	57	3	101	(118)
$15,000–34,999	40	56	4	100	(280)
$35,000–49,999	41	57	2	100	(253)
$50,000–74,999	43	55	2	100	(566)
$75,000–89,999	44	55	1	100	(269)
$90,000–124,999	42	56	2	100	(847)
$125,000–174,999	46	52	3	101	(526)
$175,000 and over	54	44	2	100	(616)
Whites, by Union Membership[a]					
Member	50	47	3	100	(587)
Nonmember	43	55	2	100	(3,104)
Whites, by Religion					
Jewish	74	24	3	101	(102)
Catholic	42	57	2	101	(769)
Protestant	32	67	2	101	(1,108)
None	66	32	2	100	(11,002)

(Continued)

Table 5.1   How Social Groups Voted for President, 2020 (Percent) (Continued)

Social Group	Biden	Trump	Other	Total	(N)
White Protestants, by Whether Born Again					
Not Born Again	49	49	2	100	(466)
Born Again	18	80	2	100	(628)
White Protestants, by Religious Commitment					
Medium or Low	50	49	1	100	(399)
High	26	72	2	100	(524)
Very High	8	90	1	99	(176)
White Protestants, by Religious Tradition					
Mainline	48	52	1	101	(422)
Evangelical	16	82	2	100	(377)

Source: Authors' analysis of the 2020 ANES survey.
[a]Respondent or family member in union.

higher percentage of people who voted by mail because of the pandemic.[6] For comparison we will sometimes reference the 2016 exit polls, for which 24,558 voters were interviewed.

Race, Gender, Region, and Age

Political differences between African Americans and whites are far sharper than any other social cleavage.[7] According to the 2020 ANES, 90 percent of black voters supported Biden (see table 5.1), similar to the pool poll, which indicates that 87 percent did, and similar to Clinton's support among black voters in 2016 (90 percent), though smaller than Obama's level of support (98 percent) as reported in the 2012 ANES. Based on the ANES survey, we estimate that 17 percent of Biden's vote came from blacks; our analysis of the pool poll suggests that 22.1 percent did. These estimates are slightly smaller than those associated with Hillary Clinton's 2016 electorate, 20 percent. Nevertheless, this is a sizable, and relatively high, contribution to the Democratic electorate and suggests that the party is heavily reliant on black voters for their electoral fortunes. Biden's electorate is estimated to have been between 53.6 (exit poll) and 58.2 (ANES) percent white.

In comparison, African Americans comprised a very small portion of the Trump coalition. Based on the ANES estimates only 7.4 percent of blacks voted for Trump, 12 percent according to exit polls. This was up slightly from four years earlier, when 6.4 percent of blacks voted for Trump (ANES), 8 percent according to the exit polls. These estimates suggest that in 2020 between 1.7 to 3.3 percent of all Trump voters were black. Based on the ANES we estimate that Trump's electoral coalition was 86.5 percent white; the exit poll estimate is 82.2 percent white. But this figure is not atypical for Republican presidential nominees. In 2012, for example, it is estimated that 90 to 93 percent of Romney voters were white, larger than the Trump electorate in 2020 and 2016 (84.5 percent). Clearly, while the Democratic Party is increasingly reliant on black voters as a part of their coalition, the Republican Party is almost wholly dependent upon white voters.

The Democrats continue to hold a decided edge among Latino voters, and Biden's level of support among Latinos was higher than Clinton's in 2016. As seen in table 5.1, the ANES reports that Biden received 75 percent of the Latino vote, a figure in line with the level of Latino support received by Obama in 2008 and 2012. The exit polls suggest that Biden won 65 percent of the Latino vote. Latinos, of course, are not a homogeneous group.[8] Cuban Americans in South Florida, for example, have traditionally voted Republican, although younger generations now lean Democrat. Unfortunately, we cannot examine differences among Latino groups using the ANES. The pool poll, however, shows that Cuban American voters in Florida split 56 percent to 42 percent in Trump's favor; four years ago, the poll reported that the group voted 54–41 percent in Trump's favor. The data do not allow us to examine the voting behavior of other Latino groups.

Based on data from the ANES and the exit polls, we estimate that Latinos (of all ethnicities) composed roughly 14.3 to 16.5 percent of Biden's 2020 electorate, depending on the data source, and between 5.1 to 8.8 percent of the Trump electorate. These estimates are similar to the support Trump received among Latinos in 2016. Trump's level of support among Latinos is likely surprising to many given that during the 2016 campaign, candidate Trump threatened to build a wall on the U.S.-Mexico border, deport undocumented immigrants, and described Mexican immigrants as "bringing drugs; they're bringing crime; they're rapists."[9] While in office, he made good on some of those promises and further received heat for his family separation polices at the US-Mexico border.[10] The battle over the Latino vote is a potentially important one. The US Census predicts that the size of the Latino electorate will continue to grow over the next twenty years. If Latinos' current rate of support for the Democrats were to continue, we estimate that nearly one in five Democratic votes will be cast by Latinos by 2028. This puts tremendous pressure on Republicans. The GOP already lags well behind Democrats in support among Latinos and African Americans; about 31 percent of Biden's voters came from these two groups according to the ANES data, whereas 6.8 percent of Trump's voters did. We observe similar patterns with Asian Americans, another group that is growing according to Census estimates, where 67 percent reported voting for Biden in the ANES, and only 33 percent for Trump. The pool poll shows that 61 percent of Asians reported voting for Biden, compared to 34 percent for Trump.[11] If Republicans cannot make inroads with these three minority groups, they will be forced to increase their support—through increased turnout and vote share—from white voters.

Gender differences in voting behavior have been pronounced in some European societies, but they have been relatively weak in the United States.[12] Gender differences, whereby men disproportionately support the Republican Party and women the Democratic Party, emerged in the 1980 election and have been found in every election since. According to the exit polls, the "gender gap" was 8 percentage points in 1980, and has hovered within about 2 percentage points of that gap in elections since, though it reached a high point of 13 points in 2016. According to the 2020 exit polls, 57 percent of women and 45 percent of men voted for Biden, a gap of 12 points. Among whites Trump received a majority of votes from both men and women, although men were significantly more likely to support him. Trump received 55 percent of the white female vote and 61 percent of the white male vote, a gap of 6 points.

As the gender gap began to emerge, some feminists hoped that women would play a major role in defeating the Republicans.[13] But as we pointed out more than three decades ago, a gender gap does not necessarily help the Democrats.[14] For example, in 1988, George H. W. Bush and Michael Dukakis each won half of the female vote, but Bush won a clear majority of the male vote. However, two decades later the role of gender was reversed. In 2008 Obama and McCain split the male vote, whereas Obama won a clear majority among women. By the same logic, then, Obama benefited from the gender gap in 2008. During the intervening elections, Clinton benefited from the gender gap in both 1992 and 1996, and George W. Bush benefited in 2000 and 2004.

Like the pool polls, the 2020 ANES (see table 5.1) finds evidence of a small gender gap in voting among whites, only a 3 percentage-point difference. In 2016, Hillary Clinton, despite being the first female major-party nominee for president, received only 41 percent of the vote from white females, who gave Trump 53 percent of their vote. Biden actually did better among white women in 2020, receiving 46 percent of the vote from white women, though a majority, 52 percent supported Trump. As Jane Junn notes, this higher level of support for Republican candidates among white women has been "hiding in plain sight" since 1952, and the greater support for Democratic candidates among women is driven by women of color.[15]

As for marital status, in all of our analyses of ANES surveys between 1984 and 2012, we found clear differences between married women and single women.[16] Among all women voters who were married, 49 percent voted for Biden; among those who were never married, 69 percent did—a 20 point difference. This difference remains large, 11 points, if we limit our analysis to white women. Interestingly, as in the 2016 election, we see a large marriage gap among men. Among all men, married voters were 19 points less likely to vote for Biden than men who had never been married. Indeed the majority of married men (51.8 percent) voted for Trump, whereas the majority of single men (65.4 percent) supported Biden. This overall difference cannot be attributed wholly to racial differences. Among white men, married voters were 19.6 percentage points less likely to vote for Biden than those who have never married.

Since the 2000 election, exit polls have shown that sexual orientation is related to the way people vote. In 2000, 70 percent of the respondents who said they were gay, lesbian, or bisexual voted for Gore; in 2004, 77 percent voted for Kerry; in 2008, 70 percent voted for Obama; and in 2012, 76 percent voted for Obama, and 77 percent said they voted for Clinton. In the 2020 exit polls, 64 percent said they voted for Biden, a percentage lower than the support received among other recent Democratic candidates. However, support looks higher in the ANES study. In 2020, 5.6 percent of the ANES respondents said they were gay, lesbian, or bisexual.[17] Among homosexual or bisexual voters ($N = 264$), 86.3 percent voted for Biden.

As described in chapter 3, in the 2020 election the political variation among states was slightly higher than in 2016 (which had been greater than in any election since 1964), suggesting that states were slightly more divided in their support for Trump in 2016 than in recent elections. And there were clear regional differences among white voters. As table 5.1 shows, Trump garnered electoral majorities from white voters in three of the five regions. Trump, like all recent Republican nominees, fared best in the South, where he won 67 percent of the white vote (a few points lower than his share in the region four years earlier). Biden won 31 percent of the vote among white southerners, higher than the 24 percent won by Clinton four years earlier. The exit polls show that he fared similarly among whites in one of the southern states he carried, Georgia, where he captured 30 percent of the white vote. However, the key to Biden's success in Georgia was his high levels of support from black voters, with 88 percent supporting him. He fared better among whites in Virginia, the other southern state he carried, with 45 percent supporting him, and 89 percent of black voters. Trump also won majorities in the border region in the South and in the north central states, but Biden won a majority in the Mountain and Pacific region and New England and the Mid-Atlantic region. Exit polls were taken in nine of the twenty-two states that define these two regions, and our analysis of these state-level results shows that Biden outpolled Trump among whites in six of these states—California, Colorado, Maine, New Hampshire, Oregon, and Washington.

Between Ronald Reagan's election in 1980 and Bill Clinton's reelection in 1996, young voters were more likely to vote Republican than their elders, and the Democrats did best among Americans who came of age before World War II (born before 1924). This was not the case in the 2000, 2004, 2008, and 2012 elections. In these elections, the ANES surveys show that Republicans did well among white voters who entered the electorate in the 1980s and who may have been influenced by the pro-Republican tide during the Reagan years. Yet among those who entered the electorate in the mid-1990s or later, Democrats outgained Republicans. If Democrats were optimistic about their future because of these trends among young voters, they were no doubt ecstatic about Obama's exceptional performance among young adults in 2008, in which he won 57 percent of the vote among whites born between 1979 and 2000 according to ANES data (those who were between the ages of eighteen and twenty-nine at the time of the election).

The ANES shows that Trump won majorities from whites in each of the four oldest cohorts (forty and over). Among white voters thirty-nine years old or younger, the candidates received an equal share of the vote, 48 percent. Biden won a clear majority in the two youngest cohorts. The pool poll also shows a relationship between age and voting behavior, but unlike the ANES, these polls suggest that whites of all ages supported Trump more than Biden (although it should be noted that the cohorts are defined differently by the survey organizations). The pool poll shows that black voters of all ages overwhelmingly supported Biden (between 78 and 92 percent), as did Latino voters (between 62 and 69 percent).

Social Class, Education, Income, and Union Membership

Traditionally, the Democratic Party has fared well among the relatively disadvantaged. It has done better among the working class, voters with lower levels of formal education, and the poor. Moreover, since the 1930s most union leaders have supported the Democratic Party, and union members have been a mainstay of the Democratic presidential coalition. We have been unable to measure social class differences using the 2012–2020 ANES surveys because the occupational codes we use to classify respondents as working class (manually employed) and middle class (non-manually employed) are restricted access for privacy concerns and unavailable at the time of this writing. But we do have substantial evidence that class differences as defined by occupation have been declining—a trend found in other advanced democracies.[18] Differences between the more educated and the less educated were relatively strong in 2020.

In 1992 and 1996 Bill Clinton fared best among whites who had not graduated from high school, whereas both George H. W. Bush and Bob Dole fared best among whites who were college graduates (but without advanced degrees). In 1992 Clinton won more than half of the major-party vote among whites with advanced degrees, and in 1996 he won almost half the major-party vote among this group. In 2000 there was a weaker relationship between education and voting preferences, and in 2004 Kerry did best among whites in the highest and lowest educational categories. The 2008

ANES survey found only a weak relationship between level of education and the vote among whites. Moreover, the only educational group among which Obama won a majority of the vote was the small number who had not graduated from high school. In 2012, the ANES showed no discernible relationship between educational attainment and vote choice among whites. There was a dramatic shift in the relationship between education and vote choice in the 2016 election, where Trump won clear majorities among whites who had not completed high school, high-school graduates, and those with some college, while Clinton carried whites with a college degree and postgraduate degree. In table 5.1, we see the relationship between education and vote choice in the 2020 ANES mirrored the patterns from 2016. The 2020 exit polls—which, again we remind readers, are not nationally representative—also show a strong relationship between education and vote choice among whites. Trump won 19 percentage points more support from those whites without college degrees than he did from those with college degrees.

Scholars such as Jeffrey M. Stonecash and Larry M. Bartels argue that voting differences according to income have been growing in the United States.[19] We find little evidence to support this claim, however. Instead, we find evidence that the relationship between income and voting has varied considerably in recent decades and in no discernible pattern. In his victories in 1992 and 1996, for example, Clinton clearly fared much better among the poor than among the affluent. The relationship between income and voting preferences was weaker in both 2000 and 2004, although whites with an annual family income of $50,000 and above were more likely to vote for Bush. In 2008, the ANES data revealed a strong relationship between the respondent's family income and voting choice. Like Clinton's victories, Obama did better among those with lower incomes than those who were wealthier. The 2012 ANES showed a weak negative relationship between annual family income and voting for Obama. In fact, across all income categories except for those making between $125,000 and $174,999, Romney won a majority of the white vote. In 2016, Trump did best among whites in the six lowest income categories, winning majorities from all income groups under $125,000, while Clinton won a majority among the top earners in our sample.

The 2020 ANES shows a relationship between income and vote choice similar to that in 2016, but Trump carried whites in all income groups except the highest income group. If we include voters of all races and ethnicities in the analysis, Biden carried those in all income groups. Low-income voters in particular were most likely to support Biden. The exit polls support this general finding, with the majority of whites making below or above $50,000 voting for Trump, while majorities of black and Latino voters in both categories being more likely to vote for Biden. Thus, as was the case in 2016, it appears that much of the relationship between social class—in this case, measured by income and education—and the vote is conditioned by race and ethnicity.

According to the ANES surveys, Bill Clinton made major gains among white union households between 1992 and 1996. But the 2000 ANES survey shows that Gore slipped 12 percentage points from Clinton's 1996 total, whereas George W. Bush gained 16 points over Dole's. The 2004 ANES survey shows that Bush made no gains among union households but gained 6 points among nonunion households. In 2008, the ANES survey shows a five-point loss for the Democrats among white union households but a 7 point gain among nonunion households. Four years later Obama's vote share among white voters in nonunion households declined markedly, a 5 percentage-point drop. This allowed Romney to dominate Obama among nonunion households: 61 to 38 percent. In 2016, Trump did no better among union members than Romney did four years earlier, capturing 47 percent of the vote, to Clinton's 49 percent plurality. In 2020, Biden did slightly better among union members, gaining 50 percent of the vote to Trump's 47 percent. The exit polls also suggest that Biden won union voters (50 percent), whereas Trump won nonmember households (58 percent).

Religion

Religious differences have long played a major role in American politics.[20] In the postwar period, Catholics tended to support the Democrats, whereas white Protestants, especially those outside the South, tended to favor the Republicans. Jews consistently voted more Democratic than any other major religious group. Yet the religious cleavages of old, partly reflecting ethnic differences between Protestants and Catholics, do not necessarily hold today. As noted by David E. Campbell, "the last thirty years have seen a re-sorting of the parties' electoral coalitions along religious lines."[21] As social and moral issues have become more politically salient, religious denomination plays a smaller role in defining partisan loyalties. Indeed, the role of religion in modern politics is not so much about denomination as it is about what Campbell calls "religious devotional style" or religiosity. Today, white Christian voters who classify themselves as devout in their beliefs and practices—regardless of denomination—tend to support the Republican Party. This has allowed the Republicans to benefit electorally from a "coalition of the religious," which brings together groups that are sometimes theologically and politically disparate (if not antagonistic), evangelical Christians, traditionalist Catholics, and Mormons, while Democrats enjoy strong support from religious "nones," those with no religious affiliation.[22]

In the 2020 election Joe Biden won a plurality of the Catholic vote compared to Trump (51.6 to 46.7 percent), somewhat larger than Hillary Clinton's support (47.6 to 45.3 percent) with the group four years earlier. But Biden's plurality support among *all* Catholics belies his relationship with *many* Catholic voters, as well as the church hierarchy, and says much about ethnic changes among American Catholics. Roughly two in ten voters in 2020 was a self-identified Catholic, but the "Catholic vote" is hardly a monolith. White Catholics voted in favor of Donald Trump, awarding him 57 percent of the vote to Biden's 42 percent. Biden did better among white Catholic voters than Clinton did four years earlier, when the 2016 ANES showed that she garnered 30.8 percent of the white Catholic vote to Trump's 55.9 percent. This is not entirely surprising given that Biden is known for being a devout Catholic. Biden's primary source of support among American Catholics was from Latinos, who represent about a third of all Catholics in the United States (and also 26 percent of Catholic voters in the 2020 ANES).[23] In the pool poll, 65 percent of Latino Catholics reported voting for Biden, and only 32 percent supported Trump.

Although the Republican Party has been successful among white Protestants, it has been more successful among some than others. The Republican emphasis on traditional values may have special appeal to Protestants who share them. George W. Bush's policies such as limiting funding for embryonic stem cell research, calling for an amendment to the US Constitution to ban same-sex marriage, and appointing conservatives to the federal courts may have appealed to Christian conservatives. But Romney's Mormon faith and previous support for abortion rights—although he consistently opposed same-sex nuptials and stem cell research—may have given some socially conservative evangelical Protestants cause for concern. In 2016 and 2020, the question was whether white Christian conservatives would lend their support to Donald Trump, a nominal mainline Protestant who has been married three times and was secretly recorded making lewd comments about his own treatment of women.

We focus here on differences among white Protestants. For the 1992, 1996, 2000, 2008, 2012, and 2016 ANES surveys, we examined differences between white Protestants who said they were "born again" and those who had not had this religious experience.[24] In all six surveys, white born-again Protestants were more likely to vote Republican than those who were not. In 2020, 49 percent of the white Protestants who said they had not had this religious experience voted for Trump; among those who said they were born again, 80 percent voted for Trump, up from the 75.3 percent four years earlier. Among born-again Protestants, Biden only received 18 percent of the vote. The 2020 pool poll also asked Protestants if they considered themselves born again or not. According to this survey, among born-again Christians, Trump outpolled Biden 76 percent to 24 percent. Finally white Protestants affiliated with evangelical denominations were 30 percentage points more likely to vote for Trump than those who were affiliated with mainline congregations. There are much smaller differences among black Protestants affiliated with evangelical denominations, and they overwhelmingly supported Biden. Among those who are born again, 86.4 percent reported voting for Biden, while the number is only slightly higher among those who are not born again, 94.8 percent.

As we noted earlier, Campbell argues that the role of religion in modern politics is not so much about denomination as it is about "religious devotional style" or religiosity. The point is similarly made by Lyman A. Kellstedt, who argues that religious commitment has an important effect on voting behavior.[25] According to the 2016 ANES, a clear majority of religious nones, who now makeup about 23 percent of the population,[26] reported voting for Biden, 66 percent compared to 32 percent supporting Trump. Table 5.1 presents the results from the ANES for all Protestants and Catholic voters, and the degree of religious commitment appears to have also mattered in 2020.[27] Trump won 90 percent of the vote from those voters who held a "very high" religious commitment; among whites who had low levels of religious commitment, Biden won 50 to 49 percent. This division is particularly pronounced among Protestants.

HOW SOCIAL GROUPS VOTED
DURING THE POSTWAR YEARS

Although we found sharp racial/ethnic and religious differences in voting, most other social differences in voting behavior were relatively modest in 2020. How does this election compare with other presidential elections? Do the relationships between social variables and the vote found in 2020 result from long-term trends that have changed the importance of social factors? To answer these questions, we will examine the voting behavior of social groups that were an important part of the Democrat's New Deal coalition during the postwar years. Understanding the nature of this broad coalition and its subsequent collapse helps place current American politics into a broader historical perspective—and, in our view, this helps us understand better that the politics that brought Joe Biden to office in 2020 are not very different from (indeed are a product of) the politics of the recent past. Our analysis, which will begin with the 1944 election between Roosevelt and Thomas Dewey, uses a simple measure to assess the effect of social forces over time.

In his lucid discussion of the logic of party coalitions, Robert Axelrod analyzed six basic groups that made up the Democrat's New Deal coalition: the poor, southerners, blacks (and other nonwhites), union members (and members of their families), Catholics and other non-Protestants such as Jews, and residents of the twelve largest metropolitan areas.[28] John R. Petrocik's more comprehensive study of the Democratic coalition identified fifteen groups and classified seven of them as predominantly Democratic: blacks, lower-status native southerners, middle- and upper-status southerners, Jews, Polish and Irish Catholics, union members, and lower-status, border-state whites.[29] A more recent analysis by Harold W. Stanley, William T. Bianco, and Richard G. Niemi analyzes seven pro-Democratic groups: blacks, Catholics, Jews, women, native white southerners, members of union households, and the working class.[30] Our own analysis focuses on race, region, union membership, social class, and religion.

The contribution that a social group can make to a party's coalition depends on three factors: the relative size of the group in the total electorate, its level of turnout compared with that of the total electorate, and its relative loyalty to the political party.[31] The larger a social group, the greater its contribution can be. For example, African Americans make up 11.3 percent of the electorate; the white working class makes up about 30 percent. Thus the potential contribution of blacks is smaller than that of the white working class. Historically, the electoral power of blacks was limited by their relatively low turnout. But black turnout has increased substantially in recent elections and has been comparable to white turnout. Moreover, because blacks vote overwhelmingly Democratic, their contribution to the Democratic Party can be greater than their group size would indicate. And the relative size of their contribution grows as whites desert the Democratic Party.

Race

We begin by examining racial differences, which we can trace back to 1944 by using the NORC study for that year.[32] Figure 5.1 shows the percentages of white and black major-party voters who voted Democratic for president from 1944 to 2020. (All figures in this chapter are based on major-party voters only.) After emancipation and the passage of the Fifteenth Amendment, most blacks voters—when not deprived of their voting right under Jim Crow—tended to vote for the Republican Party, the "Party of Lincoln." By 1932, however, those old allegiances had begun to change, and the GOP could no longer count on the solid support of black voters. Although most African Americans voted Democratic from 1944 to 1960, a substantial minority voted Republican. Yet the political mobilization of blacks, spurred by the civil rights movement and by the Republican candidacy of Barry Goldwater in 1964, evaporated black support for the Republican Party, and the residual Republican loyalties of older blacks were discarded between 1962 and 1964.[33]

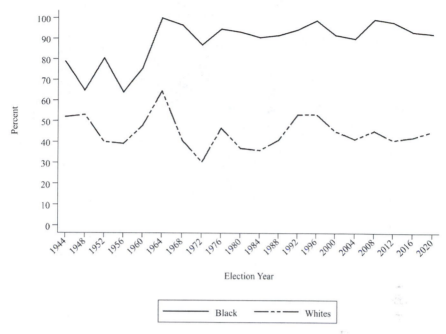

Figure 5.1 Major-Party Voters Who Voted Democratic for President, by Race, 1944–2020 (Percent).*Source*: Authors' analysis of the ANES surveys. Note: Numbers are weighted.

Although the Democrats made substantial gains among blacks, they lost ground among whites. From 1944 to 1964 the Democrats gained a majority of the white vote in three of six elections. Since 1964 the Democrats have never again won a majority of the white vote. However, in a two-candidate contest, a Democrat can win with just under half the white vote, as the 1960, 1976, 2008, 2012, and 2020 elections demonstrate. (Of course, in 2016, Hillary Clinton won the popular vote while only capturing 39.2 percent of the white vote.) In the three-candidate contests of 1992 and 1996, Bill Clinton was able to win with only about two-fifths of the white vote.[34]

The gap between the two trend lines in figure 5.1 illustrates the overall difference in the Democratic vote between whites and blacks. Table 5.2 shows the overall level of "racial voting" from 1944 to 2020 as well as four other measures of social cleavage.

From 1944 to 1964 racial differences in voting ranged from a low of 12 percentage points to a high of 40 points. These differences then rose to 56 percentage points in 1968 (61 points if Wallace voters are included with Nixon voters) and did not fall to the 40 percentage-point level until 1992.[35] Racial voting was higher in the 1996, 2000, and 2004 contests but increased markedly in the elections of Barack Obama. In 2008 there was a

Table 5.2 Relationship of Social Characteristics to Presidential Voting, 1944–2020

	Election Year (Percentage-Point Difference)																			
	1944	1948	1952	1956	1960	1964	1968	1972	1976	1980	1984	1988	1992	1996	2000	2004	2008	2012	2016	2020
Racial Voting[a]	27	12	40	25	23	36	56	57	48	56	54	51	41	47	47	49	54	57	51	47
Regional Voting[b]																				
Among Whites	—	—	12	17	6	-11	-4	-13	1	1	-9	-5	-10	-8	-20	-10	-14	-16	-22	-18
Among Entire Electorate (ANES Surveys)	—	—	9	15	4	-5	6	-3	7	3	3	2	0	0	-10	1	-11	-2	-11	-9
Among Entire Electorate (Official Election Results)	23	14	8	8	3	-13	-3	-11	5	2	-5	-7	-6	-7	-8	-8	-10	-9	-6	-8
Union Voting[c]																				
Among Whites	20	37	18	15	21	23	13	11	18	15	20	16	12	23	12	21	8	15	11	7
Among Entire Electorate	20	37	20	17	19	22	13	10	17	16	19	15	11	23	11	18	6	10	9	9
	Election Year (Percentage-Point Difference)																			
	1944	1948	1952	1956	1960	1964	1968	1972	1976	1980	1984	1988	1992	1996	2000	2004	2008	2012	2016	2020
Class Voting[d]																				
Among Whites	19	44	20	8	12	19	10	2	17	9	8	5	4	6	-6	3	3	—	—	—
Among Entire Electorate	20	44	22	11	13	20	15	4	21	15	12	8	8	9	2	4	4	—	—	—
Religious Voting[e]																				
Among Whites	25	21	18	10	48	21	30	13	15	10	16	18	20	14	8	19	15	16	7	10
Among Entire Electorate	24	19	15	10	46	16	21	8	11	3	9	11	10	7	2	5	9	7	13	13

Sources: Authors' analysis of a 1944 NORC survey, official election results, and ANES surveys.

Notes: All calculations are based upon major-party voters. "—" indicates not available.

[a]Percentage of blacks who voted Democratic minus percentage of whites who voted Democratic.

[b]Percentage of southerners who voted Democratic minus percentage of voters outside the South who voted Democratic. Comparable data for region were not available for the surveys conducted in 1944 and 1948.

[c]Percentage of members of union households who voted Democratic minus percentage of members of households with no union members who voted Democratic.

[d]Percentage of working class that voted Democratic minus percentage of middle class that voted Democratic. The data for occupation needed to classify respondents according to their social class for 2012, 2016, and 2020 are restricted for privacy concerns.

[e]Percentage of Catholics who voted Democratic minus the percentage of Protestants who voted Democratic.

54 percentage-point gap between blacks and whites, and in 2012 that gap increased to 57 points, matching the record high level of racial voting found in 1972. Obama's elections exhibit the highest levels of racial voting in any elections in which the Democratic candidate has won. In 2016 and 2020 racial differences in voting contracted only slightly, to a 51 and 47 percentage-point gap, respectively. Thus America has not experienced a racial gap in voting of less than 40 percentage points since 1964, more than a half century ago.

Not only did African American loyalty to the Democratic Party increase sharply after 1960, but black turnout rose considerably from 1960 to 1968 because southern blacks were enfranchised. And while black turnout rose, white turnout outside the South declined. Between 1960, when overall turnout was highest, and 1996, when postwar turnout was lowest, turnout fell by about 15 percentage points among the voting-age population.[36] Between 1996 and 2008, turnout in the United States rose by roughly 8 percentage points. In the 2000 and 2004 election, turnout among whites and blacks increased at approximately the same rate. Yet in the 2008 and 2012 election, the groups moved in opposite directions, with black turnout continuing to rise and white turnout declining to the point where black turnout exceeded white turnout in 2012. The trend lines reversed course between 2012 and 2016, with black voter turnout declining by 7 percentage points and white turnout increasing by 1.2 percentage points. As noted in chapter 4, in 2020, black voter turnout increased again by about 3 percentage points (according to the Census), whereas white turnout increased by 6 percentage points.

From 1948 to 1960 African Americans never accounted for more than one Democratic vote in twelve. In 1964, however, Johnson received about one in seven of his votes from blacks, and blacks contributed a fifth of the Democratic totals in both 1968 and 1972. In the 1976 election, which saw Democratic gains among whites, Jimmy Carter won only about one in seven of his votes from blacks, and in 1980, one in four. In the next three elections, about one in five Democratic votes were from blacks. In 1996 about one in six of Clinton's votes came from black voters, and in 2000 about one in five of Gore's votes did. In 2004, between a fifth and a fourth of Kerry's total vote was provided by black voters. Both Gore and Kerry came very close to winning, even with this heavy reliance on African American voters. In both 2008 and 2012, black voters accounted for about one-fourth of Obama's total vote. No Democratic presidential winner had ever drawn this large a share of his total vote from these voters. Hillary Clinton and Joe Biden received about one in five of all of their votes from blacks in 2016 and 2020, lower than the share received by Obama but comparable to that received by the Democratic nominees in 1984, 1988, 1992, 2000, and 2004. Thus it is fair to say that Obama's elections aside, the size of the Democratic Party black electoral base has been relatively consistent over the past three decades.

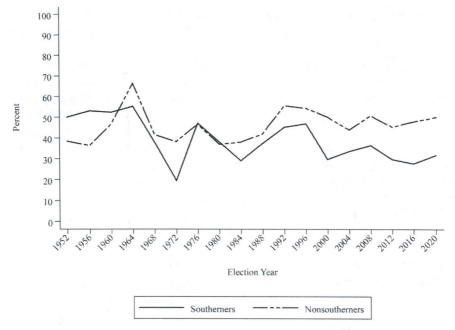

Figure 5.2   White Major-Party Voters Who Voted Democratic for President, by Region, 1952–2020 (Percent)._Source_: Authors' analysis of ANES surveys. Note: Numbers are weighted.

Region

White southerners' desertion of the Democratic Party is arguably the most dramatic change in postwar American politics and the most consequential for the electoral fortunes of the Republican Party. As we saw in chapter 3, regional differences can be analyzed using official election statistics, but these statistics are of limited use in examining race-related differences in regional voting because election results are not tabulated by race. Consequently, we rely on survey data to document the dramatic shift in voting behavior among white southerners.

As figure 5.2 reveals, white southerners were somewhat more Democratic than whites outside the South in the 1952 and 1956 contests between Dwight Eisenhower and Adlai Stevenson and in the 1960 contest between John Kennedy and Richard Nixon.[37] But in the next three elections, regional differences were reversed, with white southerners voting more Republican than whites outside the South. In 1976 and 1980, when the Democrats fielded Jimmy Carter of Georgia as their standard-bearer, white southerners and whites outside the South voted very much alike. But since 1980 southern whites have been less likely than nonsouthern whites to vote Democratic, by an average difference of 12.6 percentage points. In 1984 and 1988, white southerners were less likely to vote Democratic than whites from any other region. In 1992 and 1996 Bill Clinton and his running mate, Al Gore, were both from the South. Even so, George H. W. Bush in 1992 and Bob Dole in 1996 did better among white southerners than among whites from any other region. In 2000, Gore did even worse among white southerners, as he was competing against George W. Bush, the governor of Texas. In 2004 the Democrats ran John Kerry, the junior senator from Massachusetts, although John Edwards, his running mate, was from North Carolina. But in both these contests, the Democratic vote in the South was low, and the Democrats did substantially better outside the South. In both 2008 and 2012, neither party ran a southerner on its ticket. In Obama's 2008 election, the Democrats made gains among both white southerners and among whites outside the South; however, regional differences among whites set a record high for the modern period in 2016 when Hillary Clinton and Donald Trump competed for the presidency, with white southerners being 22 percentage points less likely to vote Democratic than white nonsoutherners. But, as figure 5.2 shows, the Democrats' support among whites in both regions improved in 2020.

Regional differences among whites from 1952 to 2020 are summarized in table 5.2. The negative signs for 1964, 1968, 1972, and 1984–2020 reveal that the Democratic candidate fared better outside the South than in the South. Table 5.2 also presents regional differences for the entire elector-ate. Here, however, we present two sets of estimates: (1) the ANES results from 1952 to 2020 and (2) the results we computed using official election statistics. Both sets of statistics indicate that regional differences have been reversed, but these results are often different and in many cases would lead to substantially different conclusions. The 2004 election provides a clear example. According to the 2004 ANES survey, voters in the South were as likely to vote Democratic as voters outside the South. But we know that this result is wrong. After all Bush won all the southern states, whereas Kerry won nineteen states outside the South as well as the District of Columbia. In fact, the official statistics show that southerners were 8 points more likely to vote Republican than voters outside the South. In this case, the ANES results, which are based on a sample of eight hundred voters, overestimated the number of Democratic voters in the South. This should remind us of a basic caution in studying elections: always turn to the actual election results before turning to the survey data.

Surveys are useful in demonstrating the way in which the mobilization of southern blacks and the defection of southern whites from the Democratic Party dramatically transformed the Democratic coalition in the South.[38] According to our analysis of ANES surveys, between 1952 and 1960, Democratic presidential candidates never received more than one in fifteen of their votes in the South from blacks. In 1964 three in ten of Johnson's southern votes came from black voters, and in 1968 Hubert Humphrey received as many votes from southern blacks as from southern whites. In 1972, according to these data, George McGovern received more votes from southern blacks than from southern whites.

Black voters were crucial to Carter's success in the South in 1976; he received about a third of his support from African Americans. Even though he won ten of the eleven southern states, he won a majority of the white vote only in his home state of Georgia and possibly in Arkansas. In 1980, Carter again received about a third of his southern support from blacks. In 1984, Walter Mondale received about four in ten of his southern votes from blacks, and in 1988, one in three of the votes Michael Dukakis received came from black voters. In 1992 and 1996, Clinton won about a third of his southern support from African Americans. In 2000, four in ten of the southern votes Gore received came from blacks, while about half of Kerry's votes in the South came from blacks in 2004.

Our analysis of the 2008 ANES survey indicates that about a third of Obama's votes in the South came from black voters. And blacks were crucial to the three southern states he carried, because he won a minority of the white vote in those states. In 2012 Obama's electorate in the South was roughly 38 percent black, an increase of 5 percentage points from his first election. This reflects a combination of factors, including increased turnout among blacks, lower turnout among whites, and a decrease in Obama's vote share among whites. Obama won two southern states in 2012. Hillary Clinton won only one southern state, Virginia, in 2016. We estimate that Clinton's electorate in the South was 41 percent black, larger than the share of blacks in Obama's electorate but primarily a product of lower levels of support among southern whites. By comparison we estimate that blacks represented only 1.3 percent of Trump's electorate in the South. In 2020, 30 percent of Biden's electorate in the South was black, 29 percent was other people of color, and 42 percent was white. In comparison, 3 percent of Trump's electorate in the South was black, 12 percent was other people of color, and the vast majority, 85 percent was white.

Union Membership

Figure 5.3 shows the percentage of white union members and nonmembers who voted Democratic for president from 1944 to 2020. Over the course of the postwar period, from 1944 through 2020, the majority of white union members (and members of their households) voted Democratic, with the exception of a few elections, 1972 and 1980. In 1968 Humphrey won a slight majority of the union vote, although his total would be cut to 43 percent

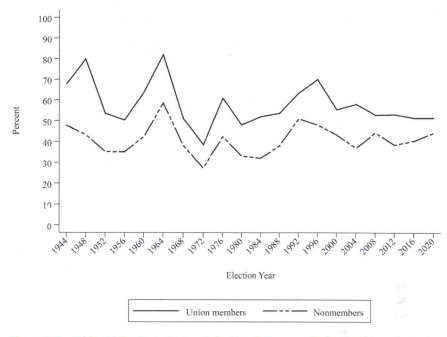

Figure 5.3 White Major-Party Voters Who Voted Democratic for President, by Union Membership, 1944–2020 (Percent).*Source*: Authors' analysis of ANES surveys. Note: "Union members" indicates that the respondent is a union member or lives in a union household. "Nonmembers" indicates that the respondent is not a union member nor lives in a union household. Data are weighted.

if Wallace voters were included. The Democrats won about three-fifths of the union vote in 1976, when Jimmy Carter defeated Gerald Ford. In 1988 Dukakis appears to have won a slight majority of the white union vote, although he fell well short of Carter's 1976 tally. In 1992 Bill Clinton won three-fifths of the major-party union vote and improved on that further in 1996, winning 70 percent. In 2000 Gore won a majority of the union vote, but he was well below Clinton's 1996 tally. In 2004 Kerry did slightly better than Gore among white union voters, but Bush did somewhat better among nonmembers. In 2008 the Democrats' support among white union members declined from 2004 levels, but Obama nonetheless won a small majority of white union voters, and made significant gains among nonmembers in 2008, obviously a net benefit for the Democrats. Obama maintained his majority support among white union members in 2012, but support from whites in nonmember households dropped precipitously, by roughly 6 points. Hillary Clinton's support among union members in 2016 was slightly less than that received by Obama in his two elections, 51.4 percent, and the same as that received by Joe Biden in 2020. Biden did slightly better among whites from nonunion households than Clinton, 44 to 40.4 percent. Clearly unions continue to be an important vehicle for mobilizing white voters' support for the Democratic Party, but the gap in support from union versus nonunion voters has contracted some since the heyday of the New Deal coalition.

Differences in presidential voting between union members and nonmembers are presented in table 5.2. Union voting was highest in 1948, a year when Truman's opposition to the Taft-Hartley Act gained him strong union support.[39] Union voting was low in 1992 and 2000, when white union members were only slightly more likely to vote Democratic than nonmembers. Because Bush did better among nonmembers in 2004, the differences between members and nonmembers rose to 21 points. Differences between members and nonmembers were sharply reduced in 2008, reaching the lowest level in any of the preceding seventeen elections, although the differences were expanded—due to a loss in vote share among white nonunion households—during his reelection bid in 2012. In 2016, the gap in member/nonmember voting differential decreased by 4 percentage points with symmetrical forces seemingly at play; union members lowered their support for the Democratic nominee by 2 points, whereas nonmembers increased their support by 2 points. In 2020, differences between members and nonmembers reached the lowest point in the time series, in part because of increased support among white nonunion households for Biden. Table 5.2 also shows the results for the entire electorate, but because blacks are about as likely to live in union households as whites, including blacks has little effect in most years.

The percentage of the total electorate composed of white union members and their families has declined during the postwar years. White union members and their families made up 25 percent of the electorate in 1952; in 2020, according to the ANES survey, they made up only 11 percent.[40] Turnout among white union members has declined at about the same rate as turnout among nonunion whites. In addition, in many elections since 1964, the Democratic share of the union vote has been relatively low. All of these factors, as well as increased turnout by blacks, have reduced the contribution of white union members to the Democratic presidential coalition. Remarkably, through 1960, a third of the total Democratic vote came from white union members and their families; between 1964 and 1984 only about one Democratic vote in four; in 1988, 1992, and 1996 only about one Democratic vote in five; and in 2000 only about one Gore vote in six. In 2004, with a drop in Democratic support among whites who did not live in union households, the share of Kerry's vote from union households rose back to one vote in five. Although Obama recorded a small majority among union voters in 2008, only 10 percent of his votes in that year came from members of a white union household.[41] Union voters were a larger portion of Obama's electorate in 2012; by our estimation 16.1 percent of Obama's votes nationally came from white union members, though they were a lower portion of Clinton's electorate in 2016, 12.3 percent. By our estimates with 2020 ANES data, 10 percent of Biden's votes nationally came from white union members, a record low. By comparison white union members composed 5.4 percent of Trump's electorate.

Of course, as with all groups, the union vote is not monolithic. Voters from union households were an important part of the electorate in the battleground states of Michigan, Ohio, and Wisconsin. Based on exit polls in those states and regardless of race, it appears that Biden won a majority of the union vote in Michigan and Wisconsin, whereas Trump won a majority of union voters in Ohio. In Wisconsin it is estimated that 14 percent of all voters were union members; of these Biden won 59 to 40 percent. Biden also did well garnering union support in Michigan, where roughly 21 percent of the electorate belong to unions. Of these voters Biden won 62 to 37 percent, doing better than Clinton did four years earlier, and he carried the state. Biden lost in Ohio, and in the Buckeye State, union voters were decidedly pro-Trump. The billionaire Republican won 55 percent of union voters to Biden's 43 percent.

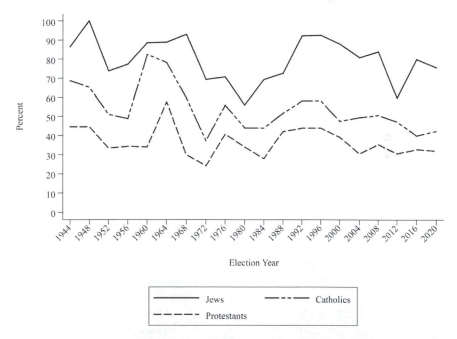

Figure 5.4 White Major-Party Voters Who Voted Democratic for President, by Religion, 1944–2020 (Percent).*Source*: Authors' analysis of a 1944 NORC survey and ANES surveys. Note: Numbers are weighted.

Religion

Voting differences among major religious groups have also declined during the postwar years. Even so, as figure 5.4 reveals, in every election since 1944, Jews have been more likely to vote Democratic than Catholics, and Catholics have been more likely to vote Democratic than Protestants.[42]

As figure 5.4 shows a large majority of Jews voted Democratic in every election from 1944 to 1968, and although the percentage declined in Nixon's landslide over McGovern in 1972, even McGovern won a majority of the Jewish vote. In 1980 many Jews were dissatisfied with Carter's performance as president, and some resented the pressure he had exerted on Israel to accept the Camp David Accords, which returned the Sinai Peninsula—captured by Israel in 1967 during the Six Day War—to Egypt, and he garnered a much lower percentage of the Jewish vote than other Democratic candidates. The Jewish Democratic vote surged in 1992, with Clinton winning nine in ten major-party voters. With Lieberman, an observant Jew, as his running mate, Gore, too, won overwhelming Jewish support in 2000. Support stayed high for the Democratic candidate among Jewish voters through 2008, but dipped to 59.8 percent in 2012. Obama had a rocky relationship with the Israeli prime minister, Benjamin Netanyahu, during his first term, and the decline in his support among Jewish voters may reflect these tensions. Hillary Clinton and Joe Biden were able to regain high levels of Jewish support in 2016 and 2020, 80.1 percent and 75.8 percent, respectively. Obviously, on the whole, Jewish voters' loyalty to the Democratic Party remains very strong.

A majority of white Catholics voted Democratic in six of the seven elections from 1944 to 1968. The percentage of Catholics voting Democratic surged in 1960, when the Democrats fielded a Catholic candidate, John Kennedy, but Catholic support was still very high in Johnson's landslide four years later.[43] In 1976 Carter won a majority among white Catholics, but the Democrats did not win a majority of the major-party vote among white Catholics again until 1992. In his 1996 reelection, Clinton again won over half of the major-party vote among white Catholics. Four years later, George W. Bush outpolled Al Gore among white Catholics. Even in 2004, when the Democrats ran a Catholic presidential candidate, Bush outscored Kerry among white Catholic voters. Based on 2008 ANES data, Obama won half the vote among white Catholics. He won slightly less than half in the 2008 pool poll. Obama's two-party vote share among white Catholics declined, however, in 2012, falling to 47.2 percentage points. Hillary Clinton's white Catholic support in 2016 declined even further to 40 percent of the two-party vote share. Joe Biden's two-party vote share among white Catholics increased slightly in 2020 to 42.4 percent, but this was much lower than prior Democratic candidates who were Catholic, like Kennedy (88.7 percent) and Kerry (49.4 percent).

Catholics had once been firmly footed in the Democrats' New Deal coalition, but the party's support for abortion rights—first formally espoused in the 1976 party platform—places it at odds with the Catholic Church and many of the faithful.[44] As we noted earlier, much of the Democrats' support from Catholics comes from those who are less devout in their religious practices as well as the Latino Catholic population. Nevertheless, on average, Democrats continue to do better among white Catholics than among white Protestants.

Our measure of religious voting shows considerable change from election to election, although there was a downward trend from 1968 to 2000, when religious differences reached their lowest level. Religious differences were somewhat higher in both 2004 and 2008 (see table 5.2), but dropped back down to low levels in 2016 and 2020. Because the Latino Catholic electorate is projected to grow, religious voting may rise in future elections.

Including African Americans in our calculations reduces religious voting. Blacks are much more likely to be Protestant than Catholic, and including blacks in our calculations adds a substantial number of Protestant Democrats. In 2020, for example, religious voting is reduced from 10 points to 7 points when blacks are included. However, when we look at the electorate as a whole, we see that religious voting increases significantly to 13 points; this is driven primarily by the inclusion of Latinos.[45]

The Jewish contribution to the Democratic Party has declined in part because Jews did not vote overwhelmingly Democratic in 1972, 1980, 1984, 1988, 2004, and 2012 and in part because Jews make up a small and declining share of the electorate. During the 1950s, Jews were about a twentieth of the electorate. But the most recent estimates suggest that only about one American in forty is Jewish.[46] Although Jews make up only about 2.4 percent of the population, three-fourths of the nation's Jews live in seven large states—New York, California, Florida, New Jersey, Pennsylvania, Massachusetts, and Illinois—which together had 178 electoral votes in 2020.[47] More important, two of these states are battleground states: Florida, where Jews make up 3.3 percent of the population, and Pennsylvania, where they make up 2.3 percent. In these close elections, even a relatively small group, like Jewish voters, can be influential in presidential politics. Overall, however, the electoral significance of Jews is lessened because five of these large states are not battleground states.

According to our estimates based on ANES surveys, in 1948 Truman received about a third of his total vote from white Catholics. In 1960, Kennedy, the first Catholic president, received 37 percent of his vote from Catholics. White Catholics provided just over a fourth of Carter's vote in his 1976 victory, but in his 1980 loss to Reagan, just over a fifth came from this source, similar to the share received by Dukakis (1988), Clinton (1992), and Kerry (2004). In 2008, less than a fifth of Obama's vote came from white Catholics, and in 2012, 17.4 percent of the votes cast for Obama were from white Catholics. White Catholics composed 16.6 percent of Hillary Clinton's electoral coalition and only 11.5 percent of Biden's electoral coalition, roughly a third of the size of the group's contribution to the New Deal coalition.

The contrast between the 1960 and 2020 elections is the most striking comparison across the eight decades in our investigation. In both elections the Democrats fielded a Catholic presidential candidate. But Kennedy received over three times as large a share of the Catholic vote as Biden. Well over a third of Kennedy's votes came from white Catholics, but only about one-ninth of Biden's did. Obviously the social characteristics of the Catholic community changed over the span of the sixty years between these elections. Of course, there were also social issues that may have led many Catholics to vote Republican in 2020 that were simply not on the political agenda six decades earlier.[48]

WHY THE NEW DEAL COALITION BROKE DOWN

The importance of race increased substantially after 1960, but all of the other factors we have examined have declined in importance. The effects of region on voting behavior have been reversed, with the Republicans now enjoying an advantage in the South, especially when we compare southern whites with whites outside the South. As the national Democratic Party strengthened its appeals to African Americans during the 1960s, party leaders endorsed policies that southern whites opposed, and many of them deserted the Democratic Party. The migration of northern whites to the South also may have reduced regional characteristics.

Although the Democratic Party's appeals to blacks may have weakened its hold on white groups that traditionally supported it, other factors were at work as well.[49] During the postwar years these groups have changed. Although union members do not hold high-paying professional and managerial jobs, they have gained substantial economic advantages. Differences in income between the working and the middle class have diminished. And Catholics, who often came from more recent European immigrant groups than Protestants, have become increasingly middle class and less identified with their ethnic roots with every passing generation. This trend is only partially offset by the growing number of Catholic Latinos.

Not only have these social groups changed, but the historical conditions that led union members, the working class, and Catholics to become Democrats have receded further into the past. Although the transmission of partisan loyalties from generation to generation gives historically based coalitions some staying power, the ability of the family to transmit partisan loyalties decreased as the strength of party identification within the electorate weakened during the 1960s and 1970s and were formed anew in a changed political environment.[50] Moreover, with the passage of time the proportion of the electorate that directly experienced the Roosevelt years and its wake has progressively declined. New policy issues, unrelated to the political conflicts of the New Deal era, have tended to erode party loyalties among traditionally Democratic groups. Edward G. Carmines and James A. Stimson provide strong evidence that race-related issues were crucial in weakening the New Deal coalition.[51] And more recently social issues such as abortion and same-sex marriage may have weakened Democratic Party loyalties among Catholic voters.

Despite the erosion of the New Deal coalition, the Democrats managed to win the presidency in 1992 and 1996, came very close to holding it in 2000, and came close to regaining it in 2004. In 2008 they did regain the presidency, winning a majority of the popular vote for the first time since 1976. And they won a popular-vote majority again in 2012 and 2020. In his 1992 victory Bill Clinton boosted his share of the major-party vote among union members, the white working class, and even among white southerners. He focused on appeals to middle America, and in both 1992 and 1996, he paid as low a price as possible to gain the black vote. Clinton was the first Democrat to win in an election in which blacks made up more than 15 percent of the Democratic vote. In 1996, Clinton once again won with more than 15 percent of his votes provided by blacks. But the 1992 and 1996 elections were three-candidate contests. Our calculations suggest that under typical levels of turnout among its various coalition groups, it would be exceedingly difficult for a Democrat to win a two-candidate contest in which blacks made up a fifth or more of his or her total coalition—difficult but not impossible.

With the 2008 and 2012 elections, we see the ingredients (and challenges) of building a modern Democratic coalition. Obama gained about a fourth of his total tally from black voters. This was possible because black turnout equaled or exceeded white turnout and because blacks voted overwhelmingly Democratic. The Democrats also enjoyed strong support from Latino voters, and population growth makes this group an increasingly larger share of the Democratic coalition. The Democrat's New Deal coalition was often described as a "coalition of minorities"—increasingly the minorities at the heart of the new Democratic electoral coalition are blacks, Latinos, and Asians.

The 2016 election brought many of the electoral challenges confronting both parties to the fore. For the Democrats, while they were able to capture the national popular vote, the party's losses in nearly every battleground state were brought about, in large measure, by the same symptoms. To win, the modern Democratic coalition must not only maintain their recent levels of support from racial and ethnic minorities, but they must turn these voters out to the polls. African American turnout declined by 7 percentage points in 2016, and Latino turnout remains low. At the same time the Democratic Party's increasing reliance on its minority constituents may exacerbate its losses among a growing number of disaffected, white working-class voters, who feel the party has lost touch with their interests. Indeed, as we have seen in our analysis, over the last forty years, the Democratic Party has lost ground with every segment of the white electorate, save the most educated (and, possibly, urban dwellers). However, Democrats did slightly better among some segments of the white electorate in 2020, likely due to concerns related to the global pandemic, and they expanded their support among racial and ethnic minorities.

With the end to racial segregation in the formerly "solid" Democratic South in the 1960, the Republican Party moved quickly (and successfully) to capture the partisan loyalties of white southerners. With the exception of the elections of its native sons, Jimmy Carter in 1976 and Bill Clinton in 1992 and 1994, the South has been solidly Republican since 1964. In the South political change was quick. But the broadening of the Republican Party's electoral coalition to include large segments of the bygone Democratic New Deal coalition, including white Catholic voters and the white working class, occurred at a much slower rate of change, indeed, decades in the making. Much has been made of Donald Trump's resonance with disaffected white voters, tired of immigration, tired of seeing jobs moving overseas, tired of a government that, in their view, seems to care little about them and cannot be trusted. Yet careful examination of the electoral record shows that these "Trump voters" have been "Republican voters" for quite some time now, although the GOP's share of these voters has grown with each passing decade. On balance, the evidence shows that the American electorate in 2020 is remarkably similar to electorates of the last few decades.

Chapter 6

Party Loyalties and the Vote

In chapter 5, we discussed the influence of social forces such as race and ethnicity on voting behavior. We noted that, for example, African Americans do not vote Democratic simply because of their race. Instead, race and other social forces provide the context for electoral politics and thus influence how voters reach their decisions. In this chapter, we move from social identities to political identity, namely partisanship, perhaps the single most important factor connecting voters' backgrounds, social settings, and their more immediate assessments of issues and the candidates. Thus a major part of the explanation of why African Americans vote overwhelmingly Democratic are the various events and actions that made the Democratic Party attractive (and the Republican Party unattractive) to them. Party is part of the triumvirate of "candidates, issues, and parties"—that is, evaluations of the parties are one of three major forces that shape voting behavior. Party identification may be more foundational even than that. Party may not only directly shape voting behavior, but as we will see in later chapters, it even has indirect effects, explaining, for example, why voters have the evaluations of candidates and of issues they do.

Partisanship is not the only force that helps connect context and evaluation, but it has proven to be by far the most important for understanding elections. Its dual role in directly and indirectly affecting voting makes it unusually critical for understanding why US citizens vote as they do. Most Americans identify with a political party—one reason why it is so central. Their identification then influences their political attitudes and, ultimately, their behavior. In the 1950s and 1960s, Angus Campbell and his coauthors of *The American Voter*, along with other scholars, began to emphasize the role of party loyalties.[1]

In this chapter, we ask three key questions: What is party identification? What are the different approaches scholars have proposed for understanding party identification? How does party identification structure other attitudes and behavior? We then examine the role that party identification played in the 2020 presidential election, compared to earlier elections.

PARTY IDENTIFICATION AS LOYALTY: THE ORIGINAL VIEW

According to Angus Campbell and his colleagues, party identification is "the individual's affective orientation to an important group-object in his environment," in this case a political party.[2] In other words, an individual recognizes that two major political parties are playing significant roles in elections (and presumably, observing its role in governing and policy making) and develops an affinity for one of them. Partisanship, therefore, represents an evaluation of the two parties, but its implications extend to a wider variety of political phenomena. Campbell and his colleagues measured partisanship by asking individuals which party they identified with and how strong that identification was.[3] If an individual did not identify with one of the parties, he or she may have either "leaned" toward a party or been a "pure" independent. Most Americans develop a preference for either the Republican or the Democratic Party. Very few identify with any third party. The rest are mostly independents who, according to this classic view, are not only unattached to a party but also relatively unattached to politics in general. They are less interested, less informed, and less active than those who identify with a party.

Partisan identification in this view becomes an attachment or loyalty similar to that between the individual and other groups or organizations in society such as a religious body, a social class, or even a favorite sports team. As we will see, partisanship attachments in this polarized era have heightened in such a fashion that some scholars see them as a part of one's political identity. We will return to this topic shortly. The major point, though, is that as with loyalties to many racial, ethnic, or religious groups, partisan affiliation often begins early and lasts perhaps over the life cycle. One of the first political attitudes children develop is partisan identification, and it develops well before they acquire policy preferences and many other political orientations. Furthermore, as with other group loyalties, once an attachment to a party develops, it tends to endure.[4] Some people do switch parties, of course, but they usually do so only if their social situation changes dramatically, if there is an issue of overriding concern that sways their loyalties, or if the political parties themselves change substantially.

Party identification, then, stands as a base or core orientation to electoral politics. Once formed, this core orientation, predicated on a general evaluation of the two parties, affects many other specific orientations. Democratic loyalists tend to rate Democratic candidates and officeholders more highly than Republican candidates and officeholders and vice versa. In effect, one is predisposed to evaluate the promises and performance of one's party leaders relatively more favorably. It follows, therefore, that Democrats are more likely to vote for Democratic candidates than are Republicans and vice versa.

PARTY IDENTIFICATION AS RETROSPECTIVE EVALUATION: A SECOND VIEW

In *The Responsible Electorate*, V. O. Key argued that party loyalties contributed to electoral inertia and that many partisans voted as "standpatters" from election to election.[5] In other words, in the absence of any information to the contrary, or if the attractions and disadvantages of the candidates are fairly evenly balanced, partisans are expected to vote for the candidate of their party. This "rule" is one of voters' having a "standing decision" to vote along party lines until and unless they are given good reasons not to follow that rule. This finding led scholars to reexamine the basis of such behavior.

In this second view, citizens who consider themselves Democrats have a standing decision to vote for the Democratic nominee because of the past positions of the Democrats and the Republicans and because of the parties' comparative past performances while in office. In short, this view of partisan identification presumes that it is a "running tally" of past experiences (mostly in terms of policy and performance), a sort of summary expression of political memory, according to Morris P. Fiorina.[6]

Furthermore, when in doubt about how, for example, a Democratic candidate is likely to handle a civil rights issue in comparison with the Republican opponent, voters can reasonably assume that the Democrat will be more liberal than the Republican—until and unless the candidates indicate otherwise. Political parties tend to be consistent with their basic historical policy cleavages for long periods of time, changing in any fundamental ways only rarely. Naturally, therefore, summary judgments of parties and their typical candidates do not change radically or often.[7] As a result a citizen's running tally serves as a good first approximation, changes rarely, and can be an excellent device for saving time and effort that would be spent gathering information in the absence of this "memory."

Many of the major findings used in support of the original interpretation of party identification are completely consistent with this more policy-oriented view.[8] Indeed the two interpretations are not mutually exclusive. Moreover, they share the important conclusion that party identification plays a central role in shaping voters' decisions and make many of the same predictions. Equally clearly they connote quite different aspects of a political attribute. The original emphasizes affective evaluations and loyalty; the second view is more substantively based in the cognition of politics and in adjusting political views to the world one experiences. We will discuss strong empirical findings in this chapter but will be unable to resolve fully just which view is correct. In part, this is because of the confluence of two newer forces in American politics: polarization of political elites and the development of a better understanding of how identity politics works and how it may have spread to include partisanship.

PARTY IDENTIFICATION, POLARIZATION, AND IDENTITY: A SYNTHESIS?

These two views are still widely studied today. The two views sometimes seem irreconcilable, but they make many similar empirical claims. We propose here a way to think about how the two might be related in concepts to match their empirical similarity.

Robert S. Erikson, Michael B. MacKuen, and James A. Stimson argued that an updated version of the Key-Downs-Fiorina view of partisanship is one of the central concepts for understanding what they call the "macro polity"—that is, an explanation of how political leaders, institutions, and policy respond to changes in aggregate public opinion.[9] They argue that partisanship in the electorate changes, as do macro-level conditions such as inflation and unemployment rates, akin to the Key-Downs-Fiorina view. In turn political elites react to changes in this "macro-partisanship," among other aspects of public opinion and beliefs. On the other side, Donald Green, Bradley Palmquist, and Eric Schickler developed an equally elegant account of the affective base of partisan identification and its stability over time, and this has recently been extended by Mason.[10] This view is therefore the modern version of the original account by Campbell et al. And, as their exchanges have shown, the authors differ substantially in their interpretations of what partisanship means, but empirical differences are slighter.[11]

Both views agree that partisan identifications are long-term forces in politics. Both agree that for most people, such identifications are formed early in life; children often develop a partisan loyalty, which they usually learn from their parents, although these loyalties are seldom explicitly taught. Both views recognize that partisan loyalties contribute to voter participation, as we demonstrated in chapter 4. Partisan choices also are often closely associated with social forces, as discussed in chapter 5, especially when a social group is actively engaged in partisan politics. An important illustration of this point is the affiliation of evangelical and other religious groups on the right with the Republican Party today, reinforcing the tendency of those who share such religious beliefs to identify with the Republican Party, much as members of labor and civil rights groups have long affiliated with the Democrats. Finally both views agree that partisanship is closely associated with more immediate evaluations, including assessments of candidates and their traits and both prospective and retrospective evaluations of the issues and candidates, as will be analyzed in chapters 7 and 8.

The two views may not disagree if also viewed in a larger perspective. We pose a way to think about party identification in this partisan-polarized era. To be sure, the hard work of actual synthesis is yet to come, but we pose this as a way forward. Partisan polarization is taken firstly to mean that the two parties present—and act in government—by taking relatively homogenous views on issues within each party with very different and thus heterogeneous views on issues between the two. But polarization means not only differentiation between the two parties on issues but on an increasingly broad and diverse array of political matters, from social groups that align with only one party (e.g., especially related to race and religiosity, see Mason 2018) to a wider and wider array of affective and evaluative judgments that distinguish a Republican from a Democrat. If Fiorina is right and the variety of experiences (no longer policy experiences alone but social and cultural experiences) that differentiate the two parties increase, then we would expect to find heightened affective support for one party (if one is close to them on policy, economic, social, and cultural dimensions) and negative feelings toward the more distant party (distant on nearly all matters). Still, if the standing decision really is a "running tally" such that this increasingly wide array of matters all go together into the calculation of which party is more like the individual than the other party, then Fiorina would be right: those pieces of evidence that push the citizen one way or the other are included but then set aside from memory and forgotten, with only the tally and perhaps a few of the most memorable pieces held in mind—those individual pieces often being those that arouse the most affect, that is, emotional reactions.

The key point, however, is that partisan polarization of elites is not just over policy—it is that to be sure—but it is a set of political, social, cultural, and economic differentiations that have grown from the 1980s to today and that make partisanship a retrospective judgment, an affective loyalty, and an all-around guide to understanding politics and especially the political choices the voter faces. Is it policy choice? Yes. Is it a loyalty? Yes. Is it part of one's political identity? Yes. All of these reinforce one another. In the jargon of politics, partisan polarization is the result of a large number of political cleavages that have grown over recent decades and that reinforce one another.[12] This makes them unlike the partisan politics of the 1950s to 1980s, when cleavages cross-cut one another, some pushing along lines of partisan cleavages but many cutting across them. Every reinforcing cleavage today adds one more dimension on which the parties polarize. As it grows across increasingly diverse arrays of topics, that reinforcement is nearly multiplicative in that it not only reinforces but adds both cognitive differentiation and increasingly emotive differentiation between the two parties.[13] The stakes in having one party or the other in power simply increase with each reinforcing cleavage.

PARTY IDENTIFICATION IN THE ELECTORATE

If partisan identification is a fundamental orientation for most citizens, then the distribution of partisan loyalties is crucial. The ANES surveys have monitored the party loyalties of the American electorate since 1952. In table 6.1, we show the basic distributions of partisan loyalties in presidential election years from 1980 to 2020, and the results for 1952 to 1976 (and every election thereafter) can be found in table A6.1 in the appendix. As the table shows, most Americans identify with a political party. In 2020, 64 percent claimed to think of themselves as a Democrat or as a Republican, and another 22 percent, who initially said they were independent or had no partisan preference, nevertheless said they felt closer to one of the major parties than to the

Table 6.1   Party Identification in Presidential Years, Pre-Election Surveys, 1980–2020 (Percent)

Party Identification	1980	1984	1988	1992	1996	2000	2004	2008	2012	2016	2020
Strong Democrat	18	17	18	17	18	19	17	19	17	21	22
Weak Democrat	24	20	18	18	20	15	16	15	12	14	11
Independent, Leans Democratic	12	11	12	14	14	15	17	17	16	11	11
Independent, No Partisan Leanings	13	11	11	12	8	12	10	11	10	15	14
Independent, Leans Republican	10	13	14	13	12	13	12	12	19	11	10
Weak Republican	14	15	14	15	16	12	12	13	12	12	11
Strong Republican	9	13	14	11	13	12	17	13	14	16	20
Total	100	100	101	100	101	98	101	100	100	100	99
(N)	(1,577)	(2,198)	(1,999)	(2,450)	(1,696)	(1,777)	(1,193)	(2,301)	(1,804)	(4,244)	(7,432)
Apolitical	2	2	2	1	1	1	a	a	b	b	a
(N)	(35)	(38)	(33)	(23)	(14)	(21)	(3)	(2)	b	b	b

Source: Authors' analysis of ANES surveys.
Note: Numbers are weighted.
[a]Less than 1 percent.
[b]The ANES survey did not use the apolitical category in 2012, 2016, or 2020.

other.[14] One in seven was purely independent of party. One of the biggest changes in partisanship in the electorate began in the mid-1960s, when more people claimed to be independents.[15] This growth stopped, however, in the late 1970s and early 1980s. There was very little change in partisan loyalties between the 1984 and 1992 surveys.

There were signs in 1996 of reversals of the trends in party identification toward greater independence. All partisan groups increased slightly in 1996 compared with 1992, and the percentage of "pure" independents (i.e., those with no partisan leanings) was at its lowest level, 8 percent, since 1968. That dip in independence stopped, however, so that the percentages of independents in 2004, 2008, and 2012 were at about the same levels as during the 1980s. There was, however, a substantial increase in (pure) independence in 2016 and 2020 to go along with a growth of strong partisans, both coming at the expense of independent leaners and weak partisans.

Table 6.1 also shows that people are rather evenly divided between the two parties with a slight edge to Democrats. When "leaners" are included, 44 percent of partisans are Democrats compared to 41 percent of Republicans in 2020. Over the last forty years, the balance between the two parties had favored the Democrats by a range of about 55/45 to about 60/40. The results from the last six presidential election years before 2012 still fell within that range, although more often at the lower part of the range. From 1984 to 2000, there was a clear shift toward the Republicans. In 1980, 35 percent of partisans were Republicans; in 2000 Republicans accounted for 42 percent. The inclusion of independents who leaned toward a party would increase the percentage of Republicans to 38 percent in 1980 and 43 percent in 2000. The high point was 47 percent in 1988. In 2004, the (strong and weak) Democrats led comparable Republicans in the ANES survey with 33 percent to 29 percent (or 54/46). The Democratic advantage increased in 2008, as the percentage of Republicans declined, while there was a one-point increase on the Democratic side. These two small differences nevertheless brought the ratio of Democrats to Republicans to 57/43. The percentage of independents who leaned toward a party remained the same as in 2004, and as a result, including them maintained the Democrats' edge over Republicans at 57/43, keeping the partisan balance within the historical range of a noticeable Democratic lead. By 2012, however, that edge was gone. It returned slightly in 2016, when the Democratic advantage among strong and weak partisans returned to 55 percent, with the number of strong Democrats reaching its highest point since 1964. Of course the edge Democrats recovered in 2016 was still at the lower end of the heretofore usual range, and it is softened again in 2020, as the percentage of weak Democrats declined.

Gary C. Jacobson has provided two excellent analyses of the shift in party loyalties away from the Republican Party from a high watermark in 2003 to a low watermark in 2009.[16] His analyses strongly suggest that the decline was driven largely by the decline in approval of George W. Bush's performance as president. Jacobson relies mainly on Gallup data, which probably capture more short-term variation than the standard Michigan SRC question.[17]

The earlier shift toward the Republican Party was concentrated among white Americans.[18] As described in chapter 5, the sharpest social division in US electoral politics is race, and this division has been reflected in partisan loyalties for decades. Moreover, the racial gap has appeared to be widening, with a sharp increase in 2004.

Although the distribution of partisanship in the electorate as a whole has changed only somewhat since 1984, this stability masks the growth in Republican identification among whites and the compensating growth of already strong Democratic loyalties among African Americans and other minorities. In tables 6.2 and 6.3 we report the party identification of whites and blacks, respectively, between 1980 and 2020. In tables A6.2 and A6.3 in the appendix, we report the party identification of whites and blacks between 1952 and 1978 (as well as through 2020). As these four tables show, black and white patterns in partisan loyalties were very different from 1952 to 2020. There was a sharp shift in black loyalties in the mid-1960s. Before then about 50 percent of African Americans were strong or weak Democrats. Since that time, 60 to 70 percent—and even higher—of blacks have considered themselves Democrats.

The party loyalties of whites have changed more slowly. Still, the percentage of self-professed Democrats among whites declined over the Reagan),

Table 6.2   Party Identification among Whites in Presidential Years, Pre-Election Surveys, 1980–2020 (Percent)

Party Identification	1980	1984	1988	1992	1996	2000	2004	2008	2012	2016	2020
Strong Democrat	14	15	14	14	15	15	13	14	13	16	17
Weak Democrat	23	18	16	17	19	14	12	14	10	12	9
Independent, Leans Democratic	12	11	10	14	13	15	17	17	15	11	11
Independent, No Partisan Leanings	14	11	12	12	8	13	8	12	10	14	11
Independent, Leans Republican	11	13	15	14	12	14	13	17	22	13	12
Weak Republican	16	17	15	16	17	14	15	13	13	14	13
Strong Republican	9	14	16	12	15	14	21	15	17	21	27
Apolitical	2	2	1	1	1	1	a	16	b	b	a
Total	101	101	99	100	100	100	99	101	100	101	100
(N)	(1,405)	(1,931)	(1,693)	(2,702)	(1,451)	(1,404)	(859)	(1,824)	(1,449)	(2,917)	(4,845)

Source: Authors' analysis of ANES surveys.
Note: Numbers are weighted.
[a]The percentage supporting another party has not been presented: it is usually less than 1 percent and never totals more than 1 percent.
[b]The ANES survey did not use the apolitical category in 2012, 2016, or 2020.

years, whereas the percentage of Republicans increased. In the five elections that followed, partisanship among whites changed. If independents who lean Republican are included, there was close to an even balance among whites between the two parties in 1984. By 1988 the numbers of strong and weak Democrats and strong and weak Republicans were virtually the same, with more strong Republicans than strong Democrats for the first time. Adding in the two groups of independent leaners gave Republicans a clear advantage in identification among whites. In 1992, however, there were slightly more strong and weak Democrats than strong and weak Republicans. In 1996 all four of the partisan categories were larger, by one to three points, than in 1992. The result was that the balance of Republicans to Democrats changed very slightly, and the near parity of identifiers with the two parties among whites remained. By 2000, the parity was even more striking. But 2002 revealed a substantial increase in Republican identification among whites, one that was constant in terms of the three Republican groups in 2004. Democratic identification declined slightly so that from 2000 to 2004, strong and weak Democrats fell by four points, partially balanced by a two-point gain among independent leaners. Pure independents declined sharply, to 8 percent, in both 2002 and 2004, a sign (along with the growth in strong Republicans) that the white electorate was polarizing somewhat on partisanship. As a result, the three Republican groups constituted very nearly half of the white electorate and led Democrats by a 49 to 42 percent margin. That changed in 2008.[19] Democratic identification (over the three Democratic categories) increased 3 percentage points to 45 percent, whereas strong Republicans fell from 21 to 15 percent, dropping their three-category total to 45 percent. Thus in 2008, Democrats had at least regained parity with Republicans among white identifiers. And pure independents increased 4 points, to 12 percent, the highest level in over a decade. That changed again in 2012. The Democrats lost ground in all three categories in 2012 compared to 2008, and pure independents also declined somewhat. The strong and not-so-strong Republican categories changed only slightly, and as a result, the entire decline among Democrats and pure independents was concentrated in one spot—among independents who leaned toward the Republican Party. As a result, the GOP held a seven-point advantage over Democrats in terms of strong and weak identifiers but a fourteen-point advantage if adding in those who lean toward a party.[20] In 2016, Democrats continued to trail Republicans among whites, by the same seven points among strong and weak partisans, but only by nine points when leaners are included. By 2020, Republicans increased their advantage among whites to a fourteen-point advantage among strong and weak identifers, and a fifteen point advantage with leaners included. Of course standing among whites is different from standing among all voters, and indeed whites continue to decline as a proportion of the total population.

Table 6.3 Party Identification among Blacks in Presidential Years, Pre-Election Surveys, 1980–2020 (Percent)

Party Identification	1980	1984	1988	1992	1996	2000	2004	2008	2012	2016	2020
Strong Democrat	45	32	39	40	43	47	30	47	53	52	53
Weak Democrat	27	31	24	24	22	21	30	23	17	19	14
Independent, leans Democratic	9	14	18	14	16	14	20	15	17	10	14
Independent, no partisan leanings	7	11	6	12	10	10	12	9	5	13	10
Independent, leans Republican	3	6	5	3	5	4	5	3	7	1	5
Weak Republican	2	1	5	3	3	3	2	1	0	2	3
Strong Republican	3	2	1	2	1	0	1	1	1	3	2
Apolitical	4	2	3	2	0	1	0	0	a	a	a
Total	100	99	101	100	100	100	100	99	100	100	101
(N)	(187)	(247)	(267)	(317)	(200)	(225)	(193)	(281)	(124)	(460)	(831)

Source: Authors' analysis of ANES surveys.
Note: The percentage supporting another party has not been presented: it is usually less than 1 percent and never totals more than 1 percent. Numbers are weighted.
a The ANES survey did not use the apolitical category in 2012, 2016, and 2020.

Party identification among blacks is very different. In 2020, there were very few black Republicans. Indeed, whereas the percentage of black Republicans increased in 2016 and 2020 over 2012 (when the percentage of black Republicans fell to near trace levels, with only 4 percent choosing any Republican option and a mere 1 percent being strong and weak Republican), they nonetheless remain a very small percentage, with only 5 percent of strong and weak partisans and 10 percent including leaners. Because the Democrats were the first major party to choose a black presidential candidate, we would expect this choice to exert a strong pull of blacks toward the party in 2008 and 2012, and that appeared to hold in 2016 and 2020. Indeed a majority of black respondents considered themselves strong Democrats, and greater than 67 percent were strong or weak Democrats, eight in ten when including those leaning toward the Democrats. This is not to say that black political preferences are monolithic. Ismail White and Chryl Laird note that even though African Americans are nearly uniform in their allegiance to the Democratic Party they are increasingly politically moderate and even conservative.[21] White and Laird argue that blacks' allegiance to the party is socially reinforced by norms within the black community that prioritize solidarity in the group's continued struggle for political equality, thus producing social pressure to affiliate with the Democrats even when one disagrees with the party.

These racial differences in partisanship are long-standing, and they have increased over time. Between 1952 and 1962 blacks were primarily Democratic, but about one in seven supported the Republicans. Black partisanship shifted massively and abruptly even further toward the Democratic Party in 1964. In that year, more than half of all black voters considered themselves strong Democrats. Since then, well over half have identified with the Democratic Party. Black Republican identification fell to barely a trace in 1964 and edged up only slightly since then, only to fall back even further in recent years.

The abrupt change in black loyalties in 1964 reflects the two presidential nominees of that year: Democrat Lyndon Johnson and Republican Barry Goldwater. President Johnson's advocacy of civil rights legislation appealed directly to black voters, and his Great Society and War on Poverty programs made only slightly less direct appeals. Arizona senator Barry Goldwater voted against the 1964 Civil Rights Act, a vote criticized even by many of his Republican peers. In 1968, Republican nominee Richard Nixon began to pursue systematically what was called the "Southern strategy"—that is, an attempt to win votes and long-term loyalties among white southerners. This strategy unfolded slowly but consistently over the years, as Republicans, particularly Ronald Reagan, continued to pursue the southern strategy. Party stances have not changed appreciably since then.[22]

In 1964 the proportion of blacks considered apolitical dropped from the teens to very small proportions, similar to those among whites. This shift resulted from the civil rights movement, the contest between Johnson and Goldwater, and the passage of the Civil Rights Act. The civil rights movement stimulated many blacks, especially in the South, to become politically active. Furthermore, the 1965 Voting Rights Act enabled many of them to vote for the first time. Party and electoral politics suddenly were relevant, and blacks responded as all others by becoming engaged with the political—and party—system.

LATINO PARTISANSHIP IN 2008–2020

One of the most important changes in American society and its politics has been the growth of the Latino community. They are now the largest ethnic or racial minority in the United States. The outcome of the 2012 election spurred a vast commentary on the future of the Republican Party based on whether and how they might be able to appeal to the Hispanic vote or seek a majority in some other way, such as through voter identification laws. The discussion of the stance of the Republican Party toward both documented (i.e., legal) and undocumented Latino immigrants turned dramatically in 2016, especially due to Trump's candidacy, where "Build the Wall!" was a common response of his audience to his calls for an end to at least illegal if not nearly all immigration and the possible deportation of up to 19 million undocumented and mostly Latino immigrants living in the United States.

We have not been able to assess the attitudes and behavior of Latino citizens eligible to vote until recently due to the small numbers that appear in the ANES and other survey opinion polls. Fortunately, in 2008 and 2012, the ANES included a supplemental sample of Hispanics so that we have access to sufficiently large numbers to support at least a modicum of analysis, whereas the large numbers involved in the ANES 2016 and 2020 surveys, considering both face-to-face and online surveys, provide sufficient numbers to analyze. Table 6.4 reports the distribution of partisan loyalties among Latinos in Part A and their voting patterns in Part B, which we consider in our analyses. As can be seen there, Latino partisanship may not be as massively Democratic as that of African Americans, but a majority of Latinos identify with or lean toward the Democratic Party, 54

Table 6.4 Party Identification among Latinos in Presidential Years, Pre-Election Surveys, 2008–2020 (Percent)

Party Identification				
Part A: Party Identification	**2008**	**2012**	**2016**	**2020**
Strong Democrat	23	27	14	23
Weak Democrat	21	23	21	19
Independent, Leans Democratic	17	16	11	12
Independent, No Partisan Leanings	16	15	18	22
Independent, Leans Republican	9	7	7	7
Weak Republican	6	6	7	7
Strong Republican	7	5	8	10
Total	99	99	100	100
(N)	(192)	(222)	(503)	(978)
Part B: Vote for Democratic Candidate	**2008**	**2012**	**2016**	**2020**
Strong Democrat	95	100	84	98
Weak Democrat	90	87	91	98
Independent, Leans Democratic	94	99	100	92
Independent, No Partisan Leanings	61	82	69	71
Independent, Leans Republican	35	39	32	30
Weak Republican	24	4	23	36
Strong Republican	20	1	5	15
Total	79	78	74	75
(N)	(104)	(107)	(227)	(535)

Source: Authors' analysis of ANES surveys.
Note: Numbers are weighted.

percent in 2020, while just under a quarter identify with or lean toward the Republican Party., A higher percentage of Latinos identify as pure independents, 22 percent, compared to whites and African Americans. Recall that to be included in the ANES survey, respondents need to be citizens so that these results are relevant to vote-eligible Latinos in 2008, 2012, 2016, and 2020, respectively. With large numbers of documented Latinos in the United States, combined with many who were born in the United States and thus native-born Americans, the number eligible to vote will only increase, likely considerably faster than any other source of new voters in the United States. Hence the Republicans must find a way to attract new voters to their camp to compensate for the growth in the total number of Latino voters election after election who tilt disproportionately to the Democrats. If the party continues to highlight an anti-immigrant platform, it will be an increasingly challenging one.

PARTY IDENTIFICATION AND THE VOTE

As we saw in chapter 4, partisanship is related to turnout. Strong supporters of either party are more likely to vote than weak supporters, and independents who lean toward a party are more likely to vote than independents without partisan leanings. Republicans are somewhat more likely to vote than Democrats. Although partisanship influences whether people vote, it is more strongly related to how people vote.

Table 6.5 reports the percentage of white major-party voters who voted for the Democratic candidate across all categories of partisanship since 1980 and table A.6.5 in the appendix reports the same for all ANES studies.[23] Clearly, there is a strong relationship between partisan identification and choice of candidate. In every election except 1972, the Democratic nominee has received more than 80 percent of the vote of strong Democrats and majority support from both weak Democratic partisans and independent Democratic leaners. In 1996 these figures were higher than in any earlier election, with nine in ten white Democratic identifiers voting for their party's nominee. Although the figures fell somewhat in 2000, especially in the independent leaning Democrat category, that reversed in 2004, with John Kerry holding onto very large majorities of those who identified with the Democratic Party, including nearly nine in ten independents who were leaning toward the Democratic Party. In 2008 this very high level of Democratic voting continued, with slight declines among strong Democrats balanced by comparable increases among weak Democrats. The 2012 election looked more similar to 1996 than any other in this regard, and was only slightly less solidly Democrat in voting than in that year. Perhaps in the absence of the pull of Obama's candidacy,

Chapter 6

Table 6.5   White Major-Party Voters Who Voted Democratic for President, by Party Identification, 1980–2020 (Percent)

Party Identification	1980	1984	1988	1992	1996	2000	2004	2008	2012	2016	2020
Strong Democrat	87	88	93	96	98	96	97	92	98	95	98
Weak Democrat	59	63	68	80	88	81	78	83	82	75	88
Independent, leans Democratic	57	77	86	92	91	72	88	8	86	88	95
Independent, no partisan leanings	23	21	35	63	39	44	54	50	42	36	46
Independent, leans Republican	13	5	13	14	26	15	13	17	11	8	12
Weak Republican	5	6	16	18	21	16	10	10	14	17	18
Strong Republican	4	2	2	2	3	1	3	2	4	2	3

Source: Authors' analysis of ANES surveys.

Democratic partisans supported Clinton at "only" the levels they supported Kerry in 2004, but that still was at very high levels. In 2020, support among strong Democrats and weak Democrats mirrored the peak in 1996, and support peaked among independent leaning Democrats.

Since 1952, strong Republicans have given the Democratic candidate less than one vote in ten. In 1988, more of the weak Republicans and independents who leaned toward the Republican Party voted for Michael Dukakis than had voted for Walter Mondale in 1984, but even so, only about one in seven voted Democratic. In 1992 Clinton won an even larger percentage of the two-party vote from these Republicans, and he increased his support among Republicans again in 1996. In 2000, George W. Bush held essentially the same level of support among the three white Republican categories as his father had in 1988 and 1992 and if anything increased his support among Republicans in 2004. In 2008 more than 90 percent of strong and weak Republicans voted for McCain, just as they did for Bush four years earlier. The 2012 data looked rather similar to 2008, with Romney doing a little worse in holding weak Republican votes but doing much better than McCain among Republican leaners. In 2016, Clinton gathered more support from weak Republicans than anyone since her husband but did quite poorly among those whites who lean toward the Republican Party. In 2020, Biden garnered slightly higher support than Clinton among strong and weak Republicans, and independent leaning Republicans.

The pure independent vote among whites, which fluctuates substantially, has been more Republican than Democratic in twelve of these seventeen elections and was strongly Democratic only in 1964. Clinton did well among major-party voters in 1992. John F. Kennedy won 50 percent of that vote in 1960, but Bill Clinton won nearly two-thirds of the pure independents' vote (between the two parties) in 1992. Kerry was able to win 54 percent of the pure independent vote. Obama, like Kennedy, won exactly half of the vote among whites who are pure independents in 2008. However, that 50-50 vote in 1960 was the same as the overall vote, whereas Obama won a higher proportion from the full electorate than from white pure independents. But, in 2012, he fell back significantly, winning only 42 percent of the "pure" independent vote among whites. Clinton did particularly poorly among whites who claimed to be "pure" independents, holding only as many of them as did Dukakis in 1988. Biden did substantially better than Clinton among this group, but still won less than a majority, 46 percent.

Thus, at least among major-party white voters, partisanship is very strongly related to the vote. In recent elections the Democrats have been better able to hold support among their partisans, perhaps because the loss of southern white support has made the party more homogeneous in its outlook. Their partisan base has become essentially as strong as the Republicans', which has been consistently strong except in the very best years for the Democrats. Partisanship, then, has become more polarized in its relationship to the vote. Biden won because he broke relatively even among independents, he held his base better than Trump, and performed strongly among independent leaning Democrats. Much of this was likely related to the national crisis of the pandemic.

Table 6.4B shows that there is a very powerful relationship between Latino party identification and their vote. Nearly all Democratic Latinos voted for Obama in 2008 and 2012. Obama was able to hold about a quarter of the relatively small number of Latinos who identified with the GOP in 2008, but Romney won nearly all of the by-now very small number of strong and weak Republican Hispanic votes in 2008. The pure independent vote broke strongly for Obama in 2008 but increased dramatically in 2012. Whereas Clinton's support among strong Democrats declined in 2016, the pattern looked similar to that of 2008. Biden did even better among Latinos in 2020, and even made inroads with weak Republicans. Our conclusion is that, whereas particular percentages are somewhat variable, presumably primarily due to the smaller numbers involved, the overall pattern is one in which Latino voting follows white voting in that partisanship is a very strong guide to voting. The big difference is that so many more Hispanics are Democrats that they are a solid and important part of the Democratic voting coalition, not as heavily pro-Democratic as blacks but certainly far more Democratic than Republican in their loyalties and their voting choices.

Although nearly all blacks vote Democratic regardless of their partisan affiliations (most are, however, Democratic identifiers), among Latinos and whites, partisanship leads to loyalty in voting. Between 1964 and 1980 the relationship between party identification and the vote was declining, but in 1984 the relationship between party identification and the presidential vote was higher than in any of the five elections from 1964 to 1980. The relationship remained strong in 1988 and continued to be quite strong in the two Clinton elections and the Gore-Bush election, at least among major-party voters. The question of whether the parties are gathering new strength at the presidential level could not be answered definitively from the 2000 election data, but the 2004 through 2020 election data now make it clear that these growing signs have become a strong trend, to the point that party identification is as strongly related to the presidential vote as it has been since the 1950s and early 1960s, and indeed may be stronger. The relationship between party identification and voting in general will be reconsidered in chapter 10, when we assess its relationship to the congressional vote.[24]

Partisanship is related to the way people vote. The question, therefore, is why do partisans support their party's candidates? As we shall see in later chapters party identification affects behavior because it helps structure (and, according to the understanding of partisanship as a running tally of experiences, is structured by) the way voters view both policies and performance.

CONCLUSION

As we saw in this chapter, there was a substantial shift toward Republican loyalties over the 1980s. Although the 2008 election suggests that there was at least a chance that the Democrats would enjoy a resurgence, that advantage was at least temporarily stemmed in 2012, as the two parties were near parity. This parity turned back toward a slight Democratic advantage in 2016 and 2020, but that advantage is substantially smaller than it was in the 1950s and 1960s.

However, these shifts in the aggregate mask even larger changes across different racial and ethnic groups. One big change, for example, was the slow transition of southern whites in the 1980s from Democratic to Republican partisanship, for the first time since before 1876, which led to more conservative candidates running for office in the south.[25] By 2020, whites were 14 percentage points more likely to identify as Republicans than Democrats. The patterns are reverse for people of color. Over time, party identification with the Democratic Party has increased greatly among African Americans, and to a lesser extent among Latinos. Furthermore, while the American National Election Study does not have large enough samples of Asian respondents over time for analysis, Pew surveys have found increases in identification with the Democratic Party.[26]

And, while we focused on differences in partisan identification by race, where whites have become increasingly aligned with the Republican Party, and people of color have become increasingly aligned with the Democratic Party, other research has found increased sorting by social groups into parties on other dimensions. For example, those who are more religious have become increasingly aligned with the Republican Party, while religious nones have become increasingly aligned with the Democratic Party. Mason (2018) calls this process of an increased alignment between social groups and partisanship social sorting. Others have found an increasing alignment between ideological and partisan identification over time.[27]

These shifts have important implications for voting behavior. There is a strong association between partisan identification and voting decisions, and this has strengthened over time. In recent elections, somewhere between 95 percent or more of strong partisans vote for their party's candidate. Support is lower, but still generally over 75 percent, among weak partisans, and increasingly even higher among independents who lean toward one of the parties. Given that most in the electorate have at least some partisan inclinations, and given that they are sorted into the same partisan groups as the parties' political candidates and officeholders, that means that even only moderately liberal Democrats will choose a partisan-polarized, liberal Democrat for office after office, in election after election, over any conservative Republican. And, of course, the same works in reverse for even modestly conservative Republicans. Thus elections are dominated by the polarized parties at the elite level and the sorted parties at the voter level (and possibly polarized voters, too, at least in some dimensions). Elections look a lot like one another because the big picture is that they are like one another—conservative Republican candidates appealing to conservative Republican voters, liberal Democratic voters appealing to liberal Democrats.[28] Increasingly polarized parties mean that each election looks a lot like the preceding one, only a bit more so, election after election. And that there are reasonably similar numbers of Democrats at the voting booth as there are Republicans holds this all in balance.[29] That is, partisan polarization has nearly locked voting patterns into place, such that once the public observed this dramatic change, the electoral world is less change and much more continuity.

This chapter has demonstrated that party loyalties affect how people vote, and increasingly so over time. However, the theories we reviewed earlier in the chapter also note the indirect ways in which partisanship can influence voters. That is, partisanship may color the way in which we evaluate issues and judge the performance of the incumbent president and his party. We will consider these more indirect effects in subsequent chapters.

Chapter 7

Candidates, Issues, and the Vote

In this chapter and the one that follows, we examine some of the concerns that underlie voters' choices for president further down the decision-making chain. Even though scholars and politicians disagree about what factors voters employ and how they employ them, there is general consensus on several points. First, voters' attitudes or preferences determine their choices. There may be disagreement over exactly which attitudes shape behavior, but most scholars agree that voters deliberately choose to support the candidate they believe will make the best president. For decades there had also been general agreement that, as Campbell et al., in *The American Voter*, originally argued, it is the tripartite attitudes toward the candidates, the issues, and the parties that is the most important set of attitudes in shaping the vote.[1] We examined partisanship in the last chapter and now turn to shorter-term forces that shape voting decisions, namely evaluations of candidate traits and issues.

We look first at the relationships among several measures of candidate evaluations and the vote, beginning with the "feeling thermometers" used by the ANES to measure affect toward the candidates. After this brief analysis, we examine aspects of the major components of these evaluations: voters' perceptions of the candidates' personal qualities and of the candidates' professional qualifications, and competence to serve as president.[2] As we will see, there is a very powerful relationship between thermometer evaluations of candidates and the vote and an only somewhat less strong one between evaluations of candidate traits and the vote. It might seem obvious that voters support the candidate they like best, but in 1968, 1980, 1992, 1996, and 2000, the presence of a significant third candidate complicated decision-making for many voters.[3]

We conceive of attitudes toward the candidates as the most direct influence on the vote itself, especially the summary evaluations encapsulated in the "feeling thermometers," as we used in chapter 1. But attitudes toward the issues and the parties help shape attitudes toward the candidates and thus the vote.[4] With that in mind we turn to the first part of our investigation of the role of issues. After analyzing the problems that most concerned voters in 2020, we discuss the two basic forms of issue voting: that based on prospective issues and that based on retrospective issues. In this chapter, we investigate the impact of prospective issues. In doing so, we consider one of the enduring questions about issue voting—how much information the public has on the issues and candidates' positions on them—and is this sufficient for casting an issues-based vote? Our analyses provide an indication of the significance of prospective issues in 2020 and compare their impact as shown in earlier election surveys. Chapter 8 examines retrospective issues and the vote.

ATTITUDES TOWARD THE CANDIDATES

Although the United States has a two-party system, there are still ways in which other candidates can appear on the ballot or run a write-in candidacy. The 2020 presidential election was a two-person race for all intents and purposes, but many other candidates were running as well.[5] Two other political parties qualified for inclusion on nearly all state ballots. The Libertarian Party nominated Jo Jorgensen for president, winning about 1.9 million votes (about 1.2 percent; by comparison Biden won about 81.3 million or 51.3 percent, whereas Trump won 74.2 million votes, or 46.9 percent). Howie Hawkins was the Green Party's presidential nominee, winning 0.4 million votes (or 0.3 percent). Both of these candidates fell far short of being competitive for a single Electoral College vote.

As a result, we consider 2020 to be a nearly pure, two-person contest, and thus we limit our attention to Joe Biden and Donald Trump. We want to know why people preferred one candidate over the other, and therefore how they voted, and by extension, why Biden won the popular vote (which is what the ANES survey, as most surveys, is designed to measure), as well as an Electoral College majority.

If attitudes determine choices, then the obvious starting point in a two-person race is to imagine that people voted for the candidate they preferred. This may sound obvious, but as we have noted, in races with three or more candidates, people do not necessarily vote for the candidate they most prefer.[6] Respondents who rank a major-party candidate highest among three candidates vote overwhelmingly for the major-party candidate. On the other hand, respondents who rank a third-party or independent candidate highest often desert that candidate to vote for one of the major-party candidates, which we believe may result from voters using strategic considerations to avoid "wasting" their vote on a candidate who has little chance of winning.

Happily for understanding the 2020 presidential election, in an essentially two-person race, people overwhelmingly vote for the candidate they prefer. This close relationship can be demonstrated by analyzing the "feeling thermometer." This measure is a scale that runs from 0 to 100 degrees, with 0 indicating "very cold" or negative feelings, 50 indicating neutral feelings, and 100 indicating a "very warm" or positive evaluation.

The data for 2020 are reported in table 7.1. As the data in Part A of the table illustrate, there was a close balance in the electorate between those ranking Biden higher than Trump (52 percent of respondents) and those ranking Trump higher (42 percent).[7] The closeness of these overall ratings of the candidates to the actual vote choice is clear in Part B of the table. In particular, it depicts the powerful relationship between these assessments and the vote, in which almost everyone supported the candidate they rated higher—all but 4 percent of those who rated the Democrat higher and 5 percent of those who rated the Republican higher voted for that party's nominee. The relatively small percentage who tied the two candidates voted much closer to the mental coin flip that would imply—43 percent for Biden.

Overall, then, these summary evaluations are quite proximate to the vote in a two-candidate race. This finding is particularly strong in 2020, but the general pattern of more than nine in ten supporting their preferred candidates is commonplace. These preferences about the major-party candidates are, therefore, but a first, very close, step back from the vote to the discovery of underlying reasons that explain how people came to the choices they did.

That is to say that we are led to the next obvious question: Why did more people rate Biden or Trump more warmly? The ANES asked a series of questions about how people view the candidates as people and as potential presidents, four of which are reported in table 7.2A. These cover different aspects of attributes we might like a president to possess: providing strong

Table 7.1 Relative Ranking of Presidential Candidates on the Feeling Thermometer: Response Distribution and Vote Choice, 2020

	Rated Biden Higher Than Trump on Thermometer	Rated Biden Equal to Trump on Thermometer	Rated Trump Higher Than Biden on Thermometer	Total	(N)
A. Distribution of Responses					
Percent	52	6	42	100	(7,453)
B. Major-Party Voters Who Voted for Biden					
Percent	96	43	5	69	(5,121)
(N)	(4,103)	(404)	(2,945)		

Source: Authors' analysis of the 2020 ANES survey.
Note: The numbers in parentheses in Part B of the table are the totals on which the percentages are based. Only respondents who rated both candidates on the scale are included. All numbers are weighted.

Table 7.2A   Distribution of Responses on Presidential Candidate Trait Evaluations, 2020 (Percent)

	Extremely Well	Very Well	Moderately Well	Slightly Well	Not Well at All	Total	(N)
Biden							
Provides strong leadership	10	18	21	14	37	100	(7,427)
Really cares about people like you	15	18	20	17	30	100	(7,423)
Knowledgeable	12	21	22	18	27	100	(7,425)
Honest	12	18	21	17	32	100	(7,431)
Trump							
Provides strong leadership	19	15	11	10	45	100	(7,432)
Really cares about people like you	14	14	11	10	51	100	(7,434)
Knowledgeable	12	15	14	12	47	100	(7,430)
Honest	8	13	15	9	54	100	(7,433)

Source: Authors' analysis of the 2020 ANES.
Note: Numbers are weighted.

leadership, caring about people, and being knowledgeable, and honest. These evaluations tend to fluctuate across elections. In 2008, for example, Obama and McCain were both perceived quite positively on most (but not all) of these traits, whereas 2012 illustrated a case in which the electorate had mixed views about both nominees. The candidates were perceived more negatively on these traits in 2016. Of all four traits for Clinton and Trump, the only case of a net positive evaluation was for Clinton on being knowledgeable.[8] Trump garnered more of a mix of positive or negative trait evaluations in 2020, though Biden had a net positive evaluation on all four traits, scoring particularly high on really cares about people [like you] and on knowledgeable.

In table 7.2B we report the percentage of major-party voters with differing assessments of these traits who voted for Biden and Trump, respectively. For Biden, the relationship is quite like what one might expect. He won the support of nearly everyone who thought the trait described him extremely well and quite high majorities among those who responded "very well" and even "moderately well." Those who responded "slightly well" or "not at all well" did not support him highly at all (except on strong leadership). For evaluations of traits describing Trump, much the same is true for each of the four traits (strong leadership, really cares, knowledgeable, and honest). As a general rule, then, we find trait evaluations provide context and underpinning for

Table 7.2B Major-Party Vote for Biden and Trump by Presidential Candidate Trait Evaluations, 2020 (Percent)

	Extremely Well	*Very Well*	*Moderately Well*	*Slightly Well*	*Not Well at All*
Biden					
Provides strong leadership	99	98	84	52	7
(*N*)	(550)	(982)	(804)	(353)	(125)
Really cares about people like you	99	94	74	37	6
(*N*)	(858)	(900)	(647)	(304)	(102)
Knowledgeable	98	93	66	32	6
(*N*)	(690)	(1,087)	(674)	(275)	(87)
Honest	98	94	79	43	6
(*N*)	(655)	(942)	(749)	(363)	(104)
Trump					
Provides strong leadership	97	94	71	29	2
(*N*)	(1,018)	(750)	(340)	(135)	(56)
Really cares about people like you	98	98	83	52	4
(*N*)	(803)	(762)	(415)	(210)	(107)
Knowledgeable	98	96	79	45	3
(*N*)	(663)	(801)	(512)	(242)	(79)
Honest	98	96	94	75	6
(*N*)	(452)	(711)	(674)	(307)	(155)

Source: Authors' analysis of the 2020 ANES.
Note: The numbers in parentheses are the totals on which the percentages are based. The numbers are weighted.

understanding why some felt warmly toward one candidate or the other, and indeed, they show the public responded to the observations of the campaign in an at least somewhat bipartisan way. However, these remain only one more step removed from the vote than the candidate thermometer questions.

What might lie even further from the vote? Candidates and their supporters campaign on the assessments of the two candidates (decidedly not bipartisan with much negative campaigning!), but they also spend a great deal of time discussing a variety of issues. These are both prospective—what I or my opponent will do if elected—and retrospective—how Trump or the Republicans succeeded or failed in handling public policy in the last four years. These, we might expect, stand farther removed from the vote and thus help shape how these global or more specific assessments of the candidates came about. The rest of this chapter examines issues as they are discussed prospectively, leaving retrospective assessments for chapter 8.

PROSPECTIVE EVALUATIONS

Public policy concerns enter into the voting decision in two very different ways. In any election, two questions become important: How has the incumbent president and party done on policy? And how likely is it that his opponent (or opponents) would do any better? Voting based on this form of policy appraisal is called retrospective voting and will be analyzed in chapter 8.

The second form of policy-based voting involves examining the candidates' policy platforms and assessing which candidate's policy promises conform most closely to what the voter believes the government should be doing. Policy voting, therefore, involves comparing sets of promises and voting for the set that is most like the voter's own preferences. Voting based on these kinds of decisions is called prospective voting because it involves examining the promises of the candidates about future actions. In this chapter, we examine prospective evaluations of the two major-party candidates in 2020 and how these evaluations relate to voter choice.

The last eleven elections show some remarkable similarities in prospective evaluations and voting. Perhaps the most important similarity is the perception of where the Democratic and Republican candidates stood on issues. In these elections, the public saw clear differences between the major-party nominees. In all cases the public saw the Republican candidates as conservative on most issues, and most citizens scored the GOP candidates as more conservative than the voters themselves. And in all elections the public saw the Democratic candidates as liberal on most issues, and most citizens viewed the Democratic candidates as more liberal than the voters themselves. As a result, many voters perceived a clear choice based on their understanding of the candidates' policy positions. The candidates presented the voters with, as the 1964 Goldwater campaign slogan put it, "a choice, not an echo." The *average* citizen, however, faced a difficult choice. For many, Democratic nominees were considered to be as far to the left as the Republican nominees were to the right. In general, the net effect of prospective issues over recent elections has been to give neither party a decided, potentially long-term, advantage on policy.

One of the most important differences among these elections, however, was the mixture of issues that concerned the public. Each election presented its own mixture of policy concerns. We focus our discussion of the issues relevant in each election from 1992 to the present.[9] Moreover, the general strategies of the candidates on issues differed in each election. In the 1992 election, President George H. W. Bush used the success of the 1991 Persian Gulf War to bolster his claim that he was a successful world leader, but Bill Clinton attacked the Bush administration on domestic issues, barely discussing foreign affairs at all. He sought to keep the electorate focused on the current economic woes and argued for substantial reforms of the health care system, hoping to appeal to Democrats and to spur action should he be the first Democrat in the White House in twelve years. At the same time, he sought to portray himself not as another "tax and spend" liberal Democrat but as a moderate "New Democrat."

In 1996, Clinton ran a campaign typical of a popular incumbent; he focused on what led people to approve of his handling of the presidency and avoided mentioning many specific new programs. His policy proposals were a lengthy series of relatively inexpensive, limited programs. Bob Dole, having difficulties deciding whether to emphasize Clinton's personal failings in the first term or to call for different programs for the future, decided to put a significant tax-cut proposal at the center of his candidacy under either of those campaign strategies.

In 2000, the candidates debated a broad array of domestic issues—education, health care, social security, and taxes the most prominent among them—often couched in terms of a newfound "problem," federal government budget surpluses. Typically, these issues (except for taxes) have favored Democratic contenders, and Republicans often avoided detailed discussions of all except taxes on the grounds that doing so would make the issues more salient to voters and would highlight the Democratic advantages. George W. Bush, however, spoke out on education, in particular, as well as health care and social security to a lesser extent, believing he could undercut the traditional Democratic advantage. For his part, Al Gore had the advantage of his belief (backed by public opinion polls) that the public was less in favor of tax cuts than usual and more in favor of allocating budget surpluses to buttress popular domestic programs.

In 2004, in contrast, Bush and Kerry had less choice about what issues to consider. With wars under way in Iraq, in Afghanistan, and against terrorism, neither candidate could avoid foreign policy considerations. Bush preferred to emphasize that Iraq was part of the war on terrorism, whereas Kerry argued that it was not and indeed that it was a costly distraction from it. Similarly, 2004 opened with the economy slumping. The Democrats, including Kerry, attacked the Bush administration's policies, while Bush countered by saying that the economy was actually improving—in large part because of his successful policies. As the year wore on, the economy did in fact improve, although not so much as to remove all criticism.

The 2008 campaign began as one in which the Democrats tried to emphasize their opposition to Bush's policies in Iraq and their concern about the war in Afghanistan. On the domestic front, Obama emphasized health care reform, improved environmental policies, and other aspects of his agenda that called for "change." McCain, conversely, began with a spirited defense of the war in Iraq, and especially the "surge" in the war effort there. By fall, however, the economy had swept aside virtually every other issue but war from consideration and replaced war as topic number one. Indeed, so worrisome were the economic events of the fall that candidates could ill afford to do anything but relate any domestic issue to their plans for fighting the economic downturn.

In 2012, both the Obama and Romney camps anticipated a close contest. Romney's side wanted to make the campaign be about Obama and his successes or failures in office—retrospective voting concerns—on the grounds that the economy had not recovered sufficiently to justify returning Obama to office. This was made problematic first by Romney's statement that Obama's supporters were 47 percent of the electorate whom he characterized as people "who live off government handouts" and do not "care for their lives," and then by Hurricane Sandy and the appearance of successful performance by Obama, reinforced by a leading Republican figure, Gov. Chris Christie (NJ), saying that Obama was doing his job very well. Obama, for his part, approached issues rather more like Clinton did in 1996, offering a series of popular but relatively small domestic initiatives ("small ball" as it was called at times) and his emphasis on how the economy was not where everyone hoped but it was improving and would do so quicker with Democrats in office.

In 2016, Clinton's nomination campaign had many positions that reflected Obama and her service to his administration. In that sense, many were retrospective or at least made attacking her through attacking Obama and his policies fair game. On the domestic side, although she had her own ideas about how to improve by building on the Affordable Care Act, "Obamacare" was the base of her position. Essentially, the same was true on many aspects of domestic policy, though she deviated on free trade given pressures she faced against Sanders in the primary. And, her advocacy of free access to community and junior colleges marked new directions from the past. Thus, her platform was a mixture of retrospective and prospective issues. Trump relentlessly attacked policies from the Obama administration. And, of course, he also had signature issues that would represent prospective policies, "repeal and replace" Obamacare, build a wall to keep new immigrants from crossing the Mexican border, deporting all illegal (undocumented) immigrants, and barring entry for all Muslims. Therefore, he was providing very strong retrospective critiquing while advocating for prospective policies.

A mix of retrospective and prospective policies were also highlighted in the 2020 election. It was near impossible to ignore the global pandemic that shut down the country and led to the death of hundreds of thousands of Americans by the fall election. For his part, Trump cast his presidency as making great strides on the economy, especially before the pandemic. He highlighted the progress he made on campaign promises such as cutting taxes, starting to build a wall along the US-Mexico border, and he appointed three conservative justices to the Supreme Court—Neil Gorsuch, Brett Kavanaugh, and Amy Coney Barrett. He highlighted the successes of his administration in helping with the development of a vaccine and pushed for the country to open up again. However, the majority of the electorate did not buy Trump's claims of success in dealing with COVID-19, which provided fodder for Biden to attack Trump on his dismal handling of the pandemic. Biden promised a more robust federal response in combating the pandemic, to build up vaccine supply, testing capacity, and support to states hardest hit. While the main thrust of Biden's campaign was retrospective, he also presented more prospective policies, which his campaign coined "building back better." He presented the electorate with a vision for a large infrastructure plan, a plan to provide affordable childcare for families, to elevate the pay and benefits to educators and caregivers, and address systemic racism.

Most Important Issues in the Public

What did the public care about most? From 1972 to 2004, we were able to use ANES surveys to assess this question. In 2012 and 2016, we examined exit polls, conducted as voters were leaving the voting booth, and the various interested parties (news media, etc.) formed a pool to conduct that poll.[10] We did so again for 2020.

In the four elections from 1984 through 2000, the great majority of responses revolved around domestic issues rather than foreign policy, perhaps because of the end of the Cold War.[11] In those elections, and even the four before them (when foreign affairs were more important) prior to 2004, two major categories of domestic issues dominated. From 1976 to 1992, in good times and bad, by far the more commonly cited issue was the economy. Yet, in 1972, 1996, 2000, and then in 2004 as well, the most frequently cited problems were in the social-issues category, such as either social-welfare issues or concerns about public order. In 2004, for example, nearly half (49 percent) cited social issues, whereas 29 percent (the highest since 1984, that is, since the Cold War) cited foreign and defense issues. Mostly that was the war in Iraq in particular (18 percent). In 2008 (shifting to the pooled exit poll) 63 percent of voters said the economy was most important, with the war in Iraq selected by 10 percent and the war on terror by 9 percent. That high a percentage selecting the economy should come as no surprise as we were in the midst of the initial decline into the "Great Recession," the most severe since the Great Depression.

Table 7.3A reports the results of the exit poll for the 2012, 2016, and 2020 elections. Foreign policy in 2012 continued to drop in concern as US involvement in Iraq was over (at least temporarily) and the war in Afghanistan was

Table 7.3A Most Important Problem as Seen by the Electorate, 2012, 2016, and 2020 and Reported Vote for Biden and Trump in 2020 (Percent)

Problem	2012	2016	2020
The economy	59	52	35
Foreign policy	5	13	—
Terrorism	—	18	—
Immigration	—	13	—
Health care	18	—	11
Federal budget deficit	15	—	—
Coronavirus	—	—	20
Racial inequality	—	—	17
Crime and safety	—	—	11

Sources: 2012, 2016, and 2020 National Election Exit Polls. Question in 2012 asked 10,798 respondents about which of the four issues were the most important issue facing the country, 24,558 respondents in 2016, and 15,590 respondents in 2020. The two percentages do not sum to 100 percent, with the rest reporting that they voted for some other candidate or did not answer the question. For 2016: http://www.cnn.com/election/results/exit-polls, Accessed 6/15/2017. For 2012: https://ropercenter.cornell.edu/polls/us-elections/how-groups-voted/how-groups-voted-2012/. Accessed June 17, 2017. For 2020: https://www.cnn.com/election/2020/exit-polls/president/national-results

diminishing (at least temporarily). Only 5 percent selected foreign policy as most important. It was the economy that remained dominant, as 59 percent selected it as their chief concern, whereas 15 percent more said it was the deficit. The latter had been a key part of the Tea Party and Republican leadership concerns through 2010 and into 2012 (it is of course an issue that touches on the economy and on the role of the government and so is not purely about the economy nor about the government). Another large portion, 18 percent, said that health care was the most important problem, whereas selection of other options was rare.

In 2016 the economy remained the most important concern, dropping only slightly to 52 percent of voters, even though the economy had improved noticeably over the intervening four years. Foreign policy increased to 13 percent as both wars rekindled and as Trump critiqued our involvement in foreign trade and international relations generally. The two issues that, in effect, replaced health care and the budget deficit as concerns (those two dropping to low percentages in 2016) were terrorism (18 percent of the voting public) and immigration (13 percent); both appear to us to be made into popular concerns not only because of media coverage of these issues (for example given terrorist attacks during the invisible primary) but because of Trump highlighting them in his campaigning. These issues are sometimes referred to as "intermestic," that is, as having both international and domestic dimensions. Indeed, one part of the partisan debate over these issues is precisely whether the international or domestic aspects of these issues are predominant.

Table 7.3B   Percent reporting voted for

	2012		2016		2020	
	Obama	*Romney*	*Clinton*	*Trump*	*Biden*	*Trump*
The economy	47%	51%	52%	41%	17%	83%
Foreign policy	56%	33%	60%	33%	—	—
Terrorism	—	—	40%	57%	—	—
Immigration		33%	64%		—	—
Health care	75%	24%	—	—	62%	37%
Federal budget deficit	32%	66%	—	—	—	—
Coronavirus	—	—	—	—	81%	15%
Racial inequality	—	—	—	—	92%	7%
Crime and safety	—	—	—	—	27%	71%

In 2020, the economy was again an important concern, though much less so than in the prior two elections, with only 35 percent of the public mentioning it. And, economic concerns were closely linked to the global pandemic, as many businesses were forced to shutter as states went on lockdowns, resulting in high job losses for many Americans. Twenty percent of the public mentioned the coronavirus as their most important concern. It may be somewhat surprising that it was not higher with cases starting to rise again in the fall, but the public was also concerned with other issues that rose on the agenda in spring and summer of 2020, most notably issues of racial inequality, mentioned by 17 percent of the public, after the killing of George Floyd by police officers sparked protests throughout the nation. Health care was also cited as a concern by many, an issue linked in part to the coronavirus, and crime and safety rose as a concern, which was likely due to the way protests for racial justice were depicted in some media outlets on the right. Most notably these newer issues displaced foreign policy concerns and immigration.

Table 7.3B illustrates that people's concerns played a role in their voting. Those concerned about two of Trump's most regularly discussed issues in 2020, crime and security and the economy, were indeed considerably more likely to support him than to vote for Biden. Conversely, Biden had a clear advantage on health care, the coronavirus, and racial inequality generally.

ISSUE POSITIONS AND PERCEPTIONS

Since 1972, the ANES surveys have included issue scales designed to measure the preferences of the electorate and voters' perceptions of the positions the candidates took on the issues.[12] The questions are therefore especially appropriate for examining prospective issue evaluations. We hasten to add, however, that voters' perceptions of where the nominees stand may be based in part on what the president has done in office as well as on the campaign promises he or she made as the party's nominee. The policy promises of the opposition party candidate may also be judged in part by what that candidate's party did when it last held the White House, and this may be more likely for Joe Biden, since he served as vice president under Obama. Nevertheless, the issue scales generally focus on prospective evaluations and are very different from those used to make the retrospective judgments examined in chapter 8.

The issue scales will be used to examine several questions: What alternatives did the voters believe the candidates were offering? To what extent did the voters have issue preferences of their own and relatively clear perceptions of candidates' positions? Finally, how strongly were voters' preferences and perceptions related to their choice of candidates?

Figure 7.1 shows the seven-point issue scales used in the 2020 ANES survey. The figure presents the average (median) position of the respondents (labeled "S" for self) and the average (median) perceptions of the positions of Biden and Trump (labeled "B" and "T"). The issues raised in 2020 probe the respondents' own preferences and perceptions of the major-party nominees on whether government should spend more or less on social services; whether defense spending should be increased or decreased; whether health insurance should be provided by the government or by private insurance; whether the government should see to it that everyone has a job and a good standard of living or let citizens get ahead on their own; whether the government should provide aid to blacks or whether they should help themselves; and whether the government should protect the environment at the cost of jobs and a good standard of living. These issues were selected for inclusion in the ANES survey because they are controversial and generally measure long-standing partisan divisions. As a result, the average citizen comes out looking reasonably moderate on these issues. In every case, the average citizen falls between the positions corresponding to the average placements of the two candidates.

Note that, on all six of the scales, the average citizen is at least very slightly to the liberal end of the scale. Because we use the median as our measure of "average," that means that more than half of the respondents were at least slightly liberal and may have been very liberal on those six issues. That is actually a slight change from 2012 to 2016 (in which all six of these issue scales were also included).[13] In both of those years, the average citizen was to the left on five of six of these issue scales, with the exception of aid to blacks in 2012 and defense spending in 2016, where they were slightly to the right. Still, in most cases, the average citizen was only slightly left of center and better seen as moderate than even moderately liberal. The exception was the jobs and environment issue, on which the average citizen was clearly to the left of center, as they have been on this issue in most elections, and the public moved a bit further to the left on government services/spending.

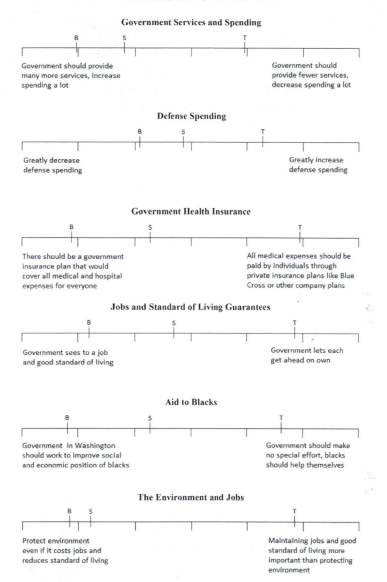

Figure 7.1   Median Self-Placement of the Electorate and the Electorate's Placement of Candidates on Issue Scales, 2020. *Source*: Author's analysis of the 2020 ANES. Note: S = median self-placement of the respondents; T = median placement of Trump; B = median placement of Biden. *Reversed from actual scoring to make a "liberal" response closer to point 1 and a "conservative" response closer to point 7.

Generally, on issue scales used between 1980 and 2020, the public has viewed the Democratic candidate as more liberal and the Republican candidate as more conservative than the average member of the public.[14] Indeed these differences are often quite large, including in 2020. Except for defense spending and government services/spending, they exceed three points (with a maximum difference of six points) on every issue scale.[15]

Perceptions of Biden generally were very similar to those of Clinton four years earlier, and Obama four years before that. The rather ironic exception is aid to blacks, where respondents saw Biden just slightly to the left of where they had placed Clinton, who they had placed just slightly to the left of where they had placed Obama. Trump, in both 2016 and 2020, was generally seen as more conservative than Romney had been seen in 2012, although often this difference was small (and on government services and spending, he was seen as very slightly more moderate). The largest difference was his more conservative stances on defense spending, the environment, and aid to blacks. Overall, the public saw quite large differences between the offerings of the two candidates. No matter how much or how little the public may have been polarized in 2020, it saw that alleged polarization dividing the two candidates, even more so than in preceding elections.

Although voters saw clear differences between the candidates, the average voter faced a difficult choice. Biden was seen to the left of the average respondent, and Trump was seen to the right on every issue, though the average voter was much closer to Biden than Trump on all six issues. Of course, we cannot at this point go much further on these overall figures. The choice is made not by a mythical average voter choosing over what the respondents as a whole thought the candidates offered, but it is made by individual voters considering what they think about these issues. To consider a voter's choices, then we must look inside these averages to assess the individual behavior that makes up those averages.

ISSUE VOTING CRITERIA

The Problem

Because voting is an individual action, we must look at the preferences of individuals to see whether prospective issues influenced their votes. In fact, the question of prospective voting is controversial. In their classic study of the American electorate, *The American Voter*, Angus Campbell and his colleagues pointed out that the public is often ill-informed about public policy and may not be able to vote on the basis of issues.[16] They asked themselves what information voters would need before an issue could influence the decision on how to vote, and they answered by posing three conditions. First, the voters must hold an opinion on the issue; second, they must learn what the government is doing on the issue; and third, they must perceive a difference between the policies of the two major parties. According to the authors' analysis, only about one-quarter to one-third of the electorate in 1956 could meet these three conditions, and they therefore concluded that relatively few were likely to vote on the basis of issues.

Although it is impossible to replicate the analysis in *The American Voter*, we can adapt the authors' procedures to the 2020 electorate. ANES data, in fact, focus even more directly on the actual choice citizens must make—the choice among the candidates. The first criterion is whether respondents claim to have an opinion on the issue. This is measured by whether they placed themselves on the issue scale as measured by Campbell et al. Second, the respondents should have some perception of the positions taken by the candidates on an issue. This is measured by whether they could place both major-party candidates on that issue. Although some voters might perceive the position of one candidate and vote on that basis, prospective voting involves a comparison between or among alternatives, so the expressed ability to perceive the stands of the contenders seems a minimal requirement of prospective issue voting. Third, the voter must see a difference between the positions of the candidates. Failing to see a difference means that the voter perceived no choice on the issue, perhaps because he or she failed to detect actual distinctions between the candidates. This failure might arise from lack of attention to the issue in the campaign. It also may arise from instances in which the candidates actually did take very similar positions on the issue, and respondents were thus, on average, reflecting that similarity, as we believe was truer of the candidates on most issues in 1976 than in other campaigns. Actual similarity of positions is rare in this era of partisan polarization, although this happens at times on specific issues. Biden and Trump, for example, both supported the development of vaccines to combat the coronavirus.

A voter might be able to satisfy these criteria but misperceive the offerings of the candidates. This leads to a fourth condition, which we are able to measure more systematically than was possible in 1956: Do the respondents accurately perceive the relative positions of the two major-party candidates—that is, do they see Trump as more conservative than Biden? This criterion does not demand that the voter have an accurate perception of what the candidate proposes, but it does expect the voter to recognize that Biden, for example, favored spending more on social services than did Trump.

In table 7.4, we report the percentages of the sample that met the four criteria on the six issue scales used in 2020.[17] We also show the average proportion that met these criteria for all scales and compare those averages

Table 7.4   Four Criteria for Issue Voting, 2020, and Comparisons with 1972–2016 Presidential Elections

	Percentage of Sample Who . . .			
Issue Scale	*I* *Placed* *Self on* *Scale*	*II* *Placed Both* *Candidates on* *Scale*[a]	*III* *Saw Differences* *between Biden* *and Trump*	*IV* *Saw Biden as* *More "liberal"* *Than Trump*
Government spending/ services	83	83	73	64
Defense spending	84	83	72	61
Government health insurance	86	86	77	71
Jobs and standard of living	87	86	76	70
Aid to blacks	88	87	76	70
Jobs and the environment	83	82	72	67
Average[b]				
2020	85	85	74	67
2016 (6)	84	83	73	71
2012 (6)	86	76	67	60
2008 (7)	88	78	61	51
2004 (7)	89	76	62	52
2000 (7)	87	69	51	41
1996 (9)	89	80	65	55
1992 (3)	85	71	66	52
1988 (7)	86	66	52	43
1984 (7)	84	73	62	53
1980 (9)	82	61	51	43
1976 (9)	84	58	39	26
1972 (8)	90	65	49	41

Source: Authors' analysis of ANES surveys.
Note: Columns II, III, and IV compare the Democratic and Republican nominees. Third-party or independent candidates John Anderson (1980), Ross Perot (1992 and 1996), and Ralph Nader (2000 and 2004) were excluded.
[a]Until 1996, respondents who could not place themselves on a scale were not asked to place the candidates on that issue scale. Although they were asked to do so in 1996, 2000, 2004, 2008, 2012, 2016, and 2020, we excluded them from further calculations to maintain comparability with prior surveys.
[b]Number in parentheses is the number of issue scales included in the average for each election year survey.

to comparable averages for all issue scales used in the twelve preceding elections.[18] Column I of table 7.4 reveals that most people felt capable of placing themselves on the issue scales, and this capability was common to all election years.[19]

Nearly as many of the public also placed both candidates on the scales. Indeed a higher percentage satisfied these two criteria in 2020 than any other election. The environmental/jobs issue yielded the lowest percentage satisfying these criteria in 2020, but even that scale yielded a higher percentage, at 82, than the average in any other year except for 2016 (after this, the highest was in 1996 with an average of 80 percent). The 85 percent average for 2020 in Column II is the highest of any election for which we have relevant data.

Although there is a decline in the percentage also seeing differences between the two candidates on these issues, the main point is that 2020 is a high watermark in this regard. Indeed considering this third criterion makes 2020 stand out even more clearly. In 2020 over three in four, on average, satisfied the first three criteria: they placed both themselves and both candidates on the issue scale, and they placed the candidates at two different positions on the scale.

Finally, a very high percentage met all four issue voting criteria, with more than two in three doing so on average. As the reader can see, the average meeting all four criteria in 2020 was higher than the average meeting the first three criteria in any other election year save 2016. And compare 2020 with 1976. In the earlier election only one in four met these criteria on average. In that year relatively few could see differences between Gerald Ford and Jimmy Carter on issues and therefore could hardly have also gotten them in the correct order! But now, the idea of polarization seems to have fully settled into the presidential electorate. That is to say they saw the candidates as taking consistently and starkly different positions on just about every major issue (or at least every one of these six), and there was very little disagreement about that point in the electorate. They saw the Republican and the Democratic Party nominees as polarized, more so than ever before over the last thirteen elections. Although it could be that Biden and Trump were uniquely ideological candidates, we believe it more likely that the sustained polarization between the two party elites is becoming clearer to the public.

The data in table 7.4 suggest that the potential for prospective issue voting was high in 2020. Therefore, we might expect these issues to be rather closely related to voter choice. We will examine voter choice on these issues in two ways. First, how often did people vote for the closer candidate on each issue? Second, how strongly related to the vote is the set of all issues taken together?

APPARENT ISSUE VOTING IN 2020

Issue Criteria and Voting on Each Issue

The first question is to what extent did people who were closer to a candidate on a given issue actually vote for that candidate—that is, how strong is apparent issue voting?[20] In table 7.5 we report the proportion of major-party voters who voted for Biden by where they placed themselves on the issue scales. We divided the seven points into the set of positions that were closer to where the average citizen placed Trump and Biden (see figure 7.1).[21] Note that whereas the average perceptions of the two candidates did vary from issue to issue, the net effect of that variation did not make a great deal of difference. In particular, on all issues, respondents who placed themselves to the left of the midpoint, that is, on points 1, 2, or 3, were closer to where the electorate as a whole thought Biden stood. Similarly, those to the right of the midpoint were always closer to the perception of Trump. On four issues, those who placed themselves at point 4, the midpoint, were closer to where the electorate thought Trump stood, on defense spending "4s" were closer to Biden's position, and on the jobs and standard-of-living scales, those at 4 were essentially equidistant from both candidates. We see this as support for the idea that the two parties and their candidates and officeholders have achieved a balanced polarization with consistent deviation for the policy center toward their party's extreme (liberal for Democrats, conservative for Republicans), on issue after issue, and that by 2020, the public sees clearly even the presidential candidates being consistent with their party's positions.

Table 7.5 reveals the clear relationship between the voters' issue positions and the candidate they supported on the six scales. Those who adopted positions at the "liberal" end of each scale were very likely to vote for Biden. If we define liberal as adopting position 1 or 2, Biden received at least 80 percent of the vote and usually more on each scale. Indeed that was even true for those at point 3 (though support sometimes was just below 80 percent). Biden received one in four votes or fewer on any issue scale from those at the two most conservative positions, whereas Trump carried a clear majority of the vote from those at point 5 on any of the scales. Those at the midpoint of 4 on any issue except the environment and government services gave Biden a majority of support, and those in this in-between position often were a plurality on that issue. The major exception was the jobs and the environment scale, in which the distribution was shifted much farther to the left than on any of the other issues. Although the midpoint was still a common position, many more were to the left than in the middle. Those at the middle position gave a two-to-one majority to Trump on this one issue. Otherwise the midpoint marked a clear transition with large majorities voting for Biden when they were to the left, and large majorities voting for Trump on the right, and the 4 position being clearly in between. Regardless of the details, these are the patterns we would expect if voters voted for the closer candidate on an issue.

The information on issues can be summarized, as it is in table 7.6, to illustrate what happens when voters met the various conditions for issue voting. In the first column of table 7.6, we report the percentage of major-party voters who placed themselves closer to the average perception of Trump or Biden and who voted for the closer candidate. To be more specific, the denominator

Table 7.5 **Major-Party Voters Who Voted for Biden, by Seven-Point Issue Scales, 2020 (Percent)**

Issue Scale	Closer to Median Perception of Biden			Closer to Median Perception of Trump				(N)
	1	2	3	4	5	6	7	
Government spending/ services[a]	84	88	75	48	23	10	5	(2,453)
(N)	(698)	(530)	(573)	(470)	(127)	(37)	(17)	
Defense spending	91	87	81	60	41	23	25	(2,404)
(N)	(406)	(309)	(407)	(631)	(340)	(167)	(142)	
Government health insurance	89	90	78	54	37	19	9	(2,526)
(N)	(906)	(461)	(383)	(417)	(197)	(87)	(77)	
Jobs and standard of living	85	91	85	68	45	22	10	(2,504)
(N)	(464)	(410)	(534)	(572)	(296)	(145)	(83)	
Aid to blacks	92	92	76	54	31	19	8	(2,603)
(N)	(862)	(492)	(465)	(495)	(143)	(86)	(60)	
Jobs and the environment	89	80	64	32	20	11	5	(2,506)
(N)	(1,299)	(534)	(322)	(210)	(83)	(38)	(20)	

Source: Authors' analysis of the 2020 ANES.
Note: Numbers in parentheses are the totals on which percentages are based. Numbers are weighted.
[a]Reversed from actual scoring to make a "liberal" response closer to 1 and a "conservative" response closer to 7.

is the total number of major-party voters who placed themselves closer to the electorate's perception of Trump or Biden. The numerator is the total number of major-party voters who were both closer to Biden and voted for him plus the total number of major-party voters who were both closer to Trump and voted for him.

If voting were unrelated to issue positions, we would expect 50 percent of voters to vote for the closer candidate on average. In 2020, on average, 77 percent voted for the closer candidate. As can be seen in the comparisons to earlier elections, this is by far the highest level of apparent issue voting since these issue scales were widely used, that is, from 1972 to date. These figures do not tell the whole story, however, because those who placed themselves on an issue but failed to meet some other criterion were unlikely to have cast a vote based on that issue. In the second column of table 7.6, we report the percentage of those who voted for the closer candidate on each issue among voters who met all four conditions on that issue. The third column reports the percentage that voted for the closer candidate among voters who placed themselves but failed to meet all three of the remaining conditions.

Table 7.6   Apparent Issue Voting, 2020, and Comparisons with 1972–2016 Presidential Elections (Percent)

Issue Scale	Percentage of Voters Who Voted for Closer Candidate and . . .		
	Placed Self on Issue Scale	Met All Four Issue Voting Criteria	Placed Self but Failed to Meet All Three Other Criteria
Government spending/services	77	81	79
Defense spending	72	80	38
Government health insurance	79	83	53
Jobs and standard of living	78	83	70
Aid to blacks	79	84	32
Jobs and the environment	76	82	55
Average[a]			
2020 (6)	77	82	55
2016 (6)	75	81	66
2012 (6)	63	68	58
2008 (7)	62	71	47
2004 (7)	67	75	51
2000 (7)	60	68	40
1996 (9)	63	74	41
1992 (3)	62	70	48
1988 (7)	62	71	45
1984 (7)	65	73	46
1980 (9)	63	71	48
1976 (9)	57	70	50
1972 (8)	66	76	55

Source: Authors' analysis of ANES surveys.
Note: An "apparent issue vote" is a vote for the candidate closer to one's position on an issue scale. The closer candidate is determined by comparing self-placement to the median placements of the two candidates on the scale as a whole. Respondents who did not place themselves or who were equidistant from the two candidates are excluded from the calculations.
In 2008, analyses conducted on the randomly selected half-sample asked questions with the traditional wording, except aid to blacks, which was asked of the full sample with same (traditional) wording.
[a]Number in parentheses is the number of seven-point issue scales included in the average for each election year survey.

As we would expect, respondents who met all four conditions were more likely to vote for the closer candidate on any issue. Indeed until 2016 there has been relatively little difference, on average, across all elections, with about seven in ten such voters supporting the closer candidate. But in 2016 and 2020 the percentage jumped to greater than eight in ten, higher even than the erstwhile most ideologically charged election in 1972. In contrast, for those respondents who failed to meet the last three of the conditions of issue voting, voting was essentially random with respect to the issues, at 55 percent.

The strong similarity of all election averages in the second and third columns suggests that issue voting seems more prevalent in some elections than others because elections differ in the number of people who clearly perceive differences between the candidates. In all elections, about seven in ten who satisfied all four conditions voted consistently with their issue preferences; in all elections, those who did not satisfy all the conditions on perceptions of candidates voted essentially randomly with respect to individual issues. As we saw earlier, the degree to which such perceptions vary from election to election depends more on the strategies of the candidates than on the qualities of the voters. Therefore, the relatively low percentage of apparent issue voting in 1976, for example, results from the perception of small differences between the two rather moderate candidates. The larger magnitude of apparent issue voting in recent elections stems primarily from the greater clarity with which most people saw the positions of the two nominees. Surely, this is a consequence of the polarization of the two parties among candidates and office holders.

The Balance-of-Issues Measure

In prospective issue voting, voters compare the full set of policy proposals made by the candidates. Because nearly every issue is strongly related to the vote, we might expect the set of all issues to be even more strongly so. To examine this relationship we constructed an overall assessment of the issue scales to arrive at what we call the balance-of-issues measure. We give individuals a score of +1 if their positions on an issue scale were closer to the average perception of Trump, a score of −1 if their positions were closer to the average perception of Biden, and a score of 0 if they had no preference on an issue or put themselves on point 4 on the two issues in which that was essentially equidistant from the two candidates' positions. The scores for all six issue scales were added together, creating a measure that ranged from −6 to +6. For example, respondents who were closer to the average perception of Biden's positions on all six scales received a score of −6. A negative score indicated that the respondent was, on balance, closer to the public's perception of Biden, whereas a positive score indicated the respondent was, overall, closer to the public's perception of Trump. We collapsed this thirteen-point measure into seven categories, running from strongly Democratic through neutral to strongly Republican. We have used this scale since 1980 (see Abramson et al., 2016, and sources cited therein). The results are reported in table 7.7.

As can be seen in table 7.7A, 39 percent of respondents were in the two most strongly Democratic positions, whereas 18 percent were strongly or moderately Republican. Approximately equal proportions were in the three middle categories, totaling together just over half the electorate. Thus the balance-of-issues measure tilted slightly in the Democratic direction, but

Table 7.7   Distribution of Electorate on Net Balance-of-Issues Measure and Major-Party Vote, 2020 (Percent)

	Net Balance of Issues								
	Strongly Democratic	*Moderately Democratic*	*Slightly Democratic*	*Neutral*	*Slightly Republican*	*Moderately Republican*	*Strongly Republican*	*Total*	*(N)*
	A. Distribution of responses								
	20	19	18	12	12	11	7	100	(7,453)
	B. Major-party voters who voted for Biden								
Percent	97	85	66	42	21	10	1	69	(5,120)
(N)	(1,082)	(796)	(512)	(226)	(133)	(65)	(5)		

Source: Authors' analysis of the 2020 ANES.
Note: Numbers are weighted. The numbers in parentheses in Part B of the table are the totals on which the percentages are based.

was much more evenly balanced than the more heavily pro-Republican tilt in 2012, and slight Republican tilt in 2016.

The balance-of-issues measure was quite strongly related to the vote, as the findings for the individual issues would suggest (see table 7.7B). Biden won the vast majority of the votes from those in the strongly, moderately, and even the slightly Democratic categories. He won a bit under half of the votes from those in the neutral category. His support dropped off dramatically from that point. Indeed, this relationship between the net balance-of-issues measure and the vote is stronger in 2020 than we have ever found before.

The Abortion Issue

Clearly abortion was not the major issue in the 2020 election that it has been in some earlier ones. One special role that it played in the last few election cycles relates to which party gets to fill open seats on the Supreme Court, which can have implications for the position the Court will likely take on this issue in the future. This issue was particularly salient in 2020 as Justice Ruth Bader Ginsberg passed away on September 18, 2020, and there was a swift effort to nominate a new justice, Amy Coney Barrett, a conservative Federal Appeals Court judge, who was confirmed in late October 2020.[22] The next justice likely to retire would be Progressive Stephen Breyer.[23] And, of course, policy about abortions plays a large role in partisan polarization. The Republican national platform has taken a strong pro-life stand since 1980, whereas the Democratic Party became increasingly strongly pro-choice. In addition it is one of a complex set of issues that define much of the social-issues dimension, one of two major dimensions of domestic policy (economics being the second) into which most domestic policies—and most controversial issues—fall. Abortion has been central to the rise of social conservatism in America, virtually back to its modern emergence in the wake of the Supreme Court decision, *Roe v. Wade* (1973), which made abortion legal throughout the United States.

The second reason for examining this issue is that it is another policy question about which respondents were asked their own views as well as what they thought Trump's and Biden's positions were—a battery that has been asked for the last several elections.[24] It differs from (and is therefore hard to compare directly with) the seven-point issue scales, however, because respondents were given only four alternatives, but each was a specified policy option:

1. By law, abortion should never be permitted.
2. The law should permit abortion only in case of rape, incest, or when the woman's life is in danger.
3. The law should permit abortion for reasons *other than* rape, incest, or danger to the woman's life but only after the need for the abortion has been clearly established.
4. By law, a woman should always be able to obtain an abortion as a matter of personal choice.

Table 7.8 reports percentages voting for Biden for various groups of respondents. For example, about 81 percent of voters who believe that abortion should be a matter of personal choice voted for him, whereas about 17 percent who thought it should never be permitted did so. Substantial numbers of voters met all four conditions on this issue and, for them, their position was even more strongly related to the vote, as 89 percent who thought abortion should be a matter of personal choice voted for Biden, but only 9 percent who thought it should not be permitted did so. For those who did not meet all conditions for casting an issue-based vote, their voting was essentially the random coin flip one would expect. Thus the abortion issue adds to our previous findings.

PARTISANSHIP AND PROSPECTIVE EVALUATIONS

Up until this point, we have treated issues stances and partisanship as separate factors. However, as noted in the last chapter, partisanship does not just have direct effects on voting, but indirect effects through other, more proximate, factors. In their study of voting in the 1948 election, Bernard R. Berelson, Paul F. Lazarsfeld, and William N. McPhee discovered that Democratic voters attributed to their nominee, incumbent Harry S. Truman, positions on key issues that were consistent with their beliefs—whether those beliefs were liberal, moderate, or conservative.[25] Similarly Republicans tended to see their nominee, Gov. Thomas E. Dewey of New York, as taking whatever positions they preferred. These tendencies toward "projection" (projecting one's own

Table 7.8   Percentage of Major-Party Voters Who Voted for Biden, by Opinion about Abortion and What They Believe Trump's and Biden's Positions Are, 2020

	Respondent's Position on Abortion						
	Abortion should never be permitted		*Abortion should be permitted only in the case of rape, incest, or danger to health of the woman*		*Abortion should be permitted for other reasons, but only if a need is established*		*Abortion should be a matter of personal choice*	
	%	(N)	%	(N)	%	(N)	%	(N)
All major-party voters	17	(95)	28	(361)	45	(287)	81	(1,994)
Major-party voters who placed both candidates, who saw a difference between them, and who saw Biden as more pro-choice than Trump	9	(41)	21	(226)	44	(222)	89	(1,751)
Major-party voters who did not meet all three of these conditions	61	(54)	57	(135)	50	(65)	49	(243)

Source: Authors' analysis of the 2020 ANES.
Note: Numbers in parentheses are the totals on which the percentages are based. Numbers are weighted.

preferences onto what one thinks the favored candidate prefers) are discomforting for those who hope that in a democracy, issue preferences shape candidate assessment and voting choices rather than the other way around. These authors did find, however, that the more the voters knew, the less likely they were to project their preferences onto the candidates. Research since then has emphasized the role of party identification not only in projection but also in shaping the policy preferences of the public in the first place.[26]

We examine the impact of partisanship on attitudes and beliefs via its relationship to positions on policy issues. In table 7.9 and table A.7.9, we report this relationship among the six partisan categories and our balance-of-issues measure, collapsed into three groupings: pro-Republican, neutral, pro-Democratic.[27] As table 7.9 and A.7.9 show for 1976–2020, there has been a steady, clear, moderately strong relationship between partisanship and the balance-of-issues measure, and it is one that, by 2000, had strengthened considerably

Table 7.9   Balance-of-Issues Positions among Partisan Groups, 2020 (Percent)

				Party Identification				
Year	Issue Positions Closer to . . .	Strong Democrat	Weak Democrat	Independent, Leans Democrat	Independent	Independent, Leans Republican	Weak Republican	Strong Republican	Total %
2020	Democratic candidate	81	68	80	44	19	17	9	47
	Neutral	7	15	10	17	10	14	8	11
	Republican candidate	12	17	9	39	71	69	83	43
	Total	100	100	99	100	100	100	100	100
	(N)	(1,616)	(829)	(833)	(953)	(757)	(782)	(1,489)	(7,258)

Source: Authors' analysis of ANES surveys.
Note: The Democratic category on the condensed balance-of-issues measures includes any respondent who is at least slightly Democratic; the Republican category includes any respondent who is at least slightly Republican. The neutral category is the same as the neutral category on the seven-point issue scale (see table 7.5). Numbers are weighted.

and continued to strengthen into 2008, with only modest weakening in 2012. In 2020, while "leaners" were more like strong than weak partisans, the relationship otherwise continued to strengthen. Until 1984 the relationship had been stronger among Republicans than among Democrats.

Prospective issues appear to be increasingly polarized by party, strikingly so by 2000. The data for the 2000 through 2020 elections are quite similar in that there is a strong relationship between party identification and the balance-of-issues measure. In 2020 more than eight in ten strong Democrats were closer to Biden's position than to Trump's; likewise, eight out of ten strong Republicans were closer to where the electorate placed Trump. Thus the degree of polarization on this measure continues to be quite strong in recent elections.

Partisan polarization characterizes not only prospective issues but also most other factors we have examined. In our balance-of-issues measure, "polarization" really means "consistency"—that is, partisans find their party's candidate closer to them than the opposing party's nominee on more and more issues. On these measures, then, what we observe as growing polarization stems from the increased differentiation and consistency of positions of the candidates and not as much from changes in the issue positions among the public. This is often called "sorting"—that is, sorting Democrats into the Democratic camp and Republican identifiers into their partisan camp.[28] It might also indicate partisan polarization—the two parties becoming more distant from each other—but we do not directly measure that.

CONCLUSION

Our findings suggest that for major-party voters, prospective issues were important in the 2020 election. In fact, 2020 stands out as one in which prospective issues played about as strong a role in shaping their vote as any other. Prospective issues are particularly important for understanding how citizens voted. Those for whom prospective issues gave a clear choice, however, voted consistently with those issues. But most people were located between the candidates as the electorate saw them. Indeed on most issues the majority of people were relatively moderate, and the candidates were perceived as more conservative and more liberal, respectively. Moreover, when the conditions for issue voting are present, there can be a strong relationship between the position voters hold and their choice between the major-party candidates. And, it appears, that perhaps due to the lengthening period for which the two parties have polarized on the most important policies facing the electorate, a remarkably high proportion of the electorate met the conditions for casting an issue-based vote on many of the issues considered here. Furthermore, strong partisans were more likely to see themselves as closer to their own party's candidate, which is also a reflection of the increased polarization of the parties. For these reasons we conclude that voters took prospective issues into account in 2020, but it is also our conclusion that they also considered other factors. In the next chapter, we will see that the second form of policy voting, that based on retrospective evaluations, was among those other factors, as it has been in previous presidential elections.

Chapter 8

Presidential Performance and Candidate Choice

In most national elections, the candidates focus more on the economy than any other issue, and with good reason. As former British Prime Minister Harold Wilson once observed, "All political history shows that the standing of a Government and its ability to hold the confidence of the electorate at a General Election depend on the success of its economic policy."[1] In the 2020 presidential election, both candidates asked voters to cast their ballots on economic performance during Trump's first term in office. Trump began the year hoping to make a booming stock market and low unemployment a centerpiece of his reelection campaign. Indeed, the public seemed to give the president high marks on the economy. Although Trump's overall approval ratings in the Gallup Poll never exceeded 50 percent at any point during his first term, in January 2020 roughly 63 percent of Americans said they approved of his handling of the economy.[2] For Trump, the state of the economy appeared to be his winning card, but it was a card he would not be able to play. The onset of the pandemic during the months that followed caused an economic collapse of record proportions, creating "a demand shock, a supply shock, and a financial shock all at once."[3] As Americans took shelter, consumer spending plunged, businesses—small and large—closed their doors, and unemployment rose from 3.5 to 14.7 percent as an estimated 22 million Americans lost their jobs.[4] The Trump campaign continued to highlight the president's economic record prior to the pandemic and argued that reelecting the president was the best way to guarantee a strong economic recovery. However, the Biden campaign claimed that the administration was ineffective in containing the COVID outbreak and that blame for the resulting economic collapse and its lingering effects could be laid squarely on Trump.[5]

This was hardly the first election in which candidates thought carefully about how they would present themselves with respect to the successes or failures of the incumbent president and his party. To the extent that voters were considering the successes and failures of the Trump presidency, perhaps in comparison to what they thought Biden and his party would have done had they been in office, voters were casting a retrospective vote.

Retrospective evaluations are inherent concerns about policy, but they differ significantly from the prospective evaluations considered in the last chapter.[6] Retrospective evaluations are, as the name suggests, concerns about the past. These evaluations focus on outcomes, with what actually happened, rather than on the policy means for achieving those outcomes, which are at the heart of prospective evaluations. For example, consider how each of the campaigns discussed the issue of climate change during the 2020 election.[7] To combat climate change, Biden put forth a $2 trillion clean energy plan with the goal of reaching net-zero carbon emissions by 2050. Biden's plan invested in wind and solar power, detailed plans to limit auto emission, and invested in infrastructure to make homes and buildings more energy efficient. By its very nature, Biden's approach was future-oriented, asking voters to think prospectively about whether these proposed policy means are likely to be effective. Trump, on the other hand, touted his administration's support for natural gas production and the country's increasing levels of clean air. He charged that previous Democratic efforts resulted in a bloated bureaucracy and over-reaching government, and he blamed California's Democratic-led state government for ineffective policies such as the state's escalating problems with wildfires.[8] Such arguments focused on policy outcomes, which are the basis of retrospective judgments. This scenario illustrates the difference between prospective and retrospective judgments but also suggests that the two are often different sides of the same policy coin, which is indeed the basic point of the Downs-Fiorina perspective.

WHAT IS RETROSPECTIVE VOTING?

A voter who casts a ballot for the incumbent party's candidate because the incumbent was, in the voter's opinion, a successful president or votes for the opposition because, in the voter's opinion, the incumbent was unsuccessful is said to have cast a retrospective vote. In other words, retrospective voting decisions are based on evaluations of the course of politics over the last term in office and on evaluations of how much the incumbent should be held responsible for what good or bad outcomes occurred. V. O. Key, Jr., popularized this argument by suggesting that the voter might be "a rational god of vengeance and of reward."[9]

The more closely a candidate can be tied to the actions of the incumbent, the more likely it is that voters will decide retrospectively.[10] The incumbent president cannot escape such evaluations, and the incumbent vice president is usually identified with (and often chooses to identify him- or herself with) the administration's performance. The electorate has frequently played the role of Key's "rational god" because an incumbent president or vice president has stood for election in twenty-six of the thirty-two presidential elections since 1900 (all but 1908, 1920, 1928, 1952, 2008, and 2016).

Key's thesis has three aspects. First, retrospective voters are oriented toward outcomes rather than the policy means to achieve them. Second, these voters evaluate the performance of the incumbent only, all but ignoring the opposition. Finally, they evaluate what has been done, paying little attention to what the candidates promise to do in the future. Does this kind of voting make sense? Some suggest an alternative, as we discuss next, but note that if everyone did, in fact, vote against an incumbent whose performance they thought insufficient, then incumbents would have very strong incentives to provide such sufficiently high levels of performance to avoid the wrath of the electorate.

Anthony Downs was the first to develop in some detail an alternative version of retrospective voting.[11] His account is one about information and its credibility to the voter. He argues that voters look to the past to understand what the incumbent party's candidate will do in the future. According to Downs, parties are basically consistent in their goals, methods, and ideologies over time. Therefore, the past performances of both parties and perhaps their nominees may prove relevant for making predictions about their future conduct. Because it takes time and effort to evaluate campaign promises and because promises are just words, voters find it faster, easier, and safer to use past performance to project the administration's actions for the next four years. Downs also emphasizes that retrospective evaluations are used in making comparisons among the alternatives presented to the voter. Key sees a retrospective referendum on the incumbent's party alone. Downs believes that retrospective evaluations are used to compare the candidates as well as to provide a guide to the future. Even incumbents may use such Downsian retrospective claims. In 1996, for example, Clinton attempted to tie his opponent, Senator Bob Dole, to the performance of congressional Republicans because they had assumed the majority in the 1994 election. Clinton pointedly referred to the 104th Congress as the "Dole-Gingrich" Congress. Twenty years later a different Clinton was trying to tie evaluations of her expected performance to those of the Obama administration in which she had served.

Morris P. Fiorina elaborates on and extends Downs's thesis.[12] Here we focus especially on Fiorina's understanding of party identification (as discussed previously in chapter 6), which was a completely new addition to the Downsian perspective. Fiorina claimed that party identification plays a central role in this perspective on retrospective voting, but his conception of party identification differs from that of Campbell et al., however.[13] Fiorina argued

that "citizens monitor party promises and performances over time, encapsu-
late their observations in a summary judgment termed 'party identification,'
and rely on this core of previous experience when they assign responsibility
for current societal conditions and evaluate ambiguous platforms designed to
deal with uncertain futures."[14]

Retrospective voting and voting according to issue positions, as analyzed in
chapter 7, differ significantly. The difference lies in how concerned people are
with societal outcomes and how concerned they are with the policy means to
achieve desired outcomes. For example, everyone prefers economic prosperity.
The disagreement among political decision-makers lies in how best to achieve
it. At the voters' level, however, the central question is whether people care
only about achieving prosperity or whether they care about, or even are able to
judge, how to achieve this desired goal. Perhaps they looked at high inflation
and interest rates in 1980 and said, "We tried Carter's approach, and it failed.
Let's try something else—anything else." They may have noted the long run of
relative economic prosperity from 1983 to 1988 and said, "Whatever Reagan
did, it worked. Let's keep it going by putting his vice president in office." In
1996 they may have agreed with Clinton that he had presided over a successful economy, and so they decided to remain with the incumbent. In 2020, just
how these concerns would play out was uncertain. Would the public judge the
economy as improving sufficiently, or was its improvement too little, too late?

Economic policy, along with foreign and defense policies, are especially
likely to be discussed in these terms because they share several characteristics.
First, the outcomes are clearer than in many policy areas, and most voters can
judge whether they approve of the results. Inflation and unemployment are
high or low; the economy is growing, or it is not. The country is at war or at
peace; the world is stable or unstable. Second, there is often near consensus on
the desired outcomes; no one disagrees with peace or prosperity, with world
stability, or with low unemployment. Third, the means to achieving these
ends are often very complex, and information is hard to understand; experts
as well as candidates and parties disagree over the specific ways to achieve the
desired ends. How should the economy be improved, and how could terrorism
possibly be contained or democracy established in a foreign land?

As issues, therefore, peace and prosperity differ sharply from policy areas such
as abortion, in which there is vigorous disagreement over ends among experts,
leaders, and the public. On still other issues, people value both ends *and* means.
The classic cases often revolve around the question of whether it is appropriate
for government to take action in a particular area at all. Ronald Reagan was fond
of saying, "Government isn't the solution to our problems; government *is* the
problem." For example, should the government provide national health insurance? After decades of trying, the Democrats, under the Obama administration,
had finally succeeded in passing the Affordable Care Act (ACA), a program

labeled "Obamacare" by the Republicans. Republicans continued to try to roll back the law or keep it from being implemented. Few disagree with the end of better health care, but they disagree over the appropriate means to achieve it. The choice of means touches on some of the basic philosophical and ideological differences that have divided Republicans and Democrats for decades.[15]

Two basic conditions must be met before retrospective evaluations can affect voting choices. First, individuals must connect their concerns with the incumbent and the actions the president and his or her party took in office.[16] This condition would not be present if, for example, a voter blamed earlier administrations with sowing the seeds that become the "Great Recession," blamed an ineffective Congress or Wall Street, or even believed that the problems were beyond anyone's control. Second, individuals, in the Downs-Fiorina view, must compare their evaluations of the incumbent's past performance with what they believe the nominee of the opposition party would do. For example, even if they viewed Trump's performance during the economic crisis caused by the pandemic as weak, voters might have compared that performance with programs supported by Biden in 2020 and concluded that his efforts would not result in any better outcome and might even make things worse.

In this second condition a certain asymmetry exists, one that benefits the incumbent. Even if the incumbent's performance has been weak in a certain area, the challenger still has to convince voters that he or she could do better. It is more difficult, however, for a challenger to convince voters who think the incumbent's performance has been strong that he or she, the challenger, would be even stronger. Would this asymmetry apply to 2020? Or perhaps would both sides have the more difficult problem of convincing the electorate they could handle important problems when current performance was judged as neither especially strong nor especially weak?

We examine next some illustrative retrospective evaluations and study their impact on voter choice. In chapter 7, we looked at issue scales designed to measure the public's evaluations of candidates' promises. For the incumbent party, the public can evaluate not only its promises but also its actions. We compare promises with performance in this chapter, but one must remember that the distinctions are not as sharp in practice as they are in principle.[17] The Downs-Fiorina view is that past actions and projections about the future are necessarily intertwined.

EVALUATIONS OF GOVERNMENT PERFORMANCE ON IMPORTANT PROBLEMS

"Do you feel things in this country are generally going in the right direction, or do you feel things have pretty seriously gotten off on the wrong track?"[18]

This question is designed to measure retrospective judgments, and the responses are presented in table 8.1A. In the appendix to this book, we report responses to the question the ANES had asked in prior surveys, comparing the respondents' evaluations of government performance on the problem that each respondent identified as the single most important one facing the country.[19] The most striking finding in table 8.1A is that in 2020 just one in four thought the country was on the right track. Remarkably, given the pandemic and economic crisis that beset the country, that level of pessimism was no worse than it was in 2016. [20]

If the voter is a rational god of vengeance and reward, we can expect to find a strong relationship between the evaluation of government performance and the vote. Such is indeed the case (see table 8.1B). Nine in ten who thought the country was on the right track voted to stay the course with Trump. Only a few more than one in four who thought the country was on the wrong track voted to keep him.

According to Downs and Fiorina, it is important for voters not only to evaluate how things have been going but also to assess how that evaluation compares with the alternative. In most recent elections, including 2020, respondents have been asked which party would do a better job of solving the problem they named as the most important. Table 8.2 shows the responses to these questions. These questions are clearly oriented toward the future, but they may call for judgments about past performance, consistent with the Downs-Fiorina view. Respondents were not asked to evaluate policy alternatives, and thus responses were most likely based on a retrospective comparison of how the incumbent party handled things with a prediction about

Table 8.1   Evaluation of Government Performance and Major-Party Vote, 2016 and 2020 (Percent)

Evaluation	2016	2020
A. Evaluation of Government Performance		
Right track	25	26
Wrong track	75	74
Total	100	100
(N)	(4,239)	(7,416)
B. Percentage of Major-Party Vote for Incumbent's Party Nominee		
Right track	94	90
(N)	(430)	(1,265)
Wrong track	30	28
(N)	(804)	(1,020)

Source: Authors' analysis of the 2016 and 2020 ANES surveys.
Note: The numbers in parentheses are the totals on which the percentages are based. Numbers are weighted.

Table 8.2   Evaluation of Party Seen as Better on Most Important Political Problem and Major-Party Vote, 2016 and 2020 (Percent)

Better Party	*2016*	*2020*
A. Distribution of Responses on Party Seen as Better on Most Important Political Problem		
Republican	35	30
No difference	35	27
Democratic	30	43
Total	100	100
(*N*)	(3,578)	(7,269)
B. Major-Party Voters Who Voted Democratic for President		
Republican	6	2
(*N*)	(923)	(38)
No difference	64	44
(*N*)	(933)	(453)
Democratic	99	98
(*N*)	(792)	(2,284)

Source: Authors' analysis of the 2016 and 2020 ANES surveys.
Note: The numbers in parentheses are the totals on which the percentages are based. Numbers are weighted. Question wording: "Which political party do you think would be the most likely to get the government to do a better job in dealing with this problem?"

how the opposition would fare. We therefore consider these questions to be a measure of comparative retrospective evaluations.

Table 8.2A shows that the public had different views about which party was better at handling their important concerns, but the advantage went to the Democrats. In 2020 roughly 43 percent of voters thought that the Democrats were the party best-suited to handle their most important concern; 30 percent believed the Republicans would be better. The 13-point difference was a strong advantage for Biden and his party. In 2016, voters were more evenly split (a 5-point difference) on which party would be better at solving the most important problem. The Democratic Party held a huge advantage on this measure in 2008—a 28 percentage point difference—when very few selected the "neither party" option and only one in four selected the Republican Party as better. The largest Republican advantage that we have seen on this measure was in 1980 when 43 percent of respondents believed that the GOP would be better at solving their most pressing problem, compared to only 11 percent who thought the Democrats would be better.

Table 8.2B reveals that the relationship between the party seen as better on the most important political problem and the vote is very strong. Biden won nearly all the votes from those who thought the Democrats would be better. Trump was able to hold nearly all of those who thought the Republican Party better able to handle the most important problem. Interestingly, Trump won a 56-44 majority among those voters in the "no difference" category.

The data presented in tables 8.1 and 8.2 have an important limitation. The first question, analyzed in table 8.1, refers to an impression of how the country is going and not the incumbent president nor even the government. The question examined in table 8.2 refers to which political party would handle the most important problem better and does not directly refer to the incumbent—and we believe it is the assessment of the incumbent that relates most directly to voters' evaluations of the candidates for president. Thus we will look more closely at the incumbent and at people's comparisons of his and the opposition's performance where the data are available to permit such comparisons.

ECONOMIC EVALUATIONS AND THE
VOTE FOR THE INCUMBENT

More than any other, economic issues have been highlighted as suitable retrospective issues. The impact of economic conditions on congressional and presidential elections has been studied extensively.[21] Popular evaluations of presidential effectiveness, John E. Mueller has pointed out, are strongly influenced by the economy.[22] A major reason for Jimmy Carter's defeat in 1980 was the perception that economic performance had been weak during his administration. Reagan's rhetorical question in the 1980 debate with Carter, "Are you better off than you were four years ago?" indicates that politicians realize the power such arguments have over the electorate. Reagan owed his sweeping reelection victory in 1984 largely to the perception that economic performance by the end of his first term had become, after a deep recession in the middle, much stronger.

If people are concerned about economic outcomes, they might start by looking for an answer to the sort of question Reagan asked. Table 8.3A presents ANES respondents' perceptions of whether they were financially better off than one year earlier, including the 2004–2016 election surveys (the appendix reports these back to 1980, see table A.8.3).[23] In 2004 more than two in five reported feeling better off, the most popular response. These numbers proved beneficial to George W. Bush, who was elected to his second term that year. The year 2008, however, was a different story, because half the respondents said they were worse off, with only a third saying they were better off and very few feeling their finances were the same. To be sure, 2008 was a terrible year for the economy, and everyone knew it (even though not everyone suffered). The situation in 2012 presented little to help or harm either side. A few more thought they were better off than worse off, but each view was held by close to two in five. Only one in four claimed his or her situation was the same as in 2008. The continued

Table 8.3   The Public's Assessment of Their Personal Financial Situation and Major-Party Vote, 2004–2020

| Response | *"Would you say that you (and your family) are better off or worse off financially than you were a year ago?"* | | | | |
	2004	*2008*	*2012*	*2016*	*2020*
A. Distribution of Responses					
Better now	43	32	41	28	26
Same	25	18	24	47	50
Worse now	32	50	36	25	24
Total	100	100	101	100	100
(N)	(1,203)	(2,307)	(1,800)	(4,256)	(7,432)
B. Major-Party Voters Who Voted for the Incumbent Party Nominee for President					
Better now	65	53	65	73	58
(N)	(354)	(491)	(456)	(681)	(825)
Same	50	52	49	50	42
(N)	(207)	(280)	(274)	(1,132)	(1,113)
Worse now	28	38	31	33	33
(N)	(219)	(778)	(414)	(560)	(357)

Source: Authors' analysis of ANES surveys.
Note: The numbers in parentheses are the totals on which the percentages are based. Numbers are weighted.

slow but steady improvement over eight years, for 2016, as compared with only four for 2012, suggests that the Obama administration should have been somewhat more favorably reviewed by the public in 2016 compared to 2012, which appears to be true, at least in terms of the decline of "worse off" responses. In some ways, 2016 was like 2000. Clinton, like Obama, had inherited a troubled economy from a Republican president, and as they left office they could point to more or less eight years of consistent growth. In 2020, roughly equal numbers of ANES respondents said they were "better off" than one year earlier as said they were "worse off." Half those surveyed said their economic situation was the "same" as the prior year. These results are surprising given the economic calamity associated with the COVID pandemic. One might have expected to see a distribution similar to that found in 2008 following "the Great Recession."

In table 8.3B, we see how the responses to this question are related to the two-party presidential vote. As expected, the incumbent party tends to do better electorally among those who say they are better off than they were one year ago, but personal economic ("pocketbook") factors were not as strongly related to vote choice in 2020 as they were four years earlier. In 2020, among those who said they were better off than a year ago, Trump earned a 58 percent majority. In the prior election, the incumbent party's nominee (Clinton) garnered 73 percent of the vote from those who said they were better off. Biden won solid majorities among those who said their financial condition was either the same or worse off, 58 percent and 66 percent respectively.

Although people may "vote their pocketbooks," voters are at least as likely (in most cases, more so) to vote retrospectively based on their judgments of how the economy as a whole has been faring across the country (see table 8.4A).[24] And personal and national economic experiences can be quite different. In 1980, for example, about 40 percent of respondents thought their own financial situation was worse than the year before, but responses to the 1980 ANES survey revealed that twice as many (83 percent) thought the national economy was worse off than the year before (see table A.8.3 in the appendix). In 1992, the public gave the nation's economy a far more negative assessment than they gave their own financial situations, and this is similar to what we see in 2020. Approximately one in five respondents in 2020 said that the national economy had gotten better over the prior year. Given the near universal decline in objective economic indicators following the onset of the pandemic—and large declines at that—the proportion of respondents giving a favorable view to the state of the economy is rather large. Again, consider 2008, which occurs during the Great Recession as a point of comparison; only 2 percent of respondents in 2008 claimed that the economy had improved. Of course, a major difference between the two elections is that the incumbent

Table 8.4   The Public's View of the State of the National Economy and Major-Party Vote, 2004–2020

Response	"Would you say that over the past year the nation's economy has gotten . . .?"				
	2004	*2008*	*2012*	*2016*	*2020*
A. Distribution of Responses					
Better	24	2	28	28	19
Stayed same	31	7	36	42	23
Worse	45	90	35	30	58
Total	100	99	99	100	100
(N)	(1,196)	(2,313)	(1,806)	(4,261)	(7,433)
B. Major-Party Voters Who Voted for the Incumbent Party Nominee for President					
Better	87	69	86	88	84
(N)	(211)	(34)	(339)	(724)	(839)
Stayed same	88	57	48	50	60
(N)	(243)	(109)	(425)	(992)	(662)
Worse	20	44	16	18	26
(N)	(319)	(1,425)	(382)	(658)	(792)

Source: Authors' analysis of ANES surveys.
Note: The numbers in parentheses are the totals on which percentages are based. Numbers are weighted.
[a]We combine the results using standard and experimental prompts that contained different word orderings in 2004, and 2008.

president (George W. Bush) was not on the ballot in 2008, whereas in 2020 he was. It is likely that at least some of those in the "better" category in 2020 were Trump supporters who did not want to provide a negative assessment of the economy during the latter part of his term. Nevertheless, 58 percent of respondents in 2020 claimed that the national economy was worse off.

In table 8.4B, we show the relationship between responses to these items and the major-party vote for president. The relationship between these measures and the vote is always strong. Moreover, a comparison of table 8.3B and table 8.4B reveals that in general, the vote is more closely associated with perceptions of the nation's economy than it is with perceptions of one's personal economic well-being. Interestingly, in 2020, the relationship was not as strong as we observed as recently as 2012 and 2016. The difference in votes cast in 2012 for Obama between the "better" and the "worse" categories was fully 70 percentage points, with the "same" category essentially splitting their votes evenly. This wide difference remained in 2016, again with those in the "same" category splitting their votes in roughly equal number between the incumbent party and the challengers. In 2020, however, the difference in votes cast for Trump between the "better" and the "worse" categories was a notably smaller 58 percentage points. Among those who said the economy had stayed about the same, Trump won a solid 60 percentage point majority. Yet, unfortunately for Trump, this would not be enough to offset the large number of voters who viewed the economy as worse off. Clearly, both personal and national economic circumstances mattered a great deal in the 2020 elections.

To this point, we have looked at personal and national economic conditions and the role of the government in shaping them. We have not yet looked at the extent to which such evaluations are attributed to the incumbent. In table 8.5A, we report responses to the question of whether people approved of the incumbent's handling of the economy from the elections of 2004 through 2020 (and the same data are reported for elections between 1984 and 2000 in the appendix, table A.8.4). Evaluations of George W. Bush's handling of the economy in 2004 were more negative than positive. By 2008, evaluations of Bush's handling of the economy were decidedly negative (84 percent). In 2012, evaluations of Obama's handling of the economy were quite like those of Bush in 2004, but in 2016 evaluations Obama's performance had improved with a small majority approving of his handling of the economy. Earlier we noted that respondents tended to give Donald Trump relatively high marks in handling the economy earlier in his term, but those numbers had declined significantly by the time of the election. The ANES data reveals that a small majority (52 percent), similar in size to Obama's, approved of Trump's handling of the economy.

Table 8.5 Evaluations of the Incumbent's Handling of the Economy and Major-Party Vote, 2004–2020

	Approval of Incumbent's Handling of the Economy				
Response	*2004*	*2008*	*2012*	*2016*	*2020*
A. Distribution of Responses					
Positive view	41	18	42	53	52
Negative view	59	82	58	47	48
Total	100	100	100	100	100
(N)	(1,173)	(2,227)	(1,698)	(4,221)	(7,414)
B. Major-Party Voters Who Voted for the Incumbent Party Nominee					
Positive view	91	89	92	89	83
(N)	(341)	(313)	(476)	(1,253)	(2,228)
Negative view	17	33	13	11	3
(N)	(431)	(1,200)	(618)	(1,109)	(67)

Source: Authors' analysis of ANES surveys.
Note: Numbers are weighted.

The bottom-line question is whether these views are related to voter choice. According to the data in table 8.5B, the answer is a resounding "yes." Among those who approved of Trump's handling of the economy roughly four out of five voted to reelect him. While this ratio is high, it is significantly lower than the nine in ten ratio observed in recent elections. Among those with a negative view of Trump's handling of the economy, his level of support was lower than any incumbent party candidate we have observed. Only 3 percent of voters with negative views of Trump's handling of the economy voted to reelect him. The relationship between perceptions of the incumbent's handling of the economy and vote choice is strong. Indeed, in 2020, the difference in votes cast for Trump between those in the "positive view" and "negative view" categories was 80 percentage points. The economy was a vitally important factor in the 2020 election as all three retrospective evaluations of the economy are clearly and strongly related to the vote.

FOREIGN POLICY EVALUATIONS AND THE VOTE FOR THE INCUMBENT

Foreign and economic policies are, as we noted earlier, commonly evaluated by means of retrospective assessments. These policies share the characteristics of consensual goals (peace and prosperity, respectively, plus security in both cases), complex technology, and difficulty in ascertaining relationships between means and ends. Foreign policy differs from economic policy in one practical way, however. As we noted in the last chapter, economic problems are invariably a major concern, but foreign affairs are salient only

Table 8.6 President's Handling of Foreign Relations and Major-Party Vote, 2020 (Percent)

	Evaluation
A. "Do you approve or disapprove of the way the president is handling foreign relations?"	
Approve	43
Disapprove	57
Total	100
(*N*)	(7,411)
B. Percentage of Major-Party Vote for Incumbent's Party Nominee	
Approve	92
(*N*)	(2,088)
Disapprove	7
(*N*)	(203)

Source: Authors' analysis of the 2020 ANES survey.
Note: The numbers in parentheses in Part B are the totals on which the percentages are based. The numbers in Parts A and B are weighted.

sporadically. In fact, foreign affairs are of sufficiently sporadic concern that most surveys, including the ANES, only occasionally have many measures to judge their role in elections. Moreover, what part of our foreign policy is under scrutiny changes from election to election, especially when there are wars that are at the center of choice.

In 2020, therefore, we report on a more general evaluation, similar to that of approval of economic performance. In particular, in table A.8.6 are responses to the question of whether the respondent approves or not of Trump's handling of foreign relations. This leaves great latitude in aggregating responses over what might well be very different parts of the world in the voters' minds.

The responses to this question indicate that a majority (57 percent) of respondents disapproved of Trump's handing of foreign policy during his presidency. Consider table B.8.6. Overall, nine in ten approvers voted to reelect Trump, whereas only one in fourteen of those who disapproved of his handling of foreign policy voted for him.

EVALUATIONS OF THE PANDEMIC RESPONSE AND THE VOTE FOR THE INCUMBENT

Donald Trump's handling of the COVID-19 pandemic was one of the central issues in the 2020 presidential election.[25] When the first confirmed US case of the virus was declared in January of 2020, the president told CNBC, "It's one person coming in from China. We have it under control. It's going to be fine."[26] By the end of March, the United States led the world in confirmed cases. Several states issued strict stay-at-home orders, triggering widespread business closures and plummeting the economy into recession.[27] The administration started conducting daily press briefings from the White House, and the president frequently dominated the podium. A national survey conducted in April showed that only 23 percent of Americans expressed a high level of trust in what the president was telling the public about the pandemic.[28] By May, over 100,000 Americans had died from the virus. During the summer months, the number of daily cases seemed to be soaring, and in September the nation's death toll passed 200,000. Shockingly, on October 2, President Trump, himself, tested positive for the virus and was hospitalized, briefly creating great uncertainty about the country's leadership. The pandemic dominated American life in 2020, and over the course of the year questions about how to manage the public health crisis—indeed, whether COVID even existed—became deeply politicized.[29] Here, we ask what role did Trump's handling of the pandemic response play in his reelection bid?

In table 8.7A, we report ANES respondents' views on Trump's handling of the COVID-19 pandemic. The data reveal that voters gave lower marks on his handling of the pandemic than they did his handling of the economy and foreign policy. An estimated 61 percent of Americans said that they disapproved of Trump's handling of the pandemic. In table 8.7b we see that voters divided sharply based on their retrospective evaluations of Trump's performance during the COVID-19 crisis. Overall, 95 percent of those who approved of Trump's performance voted to reelect him, whereas only one in ten disapprovers voted for him. Given his relatively low approval ratings on the issue and the fact that voters seemed to have been activated by this issue, the evidence strongly suggests that Trump's poor performance during the pandemic had a negative effect on his reelection bid.

Table 8.7   President's Handling of COVID-19 and Major-Party Vote, 2020 (Percent)

	Evaluation
A. "Do you approve or disapprove of the way the president is handling COVID-19?"	
Approve	39
Disapprove	61
Total	100
(N)	(7,429)
B. Percentage of Major-Party Vote for Incumbent's Party Nominee	
Approve	95
(N)	(1,968)
Disapprove	10
(N)	(329)

Source: Authors' analysis of the 2020 ANES survey.
Note: The numbers in parentheses in Part B are the totals on which the percentages are based. The numbers in Parts A and B are weighted.

EVALUATIONS OF THE INCUMBENT

Fiorina distinguishes between "simple" and "mediated" retrospective evaluations.[30] By simple, Fiorina means evaluations of the direct effects of social outcomes on the person, such as one's financial status, or direct perceptions of the nation's economic well-being. Mediated retrospective evaluations are evaluations seen through or mediated by the perceptions of political actors and institutions. Approval of Trump's handling of the economy and the assessment of which party would better handle the most important problem are examples.

As we have seen, the more politically mediated the question, the more closely the responses align with voting behavior.[31] Perhaps the ultimate in mediated evaluations is the presidential approval question: "Do you approve or disapprove of the way [the incumbent] is handling his job as president?" From a retrospective voting standpoint, this evaluation is a summary of all aspects of the incumbent's service in office. Table 8.8 reports the distribution of overall evaluations and their relationship to major-party voting in the last five elections.[32]

Table A.8.5 reveals that incumbents Ronald Reagan (1984) and Bill Clinton (1996) enjoyed widespread approval, whereas only two respondents in five approved of Jimmy Carter's and of George H. W. Bush's handling of the job in 1980 and 1992, respectively. This situation presented Carter and the senior Bush with a problem. Conversely, highly approved incumbents, such as Reagan in 1984 and Clinton in 1996—and their vice presidents as beneficiaries in 1988 and 2000, respectively—had a major advantage. Clinton dramatically reversed any negative perceptions held of his incumbency in

Table 8.8   President's Handling of the Job and Major-Party Vote, 2004–2020

	"Do you approve or disapprove of the way [the incumbent] is handling his job as president?"				
Response	*2004*	*2008*	*2012*	*2016*	*2020*
A. Distribution of Responses					
Approve	51	27	50	53	42
Disapprove	49	73	50	47	58
Total	100	100	100	100	100
(N)	(1,182)	(2,245)	(1,704)	(4,226)	(7,403)
B. Major-Party Voters Who Voted for the Incumbent Party's Nominee					
Approve	91	88	92	91	95
(N)	(408)	(441)	(537)	(1,263)	(2,117)
Disapprove	6	26	6	8	6
(N)	(372)	(1,075)	(568)	(1,102)	(174)

Source: Authors' analysis of ANES surveys.
Note: The numbers in parentheses in Part B are the totals on which percentages are based. Numbers are weighted.

1994 so that by 1996 he received the highest level of approval in the fall of an election year since Nixon's landslide reelection in 1972. Between 1996 and 2000 Clinton suffered through several scandals, one of which culminated in his impeachment in 1998. Such events might be expected to lead to substantial declines in his approval ratings, but instead his ratings remained high—higher even than Reagan's at the end of his presidency. The evaluations in 2004 present a more varied picture. For the first time in nine elections, the proportions approving and disapproving of George W. Bush were almost exactly the same. In view of what we have seen so far, it should come as no surprise that evaluations of Bush turned dramatically by 2008 so that he was by far the least approved incumbent during this period, with nearly three in four respondents disapproving of his handling of the office. Obama's approval ratings in 2012 were, again, much like Bush's in 2004, here coming out exactly evenly divided between approval and disapproval.[33] By 2016 his approval increased so that it was positive, six points higher than his disapproval rating. Thus, although there was nearly an even-up balance for Clinton to work with in 2016, it was slightly more positive than the victorious Bush in 2004. Trump's overall job approval rating of 42 percent in 2020 is similar to those held by Carter and the elder Bush during their failed bids for reelection.

If it is true that the more mediated the evaluation, the more closely it seems to align with behavior, and if presidential approval is the most mediated evaluation of all, then we would expect a powerful relationship with the vote. As table 8.8B (and table A.8.5 in the appendix) illustrates, that is true over the full set of elections for which we have the relevant data. As we have seen before, the approval ratings in 2004, 2012, 2016, and 2020 are about as strongly related to the vote as is possible. Approximately 95 percent of those who approved of Trump's performance voted to reelect him; only 6 percent who disapproved voted for him.

THE IMPACT OF RETROSPECTIVE EVALUATIONS

Our evidence strongly suggests that retrospective voting has been widespread in all recent elections. Moreover, as far as data permit us to judge, the evidence is clearly on the side of the Downs-Fiorina view. Retrospective evaluations appear to be used to make comparative judgments. Presumably, voters find it easier, less time-consuming, and less risky to evaluate the incumbent party based on what its president did in the most recent term or terms in office than on the nominees' promises for the future. But few people base their votes on judgments of past performance alone. Most use past judgments as a starting point for comparing the major contenders with respect to their likely future performances.

In analyzing previous elections, we constructed an overall assessment of retrospective voting and compared that overall assessment across elections. We then compared that net retrospective assessment with our balance-of-issues measure. Our measure is constructed by combining the question asking whether the United States is on the right or on the wrong track, the presidential approval measure, and the assessment of which party would better handle the problem the respondent thinks is the single most important.[34] The combination of responses to these three questions creates a seven-point scale ranging from strongly negative evaluations of recent and current conditions to strongly positive evaluations of performance in these various areas. For example, those who thought the nation was on the right track, approved of Trump's job performance, and thought the Republican Party would better handle the most important problem are scored as strongly supportive of Trump in their retrospective evaluations in 2020.

In table 8.9, we present the results of this measure.[35] The data in table 8.9A indicate that there was a substantial diversity of responses but that the measure was skewed against the incumbent. By this measure roughly two in five were strongly opposed to the performance of the Trump administration, with another fifth moderately or slightly opposed. One in fourteen was neutral, while a bit over one in six were slightly or moderately supportive, and another one in six was strongly supportive of the Trump administration.

Table 8.9B presents a remarkably clear example of a very strong relationship between responses and votes, with greater than 90 percent of those in any of the three supportive categories voting for Trump and very few of those moderately or strongly opposed voting for him. The sparse number of voters in these categories attests to the depth of opposition to Trump. Indeed, Trump also performed relatively poorly among those who were only slightly opposed in their evaluations. Thirty-seven percent of the voters in this category voted for Trump despite their slightly negative retrospective evaluations of his first term. Thus for six of the seven categories, the valence of evaluations alone tells you everything you need to know about their voting choices. Voters cast their ballots in

Table 8.9 Summary Measure of Retrospective Evaluations of the Trump Administration and Major-Party Vote, 2020

	Strongly Opposed	Moderately Opposed	Slightly Opposed	Neutral	Slightly Supportive	Moderately Supportive	Strongly Supportive	Total (N)
A. Distribution of Responses								
Percent	39	14	5	7	12	6	17	100 (7,262)
B. Major-Party Voters Who Voted for Trump								
Percent	1	18	37	87	93	92	99	45
(N)	(17)	(89)	(65)	(249)	(630)	(227)	(983)	(2,261)

Source: Authors' analysis of the 2020 ANES survey.
Note: Numbers are weighted. The numbers in Part B are the totals on which the percentages are based.

ways that are consistent with their appraisal of the incumbent president. Among those who were supportive of the president's performance during his first term, almost all voted to keep the president in office. For those who gave a negative assessment of the president's time in office, very large percentages decided that enough was enough and they voted for the challenger, Joe Biden.

We cannot make precise comparisons between 2020 and other elections on this measure due to alterations in measurement, but we can at least make broad generalizations.[36] In earlier years, it was reasonable to conclude that the 1980 election was a clear and strong rejection of Carter's incumbency. In 1984, Reagan won in large part because voters perceived that he had performed well and because Mondale was unable to convince the public that he would do better. In 1988, George H. W. Bush won in large part because Reagan appeared to have performed well—and people thought Bush would stay the course. In 1992, Bush lost because of the far more negative evaluations of his administration and of his party than had been recorded in any election since 1980. In 1996, Clinton won reelection in large part for the same reasons that Reagan won in 1984: He was viewed as having performed well on the job, and he was able to convince the public that his opponent would not do any better. In 2000, Gore essentially tied George W. Bush because the slightly pro-incumbent set of evaluations combined with a very slight asymmetry against the incumbent in translating those evaluations into voting choices. In 2004, there was a slight victory for the incumbent because more thought he had performed well than poorly. And 2008 was most like 1980, with a highly skewed distribution working against the Republicans (likely the most skewed measure of all, subject to wording differences). In 2012, evaluations, once again, paralleled those (with a different measure) from 2004, with an outcome not substantially different—slightly negative evaluations overall but not so negative as to cost the incumbent reelection. In many respects, one of the lessons from considering these data is that 2016 looked a great deal like a repeat of 2012 on these measures as well as others. Thus, Bush and Obama won reelection after their first terms with relatively modest pluralities. That Bush's successor lost in 2008 was due to the dramatic economic collapse of the nation during the campaign, which otherwise might have looked like 2016. In 2016, Clinton received the boost of standing with her party's incumbent president, but it was an even more modest boost than retrospective evaluations gave Obama in 2012 (and Bush in 2004), enough for her to win by 2 percentage points but not enough to ensure her victory in the Electoral College.

How do retrospective assessments compare with prospective judgments? As described in chapter 7, prospective issues, especially our balance-of-issues measure, have become more strongly related to the vote over the last few elections. There appears, that is, to be a significant extent of partisan polarization in the electorate in terms of their evaluations of the choices and their vote, even if not in terms of their own opinions about issues. Table 8.10 reports the impact of both types of policy evaluation measures on the major-party vote in 2020. Both policy measures were collapsed into three categories: pro-Democratic, neutral, and pro-Republican. Reading down each column we see that controlling for retrospective evaluations, prospective issues are modestly related to the vote in a positive direction. Or, to be more precise, they are modestly related to the vote among those whose retrospective evaluations are nearly or actually neutral, with a small but real effect among those inclined to evaluate the Trump administration negatively. It is thus really only among those whose retrospective evaluations did not even moderately incline them toward either party that prospective evaluations are related to the vote. Note, however, that even in this column, Trump received the votes of slightly more than four in five who were neutral on retrospective issues.

Reading across each row, we see that retrospective evaluations are very strongly related to the vote. This is true no matter what prospective evaluations respondents held. Thus we can conclude that in 2020, retrospective evaluations shaped voting choices to a great extent. Prospective evaluations were still important but only for those without a moderate or strong partisan direction to their retrospective judgments.

Together the two kinds of policy measures take us a long way toward understanding voting choices. Essentially everyone whose retrospective and prospective evaluations inclined them toward the same party voted for the candidate of that party. This accounting of voting choices is stronger when considering both forms of policy evaluations than when looking at either one individually.[37]

Table 8.10 Major-Party Voters Who Voted for Trump, by Balance-of-Issues and Summary Retrospective Measures, 2020

	Summary Retrospective						
	Strongly or Moderately Democratic		Slightly Supportive or Slightly Opposed or Neutral		Strongly or Moderately Republican		Total
Net Balance of Issues	%	(N)	%	(N)	%	(N)	%	(N)
Democratic	2	(34)	49	(99)	93	(84)	10	(217)
Neutral	5	(13)	74	(84)	99	(81)	39	(178)
Republican	15	(59)	93	(756)	99	(1,027)	82	(1,842)
Total	4	(106)	83	(939)	98	(1,191)	45	(2,237)

Source: Authors' analysis of the 2020 ANES survey.
Note: Numbers are weighted. Numbers in parentheses are the totals on which percentages are based. For the condensed measure of retrospective voting, we combine respondents who are strongly positive (or negative) toward Joe Biden and the Democratic Party with respondents who are moderately positive (or negative). We combine respondents who are slightly positive (or negative) with those who are neutral (see table 8.8). For the condensed balance-of-issues measure, any respondent who is closer to Trump is classified as pro-Republican. The neutral category is the same as the seven-point measure (see table 7.7).

PARTISANSHIP AND RETROSPECTIVE EVALUATIONS

Most partisans evaluate the job performance of a president from their party more highly than do independents and, especially, more highly than do those who identify with the other party. Figure 8.1A shows the percentage of each of the seven partisan groups that approves of the way the incumbent has handled his job as president (as a proportion of those approving or disapproving) in the last five presidential elections in which there was a Democratic president (1980, 1996, 2000, 2012, and 2016). Figure 8.1B presents similar results for the last five elections in which there was a Republican incumbent (1988, 1992, 2004, 2008, and 2020). Strong partisans of the incumbent's party typically give overwhelming approval to that incumbent. (table A.8.6 in the appendix presents the exact values for each year.) It is not guaranteed, however. In 1980, only 73 percent of strong Democrats approved of Jimmy Carter, which is just about the same percentage of strong Republicans who approved of Bush's job performance in 2008.

We can draw two conclusions about 2020 from the data in figures 8.1A and 8.1B. First, just as in every election, there was a strong partisan cast to evaluations of the president in 2020. Democrats are very likely to approve of

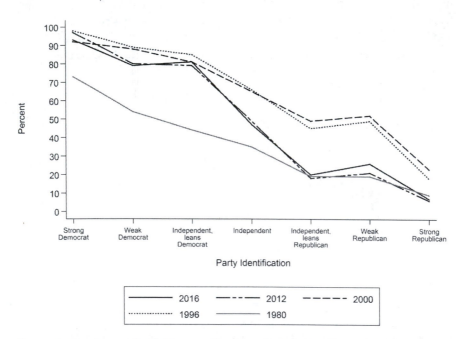

Figure 8.1A Approval of Democratic Incumbents' Handling of Job, by Party Identification, 1980, 1996, 2000, 2012, and 2016. *Source*: Authors' analysis of the ANES surveys. Note: Data are weighted.

any Democratic incumbent and very unlikely to approve of any Republican incumbent and vice versa for Republicans. This fact was perhaps even truer in 2020 than in prior elections as the degree of partisan polarization of approval of Trump's handling of his job was more dramatic than any other. Virtually all strong Republicans approved; virtually no strong Democrats did. Trump's low ratings among all Democratic identifiers (strong, weak, and leaners) is on par with that given to George W. Bush at the conclusion of his second term, essentially tying him for the lowest approval ratings any incumbent has received from out partisans. Yet, perhaps testifying to the increasingly polarized partisan environment, Trump's support from his own partisans was quite strong. In addition to his near universal support from strong GOP identifiers, three out of four Republican "leaners" and seven of ten weak Republicans approved of Trump's job performance. Bush, in contrast, received low marks from leaning and weak Republican identifiers (a majority disapproved). Strong Republicans were the only groups to give Bush majority approval of his performance, but, even then, the 74 percent support that Bush received pales in comparison to Trump's 96 percent support from this group. Pure independents did not give Trump high scores; only 33 percent of independents approved of his job performance.

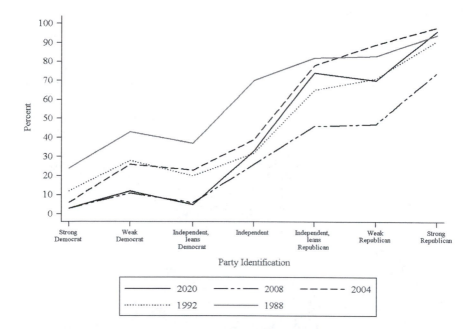

Figure 8.1B Approval of Republican Incumbents' Handling of Job, by Party Identification, 1988, 1992, 2004, 2008, and 2020. *Source*: Authors' analysis of the ANES surveys. Note: Data are weighted.

In table 8.11, we examine the relationship between partisanship and approval of the incumbent's handling of the economy. Table A.8.8 in the appendix shows the relationship among all seven partisan categories and approval of incumbent presidents' handling of the economy dating back to 1984.[38] The historical data show a trend of highly polarized partisan evaluations. In 1984 and 1988, more than three-quarters of each of the three Republican groups approved of Reagan's handling of the economy, whereas more than half—and often more than two-thirds—of the three Democratic groups disapproved. Independents generally approved of Reagan's economic efforts, albeit more strongly in 1984 than in 1988. The 1992 election was dramatically different, with overwhelming disapproval of George H. W. Bush's handling of the economy among the three Democratic groups and the pure independents. Even two-thirds of the weak and Republican-leaning independents disapproved. Only strong Republicans typically approved, and even then one in three did not. The relationship in 1996 is most like that of 1984. In 2000, the vast majority of Democrats and even three in four of the pure independents approved of Clinton's economic performance—by far the highest economic approval mark independents have given. But then most Republicans also approved. In 2004, a weak but improving economy meant that George W. Bush was approved by "only" nine in ten strong Republicans and about seven in ten weak and independent-leaning Republicans. Democratic disapproval reached very high levels, and once again pure independents did not favor Bush, only one in three approving of his handling of the economy. In 2008 the Wall Street meltdown occurred in the midst of the campaign, and its effects were devastating to President Bush's approval ratings. Only 18 percent of respondents approved of Bush's handling of the economy. Even though these ratings were lower than the overall approval ratings, they displayed a clear partisan effect. Strong Republicans still approved more than they disapproved, and one in four in the other two Republican categories approved. These are very low percentages to be sure, but they are higher than among pure independents and much higher than the mere trace levels

Table 8.11   Approval of Incumbent's Handling of the Economy among Partisan Groups, 2020 (Percent)

		Party Identification							
Year	Attitudes toward Handling of the Economy	Strong Democrat	Weak Democrat	Independent, leans Democrat	Independent	Independent, leans Republican	Weak Republican	Strong Republican	Total
2020	Approve	9	29	16	49	88	85	98	52
	Disapprove	91	71	84	51	12	15	2	48
	Total	100	100	100	100	100	100	100	100
	(N)	(1,628)	(850)	(848)	(1,014)	(761)	(797)	(1,505)	(7,403)

Source: Authors' analysis of ANES surveys.

of any type of Democrat, with about one in twenty approving. The relationship between partisanship and approval of Obama's handling of the economy in 2012 was very strong. Of the three Democrat categories of partisanship, nine in ten or more approved of Obama's performance. Nine in ten strong Republicans disapproved, but Obama was able to do marginally better among weak Republicans, being approved by two in ten of them, and even better among independents who lean Republican, being approved by a bit more than a third. And pure independents approved of Obama's performance by a two-to-one ratio. Thus, as in so many other cases we have examined, evaluations and voting in 2012 were quite polarized by party even in the electorate. In 2016, Obama's ratings continued to receive highly polarized partisan evaluations, but the relationship was not as strong as his 2012 numbers. Democratic identifiers continued to support Obama, but not as intensely as they did four years earlier.

In 2020, Trump's performance ratings on the economy were sharply colored by partisanship. Republicans strongly approved of the president's economic performance with nearly nine in ten of all GOP identifiers giving Trump favorable marks. In contrast, Democratic identifiers overwhelmingly disapproved of Trump's economic management. Interestingly, pure independents were nearly equally divided in their evaluations of Trump's handling of the economy.

Table 8.12 shows the relationship between party identification and our measure of retrospective evaluations in 2020.[39] Interestingly, the relationship is strong, but not as strong as in recent elections. As one might expect, almost all strong Democrats had negative retrospective evaluations of Trump, as did 38 percent of weak Democratic identifiers and 90 percent of Democratic leaners. But the table reveals softness in Trump's support from Republican identifiers. Among strong Republicans, only six in ten provided Trump with strong marks for his performance, and 36 percent of this group gave relatively neutral appraisals of his time in office. Among weak and leaning Republicans, assessments of Trump's performance were even weaker, with only seven in twenty giving the president highly favorable ratings. Although it is safe to say that retrospective evaluations are strongly related to partisanship, the relationship was not as strong in 2020 as it has been in 2012 and 2016, and this is largely due to weaker retrospective assessments of the incumbent from members of his own party.

Table 8.13 shows the percentage of major-party voters who voted Democratic by both party identification and retrospective evaluations in 2020. Reading down the columns reveals that party identification is strongly related to the vote, regardless of the voter's retrospective evaluations, a pattern found in the ten elections before 2020. Reading across each row reveals that retrospective evaluations are related to the vote, regardless of the voter's party identification, and once again a pattern was discovered in all ten earlier

Table 8.12   Retrospective Evaluations among Partisan Groups, 2020 (Percent)

	Party Identification							
Summary Measure of Retrospective Evaluations	*Strong Democrat*	*Weak Democrat*	*Independent, Leans Democrat*	*Independent*	*Independent, Leans Republican*	*Weak Republican*	*Strong Republican*	*Total %*
Pro-Democratic	95	83	90	60	19	23	2	54
Slightly Supportive, Opposed, or Neutral	4	13	8	26	45	43	36	23
Pro-Republican	1	4	2	14	36	35	62	23
Total	100	100	100	100	100	101	100	100
(N)	(1,606)	(838)	(826)	(981)	(753)	(777)	(1,464)	(7,246)

Source: Authors' analysis of the 2020 ANES survey.
Note: The Democratic category on the condensed measure of retrospective evaluations includes any respondent who is at least moderately opposed to the incumbent's party; the Republican category includes any respondent who at least moderately supports the incumbent's party. Numbers are weighted.

Table 8.13   Percentage of Major-Party Voters Who Voted for Trump, by Party Identification and Summary Retrospective Evaluations, 2020

	Summary Retrospective Evaluations							
	Pro-Democratic		Neutral		Pro-Republican		Total	
Party Identification	*%*	*(N)*	*%*	*(N)*	*%*	*(N)*	*%*	*(N)*
Democratic	1	(20)	25	(27)	90	(23)	4	(71)
Independent	5	(46)	83	(297)	97	(266)	41	(609)
Republican	30	(40)	93	(619)	99	(920)	91	(1,579)
Total	4	(106)	83	(943)	98	(1,209)	45	(2,259)

Source: Authors' analysis of the 2020 ANES survey.
Note: The Democratic category on the condensed measure of retrospective evaluations includes any respondent who is at least moderately opposed to the incumbent's party; the Republican category includes any respondent who at least moderately supports the incumbent's party. The numbers in parentheses are the totals on which the percentages are based. Numbers are weighted.

elections. Moreover, as in all nine elections between 1976 and 2008, party identification and retrospective evaluations had a combined impact on how people voted in 2020. Almost all Republicans with pro-Republican evaluations reported voting for Trump; among Democrats with pro-Democratic evaluations, 99 percent voted for Biden.

Finally, partisanship and retrospective assessments appear to have roughly equal effects on the vote, with partisanship slightly outweighing retrospection in 2020. It is important to note that the effect of retrospective evaluations on the vote is not purely the result of partisans having positive retrospective assessments of their party's presidents and negative ones when the opposition holds the White House. For example, Republicans who hold pro-Democratic retrospective judgments were much more supportive of Biden than other Republicans. Indeed, seven in ten of those few voted for him, and only one in ten Democrats with pro-Republican retrospective evaluations voted for Biden. Overall, then, we can conclude that partisanship is a key component for understanding evaluations of the public and their votes, but the large changes in outcomes over time must be traced to retrospective—and, as we saw in chapter 7, prospective evaluations—simply because partisanship does not change substantially over time.

CONCLUSION

In this and the previous chapter, we have found that both retrospective and prospective evaluations were strongly related to the vote in 2020. Indeed, just as 2012 presents an unusually clear case of retrospective evaluations being a very powerful reason for Obama's victory, retrospective evaluations served as a very powerful reason for Trump's loss.

Whereas retrospective evaluations are always strong, they genuinely stand out during the past three elections. In 1992, for example, dissatisfaction with George H. W. Bush's performance and with his and his party's handling of the most important problem—usually an economic concern in 1992—goes a long way toward explaining his defeat, whereas satisfaction with Clinton's performance and the absence of an advantage for the Republicans in being seen as able to deal with the most important concerns of voters go a long way toward explaining his 1996 victory. In 2000, prospective issues favored neither candidate because essentially the same number of major-party voters was closer to Bush as was closer to Gore. The Democrat had a modest advantage on retrospective evaluations, but Bush won greater support among those with pro-Republican evaluations than did Gore among those with pro-Democratic evaluations. The result was another even balance and, as a result, a tied outcome. Although Kerry was favored on prospective evaluations in 2004, his advantage was counterbalanced by Bush's slight advantage based on retrospective evaluations, leading to a Bush reelection victory with only a slight gain in the popular vote. By 2008, the public had turned quite negative on Bush's performance, and that led to a major advantage for the Democrats. In 2012, there was a return, essentially, to the 2004 patterns, except with a Democrat as incumbent and with retrospective judgments focusing more heavily on the economy and less heavily on international affairs. In a number of respects, 2016 was a continuation of the patterns of 2012, with perhaps a little more strength. In 2020, Trump received relatively favorable assessments for his handling of the economy, but voters' assessments of his overall performance (e.g., international affairs, the pandemic, and perhaps other areas) were decidedly more negative and led to his electoral loss. In 2020, the electoral gods ruled in favor of vengeance rather than reward.

Part III

THE 2020 CONGRESSIONAL ELECTIONS

Chapter 9

Candidates and Outcomes in 2020

In 1994 the Republicans unexpectedly won control of both chambers of Congress, the first time the GOP had won the House since 1952. (The only time they had controlled the Senate during that period was 1980–1986.) The electoral earthquake of 1994 shaped all subsequent congressional contests. From 1996 on, there was at least some doubt about who would control the next Congress, which had not been the case during the previous period of Democratic control. In the next five elections after 1994, the GOP retained control of the House, although they lost seats in the first three and gained in the next two. In the Senate the Republicans added to their majority in 1996, broke even in 1998, and then lost ground in 2000, leaving the chamber evenly divided. Then in 2002 the GOP made small gains to get a little breathing room, and in 2004 they gained a bit more. Going into the elections of 2006, the GOP still had control of Congress, but that year their luck ran out. The GOP suffered a crushing defeat, losing thirty seats in the House and six in the Senate, shifting control of both bodies to the Democrats, and in 2008 the Democrats achieved a second substantial gain in a row, adding twenty-one seats in the House and eight seats in the Senate.

In 2010, party fortunes reversed again. In the wake of the Great Recession, the Democrats lost the House, with the Republicans picking up a net gain of sixty-three seats. In the Senate the GOP fell short of control, but they did gain six seats. In 2012 the Republicans had hoped to continue to make gains, but that was not to be. Instead the Democrats regained some ground. In the House they won 201 seats to the Republicans' 234, a gain of eight seats. In the Senate the result was a fifty-three to forty-five division in favor of the Democrats, with two independents (both of whom sided with the Democrats on control),[1] which reflected a gain of two Senate seats. Two years later in 2014, the Republicans made a net gain of thirteen seats in the House, netting them their largest majority (247–188) since 1928. More significant, however,

233

was the Republican's capture of the Senate—they picked up nine Democratic seats while losing none of their own to take a fifty-four to forty-six majority.

Although the Republicans ended up losing six seats in the House and two in the Senate during the 2016 elections, they were able to maintain control of Congress, giving them unified control of the government for the first time since 2005–2006. This initially offered them some hope that they would be able to pass a Republican agenda, such as repealing and replacing the ACA, but such attempts were largely unsuccessful with the exception of passing tax cuts in early 2017. In 2018, Democrats picked up 40 seats in the House while Republicans managed a net gain of two seats in the Senate, yielding divided government yet again for the next two years. Despite losing about a dozen seats in the House in 2020, the Democrats were able to narrowly win control of the Senate with a 50-50 split that gave them unified majority control of government for the first time in ten years.

In this chapter, we examine the pattern of congressional outcomes for 2020 and see how it compares to previous years. We explain why the 2020 results took the shape they did—what factors affected the success of incumbents seeking to return and what permitted some challengers to run better than others. We also discuss the likely impact of the election results on the politics of the 117th Congress. Finally, we briefly consider the implications of the 2020 results for the 2022 midterm elections.

ELECTION OUTCOMES IN 2020

Patterns of Incumbency Success

One of the most dependable generalizations about American politics is that most congressional races involve incumbents and most incumbents are reelected. Although this statement has been true for every set of congressional elections since World War II, the degree to which it has held varied from one election to another. Table 9.1 presents information on election outcomes for House and Senate races involving incumbents between 1954 and 2020.[2] During this period, an average of 93 percent of House incumbents and 82 percent of Senate incumbents who sought reelection were successful.

The proportion of representatives reelected in 2020 (about 95 percent) was two points above the sixty-two year average, whereas the 85 percent success rate for senators was three points above the average for that chamber. As we discuss later in the chapter, the limited number of quality challengers running in 2020 significantly affected the results for the House. In the absence of a quality challenger, incumbents have a much easier time getting reelected.[3] In the Senate there were a disproportionate number of Republican seats up, and as we will see later, the Democrats performed slightly better than expectations.

Table 9.1   House and Senate Incumbents and Election Outcomes, 1954–2020

Year	Incumbent Running (N)	Primary Defeats %	Primary Defeats (N)	General Election Defeats %	General Election Defeats (N)	Reelected %	Reelected (N)
House							
1954	(407)	1.5	(6)	5.4	(22)	93.1	(379)
1956	(410)	1.5	(6)	3.7	(15)	94.9	(389)
1958	(394)	0.8	(3)	9.4	(37)	89.8	(354)
1960	(405)	1.2	(5)	6.2	(25)	92.6	(375)
1962	(402)	3.0	(12)	5.5	(22)	91.5	(368)
1964	(397)	2.0	(8)	11.3	(45)	86.6	(344)
1966	(411)	1.9	(8)	10.0	(41)	88.1	(362)
1968	(409)	1.0	(4)	2.2	(9)	96.8	(396)
1970	(401)	2.5	(10)	3.0	(12)	94.5	(379)
1972	(392)	3.3	(13)	3.3	(13)	93.4	(366)
1974	(391)	2.0	(8)	10.2	(40)	87.7	(343)
1976	(383)	0.8	(3)	3.1	(12)	96.1	(368)
1978	(382)	1.3	(5)	5.0	(19)	93.7	(358)
1980	(398)	1.5	(6)	7.8	(31)	90.7	(361)
1982	(393)	2.5	(10)	7.4	(29)	90.1	(354)
1984	(411)	0.7	(3)	3.9	(16)	95.4	(392)
1986	(393)	0.5	(2)	1.5	(6)	98.0	(385)
1988	(409)	0.2	(1)	1.5	(6)	98.3	(402)
1990	(407)	0.2	(1)	3.7	(15)	96.1	(391)
1992	(368)	5.4	(20)	6.3	(23)	88.3	(325)
1994	(387)	1.0	(4)	8.8	(34)	90.2	(349)
1996	(384)	0.5	(2)	5.5	(21)	94.0	(361)
1998	(401)	0.2	(1)	1.5	(6)	98.3	(394)
2000	(403)	0.7	(3)	1.5	(6)	97.8	(394)
2002	(398)	2.0	(8)	1.8	(7)	96.2	(383)
2004	(404)	0.5	(2)	1.7	(7)	97.8	(395)
2006	(404)	0.5	(2)	5.4	(22)	94.1	(380)
2008	(403)	0.9	(4)	4.7	(19)	94.2	(380)
2010	(396)	1.0	(4)	13.6	(54)	85.4	(338)
2012	(391)	4.6	(18)	5.6	(22)	89.8	(351)
2014	(395)	1.3	(5)	3.3	(13)	95.4	(377)
2016	(393)	1.5	(6)	2.0	(8)	96.4	(379)
2018	(378)	1.1	(4)	7.9	(30)	91.0	(344)
2020	(390)	2.1	(8)	3.1	(12)	94.8	(370)
Senate							
1954	(27)	—	(0)	15	(4)	85	(23)
1956	(30)	—	(0)	13	(4)	87	(26)
1958	(26)	—	(0)	35	(9)	65	(17)
1960	(28)	—	(0)	4	(1)	96	(27)
1962	(30)	—	(0)	10	(3)	90	(27)
1964	(30)	—	(0)	7	(2)	93	(28)
1966	(29)	7	(2)	3	(1)	90	(26)
1968	(28)	14	(4)	14	(4)	71	(20)
1970	(28)	4	(1)	11	(3)	86	(24)

(Continued)

Table 9.1 House and Senate Incumbents and Election Outcomes, 1954–2020 (Continued)

Year	Incumbent Running (N)	Primary Defeats %	Primary Defeats (N)	General Election Defeats %	General Election Defeats (N)	Reelected %	Reelected (N)
1972	(26)	4	(1)	19	(5)	77	(20)
1974	(26)	4	(1)	8	(2)	88	(23)
1976	(25)	—	(0)	36	(9)	64	(16)
1978	(22)	—	(1)	27	(6)	68	(15)
1980	(29)	—	(4)	31	(9)	55	(16)
1982	(30)	—	(0)	7	(2)	93	(28)
1984	(29)	—	(0)	10	(3)	90	(26)
1986	(27)	—	(0)	22	(6)	78	(21)
1988	(26)	—	(0)	12	(3)	88	(23)
1990	(30)	—	(0)	3	(1)	97	(29)
1992	(27)	4	(1)	11	(3)	85	(23)
1994	(26)	—	(0)	8	(2)	92	(24)
1996	(20)	—	(0)	5	(1)	95	(19)
1998	(29)	—	(0)	10	(3)	90	(26)
2000	(27)	—	(0)	22	(6)	78	(21)
2002	(26)	4	(1)	8	(2)	88	(23)
2004	(25)	—	(0)	5	(1)	96	(24)
2006	(28)	—	(0)	21	(6)	79	(22)
2008	(29)	—	(0)	17	(5)	93	(24)
2010	(25)	12	(3)	8	(2)	84[a]	(21)
2012	(22)	5	(1)	5	(1)	91	(20)
2014	(28)	—	(0)	18	(5)	82	(23)
2016	(29)	—	(0)	7	(2)	93	(27)
2018	(32)	—	(0)	16	(5)	84	(27)
2020	(32)	—	(0)	15	(5)	85	(27)

Source: Compiled by the authors.
[a] In 2010, Senator Lisa Murkowski (R-AK) was defeated in the primary and then won the general election as a write-in candidate. Thus, she is counted both as a primary defeat and as reelected.

During the period covered by table 9.1, House and Senate outcomes have sometimes been similar and in other instances have exhibited different patterns. For example, in most years between 1968 and 1988, House incumbents were substantially more successful than their Senate counterparts. In the three elections between 1976 and 1980, House incumbents' success averaged over 93 percent, whereas senators averaged only 62 percent. In contrast, the success rates during the 1990s were fairly similar. More recently, in all but one of the eleven elections beginning with 2000, we have again seen some divergence, with House incumbents being more successful.

These differences between the two bodies stem from at least two factors. The first is primarily statistical: House elections routinely involve around four hundred incumbents, whereas Senate contests usually have fewer than thirty.

A smaller number of cases is more likely to produce volatile results over time. Thus, the proportion of successful Senate incumbents tends to vary more than for the House. In addition, Senate races are more likely to be vigorously contested than House races, making incumbents more vulnerable. In many years many representatives had no opponent at all or had one who was inexperienced, underfunded, or both. Senators, on the other hand, often had strong, well-financed opponents. Thus, representatives were electorally advantaged relative to senators. The competitiveness of House elections increased in the early 1990s, reducing the relative advantage for representatives, although the election cycles since then still have seen competition in House contests confined to a narrower range of constituencies than Senate races.[4]

Having considered incumbency, we now consider political parties. Figure 9.1 shows the percentage of seats in the House and Senate held by the Democrats after each election since 1952. It graphically demonstrates how large a departure from the past the elections of 1994 through 2004 were. In House elections before 1994, the high percentage of incumbents running and the high rate of incumbent success led to fairly stable partisan control. Most importantly the Democrats won a majority in the House in every election

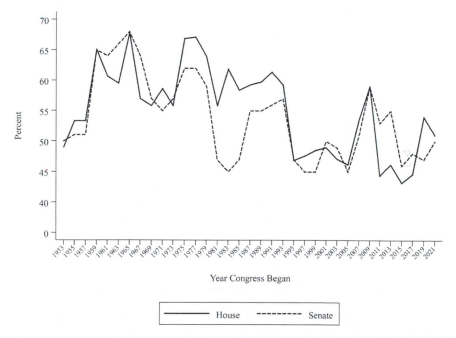

Year Congress Began

House ——— Senate - - - - - - - - -

Figure 9.1 Democratic Share of Seats in the House and Senate, 1953–2021 (in Percentages). *Sources*: Data for the House are from History, Art & Archives, United States Representatives, http://history.house.gov/Institution/Party-Divisions/Party-Divisions/. Data for the Senate are from United States Senate, https://www.senate.gov/history/partydiv.htm.

since 1954 and had won twenty consecutive national elections. This was by far the longest period of dominance of the House by the same party in American history.[5] This winning streak was ended by the upheaval of 1994, when the GOP made a net gain of fifty-two representatives, winning 53 percent of the total seats. They held their majority in each subsequent election through 2004, although there were small shifts back to the Democrats in 1996, 1998, and 2000. Then in 2006, the Democrats took back the House and expanded their margin in 2008. The huge GOP success of 2010 restored their control, and 2012 returned them as the majority with a reduced margin. They picked up thirteen additional seats during the 2014 midterm before losing a net of six seats in 2016. The Republicans lost 41 seats during the 2018 midterms but managed a net gain of 10 House seats in 2020.

In the Senate, Republican control was much more recent. They had taken the Senate in the Reagan victory of 1980 and retained it in 1982 and 1984. When the class of 1980 faced the voters again in 1986, however, the Democrats made significant gains and won back the majority. They held it until the GOP regained control in 1994, and then the Republicans expanded their margin in 1996. Then in 2000 fortune turned against them, resulting in the 50-50 division of the chamber. (This was followed a few months later by the decision of Senator James Jeffords of Vermont to become an independent, and to vote with the Democrats on organizing the chamber, shifting majority control to them until after the 2002 elections.) In 2004, the GOP gained four seats and again reached their high watermark of 55 percent. Finally, the combined Democratic gain of fourteen seats in 2006 and 2008 restored solid control for that party, which they retained for the next few years despite the difficult election of 2010. In 2014 the Republicans captured nine additional Senate seats, giving them unified congressional control for the final two years of the Obama presidency. Despite defending more than two-thirds of the seats up for reelection in 2016, the Republicans only lost two Senate seats in that election, yielding a relatively slim majority control. The Republicans also picked up two seats in the 2018 midterms but ended up losing a net of three in 2020 including the two Georgia Senate runoff elections in early January 2021.

The combined effect of party and incumbency in the general election of 2020 is shown in table 9.2. Overall, the Democrats won 51 percent of the races for House seats and 50 percent of the Senate contests. Despite the sharp partisanship of both the presidential and congressional races, incumbents of both parties did well in their House races. One hundred percent of House Republican incumbents in the general election won reelection, and 94.5 percent of House Democrats were successful. In the 2020 Senate races, ten of the eleven Democratic incumbents won, as did sixteen of the twenty GOP incumbents (more on this distinction later).

Table 9.2 House and Senate General Election Outcomes, by Party and Incumbency, 2020 (Percent)

	Democratic Incumbent	Democratic Seat	Republican Seat	Republican Incumbent	Total
		No Incumbent			
House					
Democrats	94.5	92.3	8.6	0	51
Republicans	5.5	7.7	91.4	100	49
Total	100	100	100	100	100
(N)	219	13	35	168	435
Senate					
Democrats	90.9	100	0	20	50[a]
Republicans	9.1	0	100	80	50
Total	100	100	100	100	100
(N)	11	1	3	20	35

Source: [a]Includes two independents who caucus with the Democrats. Senate values include two special elections. Compiled by the authors.

Table 9.3 Party Shares of Regional Delegations in the House and Senate, 1953, 1981, and 2021 (Percent)

	1953			1981			2021		
	Dems	Reps		Dems	Reps		Dems	Reps	
Region	(%)	(%)	(N)	(%)	(%)	(N)	(%)	(%)	(N)
House									
East	35	65	(116)	56	44	(105)	76	24	(79)
Midwest	23	76	(118)	47	53	(111)	42	58	(86)
West	33	67	(57)	51	49	(76)	68	32	(102)
South	94	6	(106)	64	36	(108)	33	67	(138)
Border	68	32	(38)	69	31	(35)	33	67	(30)
Total	49	51	(435)	56	44	(435)	51	48	(435)
Senate									
East	25	75	(20)	50	50	(20)	90	10	(20)
Midwest	14	86	(22)	41	59	(22)	36	64	(22)
West	45	55	(22)	35	65	(26)	65	35	(26)
South	100	0	(22)	55	45	(22)	18	82	(22)
Border	70	30	(10)	70	30	(10)	30	70	(10)
Total	49	51	(96)	47	53	(100)	50	50	(100)

Source: Compiled by the authors.

Regional Bases of Power

The geographic pattern of 2020 outcomes in the House and Senate can be seen in the partisan breakdowns by region in table 9.3.[6] For comparison, we also present corresponding data for 1981 (after the Republicans took control of the Senate in Reagan's first election) and for 1953 (the last Congress before 1995 in which the Republicans controlled both chambers). This series of elections reveals the enormous shifts in the regional political balance that have occurred over the last seven decades. In the House, comparing 2021 to 1981, the most pronounced shifts were in the West, the South, and the border states, with the Republican share decreasing by 17 percentage points in the West region while increasing by 31 points in the South and 36 points in the border states. Overall, the Republicans won a majority of House seats in all regions but the East and West in 2020. The pattern is roughly similar in the Senate. Between 1981 and 2021 the GOP actually made gains in three regions of the country (the Midwest, South and Border states), while they lost ground in the East and West.

The 2020 election results are even more interesting when viewed from the longer historical perspective. In 1953, there were sharp regional differences in party representation in both houses. These differences diminished significantly by 1981, but new and substantial deviations developed subsequently. The most obvious changes occurred in the East and the South. In 1953 the Republicans held nearly two-thirds of the House seats in the East, but by 2021 their share had fallen to slightly less than one-fourth. Indeed, in New England, historically a bastion of Republican strength, the GOP was unable to win any of the twenty-one House seats in 2020. The Republican decline in eastern Senate seats over the period was even greater, down from 75 percent to only 10 percent. In the South, on the other hand, the percentage of House seats held by Democrats declined from 94 percent in 1953 to 34 percent in 2021. In 1953 the Democrats held all twenty-two southern Senate seats, but in 2021 they controlled only four.

This change in the partisan share of the South's seats in Congress has had an important impact on that region's influence within the two parties. The South used to be the backbone of Democratic congressional representation. This, and the tendency of southern members to build up seniority, gave southerners disproportionate power within the Democratic Party in Congress. Because of declining Democratic electoral success in the region, the numerical strength of southern Democrats within their party in Congress has waned. In 1953, with the Republicans in control of both chambers, southerners accounted for around 45 percent of Democratic seats in the House and Senate. By the 1970s southern strength had declined, stabilizing at between 25 and 30 percent of Democratic seats. In 2021, southerners accounted for 21 percent of Democratic House seats and only 8 percent of Democratic senators.

The South's share of Republican congressional representation presents the reverse picture. Minuscule at the end of World War II, it steadily grew, reaching about 20 percent in the House after the 1980 elections and 36 percent after the 2020 election. As a consequence of these changes, southern influence has declined in the Democratic Party and grown in the GOP, to the point that southerners have often held a disproportionate share of the Republican leadership positions in both houses of Congress. Because southerners of both parties tend to be more conservative than their colleagues from other regions, these shifts in regional strength have tended to make the Democratic Party in Congress more liberal and the Republican Party more conservative.[7]

Other regional changes since 1953, although not as striking as those in the South and East, are also significant. In the 1953 House, the Republicans controlled the West by a two-to-one margin and the Midwest by three to one. In 2021 they were a 32 percent minority in the West and had a 59 percent share in the Midwest. The Senate also exhibited shifts away from substantial Republican strength in the West and Midwest. On the other hand, with the increased Republican control of the South and Democratic dominance in the East, regional differences in party shares are more prominent in 2021 than they were in 1981, and partisan representation is a bit less regionally homogeneous in the Congress of 2021 than it was in the Congress of 1953.

National Forces in Congressional Elections

The patterns of outcomes discussed here were shaped by a variety of influences. As with most congressional elections, the most important among these were the resources available to individual candidates and how those resources were distributed between the parties in specific races. We will discuss those matters shortly, but first we consider the more practical national-level influences particular to 2020.

The first national force to assess is whether there was a pattern in public opinion that advantaged one party or the other. Such "national tides" may occur in presidential years or in midterms, and they can have a profound impact on the outcomes of congressional elections. Often these tides flow from reaction to presidents or presidential candidates. For example, in 1964 the presidential landslide victory of Lyndon B. Johnson over Barry M. Goldwater carried over to major Democratic gains in both congressional chambers, and Ronald Reagan's ten-point margin over Jimmy Carter in 1980 helped Republicans achieve an unexpected majority in the Senate and major gains in the House. Similarly negative public reactions to events in the first two years of Bill Clinton's and Barack Obama's presidencies played a major part in the Republicans' congressional victories in 1994 and 2010 respectively, and dissatisfaction with President Trump significantly enhanced the Democrats' campaign to retake the House in 2018.

Clearly, 2020 was an election year that favored Democrats in a number of respects. Between President Trump's erratic and inconsistent handling of the coronavirus pandemic, the growing unemployment levels stemming from the virus and its deleterious effects on the economy, and the protests in late spring and early summer involving racial justice, Republicans had reason to be worried about the election. We saw in chapter 1 that the presidential race was close early in the year, but Biden began building a modest lead over Trump in a majority of polls during the summer and fall. Democrats initially had more House seats "in play" in 2019 and early 2020, but that number began to decline in late 2020 relative to Republicans. Figure 9.2 presents the number of Democratic and Republican House seats that political analyst Charlie Cook estimated to be highly competitive at various points in the 2019–2020 period.[8] Indeed, two weeks before the election, 33 Republican House seats were considered up for grabs compared to only 26 for the Democrats. In the Senate, the Cook Political Report indicated that 14 of the 35 Senate seats up for election 2020 were considered vulnerable—2 held by the Democrats and 12 controlled by Republicans.[9]

Another potential national influence is public reaction to the performance of Congress. In the 1996 presidential race, for example, Clinton and the Democrats tried to focus public attention on what they claimed was the extremism and excesses of the new GOP congressional majority, albeit with only very limited success.[10] In 2020, public opinion toward Congress had continued the long-term trend of being quite negative. In almost every major survey taken during the six months leading up to the election, approval of the way Congress was handling its job was between 18 and 25 percent.[11]

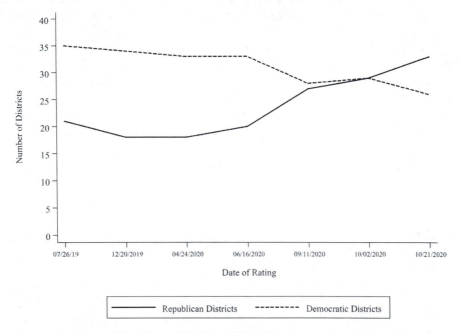

Figure 9.2   Competitive House Districts, 2019–2020. *Source*: Compiled by the authors from editions of *The Cook Political Report* on listed dates.

Additionally, according to a *Wall-Street Journal*-NBC poll conducted in June 2020 and reported by CNN, "51% of registered voters said they would prefer a Congress controlled by Democrats in 2021, while just 40% preferred a Republican-controlled Congress."[12]

Efforts of National Parties and Their Allies

One important national-level influence is the efforts of congressional party leaders and their allies to influence the races. Before the 1980s the activities of national parties in congressional elections were very limited. Individual candidates were mostly self-starters who were largely on their own in raising money and planning strategy. More recently, this situation has changed substantially, and party leaders and organizations are now heavily involved in recruiting and funding their candidates.[13] As we will see, the quality of candidates and their level of funding are two of the central determinants of election outcomes. Thus, both the short-term and long-term fates of the parties in Congress provided incentives for them to be active in efforts to improve their circumstances in these respects.

Recruiting Candidates

National party organizations are now continually active in candidate recruiting and fund-raising. As soon as the voting in one election ends, activity for the next begins. Republicans' main concern after their electoral defeat in the 2018 midterms was that many of their senior members would become frustrated by their minority status (and the expectation that it would continue) and retire. The situation was exacerbated by the fact that the Democrats had nearly a twenty-seat majority in the House and were in striking distance of controlling the Senate after the 2018 elections, especially given the number of Republican Senate seats up in 2020. The plans of individual candidates were monitored and possible strategies for eventually taking back the majority were discussed by the Republicans. The perceived prospects of success were key elements of the strategic calculations of potential recruits. It is much easier for a party to persuade a prospect to run if that party's national prospects look bright.

In the end both parties were moderately successful in staving off House retirements, with only twenty-eight representatives (twenty-three Republicans and five Democrats) opting to leave office entirely, although nine additional members sought higher office while a total of eight representatives resigned. Proportionately, retirements were greater in the Senate. There were thirty-five seats up in 2020 including two special elections, twelve held by Democrats and twenty-three by Republicans. In four of these, the sitting senator (three Republicans and one Democrat) declined to run.

The Democrats had a net gain of forty-one House seats during the 2018 midterm elections, giving them a 235–200 House majority, their largest electoral gain since 1974. In the Senate the Republicans managed to pick up four Democratic seats while losing two of their own to assume a fifty-three to forty-seven-seat majority, leading to split control in Congress. The Democratic Senatorial Campaign Committee recognized that the challenge of winning back majority control of the Senate would be far easier (at least in theory) because they had to net only four seats (or win a net of three seats and the vice presidency as it would turn out). Additionally, the Republicans had to defend nearly two times as many Senate seats as the Democrats did in 2020, which initially made their task appear that much simpler. Although a number of strong Democratic challengers considered running in 2019, many in key states such as Georgia, Iowa, and Texas ultimately decided against it, thus complicating the path for the Democrats to retake control of the chamber.[14]

For the Republicans, the challenge leading up to the 2020 elections was twofold. First, the National Republican Campaign Committee (NRCC) wanted to minimize losses in the House, especially because the majority caucus had grown increasingly heterogeneous with the election of a number of fiscally conservative, Tea Party and Freedom Caucus Republicans over the past decade. With respect to the Senate, the National Republican Senatorial Committee had the more formidable challenge of trying to defend at least nine Republican incumbents, all of which were deemed vulnerable by *Roll Call* in November 2019 (compared with only one Democratic senator, Doug Jones from Alabama). Among the most at-risk Republican senators leading up to the 2020 election were Martha McSally (AZ), Cory Gardner (CO), David Perdue (GA), Joni Ernst (IA), Susan Collins (ME), and Tom Tillis (NC). Many considered Gardner to be among the most vulnerable because he was running for reelection in a state that Hillary Clinton won in 2016 and the Democrats were expected to throw their support behind popular former Governor John Hickenlooper.[15]

Money and Other Aid

In addition to recruitment, party leaders have grown increasingly active in fund-raising, pursuing many different strategies. For example, top party leaders solicit donations to the congressional campaign committees like the NRCC and the DCCC, and they appear at fund-raisers for individual candidates in their districts. The amounts they raise are considerable. As of November 16, 2020, "Pelosi's joint fundraising committee, the Nancy Pelosi Victory Fund, raised a whopping $23.7 million through September 2020, up from $3.7 million through the entirety of the 2018 cycle. It transferred $20 million to the Democratic Congressional Campaign Committee, House Democrats' campaign arm. Pelosi's campaign committee transferred another $1.6 million to the DCCC. Then there's Pelosi's leadership PAC, PAC to the Future, which contributed the maximum $10,000 to nearly every House Democrat running in a remotely competitive race."[16] Nevertheless, majority status is an asset for fund-raising, and Speaker Nancy Pelosi did substantially better than her Californian counterpart Kevin McCarthy, amassing nearly $6.1 million more in funds raised through their campaign committees and leadership PACs.[17]

In both parties raising campaign funds for the party has become a prominent obligation for members who hold or want leadership posts and committee chairmanships, and the amounts they raise are a significant portion of money spent in campaigns. According to opensecrets.org, House Majority Leader Steny Hoyer raised more than $12 million through his reelection committee and leadership PACs during the 2020 election cycle, the bulk of which was transferred to the DCCC and liberal interest groups that both support other Democratic candidates.[18] In recent years, the parties have set contribution targets for their incumbents (which they term "dues"). Although many members would prefer to retain the money they raise for their own use, they have increasingly been pressured to share that money with other members. One interesting pattern that emerged in 2020 is that the House minority whip, Steve Scalise, raised the most money compared to every other House member including the leadership of both parties. Similar to an interesting pattern during the 2016 election cycle, the next five top earners among Republicans and Democrats included two freshmen who had been elected in 2018— Alexandria Ocasio-Cortez (D-NY) and Dan Crenshaw (R-TX).[19]

Party leaders are able to do more to help candidates' reelection efforts than just raise or spend campaign money, at least for the House majority. Because the majority party has almost total control over the floor agenda and the content of bills, it can add or remove provisions in bills that will enhance their members' reelection chances or permit vulnerable colleagues to bring their popular bills to the floor, thus enhancing their reputations.

In addition to funding by the formal party organizations like the DCCC and the NRCC, the parties' congressional candidates are receiving increasing support from outside groups and super PACs.[20] During the 2020 election cycle, more than $1.5 billion was spent by outside groups in Senate contests, nearly 30 percent of which was allocated to only two Senate races, both of which were in Georgia and one of which was a special election.[21] That was an increase of nearly 250 percent spent by outside groups during the same period in the 2016 contests.[22] Whereas the lion's share of outside spending went to

Senate contests during 2020, more than $710 million from those sources were spent on competitive House races.[23]

CANDIDATES' RESOURCES AND ELECTION OUTCOMES

Seats in the House and Senate are highly valued posts for which candidates compete vigorously. In contests for these offices, candidates draw on every resource they have. To explain the results of congressional elections, we must consider the comparative advantages and disadvantages of the various candidates. In this section, we will discuss the most significant resources available to candidates and the impact those resources have on the outcomes of congressional elections.

Candidate Quality

The personal abilities that foster electoral success can be a major political asset. Many constituencies do not offer a certain victory for one of the two major parties, and for those that do strongly tilt to one party, there is often a contested primary, so election outcomes usually depend heavily on candidate quality. A strong, capable candidate is a significant asset for a party; a weak, inept one is a liability that is difficult to overcome. In his study of the activities of House members in their districts, Richard F. Fenno, Jr., described how members try to build and establish bonds of trust between constituents and their representatives.[24] Members attempt to convey to their constituents a sense that they are qualified for their job, that they identify with their constituents, and that they empathize with constituents and their problems. Challengers of incumbents and candidates for open seats must engage in similar activities to win support. The winner of a contested congressional election will usually be the candidate who is better able to establish these bonds of support among constituents and to convince them that he or she is the person for the job (or that the opponent is not).

One indicator of candidate quality is previous success at winning elective office. The more important the office a candidate has held, the more likely it is that he or she has overcome significant competition to obtain the office.[25] Moreover, the visibility and reputation for performance that usually accompany public office can also be a significant electoral asset. For example, state legislators running for House seats can claim that they have experience that has prepared them for congressional service. State legislators may also have built successful organizations that are useful in conducting congressional campaigns. Finally, previous success in an electoral arena suggests that experienced candidates are more likely to be able to run strong campaigns than candidates without previous success or experience. Less adept candidates are likely to have been screened out at lower levels of office competition. For these and other reasons, an experienced candidate tends to have an electoral advantage over a candidate who has held no previous elected office.[26] Moreover, the higher the office previously held, the stronger the candidate will tend to be in the congressional contest.[27]

In table 9.4, we present data showing which candidates were successful in 2020, controlling for prior experience, party, and incumbency.[28] In House contests the vast majority of candidates who challenged incumbents lost regardless of their background or party, although those with previous elective experience did somewhat better when running against Democratic incumbents than those who had none. The impact of candidate quality is stronger in races without incumbents. Here, candidates with prior elective experience were more successful and won at a higher rate than those without any elective office experience. In Senate races, because there were only four incumbent losses, no clear pattern is visible there. For non-incumbent candidates those with previous elective experience generally did better.

Given the importance of candidate quality, it is worth noting that there has been substantial variation in the proportion of experienced challengers over time. During the 1980s, the proportion of House incumbents facing challengers who had previously won elective office declined. In 1980, 17.6 percent of incumbents faced such challenges; in 1984, 14.7 percent did; in 1988, only 10.5 percent did. In 1992, due largely to perceptions of incumbent vulnerability because of redistricting and scandal, the proportion rose to 23.5 percent, but in 1996, it was back down to 16.5 percent, and it remained at that level in 2000.[29] In 2004, however, there was a substantial resurgence in the number of experienced candidates in both parties, with 22.4 percent of the

Table 9.4   Success in House and Senate Elections, Controlling for Office Background, Party, and Incumbency, 2020 (Percent)

	Candidate Is Opponent of . . .		No Incumbent in District	
	Democratic Incumbent *% (N)*	*Republican Incumbent* *% (N)*	*Democratic Candidate* *% (N)*	*Republican Candidate* *% (N)*
House				
Quality	9.7 (31)	0 (22)	41.7 (12)	83.3 (18)
Amateur	2.7 (182)	0 (140)	27.8 (36)	56.7 (30)
Senate				
Quality	0 (2)	12.5 (8)	50 (2)	100 (2)
Amateur	11.1 (9)	25 (12)	0 (2)	50 (2)

Source: Data on office backgrounds were taken from issues of *The Cook Political Report* and the *Green Papers*. Compiled by the authors.

total challengers having previously held elective office, followed by a decline again in 2008 to 14.8 percent. In 2012, the proportion rebounded again to 20 percent before steadily declining to 9 percent by 2018 and modestly increasing to 13.3 percent in 2020.[30]

Whether experienced politicians actually run for the House or Senate is not an accident. These are significant strategic decisions made by politicians, and they have much to lose if they make the wrong choice. The choices will be governed by factors related to the perceived chance of success, the potential value of the new office compared to what will be lost if the candidate fails, and the costs of running.[31] The chances of success of the two major parties vary from election to election, both locally and nationally. Therefore, each election offers a different mix of experienced and inexperienced candidates from the two parties for the House and Senate.

The most influential factor in whether a potential candidate will run is whether there is an incumbent in the race. High reelection rates tend to discourage potentially strong challengers from running, which in turn makes it even more likely that the incumbents will win. In addition to the general difficulty of challenging incumbents, factors related to specific election years (both nationally and in a particular district) will affect decisions to run. For example, the Democratic Party had particular difficulty recruiting strong candidates during 2010 because of fears about a potential backlash following passage of the Affordable Health Care Act. And the 2018 decline in quality candidates was likely a function of the Republicans having less success recruiting strong candidates in many districts because the electoral environment was perceived to be negative for their party. On the other hand, some research indicates that potential House candidates are most strongly influenced in their decisions by their perceived chances of winning their party's nomination.[32] Moreover, the actions of incumbents may influence the choices of potential challengers. For example, building up a large reserve of campaign funds between elections may dissuade some possible opponents, although analysis of Senate contests indicates that this factor does not have a systematic impact in those races.[33]

As we have seen, most congressional races do not involve challengers who have previous office experience. Given their slight chance of winning, why do challengers without experience run at all? As Jeffrey S. Banks and D. Roderick Kiewiet point out, although the chances of success against incumbents may be small for such candidates, such a race may still be their best chance of ever winning a seat in Congress.[34] If inexperienced challengers were to put off their candidacies until a time when there is no incumbent, their opposition would likely include multiple experienced candidates from both parties. Moreover, as David Canon demonstrates, previous office experience is an imperfect indicator of candidate quality because some candidates without such experience can still have significant political assets and be formidable challengers.[35] For example, consider two contests from 2000, one from each chamber. The Republican candidate for the House in Nebraska's third district was Tom Osborne, the extremely popular former head coach of the University of Nebraska's football team. Osborne was elected to an open seat with a phenomenal 82 percent of the vote. In the New York Senate race, the very visible (and ultimately successful) Democratic candidate was then First Lady Hillary Rodham Clinton. In many respects this win may have set her on the path to running for the presidency in 2008 and again in 2016.

Incumbency and Electoral Margins

One reason most incumbents win is that incumbency itself is a significant resource. To be more precise, incumbency is not a single resource but rather a status that usually gives a candidate a variety of benefits. In some respects, incumbency works to a candidate's advantage automatically. For example, incumbents tend to be more visible to voters than do challengers.[36] Less automatic, but very important, incumbents usually tend to be viewed more favorably than challengers. Moreover, at least a plurality of the electorate in most districts will identify with the incumbent's political party, and this pattern has become stronger over the last couple of decades. Incumbents can also use their status to gain advantages. Incumbents generally raise and spend more money than challengers, and they usually have a better developed and more experienced campaign organization. They also have assets, provided at public expense, such as a staff and franking privileges (free postage for mail to their constituents), that both help them perform their jobs and provide electoral benefits. Incumbents also have the opportunity to introduce bills favored by their constituents and to bring "pork" home to the district, when they think it will be advantageous to do so. Challengers, in contrast, lack such advantages.

From the mid-1960s through the late 1980s, the margins by which incumbents were reelected increased (the pattern was less clear and more erratic in Senate elections than in House elections).[37] These changing patterns interested analysts primarily because they believed that the disappearance of marginal incumbents means less congressional turnover and less responsiveness to the electorate. Edward R. Tufte offered an early explanation for the increased incumbency margins by arguing that redistricting had protected incumbents of both parties.[38] This argument initially seemed plausible because the increase in margins occurred about the same time as the massive redistricting required by Supreme Court decisions of the mid-1960s. But other analysts showed that incumbents had won by larger margins both in states that had been redistricted and in those that had not as well as in Senate contests.[39] Thus redistricting was eventually dismissed as the major reason for the change.

Another explanation offered for the increase in incumbents' margins was the growth in the perquisites of members and the greater complexity of government. Morris P. Fiorina notes that in the post-New Deal period, the level of federal services and the bureaucracy that administers them had grown tremendously.[40] A more complex government means that many people will encounter problems in receiving services, and people who have problems frequently contact their representatives to complain and seek help. Fiorina contends that in the mid-1960s, new members of Congress emphasized such constituency problem-solving more than their predecessors. This expanded constituency service developed into a reservoir of electoral support. Although analyses of the impact of constituency services have produced mixed conclusions, it is likely that the growth of these services offers only a partial explanation for changing incumbent vote margins and for the incumbency advantage generally.[41]

The declining impact of party loyalties provided a third explanation for the growth in incumbent vote margins, either alone or in conjunction with other factors. Until the mid-1960s, there was a very strong linkage between party identification and congressional voting behavior. Most Americans identified with a political party, many identified strongly, and most voters supported the candidate of their chosen party. Subsequently, however, the impact of party identification decreased. John A. Ferejohn, drawing on data from the ANES, shows that the strength of party ties weakened and that within any given category of party identification, the tendency to support the candidate of one's party declined.[42] An analysis by Albert D. Cover shows that voters who did not identify with the party of a congressional incumbent were increasingly more likely to defect from their party and support the incumbent, although there had been no increase in defections from party identification by voters of the same party as incumbents.[43] Thus weakened party ties produced a substantial net benefit for incumbents,[44] although as we saw in chapter 6 (and will discuss further in chapter 10), party loyalties among the electorate have grown much stronger in recent decades.[45]

The Trend Reversed

Whatever the relative importance of these factors (and the others we will discuss) in explaining the increase in incumbents' victory margins, the increase continued through the 1980s, as the data in figure 9.3 show, peaking at 68.4 percent in 1986. These data are only for races in which both parties ran candidates. Thus, they exclude contests where an incumbent ran unopposed. Such races were also increasing in number over this period; therefore, the data actually understate the growth in incumbents' margins.

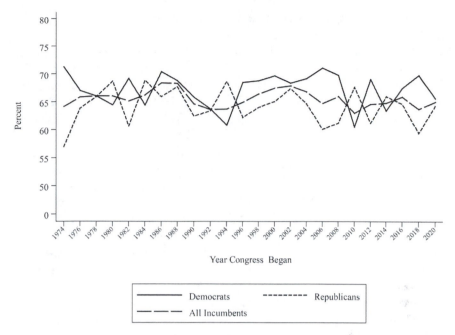

Figure 9.3 Average Vote Percentages of House Incumbents, 1974–2020. *Source*: Compiled by the authors. Note: These values include only races where both major parties ran candidates. Thus, they exclude contests in which an incumbent ran unopposed.

Then, in 1990, something changed. The average share of the vote for incumbents declined by nearly 4 percentage points. The decline was, moreover, not a result of a shift of voters toward one party, as with the decline from 1980 to 1982; both parties' incumbents suffered. Rather the shift in incumbents' electoral fortunes was apparently the result of what was called the "anti-incumbent mood" among the voters. Early in 1990 pollsters and commentators began to perceive stronger anti-Congress sentiments within the electorate.[46] For the first time, analysts began to question whether incumbency remained the asset it used to be.

There was, of course, nothing new about Congress being unpopular; Congress had long suffered ups and downs in approval, just like the president. What changed in 1990 was that Congress's unpopularity appeared to be undermining the approval of individual members by their own constituents. Yet, as the data presented in table 9.1 shows, even though there was a drop in the average percentage of the vote received by incumbents in 1990, the rate of reelection still reached 96 percent. The decline in vote margins was not great enough to produce a rash of defeats. Many observers wondered, however, whether 1990 was the beginning of a new trend: would incumbents' electoral drawing power continue to decline?

In 1992, scandals damaged many representatives of both parties, and among the public, the evaluation of Congress was very low. Opponents of incumbents emphasized that they were "outsiders" and not "professional politicians" (even when they had substantial political experience). The results from 1992 show that incumbents' share of the vote dropped a bit more. Republicans rebounded a little from their bad 1990 showing, whereas Democrats fell more than 2 percentage points. Yet again, however, the casualty rate among incumbents who ran in the general election was lower than many expected 93 percent were reelected.[47] Then, in 1994, although there was only a slight additional drop in incumbents' share of the vote overall, the drop was greater (and concentrated) for Democrats, and their casualty rate was high. The result was the loss of their majority. Next, in 1996, there was a slight rebound in incumbents' vote share, with Democrats increasing sharply, while the GOP fell. That vote shift translated into eighteen Republican incumbents defeated but only three Democrats. Finally, the results from 2000 through 2020 typically fall in between the highs of the mid-1980s and the lows of 1994 and 1996 (although 2010 and 2018 are just outside this range). Indeed, during those years, the average incumbent vote percentage has been virtually identical each year, although the averages for the parties have varied with the electoral climate.

This discussion illustrates that incumbents' vote margins and incumbents' reelection success are related but distinct phenomena.[48] When—as was true in the 1980s—the average share of the vote received by incumbents is very high, they can lose a lot of ground before a large number of defeats occur. What appears to have occurred in 1990 is that many incumbents were subjected to vigorous contests for the first time in years. Such challenges were then repeated or extended to additional incumbents in 1992, 1994, and 1996. Potential candidates apparently looked at the political situation and concluded that incumbents who had previously looked unbeatable could now potentially be defeated, and there was a substantial increase in the number of candidates for Congress. These vigorous contests by challengers who were stronger than usual resulted in a decrease in the share of the vote received by many incumbents.

Jacobson, in his *Journal of Politics* article, offers a slightly different interpretation for the reversal of fortune among incumbents since the 1990s. He argues that the increasing nationalization of elections stemming from a resurgence in party voting among the electorate has actually contributed to a decline in the incumbency advantage during the past few decades. With more constituents basing their voting decisions on partisan criteria in light of increasing levels of polarization, it has become more difficult for incumbents to win districts that lean toward the other party as was once the case. This, in turn, has contributed to a decline in the personal incumbency advantage because members of the House can no longer rely on the resources of office to carry them to victory in polarized congressional districts.[49] Indeed, the incumbency advantage declined to a record low of 1.5 percentage points in 2020 in light of the highly nationalized election featuring Donald Trump.[50] The same general pattern holds for the US Senate, although it was not quite as pronounced until 2016 when, "for the first time in history, every Senate contest was won by the party that won the state's electoral votes."[51] This pattern was nearly repeated again in the 2020 Senate elections with the exception of the Maine Senate race where Susan Collins won reelection despite Joe Biden carrying the state.

Campaign Spending

A third resource that strongly affects congressional elections is campaign spending. Campaign spending has received a great deal of attention in the last five decades because researchers gained access to more dependable data than had previously been available.[52] The data on spending have consistently shown that incumbents usually outspend their challengers, often by large margins, and that through the early 1990s, the disparity had increased.[53] (As we shall see shortly, more recent data show significant changes.)

Disparities in campaign spending are linked to the increase in incumbents' election margins. Beginning in the 1960s congressional campaigns relied more heavily on campaign techniques that cost money—for example, media time, campaign consulting, and direct mailing—and these became increasingly expensive. At the same time, candidates were progressively less likely to have available pools of campaign workers from established party organizations or from interest groups. This made using expensive media and direct mail strategies relatively more important. Most challengers are unable to raise significant campaign funds. Neither individuals nor groups interested in the outcomes of congressional elections like to throw money away; before making contributions they usually need to be convinced that the candidate has a chance. Yet we have seen that in most election years, few incumbents have been beaten. Thus, it is often difficult to convince potential contributors that their money will produce results, and contributions are often not forthcoming. Most challengers are thus at a strategic disadvantage, and they are often unable to raise sufficient funds to wage a competitive campaign.[54]

It is the ability to compete, rather than the simple question of relative amounts of spending, that is at the core of the issue. We have noted that incumbents have many inherent advantages that the challenger must overcome if he or she hopes to win. But often the money is not there to overcome them. In 2020, for example, approximately 21.6 percent of challengers spent $25,000 or less, and slightly more than 38 percent spent $75,000 or less. With so little money available, challengers are unable to make themselves visible to the electorate or to convey a convincing message.[55] Under such circumstances, most voters—being unaware of the positions, or perhaps even the existence, of the challenger—vote for the incumbent.

Data from 2020 on campaign spending and election outcomes seem consistent with this argument, and they show patterns similar to those exhibited in other recent elections.[56] Linking spending to outcomes, table 9.5 shows the relationship between the incumbent's share of the vote in the 2020 House elections and the amount of money spent by the challenger. Clearly, there is a strong negative relationship between how much challengers spend and how well incumbents do. In races where challengers spent less than $25,000, 100 percent of incumbents received 60 percent or more of the vote, the traditional cutoff for marginality. At the other end of the spectrum, in races where challengers spent $800,000 or more, 76.6 percent of the incumbents received less than 60 percent of the vote, and approximately 49 percent got less than 55 percent of the vote. These results are consistent with those in earlier House elections for which comparable data are available.[57]

These findings are reinforced by other research that shows that challenger spending has a greater influence on election outcomes than does incumbent spending.[58] This generalization has been questioned on methodological grounds,[59] but further research by Gary Jacobson reinforced his earlier findings. Using both aggregate and survey data, he found that "the amount spent by the challenger is far more important in accounting for voters' decisions than is the amount of spending by the incumbent."[60] In more recent work, Jacobson emphasized the importance of incumbent spending. He writes, "It is no mystery why winning challengers reached so many voters and were so much more familiar to them. They ran much better financed campaigns than

Table 9.5   Incumbents' Share of the Vote in the 2020 House Elections, by Challenger Campaign Spending (Percent)

Challenger Spending	Incumbents' Share of the Two-Party Vote					
	Greater than 70%	60%– <=70%	55%– <=60%	Less than 55%	Total	N
$0–$24,999	56.8 (46)	43.2 (35)	0 (0)	0 (0)	100	81
$25,000–$74,999	30.6 (19)	54.8 (34)	12.9 (8)	1.6 (1)	100	62
$75,000–$199,999	30.8 (16)	53.8 (28)	15.4 (8)	0 (0)	100	52
$200,000–$399,999	16.7 (6)	58.3 (21)	19.4 (7)	5.6 (2)	100	36
$400,000–$799,999	5.0 (1)	50.0 (10)	25.0 (5)	20.0 (4)	100	20
$800,000 and up	13.7 (17)	9.7 (12)	27.4 (34)	49.2 (61)	100	124
All	28.0 (105)	36.2 (140)	16.0 (62)	17.6 (68)	100	375

Source: Federal Election Commission, http:www.fec.gov. Compiled by the authors.
Note: Races without a major party opponent are excluded, and challenger spending that is unavailable was coded in the $0–24,999 row. *N*s are in parentheses.

did the losers."[61] In contrast, analysis of Senate elections has also resulted in somewhat more conflicting conclusions.[62]

Of course, challengers who appear to have good prospects will find it easier to raise money than those whose chances seem slim. Thus, one might wonder whether these data simply reflect the fulfillment of expectations in which money flows to challengers who would have done well regardless of spending. Other research, however, indicates that is likely not the case. In an analysis of the 1972 and 1974 congressional elections, Jacobson concluded, "Our evidence is that campaign spending helps candidates, particularly non-incumbents, by bringing them to the attention of the voters; it is not the case that well-known candidates simply attract more money; rather money buys attention."[63] From this perspective, adequate funding is a necessary but not sufficient condition for a closely fought contest, a perspective consistent with the data in table 9.6. Heavily outspending one's opponent is not a guarantee of victory; the evidence does not indicate that elections can simply be bought because money does not literally buy votes. Indeed, having to spend large sums of money in a prior race may signal to an astute challenger that the incumbent is vulnerable and likely to lose under the right circumstances. Even if an incumbent outspends the challenger, the incumbent can still lose if the challenger is adequately funded and runs a campaign that persuades the voters.[64]

The 2020 elections, for example, offer clear evidence of this, particularly in the Senate. In four of the five races in which Senate incumbents faced a non-incumbent challenger and the incumbent lost, the challenger outspent the incumbent. However, in the House, incumbents that faced a non-incumbent and lost were outspent in only three out of thirteen races.[65] The losing incumbent in each of these 13 House races spent an average of about $5 million dollars on the unsuccessful reelection bid. The losing incumbent in each of the five Senate races spent an average of about $53.8 million dollars on their

Table 9.6 Percentage of Incumbents by Vote Share, Challenger Experience, and Spending in the 2020 House Elections

Challenger	Incumbents' Share of Two-Party Vote					
Experience/ Spending	Greater than 70%	60%– <=70%	55%– <=60%	Less Than 55%	Total	N
Weak/low	43.4 (79)	49.5 (90)	6.5 (12)	0.5 (1)	100	182
Strong/low	15.4 (2)	53.8 (7)	30.7 (4)	0.0 (0)	100	13
Weak/high	14.3 (20)	26.4 (37)	27.9 (39)	31.4 (44)	100	140
Strong/high	10.0 (4)	15.0 (6)	17.5 (7)	57.5 (23)	100	40

Source: See tables 9.4 and 9.5. Compiled by the authors.
Note: Percentages read across. Strong challengers have held previous elective office. High-spending challengers spent more than $200,000. Races without a major-party opponent are excluded. *N*s are in parentheses.

unsuccessful reelection bid.[66] The fact that incumbents in each of these races had to spend as much as they did is consistent with Jacobson's argument that spending large sums of money is no guarantee of electoral victory, especially when one factors in the fund-raising prowess of their opponents.

On the other hand, raising large sums of money is not a guarantee for a challenger. In an extreme example from 2020, losing Republican challenger John Cummings spent $10.85 million against incumbent Alexandria Ocasio-Cortez of New York, who spent $16.2 million. Despite Cummings' ability to raise and spend an impressive amount of money, Ocasio-Cortez won more than 71 percent of the vote. A somewhat less extreme case occurred in 2008, when Republican Sandy Treadwell spent more than $7 million compared to incumbent Democrat Kristen Gillibrand of New York's $4.49 million. The Democrat was reelected with more than 61 percent of the vote. Based on this analysis, our view can be summarized as follows: if a challenger is to attain visibility and get his or her message across to the voters—neutralizing the incumbent's advantages in name recognition and perquisites of office— the challenger needs to be adequately funded. If both sides in a race are adequately funded, the outcome will tend to turn on factors other than just money, and the relative spending of the two candidates is unlikely to control the outcome.[67]

This argument carries us full circle back to our earlier discussion and leads us to bring together the three kinds of resources we have considered—candidate experience, incumbency, and campaign spending. Table 9.6 presents data showing the impact of these three factors in the 2020 House elections. We categorize challenger experience as strong or weak depending on previous elective-office experience; challenger spending was classified as low or high depending on whether it was below or above $200,000.[68] The data show that each element exerts some independent effect, but the impact of spending seems to be more consequential in the most recent election cycle (as was also true in 2016). When challengers had weak experience and low spending (48.5 percent of the races), all incumbents won, and nearly 93 percent won with more than 60 percent of the vote. In the opposite situation, where the challenger had both strong experience and substantial spending, 75 percent of the races were considered competitive. The combined results for the two intermediate categories fall between the extremes. In addition, incumbent defeats occur with greater frequency in situations where the challenger is experienced and has strong spending. Table 9.6 also reveals that 75 percent of the challengers with previous experience were able to raise substantial funds (forty of fifty-three), whereas only 25 percent of challengers with no elective experience were able to do so.

This combination of factors also helps explain the greater volatility of outcomes in Senate races discussed earlier. Previous analysis has shown that the effects of campaign spending in Senate contests are consistent with what we have found true for House races: if challenger spending is above some threshold, the election is often quite close; if it is below that level, the incumbent is likely to win by a large margin.[69] In Senate races, however, the mix of well-funded and poorly funded challengers is different. Senate challengers are more likely to be able to raise significant amounts of money than their House counterparts. Indeed, in recent elections, a number of challengers (and open-seat candidates) have been wealthy individuals who could provide a large share of their funding from their own resources. One of the earliest extreme examples comes from 2000, when Jon Corzine, the Democratic candidate for the open New Jersey Senate seat, spent more than $60 million of his own money to defeat his opponent. Corzine spent a total of $63 million; the Republican spent $6.4 million.[70] Nevertheless, Corzine was only elected by a 3-percentage point margin. A more recent case comes from one of the 2020 Senate runoffs in Georgia, where Republican incumbent David Perdue received 49.4 percent of the vote compared to Jon Ossoff's 50.6 percent. During the election, Perdue spent nearly $90 million compared with $149 million spent by Ossoff. However, outside spending in the race approached $270 million, bringing the total amount spent in the Georgia Senate race to approximately $507 million.[71]

Senate challengers, moreover, are also more likely to possess prior elective experience. Thus, in Senate contests, incumbents often face well-funded and experienced challengers, and the stage is then set for their defeat if other circumstances work against them. The lesson from the evidence presented here is captured by the words of David Johnson, the director of the DSCC, to Rep. Richard C. Shelby of Alabama, who was challenging Republican Senator Jeremiah Denton in 1986. Shelby, who eventually won, was concerned that he did not have enough campaign funds as Denton was outspending him two to one. Johnson responded: "You don't have as much money, but you're going to have enough—and enough is all it takes to win."[72]

THE 2020 ELECTIONS: THE IMPACT ON CONGRESS

The elections of 1994 produced huge consequences for politics and governing, and each subsequent election over the next decade was seen in relation to whether GOP control would be strengthened or weakened. The GOP retained control in the next five elections. A significant electoral tide in 2006 gave the Democrats control of both chambers, which they improved on in 2008. That was followed by the Republican congressional landslide of 2010 and the return of divided government when the GOP took the House. Divided government was maintained in 2012, with modest Democratic gains in both chambers. During the 2014 midterms, the Republicans managed to gain a net thirteen House seats and nine Senate seats, giving them control of both chambers for the first time since 2006. The Republicans lost a net of six House seats and two Senate seats in 2016, but they maintained control of both chambers, giving them unified party control of Congress coupled with a Republican president at the start of the 115th Congress. After gaining control of the House during the 2018 midterms, the Democrats won the presidency in 2020 and narrowly controlled the Senate in a 50-50 tie following the two Georgia runoff elections held in early January 2021, giving them unified Democratic control of both branches.

The modest Democratic gains in the Senate following the runoff elections yielded a 50-50 tie for the first time in twenty years and ensured a close division in which moderate senators like Joe Manchin (D-WV) and Krysten Sinema (D-AZ) would be pivotal in passing legislation. This should be viewed in the context of a long-term decline of such legislators and an increase in the number of conservative Republicans and liberal Democrats. Sixty years ago, there was more ideological "overlap" between the parties across both chambers. The Democrats had a substantial conservative contingent, mostly from the South, that was as conservative as the right wing of the Republican Party. Similarly, the GOP had a contingent (primarily northeasterners) whose members were as liberal as northern Democrats. In addition, each party had a significant number of moderate members. During the intervening years, however, this overlap between the parties began to disappear as a result of changes in the electorate and in Congress.[73] By the mid-1980s both parties in the House and Senate had become more politically homogeneous, and in each chamber there was little departure from a complete ideological separation of the two parties.[74] Thus, in the 117th Congress that resulted from the 2020 elections, substantial majorities of each party had sharply different policy preferences from those in the other party, with a very small but potentially influential group of members in the middle.

The Biden Administration and Unified Government

Following Joe Biden's election as president along with unified (albeit narrow) control of Congress, the Democrats had their best chance in several years to advance their political agenda. Throughout the 2020 presidential campaign, Biden framed his campaign as a direct challenge to the policies pursued by Donald Trump since he was elected in 2016. When Biden announced he was running for president on April 25, 2019, he said, "I believe history will look back on four years of this president and all he embraces as an aberrant moment in time. But if we give Donald Trump eight years in the White House, he will forever and fundamentally alter the character of this nation—who we are—and I cannot stand by and watch that happen."[75] At the time, this statement was directed primarily at Trump's attempts to repeal and replace the Affordable Health Care Act (Obamacare), build a wall between the United States and Mexico, and temporarily ban Muslims from entering the United States among other initiatives. It also was likely a function of how the international community viewed the Trump presidency during his time in office. Midway through 2020, this also extended to Trump's inconsistent handling of the coronavirus pandemic that would ultimately lead to over 225,000 deaths prior to the election.

Despite having Democratic control of both chambers, Biden opted to issue 19 executive orders in his first three days in office in an attempt to deliver on several of his campaign promises. One of his first executive orders, issued on January 20 within a few hours of his inauguration, sought to organize and mobilize the US government to provide a more unified and effective response to combat the COVID-19 pandemic. This had been one of his biggest priorities during his presidential campaign in light of the inconsistent response by the Trump administration in dealing with the coronavirus. He also signed executive orders on the same day that sought to prevent and combat discrimination on the basis of gender identity or sexual orientation, guarantee ethics commitments by executive branch personnel, promote scientific advances to combat the climate crisis, and revise certain immigration enforcement policies.[76] Many of these orders sought to overturn actions taken by former President Trump during the past four years as is often the case in a new presidential administration.

Over the next few months, President Biden issued additional executive orders, many of which dealt directly with combating the coronavirus and promoting public safety in light of the pandemic. He also signed a number of orders in the first few weeks of his administration that touched on issues such as worker health and safety, the gradual reopening of schools, protecting the federal workforce, and reforming the United States' prison system. On April 9, Biden responded to growing pressure from the liberal wing of his party by issuing an executive order that established a presidential commission on the Supreme Court of the United States to evaluate the possibility of increasing the size of the Court.[77] Following the death of Justice Ruth Bader Ginsberg in September 2020 and her replacement with conservative jurist Judge Amy Coney Barrett just weeks prior to the election, a large number of liberal Democrats demanded that the president consider various options to respond to Trump's controversial action, including "packing" the Court with more liberal justices.[78]

Research on the US presidency suggests that chief executives are more likely to utilize unilateral tools like executive orders during periods of unified government.[79] Part of the rationale for this behavior is that presidents have more flexibility in issuing executive orders when their party is in control of Congress, especially if Congress is unable or unwilling to act as a result of gridlock or such decisions are perceived as controversial. By mid-May, President Biden had issued 44 executive orders, making him second only to Frankin Roosevelt in the number of unilateral directives utilized in the early days of his presidency. In addition to executive orders, Biden issued a variety of proclamations and presidential memoranda to begin implementing change in light of policies enacted during the previous four years under the Trump administration.[80]

The House: Limits of a Narrow Democratic Majority

Following the historic 1994 elections, the new Republican majority instituted major institutional changes in the 104th Congress that convened in 1995.[81] By comparison, the changes in House organization for the 117th Congress were much more modest. On January 3, 2021, the House Democrats adopted rules for the chamber that included the establishment of a bipartisan Select Committee on Economic Disparity and Fairness in Growth. Several days before the start of the new Congress, Speaker Pelosi announced the creation of this committee to combat perceived disparities in economic recovery stemming from the coronavirus. At a news conference held prior to the start of the new Congress, Pelosi stated, "Clearly, the disparities in income and equity in our country are vast. We've known that. They've only gotten worse, and the pandemic, again, puts it in sharper focus."[82] She added that the committee was modeled after one created by Franklin Roosevelt and Congress during the Great Depression and would be aided by the Select Subcommittee on the Coronavirus Crisis and Select Committee on the Climate Crisis.[83]

Three days after the start of the new session, both chambers faced a crisis unlike anything the country had ever seen. As the new Congress was meeting jointly on January 6, 2021 to tally the votes cast by the Electoral College in December, a large group of protesters marched down Pennsylvania Avenue and headed to the US Capitol after being encouraged by President Trump to challenge the election returns. Even before it became apparent in November 2020 that Donald Trump was going to lose reelection, he repeatedly alleged that the election had been "stolen" and a series of voting irregularities in several states led to a fraudulent election result. While giving a speech at a "Save America" rally that day, he asserted more than once that he won the election in a landslide, that Biden could not have legitimately received 80 million votes, and that it was up to the protesters to "stop the steal." Largely in response to the president's speech, the protesters stormed the Capitol and were able to stop the counting of the Electoral votes for several hours. When counting resumed after 8:00 p.m. that evening, the country remained in shock over the actions of the president in precipitating the insurrection on one of the most sacred governmental institutions.[84]

In response to President Trump's involvement in the insurrection at the US Capitol, the US House opted to impeach the president for a second time a few days before he was to step down from office. On Wednesday, January 13, the House voted 232-197 to impeach Trump, charging him with "incitement of insurrection" over the siege of the Capitol by the protesters who had attended his speech a week before. "Ten Republicans fled Trump, joining Democrats who said he needed to be held accountable and warned ominously of a 'clear and present danger' if Congress should leave him unchecked before Democrat Joe Biden's inauguration Jan. 20."[85] Although some Democrats privately conceded that it was likely that Trump would be acquitted a second time as he had been in 2020 following his first impeachment trial over his dealings with Ukraine (which he ultimately was), the stigma of being the only president in history to be impeached twice while in office likely will have a lasting impact on his legacy. Additionally, it may also have long-term implications for electoral politics as officeholders and potential donors seek to distance themselves from the former president.[86]

Notwithstanding the siege that occurred at the Capitol on January 6 and the second impeachment of President Trump, the internal politics of the 117th Congress were less contentious than it had been two years earlier. Shortly after the Democrats picked up 40 seats in the 2018 elections, there were some rumblings about who should be the leader of the Democratic Party now that the Democrats controlled a majority of seats in the House. One senior Democratic leader, Rep. Elijah Cummings (D-MD), indicated before the midterms that Nancy Pelosi should be able to retain the speakership as long as she wants if the Democrats are successful in the election.[87] Despite this affirmation, a rebellious faction of newly elected Democrats had other views on the matter of who should be the next speaker. Less than two weeks after the midterms, sixteen Democrats released a letter "vowing to mount a coup and derail Nancy Pelosi's bid to become House speaker, the first major warning shot from the group of detractors who are trying to stop the powerful leader's bid in the new Democratic majority."[88] Many of their concerns stemmed from the view that Pelosi and others in the Democratic leadership were out of touch with many of the newly elected members as a result of both their past failures and their advanced age (at the time Pelosi was 78 and Steny Hoyer was 79).

Despite the initial concerns among some of the newly elected Democrats, Pelosi was nominated to be speaker by a majority of the Democratic caucus on November 28, 2018, which helped pave the way for her selection as speaker when the new Congress convened early the following year.[89] When the 116th Congress opened on January 3, 2019, it was Democratic divisions in the House that were most visible as expected. However, Pelosi ended up earning 220 votes as speaker, which gave her four more than she needed to become the leader of the House chamber. Two years later, Pelosi was reelected to another term as speaker at the outset of the 117th Congress by securing a narrow majority of the total votes cast, with five Democrats defecting this time around in their support.[90]

For House Republicans, there was no public contest for leadership positions as it became clear that Rep. Kevin McCarthy was again the top choice among a majority of the conference to be the House minority leader. After former Speaker Paul Ryan announced in April 2018 that he was not planning to seek reelection, he immediately endorsed McCarthy as his successor, who had held the majority leader position for the previous four years. McCarthy was elected minority leader by a 159-43 vote in November 2018, after facing a long-shot challenge from Jim Jordan (R-OH), the co-founder of the conservative Freedom Caucus. He later received the support of 192 Republicans when the 116th Congress convened. Rep. Steve Scalise was again elected to be the Republican whip in the 117 Congress and Rep. Liz Cheney, daughter of former Vice President Dick Cheney, was elected to continue her role as the conference chair (the third-ranking position in the Republican leadership) until she was removed in early May in a voice vote by House GOP members after she repeatedly criticized former President Trump. After the vote, she told reporters that she "will do everything I can to make sure the former president never again gets anywhere near the Oval Office."[91]

After four years of the Trump Presidency, the 117th Congress represented a chance for the Democrats to advance their legislative agenda. The first major bill considered and passed in the 117th Congress was the American Rescue Plan Act of 2021. Also known as the COVID-19 Stimulus Package, this $1.9 trillion stimulus plan was signed into law by President Biden on March 11, 2021 after being debated for nearly six weeks in Congress. Once the bill was introduced in mid-January, it quickly became apparent that Republicans would not be willing to support this legislation. As such, the Senate Democrats opted to pass the stimulus package without Republican support through the process of reconciliation. After several weeks of debate in both chambers, the House passed a version of the $1.9 trillion stimulus bill by a 219-212 vote on February 27 where all but two Democrats supported it and all Republicans voted against it. On March 6, a modified version of the bill passed the Senate by a vote of 50-49 and an amended version of the bill passed the House on March 10 by a final vote of 220-211 with all but one Democrat and all Republicans voting against it.[92]

In addition to COVID relief, the Democrats have a number of additional priorities during the 117th Congress including Biden's substantial infrastructure plan (which was passed by Congress in mid-November after months of negotiations), bills on voting rights and election integrity, climate change legislation, and police reform. On top of that, Democrats will have to contend with passage of the federal budget later in the year as well as potentially voting on raising the debt ceiling limit in the fall. Although the rules of the House make it easier to pass legislation compared to the Senate, time is not on the Democrats' side given the campaign promises that both President Biden and Democrats in Congress made, the sheer size of the legislative agenda, and the inevitable "preelection political paralysis" that often sets in during a midterm election year.[93] Given the close partisan divisions in the House, losing just even a few additional seats in the upcoming midterm election could put Biden's legislative agenda at risk if the Republicans are able to win back control of the chamber following the 2022 elections.

The Senate: Majority Manipulation and Legislative Stalemate

The success of the Democrats in the 2020 Senate elections, and the subsequent two Georgia runoff elections held in early January 2021, resulted in a 50-50 tie in the Senate, prompting the need for a leadership change in the upper chamber in light of the Biden-Harris ticket winning the presidency (thus allowing the Democrats to utilize existing rules and procedures to control the Senate, if albeit narrowly). At the start of the 117th Senate, Senators Chuck Schumer of New York and Dick Durbin of Illinois were elected as majority leader and majority whip, respectively. On the Republican side, Mitch McConnell of Kentucky was elected as minority leader and John Thune of South Dakota the Republican whip, the second-ranking position in the leadership.

The Senate has always been predominantly a men's club, but that has been gradually changing in recent decades. The Senate membership resulting from the 2020 elections varied significantly in gender diversity. The number of female Democrats remained the same at sixteen, whereas the number of female Republicans increased from five to eight. As a result, a record 24 percent of the senators serving in the 117th Congress were women, 32 percent of the Democrats and 16 percent of the Republicans. By comparison, 120 women were elected to the US House in 2020, which constitutes 27 percent of the 435 members.[94]

One of the first orders of business at the start of the 117th Congress was the distribution of committee seats in the chamber in light of the 50-50 split in the Senate. As had been the case in 2001 following the James Jeffords' switch, Democrats became chairs of all of the Senate committees and brought new policy goals to their posts.[95] In addition to organizational issues, one of the central procedural issues in the new Congress was whether there would be a change in the rules regarding the Senate's distinctive practice of the filibuster as had occurred with nominations in previous years. Also known as *extended debate*, the filibuster refers to an effort to prevent resolution of a measure under consideration in the Senate by refusing to end discussion of it. Unlike the House, where debate can be ended by a simple majority vote at any time, Senate consideration can only be terminated against the will of those who would continue by invoking "cloture." Under Senate rules, cloture requires sixty votes, except on a proposal to change Senate rules, when the support of two-thirds of those voting is needed.[96]

The incidence of filibusters and cloture efforts, and their relevance to the legislative process, has increased greatly over the last six decades. In the seven congresses from 1947 through 1960, motions to invoke cloture were filed only four times, and none were approved. Filibusters were rare and were almost always employed by southerners in an attempt to block civil rights bills. Then, gradually, as partisan polarization came to characterize the Senate, the scope of topics for filibusters broadened, and their frequency increased. In the seven congresses from 2007 through 2020, for instance, 1,300 cloture motions were filed and were successfully invoked 839 times.[97]

The increased use of filibusters has made it more difficult and costly for the majority party to secure passage of the bills it favors. As a consequence, some senators have sought to alter the Senate's rules to place limits on what could be filibustered or how many votes would be required to impose cloture. Of course, members of the minority would be unlikely to support such efforts and they would be likely to use the filibuster to block them. As noted, Senate rules specify that motions to invoke cloture on attempted rules changes require even more votes than such efforts on regular legislation. But some members and outside observers contend that the rule does not apply at the opening of a congress and that only the vote of a majority is then necessary to end debate and adopt an alternative rule. Whether such an interpretation (dubbed the "nuclear option") would be applied in a particular instance would depend on whether the presiding officer of the Senate, the vice president, so ruled and whether that ruling was upheld by a majority of senators. A significant proportion of the senators of both parties have accepted the view that a simple majority was sufficient to impose cloture on a rules change when they were in the minority (and the same people have often taken the opposite view when in the majority).

In 2005, the nuclear option in the Senate gained national attention when Majority Leader Bill Frist (R-TN) threatened to invoke it to put an end to Democratic filibusters of President George W. Bush's judicial nominees by a simple majority vote. When the Democrats promised to shut down the Senate and prevent any legislation from being considered if the practice was implemented, a group of seven Democratic and seven Republican senators (known as the Gang of 14) agreed in principle to oppose the nuclear option and the filibuster of judicial nominees.[98] After the GOP Senate gains of 2010, Democrats began talking about changing the cloture rules by a majority vote, but additional conflict was avoided by a "gentleman's agreement" between the two party leaders that purported to limit the scope of filibusters. Harry Reid and many Democrats were unhappy with the operation of that agreement, and after the 2012 elections, Democrats again raised the specter of a rules change. Indeed, in late November 2012, Reid flatly predicted that Senate Democrats would vote to limit Republican use of the filibuster in the new congress, although many observers questioned whether he actually had the votes to effect the change.[99]

When the new Senate convened in 2013, a confrontation over the nuclear option was initially avoided by negotiations between the party leaders and other members. However, by July of that year, the Senate Democratic majority came within hours of invoking the nuclear option in light of Republican opposition to several of President Obama's executive branch appointments. Although the president decided to withdraw two of the nominations at the last moment, thus preserving the minority's ability to filibuster nominations, the victory was short-lived. By late November 2013, Senator Reid decided that action finally had to be taken. On November 21, "the Senate approved the most fundamental alteration of its rules in more than a generation on Thursday, ending the minority party's ability to filibuster most presidential nominees in response to the partisan gridlock that has plagued Congress for much of the Obama administration."[100] As a result of the change, which passed by a narrow 52-48 vote, the Senate can effectively cut off debate on executive and judicial branch nominees with a simple majority rather than with sixty votes as had previously been necessary. However, the new rule did not then apply to Supreme Court nominations or legislation under consideration in the Senate.[101]

Republicans were initially furious with Reid's decision to "go nuclear" and warned that the Democrats would regret their action if they lost control of the Senate in the future. In fact, when the Republicans won back control of the Senate in 2014 and maintained a majority in the 2016 elections, some Democrats began to lament the decision to trigger the nuclear option.[102] Indirectly this also shaped the discussion over potential Supreme Court vacancies, especially after Justice Scalia's unexpected death in February 2016. Although some Democrats privately wished the nuclear option had included appointments to the Supreme Court as a result of the vacancy caused by Scalia's death, it ended up being a moot point because Republicans controlled a majority of the seats in the 114th Senate and would have likely blocked any of President Obama's nominees. Indeed, even before the president nominated US Court of Appeals Justice Merrick Garland on March 16, 2016, to fill

Scalia's seat on the Court, Senate Majority Leader Mitch McConnell said that the Senate should not hold a vote on any Supreme Court nominee during the president's final year in office.[103] Democrats were understandably outraged by this statement, but it later came to light that then Senator Joe Biden had made a similar remark about filling Supreme Court appointments in 1992 during President Bush's last year in office.[104] In the end, Scalia's seat remained vacant for the remainder of the year given the Republicans' reluctance to move forward with the Garland nomination.

Within days of being sworn in as the forty-fifth president of the United States, Donald Trump nominated Neil Gorsuch on January 31, 2017, to fill the vacant seat on the Supreme Court that was formerly held by Scalia. In late March, the Senate held confirmation hearings for Gorsuch, which lasted for a total of four days. On April 3, the Judiciary Committee approved Gorsuch by an eleven to nine vote, and the nomination was sent to the Senate floor for consideration the following day. When the Democrats proceeded to filibuster Gorsuch's nomination, Mitch McConnell elected to fully extend the nuclear option that had been invoked back in November 2013 to now include Supreme Court nominees. As a result, Gorsuch was confirmed on April 7, 2017, by a 54-45 vote that included three Democrats joining all the Republicans in attendance and was sworn in as the 113th justice of the Supreme Court later that day.[105] As before none of the changes adopted affected the ability of senators to filibuster final passage votes on bills, so the strength of that tactic for blocking action remains in effect.

As we previously discussed in chapter 2, Senate Majority Leader Mitch McConnell wasted no time in announcing that the Senate would move quickly to fill Ruth Bader Ginsburg's seat on the Supreme Court following her death in September 2020. The Democrats were infuriated by this decision since McConnell had effectively blocked President Obama's nomination of Merrick Garland to replace Justice Scalia, despite it occurring months before the election in March 2016.[106] A week later, President Trump announced Judge Amy Coney Barrett as his nominee to fill the seat previously held by Ginsburg and encouraged the Senate to act quickly on the nomination to ensure she was appointed prior to the election. Although the Democrats geared up for a fierce battle given Barrett's strong conservative credentials, it ultimately proved to be a futile struggle in light of the prior changes to the filibuster rule in the Senate.[107] Indeed, thirty-eight days after Ginsburg's death, Judge Barrett was confirmed by the Senate in a 52-48 vote on October 26, 2020 to the US Supreme Court.[108]

Given the 50-50 split in the 117th Senate, discussions about filibuster reform or eliminating the practice altogether continued during the first few months of the Biden presidency. Although reconciliation was a key factor in passage of the $1.9 trillion COVID relief package in early March as noted earlier, Senate parliamentarian Elizabeth MacDonough asserted in early June that use of that legislative procedure should be limited to "extraordinary circumstances" during the remainder of the year. "The new guidance . . . suggests that Democrats will get just one more try this year to pass a filibuster-proof legislative package to enact additional priorities ranging from infrastructure to immigration policy proposed by President Joe Biden and party leaders on Capitol Hill."[109] This recommendation from MacDonough, which is based on the 1974 law that established the modern budget process, increases pressure on the Democrats to attempt to eliminate the use of the filibuster on traditional legislation if they want to accomplish key pieces of their legislative agenda in light of the close partisan divisions in the Senate.

The use of reconciliation is not the only factor that has complicated the legislative process in the Senate in the early months of the 117th Congress. Since the Republicans are unified in their opposition to President Biden's agenda, it is necessary for all 50 Democratic senators to vote together if they want to have a chance at passing key legislative priorities in the months ahead. This is especially true if the Senate Democrats ultimately decide to alter the chamber rules to prevent Republicans from filibustering legislation. However, even this option appeared to be removed from the discussion when Senator Joe Manchin published an op-ed in early June where he said, "in no uncertain terms that he would not vote for the Democrats' far-reaching bill to combat voter suppression, nor would he ever end the legislative filibuster, a written promise that imperils much of President Biden's agenda."[110] As of this writing, it is unclear how President Biden or the Democrats will respond to this declaration, especially since the president had already expressed some frustration with the Senate's unwillingness to move on legislation already passed by the House.[111]

THE 2022 ELECTIONS AND BEYOND

Expectations about midterm elections are usually shaped by a strong historical pattern: The party of the president lost strength in the House in twenty-six of the thirty midterm elections since the beginning of the twentieth century. The first column in table 9.7 shows the magnitude of these midterm losses since World War II. They average twenty-six seats for the president's party. There was, however, considerable variation in the outcomes, from the sixty-three-seat loss by the Democrats in 2010 to the six-seat Republican gain in 2002. When thinking about the concept of midterm loss, one needs to keep in mind how long the president has served in office. During the first midterm election of his tenure, for instance, the president may be able to make a plausible appeal that he has not had enough time to bring about substantial change or to solidify many achievements. Moreover, even if things are not going well,

Table 9.7   House Seat Losses by the President's Party in Midterm Elections, 1946–2018

Year	All Elections	First Term of Administration	Later Term of Administration
1946	55 Democrats		55 Democrats
1950	29 Democrats		29 Democrats
1954	18 Republicans	18 Republicans	
1958	47 Republicans		47 Republicans
1962	4 Democrats	4 Democrats	
1966	47 Democrats		47 Democrats
1970	12 Republicans	12 Republicans	
1974	43 Republicans		43 Republicans
1978	11 Democrats	11 Democrats	
1982	26 Republicans	26 Republicans	
1986	5 Republicans		5 Republicans
1990	9 Republicans	9 Republicans	
1994	52 Democrats	52 Democrats	
1998	(+5) Democrats		(+5) Democrats
2002	(+6) Republicans	(+6) Republicans	
2006	30 Republicans		30 Republicans
2010	63 Democrats	63 Democrats	
2014	13 Democrats		13 Democrats
2018	41 Republicans	41 Republicans	
Average Seat Loss			
	26 seats	23 seats	29.3 seats

Source: Compiled by the authors.

voters may not be inclined to blame a president who has served for such a short time. But four years later (if the president is fortunate enough to face a second midterm), appeals of too little time are unlikely to be persuasive. After six years, if the economy or foreign policy is not going well, voters may seek a policy change by reducing the number of the president's partisans in Congress.

The second and third columns in table 9.7 indicate that this is what has usually happened in the past. Losses by the president's party in the first midterm election of a presidency have tended to be much smaller than losses in subsequent midterms.[112] In the six midterm elections besides 1994, 2002, 2010, and 2018 that took place during a first term, the president's party lost between four and twenty-six seats, with an average loss of thirteen. In the seven elections after the first term (excluding 1986 and 1998), the range of losses was between thirteen and fifty-five seats, with an average loss of thirty-eight.

Models of House Elections

In the 1970s and 1980s, political scientists constructed and tested models of congressional election outcomes, focusing especially on midterms, seeking to isolate the factors that most strongly influenced the results. The earliest models, constructed by Tufte and by Jacobson and Kernell, focused on two variables: presidential approval and a measure of the state of the economy.[113] Tufte hypothesized a direct influence by these forces on voter choice and election outcomes. The theory was that an unpopular president or a poor economy would cause the president's party to lose votes and, therefore, seats in the House. In essence, the midterm elections were viewed as a referendum on the performance of the president and his party.

Jacobson and Kernell, on the other hand, saw more indirect effects of presidential approval and the economy. They argued that these forces affected election results by influencing the decisions of potential congressional candidates. If the president is unpopular and the economy is in bad shape, potential candidates will expect the president's party to perform poorly. As a result, strong potential candidates of the president's party will often forgo running until a better year, and strong candidates from the opposition party will be more inclined to run. According to Jacobson and Kernell, this mix of weak candidates from the president's party and strong opposition candidates will lead to a poor election performance by the party occupying the White House. To measure this predicted relationship, their model related the partisan division of the vote to presidential approval and the economic situation early in the election year. This "strategic politicians" hypothesis accounts for when decisions to run for office are made, so it is not appropriate to focus on approval and the economy at the time of the election.[114]

Subsequent research built from this base. One model, developed by Alan I. Abramowitz, Albert D. Cover, and Helmut Norpoth, considered a new independent variable: short-term party evaluations.[115] They argued that voters' attitudes about the economic competence of the political parties affect the impact of presidential approval and economic conditions on voting decisions. If the electorate judges that the party holding the presidency is better able to deal with the problems voters regard as most serious, the negative impact of an unpopular president or a weak economy will be reduced. The authors concluded from their analysis of both aggregate votes and responses to surveys in midterm elections that there is evidence for their "party competence" hypothesis.

All of these models used the division of the popular vote as the variable to be predicted, and they focused only on midterm elections. Later work merged midterm results with those of presidential years, contending that there should be no conceptual distinction between them. These efforts sought to predict changes in seats without reference to the division of the vote. For example, a study by Bruce Oppenheimer, James Stimson, and Richard Waterman argued that the missing piece in the congressional election puzzle is the degree of "exposure" or "the excess or deficit number of seats a party holds measured against its long-term norm."[116] If a party wins more House seats than normal, those extra seats will be vulnerable in the next election, and the party is likely to suffer losses. Thus, the party that wins a presidential election does not automatically benefit in House elections. But if the president's party does well in the House races, it will be more vulnerable in the subsequent midterm elections. Indeed, the work by Oppenheimer et al. predicted only small Republican losses for 1986 because Reagan's large 1984 victory was not accompanied by substantial congressional gains for his party. The actual result in 1986 was consistent with this prediction, for the GOP lost only five seats.

Drawing on the insights of these various models, we can see how these factors may influence outcomes in the 2022 House elections. How well the economy is doing and what proportion of the voters approves of Biden's performance early in the year may encourage or discourage high-quality potential challengers. The same variables close to election time may lead voters to support or oppose Democratic candidates based on their judgments of the job the Biden administration is doing. The usual midterm losses happen for predictable reasons; they are not part of the laws of nature. Therefore, if the usual reasons for such losses (such as a recession, a large number of open seats, or an unpopular president) are not present in 2022, we should not expect the consequent losses to occur or at least not the magnitude of losses that history might lead us to expect. This is why the president's party gained seats in the midterms of 1998 and 2002. If, on the other hand, those reasons are present, the context will be quite different.

During the spring and early summer of his first year, Biden's average approval remained substantially higher than Trump at this early stage of the presidency, but not as high as Barack Obama's was in 2009. An average of Gallup polls during his first few months in office yielded a mean approval rating of 56 percent.[117] With respect to the economy, there has been a steady increase during the first half of 2021, especially given the deleterious effect the coronavirus had on the economy throughout much of 2020. If the economy improves further and Biden's popularity stays above 50 percent, Democrats could be insulated from significant losses in the upcoming midterm elections. Additionally, the models we discussed indicate that other considerations may be important. Democratic exposure is a bit lower than normal due to the losses from 2020, and to this point it appears that few Democratic members of the House are planning to retire. This could leave the Democrats with fewer vulnerable seats than usual.

With regard to quality candidates emerging to run, Republicans are at least as aware of the pattern of midterm losses as are political scientists, so potential candidates may regard the political landscape as encouraging—especially given the notable gains made in the House in 2020. For Democrats, on the other hand, that same landscape may be daunting and so recruiting may be somewhat difficult. Moreover, the analysis of short-term party evaluations reminds us that highly salient issues may offset the negative effects of poor economic conditions. Finally, the impact of events like a resurgence of the coronavirus or foreign crises reminds us that there are many unforeseeable events that may influence the 2022 congressional election results.

The Effects of Reapportionment and Redistricting

One thing that is likely to affect the elections of 2022 is the reapportionment and redistricting that follows from the census of 2020. Reapportionment is the redistribution of House seats among the states after even census due to the population shifts it reveals. The recent census results yielded a transfer of 7 total seats among 13 states (6 gainers and 7 losers).[118] Once the states have the census results, they begin the process of redistricting—redrawing the boundaries of their House districts (currently only forty-four states must do this because six states have only one representative).[119] By federal law, all states with more than one House seat must establish districts, one for each seat. According to the Supreme Courts' "one-person, one-vote" rulings, the population of all of the districts within a state must be as equal in population as possible. How this is carried out, however, can vary considerably across the states redrawing congressional boundaries.

In most instances districts are created through the regular process of a state law signed by the governor, although 8 states (Arizona, California, Colorado, Hawaii, Idaho, Michigan, New Jersey, and Washington) have removed districting from direct political control by the creation of independent districting commissions.[120] Given the traditional pattern of surge and decline, Democrats will likely be on the defensive leading up to the midterm elections in addition to any changes stemming from redistricting. On top of that, Republicans already maintain a structural advantage in the House of Representatives since Democrats tend to reside more in urban areas around the country. Finally, Republicans control the majority of state legislatures after the 2020 elections, giving them an additional advantage in redrawing US House boundaries following the 2020 decennial census much like the advantage they retained after the 2010 census a decade earlier.

Depending upon what happens in the 117th Congress, this could be the first redistricting cycle in over fifty years in which southern states are not affected by federal oversight when redrawing congressional district boundaries. In 2013, the Supreme Court overturned aspects of the 1965 Voting Rights Act in *Shelby County v. Holder* that required southern states to get "pre-clearance" prior to making any changes in elections or voting rules. There are currently two bills pending in the US Congress that would respond directly to the Court's 2013 decision if passed. The first bill, the For the People Act (S1), which would prevent states from gerrymandering congressional districts, is currently being debated in the Senate. The other is the John Lewis Voting Rights Act of 2021 (HR4) that would reinstate the provision requiring federal preclearance as dictated by the 1965 Voting Rights Act. Without these regulations, states would have much greater latitude in redrawing district boundaries, which could potentially lead to a significant amount of gerrymandering based on which party currently controls the districting process.[121]

Both parties want to put the best face possible on the districting situation in order to influence the decisions of potential candidates and donors ahead of the 2022 midterms. Even prior to the drawing of new seat boundaries, NRCC Chair Tom Emmer has already announced that Republicans plan to target at least 47 House Democrats in their attempt to win back control of the chamber in the midterm elections.[122] The DCCC, in contrast, plans to target 21 Republican incumbents in their bid to maintain control of the House, although their margin for error is a bit smaller than Republicans since they currently only have a narrow majority in the chamber.[123] It is important to note that these expectations may be completely overwhelmed by political forces specific to the 2022 election. Many open seats will be created by redistricting and retirements, and if there is a substantial national tide favoring one party, the effects of the line drawing could be muted or even neutralized.

Some Additional Considerations about House Races

A few further points related to the previous discussion are necessary to complete our analysis of the prospects for 2022 House races. The vulnerability of individual members varies between parties and across other attributes, and we should not expect those distributions to be similar from election to election. For example, in one year a party may have a relatively high percentage of freshmen or members who won by narrow margins in the preceding election, whereas in another year the party's proportion of such potentially vulnerable members may be low. As table 9.8 shows, both parties have a roughly similar number of members who won with less than 55 percent of the vote. Sixty-three Republicans and eighty-one Democrats fell into this category. It is in this type of district that strong challengers are most likely to come forward and where the challengers who do run are most able to raise adequate campaign funds. Thus, based solely on these election-margin figures, the current political landscape does offer a slightly more attractive prospect than usual for challengers of either party.

As our earlier analysis indicates, the parties' respective success in recruiting strong candidates for open seats and to oppose the other party's incumbents

Table 9.8   Percentage of Vote Received by Winning House Candidates, by Party and Type of Race, 2020

	Republican			Democrat		
	Reelected Incumbent	Successful Challenger	Open-Seat Winner	Reelected Incumbent	Successful Challenger	Open-Seat Winner
55 or less	42	13	8	75	0	6
55.1–60	77	0	8	63	0	5
60.1–70	31	0	7	31	0	3
70.1–100	18	0	10	37	0	1
Total	168	13	33	206	0	15

Source: Compiled by the authors.
Note: Table shows the number of districts that meet the criteria for each cell. Open seats include races in which an incumbent lost a primary.

can be expected to play a significant role in shaping outcomes for 2022. Both Democratic and Republican campaign organizations were actively pursuing recruits during 2021, with some early successes and some disappointments. The personal and financial costs of candidacies and the difficulty of defeating an incumbent often make recruitment difficult, and the unique circumstances of each party make the task harder. For the Republicans this included minority status and the difficulty of winning enough seats to take control, along with the continued influence of Donald Trump's endorsement of ideologically conservative candidates in the 2022 congressional primaries. Democrats are in a slightly better position, but they need to do what they can to mitigate any potential losses stemming from departures or retirements from Congress that might lead to an increased number of open seats.

Even when the party organizations do recruit strong challengers, this offers no guarantee of electoral success. In most congresses, one or more vacancies occur during a two-year session as a result of both voluntary and involuntary departures (i.e., appointments of legislators by the executive, unexpected retirements, or deaths of members). When a House vacancy occurs, a special election is typically held in a state and these special elections are often viewed as a bellwether of the upcoming midterm election for a new presidential administration. During the early months of the 117th Congress, there have been seven vacancies in House seats and three of those seats were filled by special elections by early June 2021—two in Louisiana (the 2nd and 5th congressional districts) and one in New Mexico's 1st congressional district. To date, Democrats have managed to win two of these special elections as expected (LA-02 and NM-01), whereas Republicans were able to win the other one (LA-05).[124] Given the close partisan division in the 117th House, these special elections have received greater scrutiny by political pundits to determine if they offer any previews regarding the upcoming midterms.

Also worth noting here is the continuing impact of term limits in the states. Although the term limits movement during the 1990s failed to impose restrictions on members of Congress, it succeeded in imposing them on state legislators in fifteen states, and those limits continue to have an impact. One potential outlet for a state legislator who is ineligible to run for reelection is to seek a congressional seat. This may lead to a greater number of strong challengers in House races than would otherwise be the case. For example, California limits state legislators to twelve years combined in the two chambers, and a number of legislators will have to leave their current positions next year. Some of them are contemplating races against Republican members of the US House as a result of enhanced recruitment efforts on the part of the DCCC.[125]

Finally one should remember that the rules that shape elections are subject to change and that such changes can have a substantial impact on the pattern of election outcomes. One source of significant change includes various attempts by state legislatures to change the way that millions of citizens vote in upcoming elections. "Republican state legislators have introduced hundreds of bills that would tighten access to voting around the country, many of them echoing then-president Donald Trump's false claims that loose election laws allowed fraud to taint the 2020 White House race."[126] A large number of these bills have targeted mail voting, which was widely used in 2020 as a result of the coronavirus pandemic and contributed to the highest level of voter turnout in over a century. Additionally, 14 states have enacted laws with provisions that could restrict voting and many others are on the agenda in at least 18 states. "Some of the bills also seek to curtail early voting, impose restrictions on voter registration efforts, limit the power of local officials to oversee elections and stop private donors from supplementing their operational budgets."[127] A few Democratic-controlled state legislatures have sought to enhance voting opportunities moving forward, but there is only so much they can do since about half of state governments are currently controlled by Republican majorities.

Senate Races in 2022

Because there are few Senate races and because they are relatively independent of one another, we have focused our discussion of 2022 on the House. We will now close with a few comments about the upper chamber's contests. Due to the six-year Senate terms, and the fact that these terms are staggered, the number of seats to be defended by each party varies from election to election. As was true in 2016, the Republicans hold more of the thirty-four seats that will be contested in 2022, with twenty seats compared to the Democrats' fourteen. Two of the Senate seats Republicans will be defending—in Pennsylvania and Wisconsin—are states that Joe Biden carried in the 2020 election whereas the Democrats will not be defending any seats that Trump won.[128] Nevertheless, two Democrats who won special elections in 2020—Mark Kelly in Arizona and Raphael Warnock in Georgia—will likely face strong challengers from the Republican Party who are eager to win back those seats that have most recently been held by members of their party.

As of early summer 2021, five Republican senators have announced their intent not to seek reelection at the end of the 117th Congress. These five senators include Richard Shelby (AL), Roy Blunt (MO), Richard Burr (NC), Rob Portman (OH), and Pat Toomey (PA), all traditional conservatives who likely would have faced a strong primary challenge from the right had they decided to run again. As a result, the Democrats have more open seat targets for potential gains in 2022, but such victories will not be easy or inexpensive if the record levels of spending during the past two elections are any indication. In light of the increasing nationalization of elections coupled with the fact that only one state split their presidential and senatorial votes in 2020, this portends to be an uphill battle for the Republicans.

Although conditions appear to favor the Democrats with respect to the 2022 Senate races at first glance, they only tell part of the story. If political circumstances shift in late 2021 or early 2022, Republicans might be able to capitalize on any anti-Biden sentiments during the midterm elections. However, one of the biggest challenges that the Republicans face is being able to recruit quality candidates to run against potentially vulnerable senators. We have seen that the kinds of candidates seeking office have a major influence on the outcome, and that parties, therefore, try to get the strongest candidates to come forward. In this cycle, however, some of the strongest potential challengers may decide 2022 does not represent the best set of circumstances to run for the Senate. Additionally, with five Republican senators choosing not to seek reelection, losing just one or two of those open seats could help the Democrats shore up their tenuous majority in the Senate.

As of early May, *Inside Elections* rated eight Senate races as battleground states in the midterm elections—four for Democrats (Arizona, Georgia, New Hampshire, and Nevada), and four for Republicans (Florida, North Carolina, Pennsylvania, and Wisconsin).[129] Whether or not they remain competitive in 2022 depends upon a variety of factors including which Senate candidates ultimately decide to run, the total amount of money raised by each side, and the continued ability of the Biden administration to tackle many of the complex problems currently facing the country. In Florida, for instance, Senator Marco Rubio has already drawn a number of Democratic and Republican challengers who are vying to replace him in 2022. Georgia, in contrast, has only a limited number of Republican challengers to date despite Raphael Warnock winning in a very close runoff election in 2020.[130] The individual circumstances of each Senate race may change, however, as the filing dead-lines approach in each state.

To summarize, then, House election results are likely to depend heavily on the political context that exists both late in 2021 (when most candidate decisions are made) and in November of 2022. The context may also deter-mine whether the historical pattern of midterm losses by the president's party occurs again or is broken as it was in both 1998 and 2002. For the Senate seats, on the other hand, the election results probably depend more on the cir-cumstances in individual races, largely fought independently of one another. Regardless of what happens in 2022, we are likely to continue to see narrow majorities in both chambers of Congress for the foreseeable future and a continuation of the polarization that has characterized politics for much of the past two decades.

Chapter 10

The Congressional Electorate in 2020

In the preceding chapter, we viewed congressional elections at the district and state levels and saw how they formed a national result. In this chapter, we consider congressional elections from the point of view of the individual voter, using the same ANES surveys we employed to study presidential voting. We discuss how social forces, issues, partisan loyalties, incumbency, and evaluations of congressional and presidential performance influence the decisions of voters in congressional elections. We also consider the existence and extent of presidential coattails in 2020.

SOCIAL FORCES AND THE CONGRESSIONAL VOTE

In general, social forces relate to the congressional vote similar to the way they do to the presidential vote (table 10.1).[1] This has been true in our previous analyses of national elections, but the relationship is somewhat stronger in 2020 than it was in the 1980s and 1990s. Even though the aggregate vote for Democratic House candidates and the vote for Biden vary across many of the categories we analyze, the relative performances are similar (see table 5.1).[2] This may reflect the closer relationship between party identification and the vote in recent elections for both the president and Congress demonstrated in analyses by Larry M. Bartels.[3]

Consider, for example, the relationship between voting and gender. In the total electorate, Joe Biden received 54 percent of the vote while House Democrats got 52 percent. Among white female voters, Democrats did 1 point worse for the presidency than for the House, and they did 1 point better among white males. (Except for the discussion of voting and race, the analysis here focuses primarily on white voters.) The gender results are

277

Table 10.1   How Social Groups Voted for Congress, 2020 (Percent)

Social Group	Democratic	Republican	Total	(N)
Total Electorate	52	48	100	(4,332)
Electorate, by Race				
African American	87	13	100	(405)
White	44	56	100	(3,139)
Other	68	32	100	(765)
Latinos (of Any Race)	69	31	100	(399)
Whites, by Gender				
Female	47	53	100	(1,633)
Male	41	59	100	(1,499)
Whites, by Region				
New England and Mid-Atlantic	53	47	100	(610)
North Central	39	61	100	(765)
South	32	68	100	(773)
Border	45	55	100	(309)
Mountain and Pacific	55	45	100	(682)
Whites, by Birth Cohort				
Before 1950	44	56	100	(509)
1951–1960	44	56	100	(606)
1961–1970	39	61	100	(632)
1971–1980	45	55	100	(486)
1981–1990	49	51	100	(444)
1991–1998	51	49	100	(251)
1999–2002	51	49	100	(123)
Whites, by Level of Education				
Not High-School Graduate	20	80	100	(103)
High-School Graduate	35	65	100	(732)
Some College	38	62	100	(905)
College Graduate	51	49	100	(864)
Advanced Degree	64	36	100	(490)
Whites, by Annual Family Income				
Less Than $15,000	43	57	100	(83)
$15,000–34,999	47	53	100	(218)
$35,000–49,999	42	58	100	(206)
$50,000–74,999	43	57	100	(473)
$75,000–89,999	43	57	100	(232)
$90,000–124,999	41	59	100	(743)
$125,000–174,999	49	51	100	(464)
$175,000 and over	51	49	100	(531)
Whites, by Union Membership[a]				
Member	50	50	100	(529)
Nonmember	43	57	100	(2,609)
Whites, by Religion				
Protestant	29	71	100	(973)
Catholic	41	59	100	(637)
Jewish	77	23	100	(85)

(Continued)

Table 10.1 How Social Groups Voted for Congress, 2020 (Percent) (Continued)

Social Group	Democratic	Republican	Total	(N)
None	67	33	100	(839)
White Protestants				
Born Again	19	81	100	(544)
Not Born Again	43	57	100	(419)
Whites, by Religious Commitment				
Low or Medium	43	57	100	(348)
High	26	74	100	(458)
Very high	9	91	100	(159)
White Protestants, by Religious Tradition				
Mainline	41	59	100	(384)
Evangelical	16	84	100	(326)

Source: Authors' analysis of the 2020 ANES.
Note: The numbers in parentheses are the totals on which the percentages are based. Numbers are weighted.
   The number in brackets is the total number in that category when there are fewer than ten total voters.
[a]Respondent or family member in union.

interesting when compared to the past. In 1988 there was a small gender gap in the presidential vote (about three points), with women more likely to vote Democratic than men, but there was no gap in the House vote. By 2000, however, the gender gap was more pronounced in the vote both for the president and for representatives; the major-party share of the vote was 9 points more Democratic for women in the former case and 10 points more Democratic in the latter. In 2004 gender differences were reduced in both types of races, with the Democratic advantage among women down to 7 points for president and 3 points in House contests. And in 2020 the differences declined even further in the vote for president. Democrats ran 4 points better among white women than among white men for president, whereas there was a gender gap of 6 percent in the congressional vote.

The presidential and congressional voting patterns are similar within many other social categories, including race, education, and income. For both the presidential and the congressional vote, African Americans were substantially more likely to vote Democratic. The difference was 56 points for the presidential race and 43 points in the House contests. Another similarity was regarding union-member voters, who were 7 points more Democratic than nonunion voters in both the presidential and House vote. In 2008 the pattern for the two offices was also similar, but it was larger: 11 percentage points better for the House and 9 points better for the presidency. In 2004, on the other hand, the relative performances were quite different, with the Democrats faring only 7 points better among union members in House contests but 19 points better in the presidential race.

There are some differences in the ways the presidential and congressional vote relate to income categories. The presidential data in chapter 5 showed

the tendency among whites to vote Democratic was strongest in the two categories near the top of the income ladder (46 and 54 percent, respectively).
For the House vote, however, the Democratic vote among lower-income voters was stronger than in the presidential vote, although the greatest amount
of support came from the two highest income categories. Moreover, this is a
great reversal from the past. As recently as the 2000 election, the tendency
to vote Democratic tended to increase as income declined across the whole
income spectrum, and in the three lowest income categories, white voters
gave the party between 50 and 60 percent of the vote.

As for education, Democratic performance was variable across categories
(except for advanced degrees, where they did 13 percentage points better
than any other category). For the presidency, on the other hand, the party's
candidates did best in the top two categories. It is important to note, however,
that some of these differences involve categories with smaller numbers of
respondents, so the results may simply be due to sampling variation. The bottom line is that overall, presidential and congressional voting among social
groups was fairly similar in 2020.

PARTY IDENTIFICATION AND THE
CONGRESSIONAL VOTE

As our previous discussion demonstrates, party identification has a significant effect on voters' decisions. Table 10.2 (corresponding to table 6.5 on
the presidential vote) reports the percentage of whites voting Democratic for
the House across all categories of partisanship from 1952 through 2020.[4] The
data reveal that the proportion of voters who cast ballots in accordance with
their party identification declined substantially over time through the 1980s.
During the 1990s and later, however, there was a resurgence of party voting
for the House, especially among Republican identifiers.

Consider first the "strong identifier" categories. In every election from
1952 through 1964, at least nine out of ten strong party identifiers supported
the candidate of their party. After that the percentage dropped, falling to
four out of five in 1980 and then fluctuating through 1992. But in the last
six elections, strong identifiers showed levels of loyalty similar to those in
the late 1960s. The relationship between party and voting among weak party
identifiers shows a more erratic pattern, although defection rates tend to be
higher in most years between 1970 and 1992 than earlier.[5] Note that during
this period the tendency to defect was stronger among Republicans, which
reflected the Democrats' greater number of incumbents, as discussed in
chapter 9. Probably reflecting the effects of the Republicans' majority status
and the corresponding increase in the number of Republican incumbents,

Table 10.2 Percentage of White Major-Party Voters Who Voted Democratic for the House, by Party Identification, 1952–2020

Party Identification	1952	1954	1956	1958	1960	1962	1964	1966	1968	1970	1972	1974	1976	1978	1980
Strong Democrat	90	97	94	96	92	96	92	92	88	91	91	89	86	83	82
Weak Democrat	76	77	86	88	85	83	84	81	72	76	79	81	76	79	66
Independent, Leans Democrat	63	70	82	75	86	74	78	54	60	74	78	87	76	60	69
Independent, No Partisan Leanings	25	41	35	46	52	61	70	49	48	48	54	54	55	56	57
Independent, Leans Republican	18	6	17	26	26	28	28	31	18	35	27	38	32	36	32
Weak Republican	10	6	11	22	14	14	34	22	21	17	24	31	28	34	26
Strong Republican	5	5	5	6	8	6	8	12	8	4	15	14	15	19	22

Party Identification	1982	1984	1986	1988	1990	1992	1994	1996	1998	2000	2002	2004	2008	2012	2016
Strong Democrat	90	87	91	86	91	87	87	87	88	88	93	92	92	89	89
Weak Democrat	73	66	71	80	80	81	73	70	60	69	73	74	82	86	68
Independent, Leans Democrat	84	76	71	86	79	73	65	70	62	71	75	74	81	75	81
Independent, No Partisan Leanings	31	59	59	66	60	53	55	42	45	50	42	46	43	21	36
Independent, Leans Republican	36	39	37	37	33	36	26	19	23	27	28	30	21	8	18
Weak Republican	20	33	34	29	39	35	21	19	25	15	26	19	22	12	12
Strong Republican	12	15	20	23	17	16	6	2	8	11	6	8	7	4	9

(Continued)

Table 10.2   Percentage of White Major-Party Voters Who Voted Democratic for the House, by Party Identification, 1952–2020 (Continued)

Party Identification	2020
Strong Democrat	93
Weak Democrat	79
Independent, Leans Democrat	90
Independent, No Partisan Leanings	51
Independent, Leans Republican	15
Weak Republican	18
Strong Republican	7

Sources: Authors' analysis of the 2020 ANES.

Note: To approximate the numbers on which these percentages are based, see tables 8.2 and A8.1 (appendix). Actual *N*s will be smaller than those that can be derived from these tables because respondents who did not vote (or who voted for a minor party) have been excluded from these calculations. Numbers also will be lower for the presidential election years because the voting report is provided in the postelection interviews that usually contain about 10 percent fewer respondents than the pre-election interviews in which party identification was measured. Except for 1954, the off-year election surveys are based on a postelection interview. *Note* that no ANES Time Series survey was conducted in 2006, 2010, and 2014.

from 1996 through 2000 the tendency of Democrats to defect rose, whereas among Republicans it fell. In five of the last six listed elections, however, the Democratic defection rate was lower in all three Democratic categories (and the GOP defection rate was lower among strong Republicans, with the exception of 2016) compared to the 1998 and 2000 elections. We consider these matters further in the next section.

Despite the increase in defections from party identification from the mid-1960s through the end of the century, strong party identifiers continued to be notably more likely to vote in accord with their party than weak identifiers. In most years weak Republicans were more likely to vote Republican than independents who leaned toward the Republican Party, although in 1996, 1998, and 2002 these groups were about equally likely to vote Republican. Weak Democrats were more likely to vote Democratic than independents who leaned Democratic in most of the elections from 1952 through 1978, but in a number of elections since, this pattern has been reversed by a small margin. In general, then, the relationship between party identification and the vote was strongest in the 1950s and early 1960s and less strong for the next several decades before showing a substantial recent rebound.

If party identifiers were defecting more frequently in House elections in recent decades, to whom have they been defecting? As one might expect from the last chapter, the answer is to incumbents.

ISSUES AND THE CONGRESSIONAL VOTE

In chapter 7, we analyzed the impact of issues on the presidential vote in 2020. Any attempt to conduct a parallel analysis for congressional elections is hampered by limited data. One interesting perspective on issues in the congressional vote is gained by asking whether voters are affected by their perceptions of where candidates stand on the issues. For a considerable time previous analysis has demonstrated a relationship between a voter's perception of House candidates' positions on a liberal-conservative issue scale and the voter's choice,[6] and we found similar relationships in 2020 (although clearly weaker for conservatives). For example, among self-identified liberals in the ANES survey who viewed the Democratic House candidate as more liberal than the Republican candidate ($N = 961$), 95 percent voted Democratic; among self-identified conservatives who saw the Republican House candidate as more conservative than the Democrat ($N = 1,369$), only 79 percent voted Republican.

Research by Alan I. Abramowitz sheds additional light on this question. In two articles, he used ANES surveys to demonstrate a relationship between candidate ideology and voter choice in both House and Senate elections.[7] For the 1978 Senate election, Abramowitz classified the contests according to the clarity of the ideological choice the two major party candidates offered to voters. He found that the higher the "ideological clarity" of the race, the more likely voters were to perceive some difference between the candidates on a liberalism-conservatism scale, and the stronger the relationship was between voters' positions on that scale and the vote.[8] Indeed, in races with a very clear choice, ideology had approximately the same impact on the vote as party identification. In an analysis of House races in 1980 and 1982, Abramowitz found that the more liberal a voter was, the more likely he or she was to vote Democratic, but the relationship was statistically significant only in 1982. Furthermore, work by Michael Ensley indicates that the degree of ideological divergence between candidates conditions the magnitude of the impact of ideology on vote choice.[9]

Another perspective was offered in analyses by Robert S. Erikson and Gerald C. Wright.[10] They examined the positions of 1982 House candidates on a variety of issues (expressed in response to a CBS News/*New York Times* poll) and found that on most issues, most of the districts had the choice between a liberal Democrat and a conservative Republican. They also found that moderate candidates did better in attracting votes than more extreme candidates. In a subsequent study, involving the 1994 House elections, Erikson and Wright showed that both the issue preferences of incumbents (measured by positions on roll call votes) and the district's ideology (measured by the district's propensity to vote for Michael S. Dukakis in the previous presidential election) are strongly related to the congressional vote.[11] The same authors, in a study of the 2002 elections, employ a measure of candidate ideology that was derived from candidates' responses to questions about issues rather than from roll calls. That analysis confirms that incumbent ideology has a substantial effect on vote share, with moderates gaining more votes relative to more extreme members. Challenger ideology does not have a consistent effect, reflecting the lesser visibility of their positions to the electorate.[12]

We examined the relationships between issues and congressional voting choices in 2020, analyzing the issues we studied in chapter 7. For the most part the relationship between issue preferences and congressional vote choices were weak and inconsistent, and these relationships were even weaker when we controlled for the tendency of Democratic identifiers to have liberal positions on these issues and of Republicans to have conservative issue preferences. However, partisan loyalties clearly affect congressional voting, even when we take issue preferences into account. Therefore, before considering the effects of other factors, we will provide more information about the effects of party identification on House voting.

INCUMBENCY AND THE CONGRESSIONAL VOTE

In chapter 9, we mentioned Albert D. Cover's analysis of congressional voting behavior from 1958 through 1974.[13] Cover compared the rates of defection from party identification among voters who were of the same party as the incumbent and those who were of the same party as the challenger. The analysis showed no systematic increase over time in defection among voters who shared identification with incumbents, and the proportions defecting varied between 5 and 14 percent. Among voters who identified with the same party as challengers, however, the rate of defection—that is, the proportion voting for the incumbent instead of the candidate of their own party—increased steadily from 16 percent in 1958 to 56 percent in 1972 then dropped to 49 percent in 1974. Thus the declining relationship between party identification and House voting resulted largely from increased support for incumbents. Because there were more Democratic incumbents, this tendency was consistent with the higher defection rates among Republican identifiers, as seen in table 10.2.

Controlling for party identification and incumbency, in table 10.3 we present data on the percentage of respondents who voted Democratic for the House and Senate in 2020 that confirm this view. In both House and Senate voting, we find the same relationship as Cover did.[14] For the House, the proportion of voters defecting from their party identification is low when that identification is shared by the incumbent: 7 percent among Democrats and

Table 10.3 Percentage Who Voted Democratic for the House and Senate, by Party Identification and Incumbency, 2020

| | Party Identification | | | | | |
| | Democrat | | Independent | | Republican | |
Incumbency	%	(N)	%	(N)	%	(N)
House						
Democrat	93	(890)	66	(608)	21	(475)
None	90	(104)	48	(113)	7	(161)
Republican	80	(423)	43	(494)	7	(810)
Senate						
Democrat	94	(357)	64	(298)	13	(294)
None	95	(46)	57	(46)	1	(71)
Republican	93	(309)	51	(359)	8	(403)

Source: Authors' analysis of the 2020 ANES.

Note: The numbers in parentheses are the totals on which the percentages are based. Numbers are weighted. In this table and in subsequent tables in this chapter, strong and weak Democrats and strong and weak Republicans are combined. Independents include those who lean toward either party and "pure" independents. We include only voters who lived in congressional districts in which both major parties ran candidates.

7 percent among Republicans.[15] When, however, the incumbent belongs to the other party, the rates are much higher: 20 percent among Democrats and 21 percent among Republicans. Note also that the support among independents is skewed sharply in favor of the incumbent. When there was an incumbent Democrat running, 66 percent of the independents voted Democratic; when there was an incumbent Republican, 57 percent of the independents voted Republican.

The pattern is quite similar in the data on Senate voting. When given the opportunity to support a Republican House incumbent, 20 percent of the Democratic identifiers defected. Faced with the opportunity to support an incumbent Republican senator, only 7 percent defected. Similarly, 21 percent of Republicans supported a Democratic House incumbent, whereas 13 percent backed an incumbent Democratic senator. Because the proportion of the electorate that has the chance to vote for Democratic and Republican senatorial candidates will vary greatly from election to election, it is difficult to generalize about the overall effects of incumbency in Senate contests from this type of data. In the remainder of this chapter, we continue to explore this relationship among party identification, incumbency, and congressional voting.

THE CONGRESSIONAL VOTE AS REFERENDUM

In chapter 8, we analyzed the effect of perceptions of presidential performance on the vote for president in 2020, viewing that election as a referendum on Trump's job performance. A similar approach can be applied here, employing different perspectives. On one hand, a congressional election can be considered as a referendum on the performance of a particular member of Congress; on the other hand, it can be viewed as a referendum on the president's performance. We will consider both possibilities here.

As we noted in chapter 9, for some time, public opinion surveys have shown that the approval ratings of congressional incumbents by their constituents are very high, even when judgments on the performance of Congress as an institution are not. While traveling with House incumbents in their districts, Richard F. Fenno, Jr., noted that the people he met overwhelmingly approved of the performance of their own representative, although at the time the public generally disapproved of the job the institution was doing.[16] Data in the 2020 ANES survey again indicate widespread approval of House incumbents: among respondents who had an opinion, 60 percent endorsed their member's job performance.[17] Approval was widespread, regardless of the party identification of the voter or the party of the incumbent. Indeed, as table 10.4 shows, approval is well above 50 percent even among identifiers of the incumbent's opposition party.[18]

Table 10.4 Percentage of Voters Who Supported Incumbents in House Voting, by Party Identification and Evaluation of Incumbent's Performance, 2020

| | *Voters' Evaluation of Incumbent's Job Performance* | | | |
| | *Approve* | | *Disapprove* | |
	%	(N)	%	(N)
Incumbent is of same party as voter	96	(1,540)	63	(145)
Incumbent is of opposite party	73	(1,050)	9	(898)

Source: Authors' analysis of the 2020 ANES.

Note: The numbers in parentheses are the totals on which the percentages are based. Numbers are weighted. The total number of cases is somewhat lower than for previous tables because we have excluded respondents who did not evaluate the performance of the incumbent and those who live in a district that had no incumbent running. We include only voters who lived in congressional districts in which both major parties ran candidates.

Further evidence indicates that the level of approval has electoral consequences. Table 10.4 presents the level of pro-incumbent voting among voters who share the incumbent's party and among those who are of the opposite party, controlling for whether they approve or disapprove of the incumbent's job performance. If voters approve of the member's performance and share his or her party identification, support is at 96 percent. At the opposite pole, among voters from the opposite party who disapprove, support is low (only 9 percent). In the mixed categories, the incumbents receive intermediate levels of support. Because approval rates are very high, even among voters of the opposite party, most incumbents are reelected by large margins, even in a difficult year such as 2014 for the Democrats or 2018 for the Republicans.

In chapter 9, we pointed out that midterm congressional elections were influenced by public evaluations of the president's job performance. Voters who think the president is doing a good job are more likely to support the congressional candidate of the president's party. Less scholarly attention has been given to this phenomenon in presidential election years, but the 2020 ANES survey provides us with the data needed to explore the question.

On the surface at least, a strong relationship is apparent. Among voters who approved of Trump's job performance ($N = 1,599$), only 13 percent voted Democratic for the House; among those who disapproved of the president's performance ($N = 2,092$), 83 percent supported Democrats.[19] In 1980 there was a similar relationship between the two variables, but when controls were introduced for party identification and incumbency, the relationship disappeared.[20] Approval of Carter increased the Democratic House vote by a small amount among Democrats but had virtually no effect among independents and Republicans. In 2020, however, the results are different. Table

Table 10.5 Percentage Who Voted Democratic for the House, by Evaluation of Trump's Job Performance, Party Identification, and Incumbency, 2020

	Evaluation of Trump's Job Performance							
	Incumbent Is Republican				Incumbent Is Democrat			
	Approve		Disapprove		Approve		Disapprove	
Party Identification	%	(N)	%	(N)	%	(N)	%	(N)
Democrat	33	(25)	83	(398)	88	(37)	94	(853)
Independent	13	(212)	67	(276)	21	(188)	86	(418)
Republican	4	(735)	33	(74)	16	(402)	48	(73)

Source: Authors' analysis of the 2020 ANES.
Note: The numbers in parentheses are the totals on which the percentages are based. Numbers are weighted. We include only voters who lived in congressional districts in which both major parties ran candidates.

10.5 presents the relevant data on House voting, controlling for party identification, incumbency, and evaluation of Trump's job performance. They show that even with these controls, evaluations of the president's job had a pronounced effect on House voting among all groups of identifiers.

PRESIDENTIAL COATTAILS AND THE CONGRESSIONAL VOTE

Another perspective on the congressional vote, somewhat related to the presidential referendum concept we just considered, is the effect of the voter's presidential vote decision, or the length of a presidential candidate's "coattails." That is, does a voter's decision to support a presidential candidate make him or her more likely to support a congressional candidate of the same party so that the congressional candidate, as the saying goes, rides into office on the president's coattails?

Expectations about presidential coattails have been shaped in substantial measure by the period of the New Deal realignment. Franklin D. Roosevelt won by landslide margins in 1932 and 1936 and swept enormous congressional majorities into office with him. Research has indicated, however, that such strong pulling power by presidential candidates may have been a historical aberration and, in any event, that presidential candidates' pulling power has declined in recent decades.[21] In an analysis of the coattail effect since 1868, John A. Ferejohn and Randall L. Calvert point out that the effect is a combination of two factors: how many voters a presidential candidate can pull to congressional candidates of his party and how many congressional seats can be shifted between the parties by the addition of that number of voters.[22] (The second aspect is called the seats/votes relationship, or the swing ratio.)

Ferejohn and Calvert discovered the relationship between presidential and congressional voting from 1932 through 1948 was virtually the same as it was from 1896 through 1928 and the impact of coattails was strengthened by an increase in the swing ratio. In other words, the same proportion of votes pulled in by a presidential candidate produced more congressional seats in the New Deal era than in the past. After 1948, they argued, the coattail effect declined because the relationship between presidential and congressional voting decreased. Analyzing data from presidential elections from 1956 through 1980, Calvert and Ferejohn reached similar conclusions about the length of presidential coattails.[23] They found that although every election during the period exhibited significant coattail voting, the extent of such voting declined over time. More recently, James E. Campbell and Joe A. Sumners concluded from an analysis of Senate elections that presidential coattails exert a modest but significant influence on the Senate vote.[24] And Franco Mattei and Joshua Glasgow showed that coattails exerted a systematic effect in open districts, an effect that persisted into the twenty-first century.[25]

Data on the percentage of respondents who voted Democratic for the House and Senate in 2020, controlling for their presidential vote and their party identification, are presented in table 10.6. For both chambers the expected relationship is apparent. Within each party identification category, the proportion of Biden voters who supported Democratic congressional candidates is significantly higher than the proportion of Trump voters who supported Democratic candidates.

Because we know that this apparent relationship could be just an accidental consequence of the distribution of different types of voters among Democratic and Republican districts, we present the same data on House voting in 2020 in table 10.7. However, this time we control for the party of

Table 10.6 Percentage Who Voted Democratic for the House and Senate, by Party Identification and Presidential Vote, 2020

| | Party Identification | | | | | |
| | Democrat | | Independent | | Republican | |
Presidential Vote	%	(N)	%	(N)	%	(N)
House						
Trump	38	(50)	13	(465)	7	(1,286)
Biden	91	(1,335)	85	(668)	55	(127)
Senate						
Trump	36	(33)	10	(263)	5	(702)
Biden	97	(665)	89	(397)	62	(54)

Source: Authors' analysis of the 2020 ANES.
Note: The numbers in parentheses are the totals on which the percentages are based. Numbers are weighted.
We include only voters who lived in congressional districts in which both major parties ran candidates.

Table 10.7 Percentage Who Voted Democratic for the House, by Presidential Vote, Party Identification, and Incumbency, 2020

Party Identification	Voted for Trump		Voted for Biden	
	%	(N)	%	(N)
Incumbent is Democrat				
Democrat	55	(21)	94	(846)
Independent	19	(186)	90	(383)
Republican	13	(398)	63	(68)
Incumbent is Republican				
Democrat	22	(23)	84	(392)
Independent	10	(238)	79	(221)
Republican	4	(736)	50	(51)

Source: Authors' analysis of the 2020 ANES.
Note: The numbers in parentheses are the totals on which the percentages are based. Numbers are weighted. The number in brackets is the total number voting for either Trump or Biden when there are fewer than ten total voters. We include only voters who lived in congressional districts in which both major parties ran candidates.

the House incumbent. In 1996, we found that—despite this additional control—the relationship held up very well. Within every category for which comparisons were possible, Dole voters supported Democratic candidates at substantially lower rates than did Clinton voters. In 2020 (as well as in 2000–2008), however, there are so few defectors within the two major parties that the comparisons are largely limited to independents, where the effect remains substantial. These limited data are consistent with the interpretation that the presidential vote exerted some small influence on the congressional vote although not as strong an influence as partisanship and congressional incumbency. In sum it appears that partisanship has become so pervasive and reliable as a predictor of voting behavior during the past two decades that there simply is little or no room for defection, which greatly limits the possibility for coattail effects. This is consistent with Gary Jacobson's argument that the resurgence of partisanship during the past few decades has contributed to the increasing nationalization of congressional elections.[26]

CONCLUSION

In this chapter, we have considered a variety of possible influences on voters' decisions in congressional elections. We found that social forces have some impact on that choice. There is evidence from the work of other researchers that issues also have an effect. Incumbency has a major and consistent impact on voters' choices. It solidifies the support of the incumbent's partisans, attracts independents, and leads to defections by voters who identify with the challenger's party. Incumbent support is linked to a positive evaluation of the representative's job by the voters. The tendency to favor incumbents currently appears to benefit the Democratic Party in House races, although that effect is smaller than it once was. Within the context of this incumbency effect, voters' choices also seem to be affected by their evaluations of the job the president is doing and by their vote for president. Partisanship has some direct impact on the vote even after controlling for incumbency. The total effect of partisanship is, however, larger, because most incumbents represent districts that have more of their partisans than of the opposition. Thus the current advantage of Democrats in congressional elections was built on a three-part base: there were more Democrats than Republicans in the electorate; most incumbents of both parties achieved high levels of approval in their constituencies; and the incumbents had resources that made it possible for them to create direct contacts with voters.

Chapter 11

The 2020 Elections and the Future of American Politics

While the *Change and Continuity* series has considered the entirety of American national elections (see especially chapters 3, 4, and 5), it has been primarily focused on elections since the advent of high-quality polling, especially the ANES, which had its first full national survey of public opinion and voting behavior in 1952.[1] In that sense, we are examining elections that extend into what is now eight decades. And we are studying national elections in their entirety—presidential nomination campaigns, presidential general election campaigns, and congressional general election campaigns in particular. That means our analyses make it possible to speak of long-term changes and continuities in the politics of American national elections.

THE GREAT CONTINUITIES: THE ELECTORAL SYSTEM AND THE PARTY SYSTEM

Continuity of the Electoral System

While much has changed in the nature of political campaigns and in the way citizens relate to issues, candidates, and the political parties since 1952, there are two great continuities. First, the electoral system—that is, the means of access to winning the three sets of national offices—is governed, for all intents and purposes, by the same constitutional design: members of the House are elected for two-year terms in single-member districts by plurality rule;[2] Senators are elected for terms of six years, rotating so that one-third are up for election every two years,[3] and the president is elected for up to two four-year terms every four years through public votes that determine who will be the members of the Electoral College.[4] In practice, it is the state parties that determine slates of candidates for electors. The winners of these various contests have successfully cast a majority of their votes for one candidate for president and for one candidate for vice president throughout this period and, thus, have been the voting body that elected the president and vice president every four years.[5]

The only major change in this fundamental design of the electoral system in this postwar era has been in the presidential nominating process, which changed most dramatically in the 1970s, as described in chapter 1. And that process is not a constitutional issue and so can be changed simply because the various state and national party organizations have chosen to do so, perhaps in concert with the state legislatures (which set the legal terms for presidential primary elections). Of course, in another sense, presidential nominations are still done exactly the same way as always, or at least since 1832. The nomination is determined by vote of the delegates to the parties' national conventions (and since 1936, decided by the vote of a simple majority of delegates). What has changed is the way in which the two parties select and perhaps instruct their delegates. With the exception of the new nomination system of 1972, the electoral system has been broadly continuous since our primary data began to be collected, in 1952.

Changes in Systems Supporting the Electoral System

To be sure, two additional systems that are related to the effective operation of the electoral system have changed dramatically since 1952: the media of mass communications and campaign finance. In 1952, television was just beginning its massive growth, and its potential effects on campaigns and elections became apparent in 1960. By that point, a majority of American households had a television. John Kennedy and Richard Nixon were of the new generation that would understand the power of television, although it was Kennedy who was truly comfortable with—indeed would be considered a master of—that medium. The first televised debates were held that year and demonstrated just how powerful the medium was.

Cable television further transformed how campaigns are conducted and how the public views them. By 1970, television was universal, and 80 percent of viewing was watching one of the three broadcast networks—ABC, CBS, and NBC—while only 6 percent subscribed to cable television. But the first all-news cable network, CNN, started in 1980, and by 2005, seven in eight homes received cable or satellite television, coming with 100 channels on average, and including an increasing variety of 24-hour news stations. More viewing was done that year on cable channels than on broadcast networks. And, the Internet, even more recently, is again altering patterns of news gathering and political engagement.[6] We know that it is now possible for a large number to select news attuned to their already established political opinions, which not only reinforce and extend those views in a liberal or conservative, Democrat or Republican, direction, but also reduce the set of agreed-upon political facts that heretofore provided a shared basis for tempering the intensity of political disagreements. The Internet has had (and is still having) great consequences for newspapers, news magazines, television, and even cable television. The rise of social media, established as a core part of Barack Obama's 2008 and 2012 campaigns and expanded in 2016 and 2020 by Donald Trump's use of the social messaging system, Twitter, to actively rally his supporters, is still transforming the way campaigns are conducted.

The second system to change radically and repeatedly has been that of campaign finance. This, too, is transformative in ways yet to be fully revealed. In chapter 1, we discussed briefly the system of campaign finance based on the Federal Election Campaign Act of 1972, its amendments in 1974 and 1976, and its modification in the wake of the Supreme Court case, *Buckley v. Valeo*, from later that year.[7] That regulatory system evolved over the years, in both presidential and congressional campaigns, particularly noted by the growth of PACs in the 1970s, the spreading use of "soft money" by the political parties as a way to acquire and spend money on campaign-related projects (e.g., turnout drives) that did not have federal limits, and the spread of issue advocacy ads, independent of the parties and candidates, that dramatically increased political campaign expenditures during election campaigns. In 2002, the Bipartisan Campaign Reform Act (BCRA) was passed to regulate some of these changes (sparking yet other changes), especially changing the latter two features described above. The Supreme Court issued a series of rulings about BCRA, but the major decision is the 2009 case (with the ruling issued in 2010) *Citizens United v. Federal Election Commission* (commonly called *Citizens United*), which invalidated many of the central features of the BCRA.[8] The decision in *Citizens United* ruled that "money is speech" and thus under the protection of the First Amendment—even when contributed by corporations or unions—has opened financial avenues in ways barely imaginable only a decade or so ago as reflected by the sheer growth in the number of super PACs since the 2010 ruling. In 2014, the Supreme Court struck down limits on the total amount of contributions that donors can give to candidates and political committees during a (two-year) election period in *McCutcheon vs. FEC*.[9] As such, how changes in the media and campaign finance will affect public opinion and voting behavior is a work very much still in progress.

Continuity in the Party System

The second great continuity is that the United States has one of the most nearly pure two-party systems in the world. The simple fact that the Democratic and the Republican Parties form this two-party system and that the constitutional design of American elections has been largely constant provide the basis of this continuity in national elections. Indeed, that these two have continued as America's two major parties since about 1860 means that not only is there a two-party system but also that it is the same two parties that have dominated the American electoral system for a time longer than virtually any other nation can claim even to be a democracy at all.

The ambition of candidates to seek election and reelection, as discussed in chapters 1 and 9, means that the overwhelming majority of state and national candidates and officeholders for elections to those offices are affiliates of one or the other of these two parties. As we noted earlier, there actually are often a great many more candidates for major office, including the presidency, but the role of these third-party candidates is ordinarily tangential or simply trivial. To be sure, third-party presidential candidates have won considerable numbers of votes in the last seventy years, peaking at the quite remarkable 19 percent of votes cast for H. Ross Perot in 1992 (albeit 0 electoral votes), and the 13.5 percent cast for George Wallace in 1968 (and 46 electoral votes),[10] but even they did not prevent a major-party candidate (Bill Clinton and Richard Nixon, respectively) from winning an outright majority of the electoral votes and thus the presidency. And in the Congress, the percentage of third-party candidates elected to either the House or the Senate has not risen above a paltry 2 percent in this period, and these few winners almost always caucused with one of the two political parties, acting, that is, as at least a pseudo-partisan (including Senator Bernie Sanders, an independent and self-described "democratic social-ist," who sought the Democratic nomination in 2016 and again in 2020).

As a result, the typical general election campaign is effectively, and often exclusively, a contest between a Republican and a Democrat. This structures how politicians act as candidates and officeholders. This structures how campaigns are conducted and observed by the media. And this structures how the citizens observe the candidates and campaigns, how they evaluate the alterna-tives, and how they vote. In other words, the two-party system permeates the full range of electoral behavior, in all its manifestations.

The electoral and the party systems interact and reinforce one another. That all national and most state and local races are conducted under a plurality-winner-take-all, or a near equivalent, means that all offices are subject to what Maurice Duverger referred to as the mechanical effect from counting votes and the psychological effect among voters that generate a two-party system.[11] Added to this are, of course, the candidates. They have incentives to cement that two-party system into place, largely as they enter elective politics as a career choice. Doing so gives them every incentive to seek to climb the informal hierarchy of offices that Joseph Schlesinger called the "opportunity structure." Because that is headed by the presidency, the general idea is that looking forward to a long successful career in politics, hopefully climbing to the top of the ladder, all but requires entering politics as a Democrat or as a Republican and staying that way for most people, most of the time.[12]

THE GREAT CHANGE: DEPOLARIZATION AND THE RETURN OF PARTISAN POLARIZATION

In 1952, the two political parties were structured primarily along the lines set during the Great Depression and the creation of the New Deal party system during Franklin Roosevelt's presidency, which in turn formed in light of the decline of a Republican majority coalition. The Republican Party achieved majority status at the turn of the twentieth century and held power in the national government for most of the first third of the century. A durable Democratic Party majority emerged by 1932 in a replacement (or as it was known then, a "partisan realignment") sparked by the Great Depression. Roosevelt created a majority party that drew its support most heavily from the cities and from working-class voters, especially those in blue-collar jobs belonging to the industrial and trade unions, and thus largely in the Northeast, Middle Atlantic, and those Midwest states that border the Great Lakes. These tended to include Catholics and Jews and others who were often the children and grandchildren of the great migration at the end of the nineteenth century and thus of the eastern and southern European immigrants, particularly those organized in Democratic machines. In the middle to late 1930s, Roosevelt added the African American population that had recently migrated from the South to the North to this set of groups that made up the New Deal coalition.

This collective grouping was added to the core of the Democratic Party, the solid, one-party South. The great majority of the white South had been overwhelmingly Democratic since the 1860s. It became the only competitive party in the South at the turn of the twentieth century, when it defeated a burgeoning threat from the Populist Party, which was the only serious threat to Democratic hegemony in that region. At the same time, it also reinforced itself as a "lily-white" party in that region, through the passage of Jim Crow Laws (and other aspects, including the systematic use of violence, that created the Jim Crow system of segregation) to disenfranchise African Americans, along with a good number of poor whites. As the 1950s opened, then, the South made up a very large portion of the Democratic Party, both in terms of electoral votes Democratic presidential candidates could win and in terms of seats controlled in both houses of Congress (see chapter 9). The Republicans held a majority in the House after World War II for two congresses, in 1947–1948 and 1953–1954. In those years, the South made up a majority of Democratic members. While they were not a majority of all

Democrats in other years, they came very close. The result is that, even then, they held a very large minority, so large that the Democratic Party could rarely act in the House or Senate without southern support.

The Republican Party could, in some sense, be defined as the rest of the country, but should largely be understood as a mixture of two groups. These groupings were sometimes called the Main Street and Wall Street wings of the party, and sometimes referred to by the peak leader of each of the two groups, the Taft Republicans (after Ohio Senator Robert Taft), typically economically conservative, Middle America, and isolationist, and the Rockefeller Republicans (after New York Governor and US Vice President Nelson Rockefeller), typically highly educated, residing in or near cities of the coasts, socially liberal and internationalist in outlook.

Both parties thus had internal divisions in this period—indeed, it is hard to imagine a party seeking to win electoral majorities that does not have diversity of views within it. But by the 1950s, both were stretched particularly broadly and thus were unusually vulnerable to internal divisions. The Democratic Party had been reasonably united early in the New Deal, in large part because southern Democrats were supportive of the first wave of New Deal legislation. The party began to split regionally during the second wave of New Deal legislation after the 1936 elections, and over social issues, particularly those related to race. Thus as the 1950s opened, the party had a semblance of remaining unity, and it could still be well described by the coalition that FDR had put together, even though it was under strain.

But the 1950s was the time of the civil rights movement, and this drove a first wedge deeply into the party that culminated with the passage of the Civil Rights and Voting Rights Acts along with other legislation making up Lyndon Johnson's Great Society programs in the mid-1960s.[13] This led directly to a dramatic and nearly instantaneous increase of African Americans in the Democratic Party, going from a small to an overwhelming majority who identified themselves as Democrats, and they voted accordingly. It was accompanied by the slow exit of white southerners from the party. In addition, time and prosperity weakened the ties of Catholics along with others who made up the former working class, but who were now moving up to the middle class. Manufacturing jobs also waned and associated unions lost their political vitality. Thus, their ties to the party weakened.

Democrats were therefore internally polarized in the 1950s and 1960s, as it consisted of elected officials and other party leaders moving toward both ideological poles. The Republican Party was, as noted above, split in two groups too, although less fully divided than the Democrats. Nonetheless, from 1952 well into the 1970s, the spread of opinion among elected officials (and among the public) in both parties was sufficiently great as to call this an era of depolarization of the two parties. The movement of conservative southerners from Democrat to Republican loyalties, and the associated chain of events affecting the two parties reversed, first slowly, and then dramatically, the depolarization, leading to the current partisan polarization.

The Republican Party changed, in large measure as the mirror image of changes in the Democratic Party. Thus, they picked up much of what the Democrats lost in the South, such that, by 1995 when it finally reemerged with a legislative majority, the Republican Party in the Congress was led almost in its entirety by southern Republicans. Conversely, the loss of social liberalism in the party effectively cost it any serious chance of majority support in the Northeast and especially New England, where the GOP's huge advantage in 1952 became a dramatic Democratic advantage by 1992, one that has continued—with very few exceptions—through 2020.

The great change described thus far was that the Democrats lost their most conservative elements, the Republicans their most liberal wing. The members of the two parties, that is, *sorted* themselves out on ideology, so that the parties hold much less diversity within their ranks, and virtually all Democrats are toward the left half of the ideological spectrum, virtually all Republicans are toward the right half. What Ronald Regan referred to as the "big tent" of a party became a much smaller and more cohesive tent on each side.

This sorting was true at all levels, from the top level of the political elites to the base of political publics. It happened first at the elite level, appearing quite clearly in the Congress, for example, beginning in the 1980s and proceeding through to today. The sorting is also true in the public, albeit moving into place more slowly but nonetheless decisively. The major difference is that the elected officials and the rest of the party elites have become more *polarized*—that is the two parties in Congress not only vote differently from one another, they appear to be taking ever-more extreme positions, moving, that is, farther and farther apart. The result is that few moderates are elected to national office (and likely to state legislatures, either).[14] The public has not polarized to anywhere near the same degree, if they have polarized at all—on this latter issue political scientists disagree.[15] No one disagrees that the public is much more sorted, however, and to that extent, the public is a reasonably close approximation to the elites in terms of sorting.[16]

This section has reviewed the kinds of changes discussed in chapters 1, 3, and 5, and parts of 9 and 10.[17] The rest of this chapter lays out additional features we have studied that reflect these continuities and changes. We turn first to consider turnout, as in chapter 4, which has some remaining features of institutional development, along with a considerable degree of continuity with some relevant changes along the lines of the "great sort." We then turn to the public opinion and voting behavior considered in chapter 6–8 and then remaining features of congressional campaigns and elections in chapter 9 and 10.

CHANGE AND CONTINUITY IN TURNOUT

Here, we highlight three basic aspects of our analysis in turnout from chapter 4. The first is that, over the course of American political history, the dominant flow has been toward expansion of suffrage, albeit with several notable exceptions, with a major political question of this sort looming today. The second is that, in many ways, turnout since the 1950s has a great deal of continuity, in no small measure due to the continuity in the party system. However, and thirdly, there are some signs that even turnout is being affected by the "great sort."

One of the central questions for understanding turnout at any time is who is eligible to vote—asking both who is eligible for citizenship and which citizens are eligible to vote. The primary thrust of American democracy has been expansion of both. Thus, for example, in the eighteenth and early nineteenth centuries, the United States may have been the first Democratic republic in the modern era, but slaves were excluded from citizenship and suffrage was limited to males (and in many places to white males), often requiring them to hold property and/or have paid taxes. By the middle of the nineteenth century property-holding requirements were gone, and we had essentially achieved one version of "universal suffrage"—all white male citizens were eligible to vote. The Civil War Amendments (especially the 15th) extended that right to all males, the 19th Amendment (ratified in 1920) extended suffrage to women, and the one amendment within our primary time frame is the 26th (1972) which provided suffrage for eighteen, nineteen, and twenty year olds.

This general expansion of the suffrage is counterbalanced in part by two major kinds of legislation that have reduced turnout from what it otherwise might have been. The most direct were the Jim Crow Laws that were intended (successfully) to all but eliminate freed slaves and their offspring from the franchise, sweeping up poor whites and others along the way, and undermining the effect of the Civil War Amendments. The second form has been one kind or another of registration laws. These laws were the centerpiece of the third-party known as the American (or "Know-nothing") Party in the 1850s, which contested against the new found Republican Party to replace the Whigs as America's second major party. Their proposals were to reduce or eliminate the then-recent wave of immigration (largely of Irish and Germans, but also other central and eastern Europeans) from becoming voters. While immigrant movement to citizenship and voting was slowed in this period, the American Party failed, and the Republicans adopted only parts of the American Party's proposed restrictions as they moved to defeat that party at the polls. Registration latched more firmly into the American voting regime in the early part of the twentieth century, as part of the Progressive and other parties' "good government" reforms. It was during this time that voting registration became commonplace throughout the nation, and the design of these registration laws was to make it the responsibility of the individuals who wanted to vote to ensure their registration, rather than it being the responsibility of the government to ensure registration of all eligible voters, as in most of the rest of the advanced democracies. These registration laws had the intended effect of reducing turnout among the poorer and the immigrant populations, especially in the North. In that way, they were similar to the Jim Crow Laws in the South, which were directed at a somewhat different population, but designed to give an edge to upper and middle-class voters over working- and lower-class voters. This "opt in" system of registration to vote was justified as "good government" on the grounds that it would reduce fraudulent voting.

The post-1952 period has been typified by attempts to increase turnout through easing of registration requirements and other aspects that increase the cost and complication of turnout. Most notable is the so-called "motor-voter" bill (1993), which got its nickname because the law's provisions allowed voter registration at various places, including where one gets a driver's license. Current legislative initiatives, however, are moving mostly in the opposite direction, particularly voter identification laws which, in the name of avoiding fraudulent voting, require voters to present a state-issued voter identification card in order to vote. Such laws are likely to have their greatest effects on both immigrants becoming citizens and on minority and poor voters (and also on the youngest voters), thus blending both targets from prior eras and also hitting disproportionately on those more likely to vote Democratic than on others. This is especially true after the 2020 elections in light of repeated and unsubstantiated claims made by former President Trump that he lost the election as a result of fraudulent voting.

Actual turnout rates thereby fluctuate in part as a function of who are eligible voters. As we have seen, since 1952, turnout for presidential elections has hewed to a fairly restricted range of the mostly mid-50s to the lower to mid-60s in terms of percent politically eligible and voting-eligible population (see figure 4.2). Congressional elections are typically in the low to mid-40 percentile ranges.

This limited variation is nonetheless important, as 10 percent of our population represents tens of millions of people. The major explanations for the over time changes (amid over time continuity) relate to political parties and to how the public views the government, as well as the large-scale changes in population reviewed elsewhere. Two general trends are the decline in such measures as trust and sense of external efficacy of the government, notable from the mid-1960s on (and at extraordinarily low levels in 2020), and the decline and re-gathering of strength of partisanship from the early 1970s to the most recent decades. The two together suggest a decline and the resurgence of turnout, as partisanship declined and then resurged, but to a somewhat lower peak, due to the declining views of government overall. We will see again this idea that partisanship declined in relevance and importance to the public, just as the divisions within the parties grew most pronounced, and the parties became more important once again, as the "great sort" and polarization of partisan elites gathered strength. So let us turn to those continuities and changes now.

CONTINUITIES IN ELECTORAL PARTISANSHIP

Perhaps the single most important fact for understanding American electoral behavior is the continuing relevance of partisan attachments. As we discussed in chapter 6, the way we as election observers understand partisanship has undergone several important changes over the last decades. But the three major continuities stand out.

The first is that substantial majorities have and continue to find the two political parties and their own partisanship of central importance for their relationship to the political system and especially to electoral politics. The proportion of "pure" independents increased from 10 percent in 2012 to 14 percent in 2020 (see table 6.1). That is, of course, a significant increase, and it could foretell the beginnings of real change. Still, that proportion is barely higher than it was in 1980 and is close to what it was in 1972. Thus, we must be cautious in interpreting the meaning and durability of this change. Moreover, this increase is accompanied by an even larger decline in the percentage of independents who said that they lean toward one party or the other (a decline of a total of 14 percent of the electorate choosing those responses from 2012; 5 percent on the Democratic side, 9 percent on the Republican side). Furthermore, the proportion of the electorate who said they were strong partisans peaked in 2020. Thus, we can say that partisanship was more "polarized" in 2020, but whether that was due to the unusual heat of the campaign or the beginnings of a long-term trend is unclear.

The second and related continuity is that the balance of partisanship between the two parties has fluctuated about an overall continuously modest but real advantage for Democrats. That is, as we noted in chapter 6, since 1952, the balance of Democrats to Republicans has been in the range of 55-45 to 60-40 or even more. It is very important to note that there has been a long-term move toward parity between the two parties. Thus, the balance was typically closer to 60-40 earlier, and is now more regularly at the bottom end of that range. If independent "leaners" are included, Democratic identifiers make up 44 percent of the electorate to 41 percent among Republican identifiers, again just at the bottom edge of the historical range. In short, 2020 looked like an increasingly balanced two-party system.

The third major continuity is that partisanship is closely related to the choices voters make. Being a partisan is just as strongly related to turnout as ever. Claiming to be a Democrat is just as closely related to how one evaluates candidates and issues and as closely related to the vote—for president and for Congress—as ever. Indeed, this is another set of cases in which these relationships were strong in the 1950s and 1960s and began to sag in strength into the 1970s and 1980s but have reasserted themselves to approximately their earlier levels. This broad but not unvarying stability is sort of the fly-wheel that keeps a balance both in the public and in office. But there are some very important changes in the electorate, too.

CHANGES IN THE PARTISAN ELECTORATE

We have already discussed some very important changes in the makeup of the electorate, those that underlie the analyses in chapter 5 in particular. One aspect of some of these changes that has become apparent only recently is that people are sorting themselves by their decisions as to where to live in ways that reinforce partisan sorting in the public. Thus, the regeneration of cities is due in significant degree to the attraction urban areas have for the young, the professionals, and others who are likely to be Democrats. Smaller towns and rural areas are either attracting more conservative (often older) voters who are likely to identify as Republican or they are disproportionately losing potential Democratic votes. In either event, geographic mobility has played a major role in public sorting and in creating more solid one-party areas. This sort of "micro-change" goes along with the changes in overall configuration of the population already noted, particularly the coming of the baby boomers to voting age in the 1960s and 1970s, and then the increasing aging of that population as baby boomers near retirement. This generational shift accompanies other changes, such as the huge new immigration, and thus the coming not only of Latino as a growing electoral force, but also the apparently soon-to-come era in which whites no longer are a majority of the voting-age population. Each of these is directly or indirectly related to the partisan nature of the electorate and ultimately to its vote.

If these changes help us understand the dynamics of party identification in postwar America, the "great sort" they helped induce in the public's partisanship has had effects on other variables, often those directly related to the vote. It appears, for example, that elite polarization has led to a truly substantial increase in the proportion of the public who see the parties and their candidates taking different positions (and seeing those positions "correctly") and thus being able to cast a vote based on one or more prospective issues. It is simply much easier to know or correctly guess where a Republican and where a Democrat stands on issue after issue, and thus incorporate prospective issues into their decision calculus. Or, while retrospective voting has been continuously important, partisan sorting has increased its distribution, with incumbent-party partisans likely to want to reward their party more strongly and out-party partisans opposing more strongly, and thus strengthening the potency of retrospective voting as well. Finally, the "great sort" and increased partisan polarization of elites has appeared to make all kinds of political judgments easier. Examples we illustrated include evaluations of the president's performance overall and in particular areas, such as the economy or war-making, and judgments about which party will best handle highly important problems or put the country on the right track. In short, elite partisan polarization and public sorting has permeated throughout the electoral arena. We suggest that this means that the political parties are seen sending signals to the electorate with greater relevance and meaning and the public is conditioning their beliefs and choices on partisanship in ways quite different from the 1970s. We conclude this section, however, by noting that all this is a question of relative balance, that partisanship has always been important, waxing and waning within relatively confined ranges.

CHANGE AND CONTINUITY IN THE US CONGRESS

It is not surprising that the significant changes we have outlined, particularly the polarization of elites and the shifts in the partisan electorate, have had substantial impacts on the institutional operation of the Congress and on congressional elections. Indeed, these institutional and electoral forces have interacted to amplify the effects, feeding back on one another over time. However, it is also true that many of the most significant patterns of the past have persisted into this new polarized era.

Despite the fact that four of the last seven congressional election years (2006, 2008, 2010, and 2018) have resulted in "wave elections" in which one party was hit with the loss of a large number of House seats, the advantages of incumbency we discussed in chapter 9 still persist. It is still true that most elections involve incumbents and that the great majority of incumbents win, both in the House and the Senate. This fact affects the governing choices of the incumbents, the decisions of potential candidates about whether to run or not, and the choices of individuals who control campaign-relevant resources about whom to support.

Still, the great changes have had profound consequences, and have produced a new equilibrium in governing and elections. The realignment of the South from a Democratic bastion to a Republican one, coupled with its echo in parts of the North leading to increased Democratic support there, created the much more ideologically homogeneous legislative party coalitions we have today, with little or no overlap between those coalitions. This development, in turn, led to the transformation of legislative governance in both chambers. The weak party organizations and the dominant role of committees in the period from World War II through the early 1970s gradually gave way to a pattern of majority-party dominance in which committee contingents were responsive to their respective party caucuses in most matters.

When the party coalitions were very diverse and overlapping, members were reluctant to vest party leaders with significant powers because those members could not confidently predict what ideological orientation future leaders would have. Conservative Democrats might be satisfied with one of their own being a powerful leader, but they could not be sure that a liberal northerner would not be chosen subsequently, and that could lead to policies they would dislike. Republicans were in a parallel situation. When partisan realignment gradually reduced party heterogeneity, however, members' reluctance to delegate power to leaders also declined. This resulted in the reform era of the 1970s, when the House Democrats undermined the protections that the seniority system gave to committee leaders, forcing them to become responsive to party opinion. The reforms also greatly increased the influence of party leaders, particularly by transferring control over the legislative agenda from independent committees to those leaders. The Senate experienced some parallel, but less extensive, reforms at the same time, and the effects of these moves were reinforced when the Republicans took congressional control in the 1994 elections and they moved even further in strengthening the parties than the Democrats had. Since then these patterns (which we have labeled "conditional party government") have been further reinforced.[18]

In this more partisan governing environment, the policies each party pursued became more divergent. This presented clearer pictures of the orientations of the parties to the electorate, as we discussed above, making it easier for voters to make their vote choice in light of their policy preferences. This enhanced party sorting, making rank-and-file preferences also more homogeneous, although not nearly so much as among elites. This was especially true of the most politically active citizens, the type who were most likely to vote in party primaries. As a result, the more extreme elements of each party's voter base had an increasingly strong influence over candidate selection. And the parties' increasing success at political gerrymandering, creating more districts that were safe for each party, created conditions that put even greater emphasis on the opinions of primary electorates.

Another area in which the enhancement of party government had an electoral impact was in campaign funding. Before the reform era, congressional candidates were largely on their own in fund-raising; the portion of such funds that came from parties and independent spending was minuscule. But as parties became more important (and more dependable) in governing, their role in raising money and channeling it to their candidates expanded as well. The parties also became more active in candidate recruiting, training, and advising, as we discussed in chapter 9. This trend was paralleled by the rise of campaign spending by independent ideological groups and later the super PACs. Both the party spending and the independent spending enhanced incentives for members to support their parties within the government, or at least not to work independently with members of the other party, furthering the development of polarization.

Thus due to electoral developments we have experienced the rise of stronger, more homogeneous, and more policy-motivated parties in Congress, parties that are more divergent from one another regarding preferred policy outcomes. When unified government occurs, the majority party can often achieve a large part of their legislative program (although the narrow Democratic majority in the House and the current 50-50 split in the Senate has made it rather challenging for the Democrats to accomplish their ambitious agenda so far in 2021). When, however, divided government is in effect, a compromise outcome is often difficult to achieve because a result that is desirable to one side is often anathema to the other, and an outcome in the middle is far from what a large portion of the members on both sides want. History is also not on the Democrats' side in the upcoming midterm elections. With the extremely close partisan divisions in both chambers of Congress, losing a few House seats or a net of just one Senate seat in the upcoming midterm election could put Biden's legislative agenda at risk if the Republicans are able to make an electoral comeback following the 2022 elections.

Appendix

Table A.6.1 Party Identification in Presidential Years, Pre-Election Surveys, 1952–2020 (Percent)

Party Identification	1952	1956	1960	1964	1968	1972	1976	1980	1984	1988	1992	1996	2000	2004	2008	2012	2016	2020
Strong Democrat	23	22	24	27	20	15	15	18	17	18	17	18	19	17	19	17	21	22
Weak Democrat	26	24	25	25	26	25	24	24	20	18	18	20	15	16	15	12	14	11
Independent, Leans Democratic	10	7	6	9	10	11	12	12	11	12	14	14	15	17	17	16	11	11
Independent, No Partisan Leanings	5	9	9	8	11	15	15	13	11	11	12	8	12	10	11	10	15	14
Independent, Leans Republican	8	9	7	6	9	10	10	10	13	14	13	12	13	12	12	19	11	10
Weak Republican	14	14	14	14	15	13	14	14	15	14	15	16	12	12	13	12	12	11
Strong Republican	14	16	15	11	10	10	9	9	13	14	11	13	12	17	13	14	16	20
Total	100	101	100	100	101	99	99	100	100	101	100	101	98	101	100	100	100	99
(N)	(1,689)	(1,690)	(1,132)	(1,536)	(1,531)	(2,695)	(2,218)	(1,577)	(2,198)	(1,999)	(2,450)	(1,696)	(1,777)	(1,193)	(2,301)	(1,804)	(4,244)[a]	(7,432)
Apolitical								2	2	2	1	1	1	b	b	c	c	c
Apolitical N								35	38	33	23	14	21	3	2	c	c	c

Source: Authors' analysis of ANES surveys.

[a] The percentage supporting another party has not been presented; it usually totals less than 1 percent and never totals more than 1 percent.

[b] Numbers are weighted.

[c] The ANES survey did not use the apolitical category in 2012, 2016, or 2020.

Table A.6.2 Party Identification among Whites, 1952–2020 (Percent)

Party Identification[a]	1952	1954	1956	1958	1960	1962	1964	1966	1968	1970	1972	1974	1976	1978	1980	1982	1984	1986	1988	1990	1992	1994	1996	1998	2000	2002	2004	2008	2012	2016	2020
Strong Democrat	21	22	20	26	20	22	24	17	16	17	12	15	13	12	14	16	15	14	14	17	14	12	15	15	15	12	13	14	13	16	17
Weak Democrat	25	25	23	22	25	23	25	27	25	22	25	20	23	24	23	24	18	21	16	19	17	19	19	18	14	16	12	14	10	12	9
Independent, Leans Democrat	10	9	6	7	6	8	9	9	10	11	12	13	11	14	12	11	11	10	10	11	14	12	13	14	15	14	17	17	15	11	11
Independent, No Partisan Leaning	6	7	9	8	9	8	8	12	11	13	13	15	15	14	14	11	11	12	12	11	12	10	8	11	13	8	8	12	10	14	11
Independent, Leans Republican	7	6	9	5	7	7	6	8	10	9	11	9	11	11	11	9	13	13	15	13	14	13	12	12	14	15	13	13	22	13	12
Weak Republican	14	15	14	17	14	17	14	16	16	16	14	15	16	14	16	16	17	17	15	16	16	16	17	18	14	17	15	15	13	14	13
Strong Republican	14	13	16	12	17	13	12	11	11	10	11	9	10	9	9	11	14	12	16	11	12	17	15	11	14	17	21	16	17	21	27
Apolitical	2	2	2	3	1	3	1	1	1	1	1	3	1	3	2	2	2	2	1	1	1	1	1	2	1	1	a	a	b	b	abc
Total	99	99	99	100	99	101	99	101	100	99	99	99	100	101	101	100	101	101	99	99	100	100	100	101	100	100	99	101	100	101	100
N	(1,615)	(1,015)	(1,610)[b]	(1,638)[b]	(1,739)[b]	(1,168)	(1,394)[b]	(1,131)	(1,131)	(1,387)	(1,395)	(2,397)	(2,246)[b]	(2,490)[b]	(1,405)	(1,248)	(1,931)	(1,798)	(1,693)	(1,663)	(2,702)	(1,510)	(1,451)	(1,091)	(1,404)	(1,129)	(859)	(1,824)	(1,449)	(2,917)	(4,845)

Source: Authors' analysis of ANES surveys.

Note: The percentage supporting another party has not been presented; it usually totals less than 1 percent and never totals more than 1 percent.

[a] Less than 1 percent.

[b] Numbers are weighted.

[c] ANES survey did not use the apolitical category in 2012, 2016, or 2020.

Table A.6.3 Party Identification among Blacks, 1952–2020 (Percent)

Party Identification[a]	1952	1954	1956	1958	1960	1962	1964	1966	1968	1970	1972	1974	1976	1978	1980	1982	1984	1986	1988	1990	1992	1994	1996	1998	2000	2002	2004	2008	2012	2016	2020
Strong Democrat	30%	24%	27%	32%	25%	35%	52%	30%	56%	41%	36%	40%	34%	37%	45%	53%	32%	42%	39%	40%	40%	38%	43%	48%	47%	53%	30%	47%	53%	52%	53
Weak Democrat	22	29	23	19	19	25	22	31	29	34	31	26	36	29	27	26	31	30	24	23	24	23	22	23	21	16	30	23	17	19	14
Independent, Leans Democratic	10	6	5	7	7	4	8	11	7	7	8	15	14	15	9	12	14	12	18	16	14	20	16	12	14	17	20	15	17	10	14
Independent, No Partisan Leaning	4	5	7	4	16	6	6	14	3	12	12	12	8	9	7	5	11	7	6	8	12	8	10	7	10	6	12	9	5	13	10
Independent, Leans Republican	4	6	1	4	4	2	1	2	1	1	3	ª	1	2	3	1	6	2	5	7	3	4	5	3	4	2	5	3	7	1	5
Weak Republican	8	5	12	11	9	7	5	7	1	4	4	ª	2	3	2	2	1	2	5	3	3	2	3	3	4	1	2	1	0	2	3
Strong Republican	5	11	7	7	7	6	2	2	1	0	4	3	2	3	3	0	2	2	1	2	2	3	1	1	0	1	1	1	1	3	2
Apolitical	17	15	18	16	14	15	4	3	3	1	2	4	1	2	4	1	2	2	3	2	2	3	0	2	1	a	a	a	b	b	a
Total	100%	101%	100%	101%	101%	100%	100%	100%	101%	100%	100%	100%	99%	100%	100%	100%	99%	99%	101%	101%	100%	101%	100%	99%	100%	100%	100%	99%	100%	100%	101
(N)	(171)	(101)	(146)	(161)ᵇ	(171)ᵇ	(110)	(156)	(132)	(149)	(157)	(267)	(224)ᵇ	(290)ᵇ	(230)	(187)	(148)	(247)	(322)	(267)	(270)	(317)	(203)	(200)	(149)	(225)	(161)	(193)	(281)	(124)	(460)	(831)

Table A.6.4 White Major-Party Voters Who Voted Democratic for President, by Party Identification, 1952–2020 (Percent)

Party Identification	1952	1956	1960	1964	1968	1972	1976	1980	1984	1988	1992	1996	2000	2004	2008	2012	2016	2020
Strong Democrat	82	85	91	94	89	66	88	87	88	93	96	98	96	97	92	98	95	98
Weak Democrat	61	63	70	81	66	44	72	59	63	68	80	88	81	78	83	82	75	88
Independent, Leans Democratic	60	65	89	89	62	58	73	57	77	86	92	91	72	88	8	86	88	95
Independent, No Partisan Leanings	18	15	50	75	28	26	41	23	21	35	63	39	44	54	50	42	36	46
Independent, Leans Republican	7	6	13	25	5	11	15	13	5	13	14	26	15	13	17	11	8	12
Weak Republican	4	7	11	40	10	9	22	5	6	16	18	21	16	10	10	14	17	18
Strong Republican	2	a	2	9	3	2	3	4	2	2	2	3	1	3	2	4	2	3

Source: Authors' analysis of ANES surveys.
a Less than 1 percent.

Table A.7.1 Balance-of-Issues Positions among Partisan Groups, 1976–2020 (Percent)

Year	Issue Positions Closer to . . .	Strong Democrat	Weak Democrat	Independent, Leans Democrat	Independent	Independent, Leans Republican	Weak Republican	Strong Republican	Total
1976	Democratic candidate	28	27	22	15	12	9	3	18
	Neutral	32	26	37	29	27	23	27	29
	Republican candidate	39	47	40	55	61	67	69	53
	Total	99	100	99	99	100	99	99	100
	(N)	(422)	(655)	(336)	(416)	(277)	(408)	(254)	(2,778)
1980	Democratic candidate	26	23	27	20	12	10	9	19
	Neutral	34	37	33	43	40	43	31	37
	Republican candidate	40	40	40	37	48	48	60	43
	Total	100	100	100	100	100	101	100	99
	(N)	(245)	(317)	(161)	(176)	(150)	(202)	(127)	(1,378)
1984	Democratic candidate	57	49	59	35	23	29	14	39
	Neutral	32	37	28	48	46	40	39	38
	Republican candidate	11	14	13	17	32	32	47	23
	Total	100	100	100	100	101	101	100	100
	(N)	(331)	(390)	(215)	(213)	(248)	(295)	(256)	(1,948)
1988	Democratic candidate	49	36	50	33	21	21	11	32
	Neutral	34	40	38	48	46	43	35	40
	Republican candidate	17	24	12	19	33	36	53	29
	Total	100	100	100	100	100	100	99	101
	(N)	(355)	(359)	(240)	(215)	(270)	(281)	(279)	(1,999)
1992	Democratic candidate	40	36	30	26	13	13	9	25
	Neutral	55	57	65	70	74	77	74	67
	Republican candidate	5	7	4	5	13	11	17	9
	Total	100	100	99	101	100	101	100	101
	(N)	(380)	(389)	(313)	(235)	(283)	(335)	(238)	(2,192)

Table A.7.1   Balance-of-Issues Positions among Partisan Groups, 1976–2020 (Percent) (Continued)

Year	Issue Positions Closer to . . .	Strong Democrat	Weak Democrat	Independent, Leans Democrat	Independent	Independent, Leans Republican	Weak Republican	Strong Republican	Total
1996	Democratic candidate	44	27	35	17	13	9	1	22
	Neutral	27	36	34	43	27	23	14	29
	Republican candidate	30	37	31	40	60	68	85	49
	Total	101	100	100	100	100	100	100	100
	(N)	(313)	(333)	(229)	(140)	(195)	(268)	(217)	(2,696)
2000	Democratic candidate	30	26	25	20	8	10	2	19
	Neutral	47	48	46	49	40	33	25	43
	Republican candidate	23	25	29	31	51	57	73	38
	Total	100	101	100	100	99	100	100	100
	(N)	(188)	(161)	(157)	(113)	(134)	(101)	(99)	(953)
2004	Democratic candidate	72	55	57	40	19	21	9	40
	Neutral	8	11	9	10	9	6	5	8
	Republican candidate	21	33	34	50	73	73	86	52
	Total	100	99	101	100	100	99	100	100
	(N)	(168)	(157)	(180)	(100)	(124)	(136)	(179)	(1,046)
2008[a]	Democratic candidate	60	46	47	28	16	14	8	34
	Neutral	6	9	14	10	17	9	(2)	9
	Republican candidate	34	45	40	63	67	77	90	56
	Total	100	100	101	101	100	100	99	99
	(N)	(219)	(163)	(203)	(135)	(143)	(148)	(142)	(1,153)
2012	Democratic candidate	47	36	29	22	6	7	5	22
	Neutral	16	18	17	10	10	5	3	11
	Republican candidate	37	46	54	68	85	88	93	67
	Total	100	100	100	100	100	100	100	100
	(N)	(307)	(214)	(282)	(182)	(342)	(210)	(258)	(1,795)

(Continued)

Table A.7.1 Balance-of-Issues Positions among Partisan Groups, 1976–2020 (Percent) (Continued)

Year	Issue Positions Closer to . . .	Strong Democrat	Weak Democrat	Independent, Leans Democrat	Independent	Independent, Leans Republican	Weak Republican	Strong Republican	Total
2016	Democratic candidate	64	48	56	34	13	13	7	35
	Neutral	14	19	19	24	11	17	6	16
	Republican candidate	22	33	24	42	76	70	87	49
	Total	100	100	99	100	100	100	100	100
	(N)	(902)	(587)	(462)	(620)	(472)	(501)	(696)	(4,242)
2020	Democratic candidate	81	68	80	44	19	17	9	47
	Neutral	7	15	10	17	10	14	8	11
	Republican candidate	12	17	9	39	71	69	83	43
	Total	100	100	100	100	100	100	100	100
	(N)	(1,616)	(829)	(833)	(953)	(757)	(782)	(1,489)	(7,258)

Source: Authors' analysis of ANES surveys.

Note: In the one instance in which the category included fewer than ten observations, we show the total number of people in that category in brackets.

[a]The Democratic category on the condensed balance-of-issues measure includes any respondent who is at least slightly Democratic; the Republican category includes any respondent who is at least slightly Republican. The neutral category is the same as the neutral category on the seven-point issue scale (see table 6.5). In 2008, the issue questions that were used to form the balance-of-issues scale were asked of a randomly selected half-sample.

[b]Numbers are weighted.

Table A.8.1 Evaluation of Government Performance on Most Important Problem and Major-Party Vote, 1972–2008

Government Performance	1972[a]	1976	1980	1984	1988	1992	1996[a]	2000[a]	2004[a]	2008[a]
A. Evaluation of government performance on most important problem (percent)										
Good job	12	8	4	16	8	2	7	10	60	26
Only fair job	58	46	35	46	37	28	44	44	42	31
Poor job	30	46	61	39	56	69	48	47	40	31
Total	100	100	100	101	101	99	99	101	100	100
(N)	(993)	(2,156)	(1,319)	(1,797)	(1,672)	(1,974)[b]	(752)[b]	(8,56)[b]	(1,024)[b]	(2,083)[b]
B. Percentage of major-party vote for incumbent party's nominee										
	Nixon[a]	Ford	Carter	Reagan	Bush	Bush	Clinton[a]	Gore[a]	Bush	McCain
Good job	85	72	81	89	82	70	93	70	76	74
(N)	(91)	(128)[b]	(43)	(214)	(93)	(27)[b]	(38)[b]	(58)[b]	(460)[b]	(383)[b]
Only fair job	69	53	55	65	61	45	68	60	47	
(N)	(390)	(695)[b]	(289)	(579)	(429)	(352)[b]	(238)[b]	(239)[b]	(658)[b]	
Poor job	46	39	33	37	44	39	44	37	11	21
(N)	(209)	(684)[b]	(505)	(494)	(631)	(841)[b]	(242)[b]	(230)[b]	(305)[b]	(512)[b]

Source: Author's analysis of ANES surveys.

Note: The numbers in parentheses are the totals on which the percentages are based.

[a] In 1972, 1996, 2000, and 2004, the questions were asked of a randomly selected half-sample. In 1972, respondents were asked whether the government was being (a) very helpful, (b) somewhat helpful, or (c) not helpful at all in solving this most important problem. In 2004, respondents were asked whether the government was doing (a) a very good job, (b) a good job, or (d) a very bad job. "Good job" includes both "very good" and "good job"; "poor job" includes both "bad" and "very bad."

[b] Number is weighted.

Table A.8.2 Evaluation of Party Seen as Better on Most Important Problem and Major-Party Vote, 1980–2000 and 2008–2016

Party Better	1980	1984	1988	1992	1996[a]	2000[a]	2008	2012	2016
Republican	43	32	22	13	22	23	27	31	35
No Difference[c]	46	44	54	48	54	50	18	31	35
Democratic	11	25	24	39	24	27	55	38	30
Total	100	101	100	100	100	100	100	100	100
(N)	(1,251)	(1,785)	(1,655)	(1,954)[b]	(746)	(846)[b]	(1,932)[b]	(1,884)[b]	(3,578)[b]
Major-party voters who voted Democratic for president									
Republican	12	5	5	4	15	9	6	7	6
(N)	(391)	(464)	(295)	(185)[b]	(137)[b]	(143)[b]	(429)[b]	(436)[b]	(923)[b]
No Difference[c]	63	41	46	45	63	52	29	56	64
(N)	(320)	(493)	(564)	(507)[b]	(250)[b]	(227)[b]	(237)[b]	(405)[b]	(933)[b]
Democratic	95	91	92	92	97	94	87	98	99
(N)	(93)	(331)	(284)	(519)[b]	(133)[b]	(153)[b]	(800)[b]	(429)[b]	(792)[b]

Source: Authors' analysis of ANES surveys.

Notes: The numbers in parentheses are the totals on which the percentages are based. Question wording, 1972–2000: "Thinking of the most important political problem facing the United States, which party do you think is best in dealing with it?"; 2008: "Thinking of the most important political problem facing the United States, which party do you think is best in dealing with it?"

[a] In 1972, 1996, and 2000, the questions were asked of a randomly selected half-sample. In 1972, respondents were asked which party would be more likely to get the government to be helpful in solving the most important problem. This question was not asked in 2004.

[b] Number is weighted.

[c] In 2008, the middle response allowed was "other."

Table A.8.3 The Public's Assessment of Their Personal Financial Situation and Major-Party Vote, 1980–2020

"Would you say that you (and your family) are better off or worse off financially than you were a year ago?"

Response	1980	1984	1988	1992	1996	2000	2004	2008	2012	2016	2020
Distribution of responses											
Better now	33	44	42	31	46	33	43	32	41	28	26
Same	25	28	33	34	31	53	25	18	24	47	50
Worse now	42	27	25	35	24	14	32	50	36	25	24
Total	100	99	100	100	101	100	100	100	101	100	100
(N)	(1,393)	(1,956)	(2,025)	(2,474)	(1,708)	(907)	(1,203)	(2,307)	(1,800)	(4,256)	(7,432)
Major-party votes who voted for the incumbent party nominee for president											
Better now	46	74	63	53	66	56	65	53	65	73	36
(N)	(295)	(612)	(489)	(413)	(462)	(164)	(354)	(491)	(456)	(681)	(825)
Same	46	55	50	45	52	51	50	52	49	50	49
(N)	(226)	(407)	(405)	(500)	(348)	(291)	(207)	(280)	(274)	(1,132)	(1,113)
Worse now	40	33	40	27	47	45	28	38	31	33	16
(N)	(351)	(338)	(283)	(453)	(225)	(56)	(219)	(778)	(414)	(560)	(357)

Source: Authors' analysis of ANES surveys.
Note: The numbers in parentheses are the totals on which the percentages are based. This question was asked of a randomly selected half-sample in 2000. Numbers are weighted.

Table A.8.4 The Public's View of the State of the National Economy and Major-Party Vote, 1980–2016

Response	1980	1984	1988	1992	1996	2000	2004	2008	2012	2016	2020
	"Would you say that over the past year the nation's economy has gotten . . .?"										
Distribution of responses											
Better	4	44	19	4	40	39	24	2	28	28	19
Stayed same	13	33	50	22	44	44	31	7	36	42	23
Worse	83	23	31	73	16	17	45	90	35	30	58
(N)	(1,580)	(1,904)	(1,956)	(2,465)	(1,700)	(1,787)	(1,196)	(2,313)	(1,806)	(4,261)	(7,433)
Major-party voters who voted for the incumbent party nominee for president											
Better	58	80	77	86	75	69	87	69	86	88	36
(N)	(33)	(646)	(249)	(62)	(458)	(408)	(211)	(34)	(339)	(724)	(839)
Stayed same	71	53	53	62	45	45	88	57	48	50	29
(N)	(102)	(413)	(568)	(318)	(443)	(487)	(243)	(109)	(425)	(992)	(662)
Worse	39	21	34	32	33	31	20	44	16	18	35
(N)	(732)	(282)	(348)	(981)	(130)	(154)	(319)	(1,425)	(382)	(658)	(792)

Source: Authors' analysis of ANES surveys.
Note: The numbers in parentheses are the totals on which percentages are based. We combine the results using standard and experimental prompts that contained different word orderings in 2000, 2004, and 2008. Numbers are weighted.

Table A.8.5 Evaluations of the Incumbent's Handling of the Economy and Major-Party Vote, 1984–2020

Response	1984	1988	1992	1996	2000	2004	2008	2012	2016	2020
Distribution of responses										
Positive view	58	54	20	66	77	41	18	42	53	52
Negative view	42	46	80	34	23	59	82	58	47	48
Total	100	100	100	100	100	100	100	100	100	100
(N)	(1,858)	(1,897)	(2,425)	(1,666)	(1,686)	(1,173)	(2,227)	(1,698)	(4,221)	(7,414)
Major-party voters who voted for the incumbent party nominee										
Positive view	86	80	90	79	67	91	89	92	89	83
(N)	(801)	(645)	(310)	(688)	(768)	(341)	(313)	(476)	(1,253)	(2,228)
Negative view	16	17	26	13	11	17	33	13	11	3
(N)	(515)	(492)	(1,039)	(322)	(233)	(431)	(1,200)	(618)	(1,109)	(67)

Source: Authors' analysis of ANES surveys.
Note: Numbers are weighted.

Table A.8.6   President's Handling of the Job and Major-Party Vote, 1980–2020

Response	1980	1984	1988	1992	1996	2000	2004	2008	2012	2016	2020
"Do you approve or disapprove of the way the president is handling his job?"											
Approve	41	63	60	43	68	67	51	27	50	53	42
Disapprove	59	37	40	57	32	33	49	73	50	47	58
Total	100	100	100	100	100	100	100	100	100	100	100
(N)	(1,475)	(2,091)	(1,935)	(2,419)	(1,692)	(1,742)	(1,182)	(2,245)	(1,704)	(4,226)	(7,403)
Percentage of major-party vote for incumbent's party nominee											
Approve	81	87	79	81	84	74	91	88	92	91	95
(N)	(315)	(863)	(722)	(587)	(676)	(662)	(408)	(441)	(537)	(1,263)	(2,117)
Disapprove	18	7	12	11	4	13	6	26	6	8	6
(N)	(491)	(449)	(442)	(759)	(350)	(366)	(372)	(1,075)	(568)	(1,102)	(174)

Source: Authors' analysis of ANES surveys.
Note: The numbers in parentheses in Part B are the totals on which percentages are based. Question was asked of a randomly selected half-sample in 1972. Numbers are weighted.

Table A.8.7 Approval of Incumbent's Handling of Job, by Party Identification, 1972–2020 (Percent)

			Party Identification				
Year	Strong Democrat	Weak Democrat	Independent, Leans Democrat	Independent	Independent, Leans Republican	Weak Republican	Strong Republican
2020	3	12	5	33	74	70	96
2016	93	79	81	47	20	26	7
2012	97	80	79	49	18	21	6
2008	3	11	6	26	46	47	74
2004	6	26	23	39	78	89	98
2000	92	88	81	65	49	52	23
1996	98	89	85	66	45	49	18
1992	12	28	20	32	65	71	91
1988	24	43	37	70	82	83	94
1984	22	48	32	76	90	93	96
1980	73	54	44	35	19	19	9
1976	24	55	46	69	87	85	96
1972	38	65	52	73	87	92	94

Source: Authors' analysis of ANES surveys.
Note: To approximate the numbers upon which these percentages are based, see tables 8.2, 8.3, A8.2, and A8.3.

Table A.8.8 Approval of Incumbent's Handling of the Economy among Partisan Groups, 1984–2020 (Percent)

				Party Identification				
Year	Attitudes toward Handling of the Economy	Strong Democrat	Weak Democrat	Independent, Leans Democrat	Independent	Independent, Leans Republican	Weak Republican	Strong Republican	Total
1984	Approve	17	41	32	68	84	86	95	58
	Disapprove	83	59	68	32	16	14	5	42
	Total	100	100	100	100	100	100	100	100
	(N)	(309)	(367)	(207)	(179)	(245)	(277)	(249)	(1,833)
1988	Approve	19	35	32	57	76	79	92	54
	Disapprove	81	65	68	43	24	21	8	46
	Total	100	100	100	100	100	100	100	100
	(N)	(337)	(332)	(229)	1(85)	(262)	(262)	(269)	(1,876)
1992[a]	Approve	3	9	6	9	31	34	66	20
	Disapprove	97	91	94	91	69	66	34	80
	Total	100	100	100	100	100	100	100	100
	(N)	(425)	(445)	(340)	(267)	(310)	(347)	(266)	(2,401)
1996[a]	Approve	96	82	76	58	46	49	30	66
	Disapprove	4	18	24	42	54	50	70	34
	Total	100	100	100	100	100	100	100	100
	(N)	(310)	(325)	(228)	(131)	(188)	(263)	(209)	(1,655)
2000[a]	Approve	95	90	84	73	60	70	47	77
	Disapprove	5	10	16	27	40	30	53	23
	Total	100	100	100	100	100	100	100	100
	(N)	(342)	(265)	(264)	(198)	(206)	(184)	(200)	(1,659)

Table A.8.8   Approval of Incumbent's Handling of the Economy among Partisan Groups, 1984–2020 (Percent) (Continued)

				Party Identification				
Year	Attitudes toward Handling of the Economy	Strong Democrat	Weak Democrat	Independent, Leans Democrat	Independent	Independent, Leans Republican	Weak Republican	Strong Republican	Total
2004[a]	Approve	5	18	10	34	68	72	89	40
	Disapprove	95	82	90	66	32	28	11	60
	Total	100	100	100	100	100	100	100	100
	(N)	(197)	(176)	(204)	(107)	(139)	(141)	(194)	(1,158)
2008[a]	Approve	4	7	5	16	27	25	58	18
	Disapprove	96	93	95	84	73	75	42	82
	Total	100	100	100	100	100	100	100	100
	(N)	(428)	(338)	(381)	(240)	(255)	(274)	(291)	(2,208)
2012[a]	Approve	98	89	89	64	36	22	8	64
	Disapprove	2	11	11	36	64	78	92	36
	Total	100	100	100	100	100	100	100	100
	(N)	(287)	(167)	(176)	(74)	(129)	(116)	(173)	(1,655)
2016[a]	Approve	93	75	79	44	21	29	10	53
	Disapprove	7	25	21	56	79	71	90	47
	Total	100	100	100	100	100	100	100	100
	(N)	(896)	(582)	(460)	(606)	(470)	(499)	(691)	(4,221)
2020[a]	Approve	9	29	16	49	88	85	98	52
	Disapprove	91	71	84	51	12	15	2	48
	Total	100	100	100	100	100	100	100	100
	(N)	(1,628)	(850)	(848)	(1,014)	(761)	(797)	(1,505)	(7,403)

Source: Authors' analysis of ANES surveys.
[a]Numbers are weighted.

Notes

INTRODUCTION

1. For an analysis of the strategies in this election, see John H. Kessel, *The Goldwater Coalition: Republican Strategies in 1964* (Indianapolis, IN: Bobbs-Merrill, 1968).

2. See, for example, Benjamin Ginsberg and Martin Shefter, *Politics by Other Means: The Importance of Elections in America* (New York, NY: Basic Books, 1990); and Matthew A. Crenson and Benjamin Ginsberg, *Downsizing Democracy: How America Sidelined Its Citizens and Privatized Its Public* (Baltimore, MD: Johns Hopkins University Press, 2002).

3. The COVID-19 coronavirus is a severe acute respiratory syndrome coronavirus 2 (SARS-CoV-2) that originated in Wuhan, China in December 2019. At the time of our writing, COVID has claimed an estimated 760,000 Americans and approximately 5 million lives worldwide. Ben Hu, Hua Guo, Peng Zhou, and Zheng-Li Shi, "Characteristics of SARS-CoV-2 and COVID-19," *Nature Reviews Microbiology* 19 (2021): 141–154. For COVID case and death counts, see https://www.worldometers .info/coronavirus/

4. The Federal Reserve Bank of St. Louis, Economic Research provides data on a variety of economic indicators. For the US civilian unemployment rate, see https:// fred.stlouisfed.org/series/UNRATE. For the S&P 500, see https://fred.stlouisfed.org/ series/SP500. And, for the US gross domestic product, see https://fred.stlouisfed.org/ series/GDP

5. C-SPAN maintains an archive of Trump's appearances during the Coronavirus Task Force briefings, see https://www.c-span.org/person/?20967/DonaldJTrump. For an analysis of Trump's performance during briefings, see Philip Bump and Ashley Parker, "13 Hours of Trump: The President Fills Briefings with Attacks and Boasts, but Little Empathy," *Washington Post*, April 26, 2020, https://www.washington-post.com/ politics/13-hours-of-trump-the-president-fills-briefings-with-attacks-and-b oasts-but-little-empathy/2020/04/25/7eec5ab0-8590-11ea-a3eb-e9fc93160703_st ory.html

6. It was later revealed that in February 2020 Trump told the famed Watergate reporter Bob Woodward, "You just breathe the air and that's how it's passed. And so that's a very tricky one. That's a very delicate one. It's also more deadly than even your strenuous flus. . . . This is deadly stuff!" Weeks later, the president told Woodward, who was given White House access while writing a book on the Trump administration, "I wanted to always play it down. I still like playing it down because I don't want to create a panic." See Kevin Freking and Zeke Miller, "Book: Trump Said of Virus, 'I Wanted to Always Play It Down,'" *Associated Press*, September 9, 2020, https://apnews.com/article/ap-travel-virus-outbreak-donald-trump-ap-top-news -bob-woodward-c9f35842f7bb355be72842d15a8f7c02

7. William J. Broad and Dan Levin, "Trump Muses about Light as Remedy, But Also Disinfectant, Which is Dangerous," *New York Times,* April 24, 2020, https:// www.nytimes.com/2020/04/24/health/sunlight-coronavirus-trump.html?searchResul tPosition=1

8. Jan Wolfe, "Trump Brags about High TV Viewership of Coronavirus Briefings," *Reuters*, March 29, 2020, https://www.reuters.com/article/us-health -coronavirus-trump-tv/trump-brags-about-high-tv-viewership-of-coronavirus-brief- ings-idUSKBN21G0TR

9. Julie Pace and Hannah Fingerhut, "AP-NORC Poll: Few Americans Trust Trump's Info on Pandemic," *Associated Press*, April 23, 2020, https://apnews.com/ article/virus-outbreak-donald-trump-us-news-ap-top-news-politics-87f1545cea4b5e8 c96e6e902a8d9e9bd

10. "Presidential Approval Ratings—Donald Trump," *Gallup*, https://news.gal- lup.com/poll/ 203198/presidential-approval-ratings-donald-trump.aspx#longdesc_1 610999683184

11. The tweet from Trump is from March 22, 2020. In the wake of the storm- ing of the US Capitol on January 6, 2021, Twitter permanently suspended Trump's account for breaking its terms of service and inciting violence. See Sarah E. Needleman, "Twitter Bans President Trump's Personal Account Permanently," *Wall Street Journal*, January 8, 2021, https://www.wsj.com/articles/twitter-says-it-is-per- manently-suspending-account-of-president-trump-11610148903

12. Michael D. Shear and Sarah Mervosh, "Trump Encourages Protest against Governors Who Have Imposed Virus Restrictions," *New York Times*, April 17, 2020, https://www.nytimes.com/2020/04/17/us/politics/trump-coronavirus-gover- nors.html

13. Mike Memoli and Marianna Sotomayor, "Biden Campaign Launches New Video Attacking Trump on Coronavirus Response," *NBC News*, April 17, 2020. See also Emily Baumbaertner, and James Rainey, "Trump Administration Ended Pandemic Early-Warning Program to Detect Coronaviruses," *Los Angeles Times*, April 2, 2020, https://www.latimes.com/science/story/2020-04-02/coronavirus-trump -pandemic-program-viruses-detection

14. Christina Wilkie, "Joe Biden Rips Trump as Coronavirus Surges: 'The Wartime President Has Surrendered,'" *CNBC*, June 30, 2020, https://www.cnbc.com /2020/06/30/joe-biden-rips-trump-on-coronavirus-the-wartime-president-has-surren- dered.html

15. For a record of national polling data during the 2020 general election, see Real Clear Politics, "General Election: Trump vs. Biden," https://www.realclearpolitics.com/ epolls/2020/president/us/general_election_trump_vs_biden-6247.html

16. See "George Floyd: What Happened in the Final Moments of His Life," *BBC News*, July 16, 2020, https://www.bbc.com/news/world-us-canada-52861726

17. Erica Chenoweth and Jeremy Pressman, "This Summer's Black Lives Matter Protesters Were Overwhelmingly Peaceful, Our Research Finds," *Washington Post*, October 16, 2020, https://www.washingtonpost.com/politics/2020/10/16/this-summers-black-lives-matter-protesters-were-overwhelming-peaceful-our-research-finds/

18. See Catalina Gaitán, "After a Year of Portland Protests, Activists See No End in Sight," *The Oregonian*, May 28, 2021, https://www.oregonlive.com/portland /2021/05/after-a-year-of-portland-protests-activists-see-no-end-in-sight.html; Mike Carter, Daniel Beekman, Heidi Groover, and Paul Roberts, "How a Year of Protests Changed Seattle," *The Seattle Times*, December 29, 2020, https://www.seattletimes .com/ seattle-news/how-a-year-of-protests-changed-seattle/; Frank Morris, "A Look Back at Three Weeks of Black Lives Matter Protests in Kansas City," *NPR*, June 19, 2020, https://www.kcur.org/news/2020-06-19/a-look-back-at-three-weeks-of-black -lives-matter-protests-in-kansas-city

19. Jonathan Martin, Alexander Burns, and Thomas Kaplan, "Biden Walks a Cautious Line as He Opposes Defunding the Police," *New York Times*, June 8, 2020, https://www.nytimes.com/2020/06/08/us/politics/biden-defund-the-police.html

20. Scott Detrow and Barbara Sprunt, "'He Thinks Division Helps Him': Biden Condemns Trump's Protest Response," *NPR*, June 2, 2020, https://www.npr.org/2020 /06/02/ 867671792/biden-to-condemn-trumps-protest-response-in-speech

21. Max Cohen, "Trump: Black Lives Matter is a 'Symbol of Hate,'" *Politico*, July 1, 2020, https://www.politico.com/news/2020/07/01/trump-black-lives-matter -347051

22. "Trump Says He's 'President of Law and Order,' Declares Aggressive Action on Violent Protests," *CBS News*, June 2, 2020, https://www.cbsnews.com/news/ trump-protest-president-law-and-order/

23. "Full Call Audio: Trump Berates Governors over Protests," *Washington Post*, June 1, 2020, https://www.washingtonpost.com/video/politics/full-call-audio -trump-berates-governors-over-protests/2020/06/01/1e6e9fb6-bd8f-4349-a5ff-5bed-de5b8516_ video.html

24. Peter Hermann, Sarah Pulliam Bailey, and Michelle Boorstein, "Fire Set at Historic St. John's Church during Protests of George Floyd's Death," *Washington Post*, June 1, 2020, https://www.washingtonpost.com/religion/fire-set-at-historic -st-johns-church-during-protests-of-george-floyds-death/2020/06/01/4b5c4004-a3b6 -11ea-b619-3f9133bbb482_story.html

25. See Jill Colvin and Darlene Superville, "Tear Gas, Threats for Protesters Before Trump Visits Church," *Associated Press*, June 2, 2020, https://apnews.com /article/donald-trump-ap-top-news-dc-wire-religion-politics-15be4e293cdebe72c10 304fe0ec668e4; Charles Creitz, "St. John's Church Rector on Aftermath of Fire, Impromptu Trump Visit: 'Like I'm in Some Alternative Universe,'" *Fox News*, June 1, 2020, https://www.foxnews.com/media/st-johns-rector-fire-impromptu-trump-visit

26. See Rebecca Ballhaus and Alex Leary, "Trump Broadens His Efforts to Overturn Election Outcome," *Wall Street Journal*, November 19, 2020, https://www.wsj.com/articles/ trump-broadens-his-efforts-to-overturn-election-outcome -11605800104; and The Editorial Board, "Trump's Challenge Is Over," *Wall Street Journal*, December 13, 2020, https://www.wsj.com/articles/trumps-challenge-is -over-11607898467? mod=hp_opin_pos_1. For an international view, see "Donald Trump's Refusal to Concede is Harming America," *The Economist*, November 21, 2020, https://www.economist.com/united-states/2020/11/21/donald-trumps-refusal -to-concede-is-harming-america

27. Adam Winkler, "Trump's Wildest Claims Are Going Nowhere in Court. Thank Legal Ethics." *Washington Post*, November 20, 2020, https://www.washing-tonpost.com/ outlook/trump-lawyers-legal-ethics/2020/11/20/3c286710-2ac1-11eb-92b7-6ef17b3fe3b4_story.html

28. The Democrats technically hold 48 seats in the Senate, but the two independents, Sen. Bernie Sanders (VT) and Sen. Angus King (ME) caucus with the party, thus bringing their seat share to 50.

29. See, for one example, Lee Drutman, "Donald Trump Will Dramatically Realign America's Political Parties," *Foreign Policy*, November 11, 2016, http://foreignpolicy.com/2016/11/11/why-democrats-should-abandon-angry-working-class -whites

30. See E.J. Dionne, Jr., "Biden Could Be the One to Finally Begin Poaching the GOP's Core Voters," *Washington Post*, May 2, 2021, https://www.washingtonpost .com/opinions/ 2021/05/02/stranded-trump-island-gop-lets-biden-play-long-game/

31. Lanny J. Davis, "The Obama Realignment," *Wall Street Journal,* November 6, 2008, A19.

32. Paul R. Abramson, John H. Aldrich, and David W. Rohde, *Change and Continuity in the 2008 and 2010 Elections* (Washington, DC: CQ Press, 2012), 284.

33. Kevin P. Phillips, *The Emerging Republican Majority* (New Rochelle, NY: Arlington House, 1969).

34. Phil Gailey, "Republicans Start to Worry about Signs of Slippage," *New York Times*, August 25, 1988, E5.

35. For a discussion of the history of this concept, see Theodore Rosenof, *Realignment: The Theory That Changed the Way We Think about American Politics* (Lanham, MD: Rowman and Littlefield, 2003).

36. V. O. Key, Jr., "A Theory of Critical Elections," *Journal of Politics* 17 (February 1955): 3–18.

37. V. O. Key, Jr., "Secular Realignment and the Party System," *Journal of Politics* 21 (May 1959): 198–210.

38. These states were, and still are, the most heavily Democratic states. Both voted Republican in seventeen of the eighteen presidential elections between 1856 and 1924, voting Democratic only when the Republican Party was split in 1912 by Theodore Roosevelt's Progressive Party candidacy. For a discussion of partisan change in the New England states, see chapter 3.

39. V. O. Key, Jr., *Parties, Politics, and Pressure Groups*, 5th ed. (New York, NY: Thomas Y. Crowell, 1964), 186.

40. In addition to the eleven states that formed the Confederacy (Alabama, Arkansas, Florida, Georgia, Louisiana, Mississippi, North Carolina, South Carolina, Tennessee, Texas, and Virginia), Delaware, Kentucky, Maryland, and Missouri were slave states. The fifteen free states in 1848 were Connecticut, Illinois, Indiana, Iowa, Maine, Massachusetts, Michigan, New Hampshire, New Jersey, New York, Ohio, Pennsylvania, Rhode Island, Vermont, and Wisconsin. By 1860 three additional free states—California, Minnesota, and Oregon—had been admitted to the Union.

41. John H. Aldrich, *Why Parties? A Second Look* (Chicago, IL: University of Chicago Press, 2011), 282–287.

42. Thomas G. Hansford and Brad T. Gomez, "Estimating the Electoral Effects of Voter Turnout," *American Political Science Review* 104 (May 2010): 268–288.

43. Byron E. Shafer, ed., *The End of Realignment? Interpreting American Electoral Eras* (Madison, WI: University of Wisconsin Press, 1991).

44. David R. Mayhew, *Electoral Realignments: A Critique of an American Genre* (New Haven, CT: Yale University Press, 2002).

45. Edward G. Carmines and James A. Stimson, *Issue Evolution: Race and the Transformation of American Politics* (Princeton, NJ: Princeton University Press, 1989), 12–13.

46. Ibid., 13.

47. Key, "Secular Realignment and the Party System," 198–199.

48. The theory of punctuated equilibrium was first developed by the evolutionary biologists and paleontologists Niles Eldredge and Stephen Jay Gould. See Niles Eldredge and Stephen Jay Gould, "Punctuated Equilibria: An Alternative to Phyletic Gradualism" in Thomas J. M. Schropf, ed., *Models of Paleobiology* (San Francisco, CA: Freeman, Cooper, and Company, 1972).

49. Carmines and Stimson, *Issue Evolution*, 13.

50. John H. Aldrich argues that the decline of local party machines, technological innovations—particularly, the advent of television—and the rise of a policy-motivated activist class allowed ambitious politicians to bypass the party organization and create "candidate-centered" campaigns. The result was the demise of the traditional "mass political party" (i.e., the party as organization), and in its place followed a new type of party, one that provides services (e.g., expertise and financial and in-kind resources) to its candidates. The emergent activist class also pressured the parties to democratize their presidential nomination systems. Reforms, such as the Democratic Party's McGovern-Fraser Commission, resulted in the proliferation of primaries as the main vehicle by which party nominees are chosen. See Aldrich, *Why Parties: A Second Look*, 255–292.

51. Aldrich, *Why Parties: A Second Look,* 263.

52. See Russell J. Dalton, Paul Allen Beck, and Scott C. Flanagan, "Electoral Change in Advanced Industrial Democracies," in *Electoral Change in Advanced Industrial Democracies: Realignment or Dealignment?* eds. Russell J. Dalton, Scott C. Flanagan, and Paul Allen Beck (Princeton, NJ: Princeton University Press, 1984), 14.

53. Ronald Inglehart and Avram Hochstein, "Alignment and Dealignment of the Electorate in France and the United States," *Comparative Political Studies* 5 (October 1972): 343–372.

54. We estimated the distribution of major-party identifiers (i.e., excluding pure independents) in both the general public and among voters. In both cases, we estimate approximately 53 percent identify with the Democratic Party.

55. Jens Manuel Krogstad, Ana Gonzalez-Barrerra, and Christine Tamir, "Latino Democratic Voters Place High Importance on 2020 Presidential Election," *Pew Research Center*, January 17, 2020, https://www.pewresearch.org/fact-tank/2020/01/17/latino-democratic-voters-place-high-importance-on-2020-presidential-election/

56. According to Michael P. McDonald, 239,247,182 Americans were eligible to vote. See McDonald, "2020 General Election Turnout Rates," United States Election Project, http://www.electproject.org/home/voter-turnout/voter-turnout-data. We say "on or before" November 3 because in 2020 about 24 percent of voters voted in person before election day and 42 percent voted by mail.

57. Voters may also be influenced by random factors as well, but by their very nature, these random factors cannot be systematically explained.

58. For two excellent summaries of research on voting behavior, see Russell J. Dalton and Martin P. Wattenberg, "The Not So Simple Act of Voting," in *Political Science: The State of the Discipline II,* ed. Ada W. Finifter (Washington, DC: American Political Science Association, 1993), 193–218; and Morris P. Fiorina, "Parties, Participation, and Representation in America: Old Theories Face New Realities," in *Political Science: The State of the Discipline,* eds. Ira Katznelson and Helen V. Milner (New York, NY: Norton, 2002), 511–541.

59. For a more extensive discussion of our arguments, see Paul R. Abramson, John H. Aldrich, and David W. Rohde, "Studying American Elections," in *The Oxford Handbook of American Elections and Political Behavior,* ed. Jan E. Leighley (New York, NY: Oxford University Press, 2010), 700–715.

60. Paul F. Lazarsfeld, Bernard R. Berelson, and Hazel Gaudet, *The People's Choice: How the Voter Makes Up His Mind in a Presidential Campaign* (New York, NY: Duell, Sloan, and Pearce, 1944), 27. See also Bernard R. Berelson, Paul F. Lazarsfeld, and William McPhee, *Voting: A Study of Opinion Formation in a Presidential Campaign* (Chicago, IL: University of Chicago Press, 1954).

61. See Robert R. Alford, *Party and Society: The Anglo-American Democracies* (Chicago, IL: Rand McNally, 1963); Richard F. Hamilton, *Class and Politics in the United States* (New York, NY: Wiley, 1972); and Seymour Martin Lipset, *Political Man: The Social Bases of Politics,* exp. ed. (Baltimore, MD: Johns Hopkins University Press, 1981). For a more recent book using the perspective, see Jeff Manza and Clem Brooks, *Social Cleavages and Political Change: Voter Alignments in U.S. Party Coalitions* (Oxford, UK: Oxford University Press, 1999).

62. Angus Campbell et al., *The American Voter* (New York, NY: Wiley, 1960). For a recent assessment of the contribution of *The American Voter,* see William G. Jacoby, "The American Voter," in Leighley, *Oxford Handbook of American Elections and Political Behavior,* 262–277.

63. The Michigan model conceptualizes party identification as the individual's enduring attachment to a political party. The theory contends that party identification is socialized early in life and remains stable throughout adulthood. Dissatisfied with this static view of party loyalties, Morris P. Fiorina reconceptualized party identification as "a running tally of retrospective evaluations of party promises and

performance." Fiorina, *Retrospective Voting in American National Elections* (New Haven, CT: Yale University Press, 1981), 84. For a counterargument to Fiorina, see Larry M. Bartels, "Beyond the Running Tally: Partisan Bias in Political Perceptions," *Political Behavior* 24 (June 2002): 117–150.

64. Anthony Downs, *An Economic Theory of Democracy* (New York, NY: Harper and Row, 1957); William H. Riker, *A Theory of Political Coalitions* (New Haven, CT: Yale University Press, 1962). See also William H. Riker and Peter C. Ordeshook, "A Theory of the Calculus of Voting," *American Political Science Review* 62 (March 1968): 25–32; John A. Ferejohn and Morris P. Fiorina, "The Paradox of Not Voting: A Decision Theocratic Analysis," *American Political Science Review* 68 (June 1974): 525–536; and Fiorina, *Retrospective Voting in American National Elections*. For an excellent introduction to American voting behavior that relies on a rational choice perspective, see Rebecca B. Morton, *Analyzing Elections* (New York, NY: Norton, 2006).

65. For a more extensive discussion of the merits and limitations of these approaches, see Paul R. Abramson, John H. Aldrich, and David W. Rohde, "Studying American Elections," in *The Oxford Handbook of American Elections and Political Behavior*, ed. Jan E. Leighley (New York, NY: Oxford University Press, 2010), 700–715.

66. American National Election Studies, 2020 Time Series Study, https://electionstudies.org /data-center/2020-time-series-study/. The 2020 ANES represents the first time that organization has not conducted at least some face-to-face interviews. Due to the COVID-19 pandemic, ANES conducted interviews using three modes: video, web, and phone.

67. For an overview of how the ANES is currently constructed and its recent innovations in measurement, see the collection of essays found in John H. Aldrich and Kathleen M. McGraw, eds., *Improving Public Opinion Surveys: Interdisciplinary Innovation and the American National Election Studies* (Princeton, NJ: Princeton University Press, 2012). For a brief nontechnical introduction to polling, see Herbert Asher, *Polling and the Public: What Every Citizen Should Know*, 7th ed. (Washington, DC: CQ Press, 2007). For a more advanced discussion, see Herbert F. Weisberg, *The Total Survey Error Approach: A Guide to the New Science of Survey Research* (Chicago, IL: University of Chicago Press, 2005).

68. For a brief discussion of the procedures used by the Survey Research Center, which conducted the surveys from 1952 to 2004, to carry out its sampling for in-person interviews, see Paul R. Abramson, *Political Attitudes in America: Formation and Change* (San Francisco, CA: W. H. Freeman, 1983), 18–23. For a more detailed description of the design and implementation of the 2020 ANES election study, see https://electionstudies.org/anes_timeseries_2020_userguidecodebook_20210719/

69. For an excellent table that allows us to evaluate differences between two groups, see Leslie Kish, *Survey Sampling* (New York, NY: Wiley, 1965), 580. Kish defines differences between two groups to be significant if the results are more than two standard errors apart.

70. For 2020—as well as for 1958, 1960, 1974, 1976, 1992, 1994, 1996, 1998, 2000, 2002, 2004, 2008, 2012, and 2016—a weighting procedure is necessary to obtain a representative result, and so we report the "weighted" number of cases.

71. There also were numerous state-level ballot measures—initiatives, referenda, and state constitutional amendments—for which to vote.

Chapter 1

1.   Note that many states that have presidential primaries also hold primary elections for many other offices. Most of these primaries, such as for the US House and Senate, select the actual nominees of the two parties for those offices. Thus the party leadership plays no direct role at all in selecting the party's candidates.

2.   Parties have ceded control to the substantial majority of potential voters who are eligible to vote in primary elections. They have ceded effective control to the substantial minority who actually participate in those elections. On how the party still tries to shape presidential nomination outcomes, see Marty Cohen, David Karol, Hans Noel, and John Zaller, *The Party Decides: Presidential Nominations Before and After Reform* (Chicago: University of Chicago Press, 2008).

3.   George H. W. Bush in 1992 faced one challenger, Patrick Buchanan, who did have an impact on the race, although Bush defeated him rather easily.

4.   Gov. Jerry Brown (then, as in 2016, governor of California) did run as a third Democrat in 1980. Although obviously a formidable politician over a long career, and even though he was also a very serious threat for the Democratic nomination in 1976, he was much less formidable in 1980, picking up the nickname "Governor Moonbeam."

5.   The nine who had declared their candidacy, participated in at least one presidential "debate" in 2019, and withdrew in 2019 were: Senator Kamala Harris (California), who withdrew on December 3, 2019; Governor Steve Bullock (Montana), who withdrew on December 2; former US Representative Beto O'Rourke (Texas), who withdrew on November 1; US Representative Tim Ryan (Ohio), who withdrew on October 24; Mayor Bill de Blasio (New York), who withdrew on September 20; US Senator Kirsten Gillibrand (New York), who withdrew on August 28; Governor Jay Inslee (Washington), who withdrew on August 21; former Governor John Hickenlooper (Colorado), who withdrew on August 15; and US Representative Eric Swalwell (California), who withdrew on July 8.

6.   One other declared and dropped out in 2019: former Governor and US Representative Mark Sanford (South Carolina), who withdrew on November 12.

7.   An additional two women ran but dropped out before January 1, 2021, Kamala Harris (US Senator, CA), who Biden would later select as his running mate, and Kirsten Gillibrand (US Senator, NY).

8.   Joseph A. Schlesinger, *Ambition and Politics: Political Careers in the United States* (Chicago: Rand McNally, 1966); Joseph A. Schlesinger, *Political Parties and the Winning of Office* (Ann Arbor: University of Michigan Press, 1991).

9.   In addition to the fifty states, also included are events for the District of Columbia, various territories, and for the Democrats, even Americans Living Abroad.

10.   https://www.ncsl.org/research/elections-and-campaigns/2020-state-primary-election-dates.aspx#Chronological; Accessed, July 10, 2021.

11.   Though the rules often fall well short of being truly proportional.

12.   Theodore H. White, *The Making of the President, 1968* (New York: Pocket Books, 1970).

13. For a discussion of the importance of superdelegates in 1984 and 2008, see Paul R. Abramson, John H. Aldrich, and David W. Rohde, *Change and Continuity in the 1984 Elections*, rev. ed. (Washington, DC: CQ Press, 1987), 25; Abramson, Aldrich, and Rohde, *Change and Continuity in the 2008 and 2010 Elections*, 30–33.

The Republican Party does have its own superdelegates, but it limits them to the Republican National Committee membership, per se, which is a much smaller proportion of the total convention delegations.

14. https://www.cnn.com/2018/08/25/politics/democrats-superdelegates-voting -changes/index.html, Accessed July 19, 2021.

15. Cohen, Karol, Noel, and Zaller, *The Party Decides*.

16. Phil Paolino, "Candidate Name Recognition and the Dynamics of the Pre-Primary Period of the Presidential Nomination Process" (PhD diss., Duke University, 1995).

17. In addition a second primary for other offices often attracts very few voters, especially in the absence of a hotly contested gubernatorial or senatorial contest.

18. John Aldrich, "The Invisible Primary and Its Effects on Democratic Choice," *PS: Political Science and Politics* 42 (2009): 33–38.

19. In retrospect asking candidates to share chances and even delegates to defeat a front-runner before necessarily turning on one another to secure the single prize of presidential nomination may work in parlor games such as Risk but seems implausible in the case of seeking the most powerful office in the world.

20. https://www.nytimes.com/2020/04/08/us/politics/bernie-sanders-drops-out .html, Accessed, July 12, 2021.

21. John H. Aldrich, *Before the Convention: Strategies and Choices in Presidential Nomination Campaigns* (Chicago: University of Chicago Press, 1980); Larry M. Bartels, *Presidential Primaries and the Dynamics of Public Choice* (Princeton, NJ: Princeton University Press, 1988).

22. EMILY's List, a group that supports female candidates, draws its name from an acronym of this observation.

23. Thomas E. Mann, "Money in the 2008 Elections: Bad News or Good?," July 1, 2008, https://www.brookings.edu/opinions/money-in-the-2008-elections-bad-news -or-good/

24. Michael Muskal and Dan Morain, "Obama Raises $55 Million in February; Clinton Reports Surge in Funds," *Los Angeles Times*, March 7, 2008, http://articles .latimes.com/2008/mar/07/nation/na-money

25. https://www.npr.org/2019/04/16/711812314/tracking-the-money-race -behind-the-presidential-campaign, Accessed, July 19, 2021.

26. US Court of Appeals for the District of Columbia Circuit, *Speechnow.org v. Federal Election Commission*, March 26, 2010.

27. Center for Responsive Politics, "What Are Independent Expenditures and Communications Costs?," January 29, 2014, http://www.opensecrets.org/pacs/index-pend.php?strID=C00490045&cycle=2012

28. Jenkins, Nick. 2020. "Minimizing Whose Influence? How Rejecting PAC Contributions Affects Contribution Patterns." Working Paper. https://osf.io/preprints /socarxiv/cf3jn/

29.   See, e.g., Christopher Hare and Keith T. Poole, "The Polarization of Contemporary American Politics," *Polity* 46, no. 3 (July 2014): 411–429.

30.   Alan I. Abramowitz and Kyle L. Saunders, "Is Polarization a Myth?" *Journal of Politics* 70, no. 2 (2008): 542–555.

31.   The ANES conducted a four-wave panel beginning in January 1980, and here we use wave 1: Interview P1 (wave 1) January 22 to February 25; personal interview; 1,008 completed cases. We also use the 2020 ANES pilot study: Data collection was conducted between April 10 and April 18, 2020. The sample consisted of 3,080 individuals who were part of an opt-in Internet panel.

32.   Democrat and Republican here are those who answered the first question in the standard battery of questions about partisan identification used by the ANES as "Democrat" or as "Republican," with other responses including "independent" and so on. See chapter 6 and note these are equivalent to using "strong" and "weak" Democratic and Republican responses. The differences are in absolute value, thus measuring the size of the gap between the two sets of partisans' responses.

33.   Chapter 7 includes reports and more details about candidate thermometer measures.

34.   https://thehill.com/hilltv/what-americas-thinking/444295-poll-democratic -voters-prioritize-defeating-trump-over-their. Accessed July 14, 2021.

35.   https://www.realclearpolitics.com/epolls/2020/president/us/2020_democratic _presidential_nomination-6730.html. Accessed, July 19, 2021.

36.   https://www.theguardian.com/us-news/2019/may/11/i-have-a-plan-for-that -elizabeth-warren-democratic-policy-primary. Accessed, July 19, 2021.

37.   https://www.realclearpolitics.com/epolls/2020/president/us/2020_democratic _presidential_nomination-6730.html. Accessed, July 19, 2021.

38.   https://www.klobuchar.senate.gov/public/index.cfm/2019/3/study-klobuchar -most-effective-democratic-senator. Accessed, July 19, 2021.

39.   https://www.nytimes.com/2020/03/01/us/politics/pete-buttigieg-drops-out .html. Accessed, July 19, 2021.

40.   https://www.cnn.com/election/2020/primaries-caucuses/entrance-and-exit -polls/iowa/democratic. Accessed July 17, 2021.

41.   https://www.cnn.com/election/2020/primaries-caucuses/entrance-and-exit -polls/new-hampshire/democratic. Accessed July 17, 2021.

42.   https://www.cnn.com/election/2020/primaries-caucuses/entrance-and-exit -polls/nevada/democratic. Accessed July 17, 2021.

43.   https://www.politico.com/news/2020/02/26/jim-clyburn-endorses-joe-biden -117667

44.   According to exit poll data, 61 percent of African Americans supported Biden, and this group constituted more than half of the Democratic electorate in South Carolina.   https://www.cnn.com/election/2020/primaries-caucuses/entrance-and-exit -polls/south-carolina/democratic

45.   https://www.washingtonpost.com/graphics/politics/exit-polls-2020-super -tuesday-primary/. Accessed July 17, 2021.

46.   https://www.realclearpolitics.com/epolls/2020/president/us/2020_democratic _presidential_nomination-6730.html

47.   Most states impose such constraints only for one ballot or have some other short-run obligation, after which delegates are freed from such laws to vote as they please. However, no nomination has taken more than one ballot since 1952 and thus within the new nomination system of 1972. So, in that sense, delegate votes have indeed been so constrained. Of course, Republicans have a small number and Democrats a larger number of superdelegates who are free to vote as they choose.

48.   Although there are sometimes nominations serving as protests to the party, the last time there was an open vote for vice president was in the 1956 Democratic Convention, when nominee Adlai Stevenson (Gov., IL) threw the choice to the delegates, who were choosing between Estes Kefauver (Sen., TN) and John Kennedy (Sen., MA).

49.   The party holding the presidency, by tradition, holds its convention second.

50.   On May 25, 2020, George Floyd, a forty-six-year-old unarmed black man was killed in police custody. Floyd's death, which was captured on cell phone video, ignited protests about police brutality and racial injustice, generally, both in the United States and globally. The police officer responsible for Floyd's death was later convicted of two counts of murder and one count of manslaughter.

Chapter 2

1.   Until 2008 neither Maine nor Nebraska had divided their electoral vote under these systems, but in that year Obama succeeded in carrying one of Nebraska's congressional districts, thus gaining one of the state's votes. In 2020 Donald Trump won the second congressional district in Maine, giving him one of the state's electoral votes as had been the case in 2016.

2.   The eight states were Arizona, Florida, Georgia, Michigan, Minnesota, North Carolina, Pennsylvania, and Wisconsin. On this point, see https://www.politico.com /news/2020/09/08/swing-states-2020-presidential-election-409000. Some accounts had Nevada, Ohio, and Texas listed as battleground states as well.

3.   For a discussion of electoral-vote strategies, see Daron R. Shaw, "The Methods Behind the Madness: Presidential Electoral-College Strategies, 1988–1996," *Journal of Politics* 61 (November 1999): 893–913.

4.   The five successful incumbents (and their average approval in Gallup surveys conducted in March, April, and May) were Eisenhower 1956 (70), Johnson 1964 (76), Nixon 1972 (56), Reagan 1984 (54), and Clinton 1996 (54). The unsuccessful candidates were Johnson 1968 (36), Ford 1976 (48), Carter 1980 (40), and Bush 1992 (40). The approval data are from monthly Gallup polls (www.gallup.com).

5.   Data obtained from news.gallup.com/poll/116500/presidential-approval-ratin gs-george-bush.aspx.

6.   Data obtained from news.gallup.com/poll/203198/presidential-approval-ratin gs-donald-trump.aspx.

7.   Sean McMinn, Alyson Hurt, and Ruth Talbot, "Money Tracker: How Much Trump and Biden Have Raised in the 2020 Election," *NPR*, December 4, 2020, https://www.npr.org/2020/05/20/858347477/money-tracker-how-much-trump-and -biden-have-raised-in-the-2020-election.

8.   Gary C. Jacobson, "Donald Trump and the Parties: Impeachment, Pandemic, Protest, and Electoral Politics in 2020," *Presidential Studies Quarterly* 50 (December 2020): 762–795.

9.   Alex Isenstadt, "Trump Campaign to Unload on Biden with Negative Ad Onslaught," *Politico*, May 7, 2020, https://www.politico.com/news/2020/05/07/trump-campaign-to-unload-on-biden-with-negative-ad-onslaught-242976

10.   Thomas Kaplan and Alexander Burns, "Joe Biden is Trying to Be Heard on the Virus. Can He Break Through?" *The New York Times*, March 23, 2020, https://www.nytimes.com/2020/03/23/us/politics/joe-biden-2020-virus.html

11.   Gary C. Jacobson, "Donald Trump and the Parties: Impeachment, Pandemic, Protest, and Electoral Politics in 2020," *Presidential Studies Quarterly* 50 (December 2020): 762–795.

12.   Jonathan Swan, "Team Trump's Era of Good Feelins," *Axios*, August 30, 2020, https://www.axios.com/trump-advisers-polling-biden-ff533c39-9b06-4bb7-9e8d-2936161ee3f2.html?utm_campaign=organic&utm_medium=socialshare&utm_source=facebook

13.   Nate Cohn, "A Wave of Polls Taken After the Conventions Show Little Change in Biden's Lead," *The New York Times*, September 3, 2020, https://www.nytimes.com/2020/09/03/us/elections/a-wave-of-polls-taken-after-the-conventions-show-little-change-in-bidens-lead.html

14.   Tara Subramaniam and Holly Yan, "'It Affects Virtually Nobody': Fact-Checking Trump's Continued Efforts to Downplay the Risks of Coronavirus." *CNN*, September 22, 2020, https://www.cnn.com/2020/09/22/politics/trump-covid-19-statement-fact-check/index.html

15.   Ibid.

16.   Jim Acosta, Kevin Liptak, Kaitlan Collins, and Paul LeBlanc, "Trump Lauds Ginsburg but is Eager to Nominate Her Replacement, Source Says," *CNN*, September 19, 2020, https://www.cnn.com/2020/09/18/politics/trump-ruth-bader-ginsburg/index.html

17.   Ibid.

18.   Jordan Carney, "McConnell says Trump Nominee to Replace Ginsburg will get Senate Vote," *The Hill*, September 18, 2020, https://thehill.com/homenews/senate/517178-mcconnell-says-trump-nominee-to-replace-ginsburg-will-get-senate-vote

19.   Ibid.

20.   Maeve Reston, "Trump Vows to Appoint a Woman to Supreme Court as Vacancy Re-energizes his Political Prospects," *CNN*, September 20, 2020, https://www.cnn.com/2020/09/20/politics/trump-supreme-court-woman-nominee-2020/index.html

21.   Ibid.

22.   Sam Gringlas, "Trump Announces Amy Coney Barrett as His Supreme Court Nominee," *NPR*, September 26, 2020, https://www.npr.org/sections/supreme-court-nomination/2020/09/26/916921211/trump-set-to-formally-announce-his-supreme-court-nominee

23.   Jeff Greenfield, "How Democrats Could Pack the Supreme Court in 2021," *Politico*, September 19, 2020, https://www.politico.com/news/magazine/2020/09/19/how-democrats-could-pack-the-supreme-court-in-2021-418453

24. Russ Buettner, Susanne Craig, and Mike McIntire, "Long-Concealed Records Show Trump's Chronic Losses and Years of Tax Avoidance." *The New York Times*, September 27, 2020, https://www.nytimes.com/interactive/2020/09/27/us/donald -trump-taxes.html

25. Ibid.

26. Noah Bierman and Eli Stokols, "Biden is Prepping for First Debate. Trump is Watching TV News and Testing Attack Lines," *Los Angeles Times*, September 23, 2020, https://www.latimes.com/politics/story/2020-09-23/biden-prepping-for-first -debate-trump-is-watching-tv

27. Ibid.

28. Libby Cathey, "Trump and Biden to Face Off in 1st 2020 Presidential Debate." *ABCNews*, September 28, 2020, https://abcnews.go.com/Politics/trump -biden-face-off-1st-2020-presidential-debate/story?id=73293437

29. Domenico Montanaro, "Trump Derails 1st Presidential Debate with Biden, And 5 Other Takeaways," *NPR*, September 30, 2020, https://www.npr.org/2020 /09/30/918500976/trump-derails-first-presidential-debate-with-biden-and-5-other -takeaways

30. Ibid.

31. Ibid.

32. Ibid.

33. Melissa Macaya, Veronica Rocha, Kyle Blaine, and Jessica Estepa, "First 2020 Presidential Debate," *CNN*, September 30, 2020, https://www.cnn.com/politics /live-news/presidential-debate-coverage-fact-check-09-29-20/h_3db54de7e88d5ff b6e643c197dd2bf5c

34. "Media Advisory: First Presidential Debate of 2020 Draws 73.1 Million Viewers," *Nielsen*, September 30, 2020, https://www.nielsen.com/us/en/press -releases/2020/media-advisory-first-presidential-debate-of-2020/

35. Jennifer de Pinto, Anthony Salvanto, Fred Backus, Kabir Khanna, and Elena Cox, "Debate-Watchers say Biden Won First Debate, but Most Felt 'Annoyed'— CBS News Poll," *CBS News*, September 30, 2020, https://www.cbsnews.com/news/ who-won-debate-first-presidential-biden-trump/

36. Sam Gringlas, "Timeline: What We Know of President Trump's COVID-19 Diagnosis, Treatment," *NPR*, October 5, 2020, https://www.npr.org/sections/latest -updates-trump-covid-19-results/2020/10/03/919898777/timeline-what-we-know-of -president-trumps-covid-19-diagnosis

37. Ibid.

38. Laura Bronner, Aaron Bycoffe, Elena Mejia, and Julia Wolfe, "Won Won the Vice Presidential Debate," FiveThirtyEight.com, October 8, 2020, https://projects .fivethirtyeight.com/harris-pence-vp-debate-poll/

39. Dan Merica and Kevin Bohn, "Commission Cancels Second Debate Between Trump and Biden," *CNN*, October 9, 2020, https://www.cnn.com/2020/10/09/politics /second-presidential-debate-canceled/index.html

40. Kevin Breuninger, "Here are the Key Moments from the Final Trump-Biden Presidential Debate," *CNBC*, October 22, 2020, https://www.cnbc.com/2020/10/22/ final-presidential-debate-highlights-trump-vs-biden.html

41. Ibid.

42. Jennifer Agiesta, "CNN Poll: Biden Wins Final Presidential Debate," *CNN,* October 23, 2020, https://www.cnn.com/2020/10/22/politics/cnn-poll-final-presidential-debate/index.html

43. See Robert S. Erikson and Christopher Wlezien, *The Timeline of Presidential Elections* (Chicago: University of Chicago Press, 2012), 79–81, and the references cited therein. Also see John Sides, "Do Presidential Debates Really Matter?," *Washington Monthly*, September/October 2012, 19–21.

44. See Ibid.

45. Ibid.

46. Kevin Breuninger, "Here's What to Watch During the Final Two Weeks of the Trump-Biden Campaign," *CNBC*, October 20, 2020, https://www.cnbc.com/2020/10/20/trump-biden-election-what-to-watch-in-the-final-two-weeks.html

47. Ibid.

48. The Pfizer/BioNTech vaccine was approved for emergency use on December 11, 2020: https://www.washingtonpost.com/health/2020/12/11/trump-stephen-hahn-fda-covid-vaccine/

49. Ibid.

50. Emma Jo Morris and Gabrielle Fonrouge, "Smoking-Gun Email Reveals How Hunter Biden Introduced Ukrainian Businessman to VP Dad." *New York Post,* October 14, 2020, https://nypost.com/2020/10/14/email-reveals-how-hunter-biden-introduced-ukrainian-biz-man-to-dad/

51. Kevin Breuninger, "Here's What to Watch During the Final Two Weeks of the Trump-Biden Campaign," *CNBC*, October 20, 2020, https://www.cnbc.com/2020/10/20/trump-biden-election-what-to-watch-in-the-final-two-weeks.html

52. Katie Dangerfield, "Here is Where Trump, Biden Stand in the Polls 1 Day Before U.S. Election," *Global News*, November 2, 2020, https://globalnews.ca/news/7436697/us-election-one-day-before-trump-biden-polls/

53. The data are from Michael McDonald's website: http://www.electproject.org/national-1789-present

54. See Paul R. Abramson, John H. Aldrich, Brad T. Gomez, and David W. Rohde, *Change and Continuity in the 2012 Elections* (Washington, DC: CQ Press, 2015), chapter 2.

55. Quoted in Michael Scherer, "Inside the Secret World of Quants and Data Crunchers Who Helped Obama Win," *Time*, November 19, 2012, 58.

56. Ibid.

57. Miles Parks, "Trump, While Attacking Mail Voting, Casts Mail Ballot Again," *NPR*, August 19, 2020, https://www.npr.org/2020/08/19/903886567/trump-while-attacking-mail-voting-casts-mail-ballot-again

58. William Galston, "Election 2020: A Once-in-a-Century, Massive Turnout?" *Brookings*, August 14, 2020, https://www.brookings.edu/blog/fixgov/2020/08/14/election-2020-a-once-in-a-century-massive-turnout/

59. Ibid.

60. Ibid.

61. Ibid.

62. There has been a lot of interesting research in recent years on the impact of presidential campaigns on outcomes. In addition to the Erikson and Wlezien volume

already cited, see Lynn Vavreck, *The Message Matters* (Princeton, NJ: Princeton University Press, 2009); Thomas H. Holbrook, *Do Campaigns Matter?* (Thousand Oaks, CA: Sage Publications, 1996); James E. Campbell, *The American Campaign* (College Station: Texas A&M University Press, 2000); and Darron R. Shaw, "A Study of Presidential Campaign Effects from 1956 to 1992," *Journal of Politics* 61 (May 1999): 387–422.

63.   John Aldrich, Jamie Carson, Brad Gomez, and David Rohde. 2019. *Change and Continuity in the 2016 Elections* (Los Angeles: CQ Press/Sage).

64.   Lazaro Gamio, John Keefe, Denise Lu, and Rich Harris, "Record-Setting Turnout: Tracking Early Voting in the 2020 Election," *The New York Times*, November 12, 2020, https://www.nytimes.com/interactive/2020/us/elections/early-voting-results.html

65.   Ibid.

66.   The figure used here is the Voting Eligible Population Highest Office Turnout Rate. The data are from the United States Elections Project: http://www.electproject.org/

67.   Ford Fessenden, Lazaro Gamio, and Rich Harris, "Even in Defeat, Trump Found New Voters Across the U.S.," *The New York Times*, November 16, 2020, https://www.nytimes.com/interactive/2020/11/16/us/politics/election-turnout.html

68.   Emily Stewart, "Undecided Voters Explain Themselves: There are Fewer Undecided Voters in 2020 than there were in 2016. It doesn't Mean they can't Make a Difference," *VOX*, October 23, 2020, https://www.vox.com/21528722/undecided-voters-2020-election-trump-biden

69.   We thank Joshua Darr for generously sharing the data used in this discussion. For related work on field office placement in the 2016 presidential campaign, see Joshua Darr, 2020, *"Polls and Elections*: Abandoning the Ground Game? Field Organization in the 2016 Election." *Presidential Studies Quarterly* 50(1): 163–175.

Chapter 3

1.   Barbara Sprunt, "93 Million and Counting: Americans Are Shattering Early Voting Records," *National Public Radio*, November 1, 2020, https://www.npr.org/2020/10/26/927803214/62-million-and-counting-americans-are-breaking-early-voting-records

2.   Alexa Corse, "Biden Supporters More Likely than Trump's to Vote by Mail, Poll Shows," *Wall Street Journal*, August 17, 2020, http://www.wsj.com/amp/articles/biden-supporters-more-likely-than-trumps-to-vote-by-mail-poll-shows-11597683600

3.   Real Clear Politics, "General Election: Trump vs. Biden," https://www.realclearpolitics.com/ epolls/2020/president/us/general_election_trump_vs_biden-6247.html

4.   In 2016, polling estimates gave Hillary Clinton a 90 percent probability of winning. Donald Trump's Electoral College victory—Clinton won the popular vote—created a widespread perception that the polls had failed. An ad hoc

committee of the American Association for Public Opinion Research analyzed of the performance of pre-election polls in 2016, investigating several theories about why the polls underestimated Trump's vote share. The committee found a late swing in voters' preferences toward Trump was the primary reason, along with a "pervasive failure to adjust for overrepresentation of college graduates (who favored Clinton)." The committee found little evidence in support of the claim that Trump voters were "shy" about expressing their true preferences for their candidate, thus contributing to polling error. See Courtney Kennedy, Mark Blumenthal, Scott Clement, Joshua D. Clinton, Claire Durand, Charles Franklin, Kyley McGenney, Lee Miringoff, Kristen Olson, Douglas Rivers, Lydia Saad, G. Evans Witt, and Christopher Wlezien, "An Evaluation of the 2016 Election Polls in the United States," *Public Opinion Quarterly* 82 (Spring): 1–33.

5. Ruth Dassonneville and Charles Tien, "Forecasting the 2020 US Elections," *PS: Political Science and Politics* 54 (January): 47–51. The forecasts begin on p. 52. Opinion polls offer a snapshot of the electorate at the time of the survey and thus vary with the ebbs and flows of the campaign. Statistical forecast models are typically based on "fundamentals," factors that have been shown to be predictive across many elections. Most of these fundamentals, such as leading economic indicators, war fatalities during the past presidential term, and presidential approval, to name a few, are often known and measured before the general election campaign even begins. Many of the 2020 academic forecasts deemphasized the fundamentals in order to account for increased partisan polarization and the COVID-19 pandemic.

6. Thomas Kaplan, Katie Glueck, and Michael Cooper, "Nearing the Finish Line in Scranton, Pa., Biden says, 'You Got to Run through the Tape, Man,'" *New York Times*, November 3, 2020, https://www.nytimes.com/2020/11/02/us/politics/biden-pennsylvania-results.html?searchResultPosition=175

7. Alan Blinder, "'I Feel Very Good,' President Trump Tells Campaign Workers during an Election Day Visit to a Republican Office," *New York Times*, November 3, 2020, https://www.nytimes.com/2020/11/03/us/politics/donald-trump-president.html?searchResultPosition=86

8. Rebecca Shabad, "Biden Hits Key Swing States in Fight for Final Votes, Trump Sticks to Lower-Key Election Day Schedule," *NBC News*, November 3, 2020, https://www.nbcnews.com/politics/2020-election/biden-hits-key-swing-states-fight-final-votes-trump-sticks-n1245927

9. On its face, the tallying of votes and reporting of election returns would seem to be rather mundane. Yet the processing, verification, and counting of ballots can differ markedly across and even within states. Indeed, the 2020 elections serve to remind us of one of the peculiarities of the American system of federalism: in the United States, national elections are administered primarily at the state and local (mostly county) levels. See National Conference of State Legislatures, "Election Administration at State and Local Levels," February 3, 2020, https://www.ncsl.org/research/elections-and-campaigns/election-administration-at-state-and-local-levels.aspx. It has always been the case that the flow of results on election night is subject to the state laws that govern the tallying process and the resources (i.e., people, machines, etc.) available at the county level to count the ballots. This often leads to

systematic differences when precinct returns are added to the tally. Some counties—often smaller, rural counties—may be able to report their results soon after the polls close while others may take days to validate and report.

10.   E.g., Alexa Corse and Chad Day, "How Early Votes are Tallied is Likely to Cause Shifts in Election Night Results," *Wall Street Journal*, November 2, 2020, https://www.wsj.com/articles/how-early-votes-are-tallied-is-likely-to-cause-shifts-in-election-night-results-11604357620; Abby Vesoulis, November 3, 2020, "'Be Patient.' Why Early Election Results Will Be Misleading," *Time*, https://time.com/5906404/early-election-results-vote-count/; Benjamin Swasey, "Election Night Viewer's Guide: Why You May Need to Be Patient," *NPR*, November 3, 2020, https://www.npr.org/2020/11/03/929740947/election-night-viewers-guide-why-you-may-need-to-be-patient

11.   The *New York Times* website presents the candidates' vote shares as they were reported over time. See https://www.nytimes.com/interactive/2020/11/03/us/elections/results-president.html

12.   Within minutes, Twitter appended a warning to Trump's tweet labeling is "potentially misleading." In fact, ballots are never fully counted on election day; news organizations simply declare the "projected winner" on election night. Most states take several days or weeks to certify their election results. In 2016, for instance, only four states certified their election results within a week of election day; twenty-six states took at least three weeks to certify their results, and eleven states took at least one month to do so. See Ballotpedia, "Election Results Certification Dates," https://ballotpedia.org/Election_results_certification_dates,_2016. It should also be noted that eighteen states, including Republican strongholds, such as Mississippi and Texas, allow absentee ballots to arrive after election day. See National Conference of State Legislatures, "Table 11: Receipt and Postmark Deadlines for Absentee Ballots," https://www.ncsl.org/research/elections-and-campaigns/vopp-table-11-receipt-and-postmark-deadlines-for-absentee-ballots.aspx

13.   *BBC News*, "US Election 2016: Cruz Wins Wisconsin in Blow to Trump," https://www.bbc.com/news/election-us-2016-35975052

14.   John H. Aldrich, Jamie L. Carson, Brad T. Gomez, and David W. Rohde. 2019. *Change and Continuity in the 2016 Elections*. Thousand Oaks, CA: Sage/CQPress.

15.   Jane C. Timm, "With States Still Counting, Trump Falsely Claims He Won," *NBC News*, November 4, 2020, https://www.nbcnews.com/politics/2020-election/10-states-still-counting-millions-votes-trump-falsely-claims-he-n1246336. Tom McTague, "The President Confirms the World's Fears." *The Atlantic*, November 4, 2020, https://www.theatlantic.com/international/archive/2020/11/american-decline-trump-biden/616984/

16.   Michael M. Grynbaum and John Koblin, "TV Anchors and Pundits Criticize Trump's Baseless Claims of Fraud." *New York Times*, November 4, 2020, https://www.nytimes.com/2020/11/04/business/media/trump-tv-anchors-criticism.html?searchResultPosition=45

17.   Stephen Battaglio, "How the Networks Decided to Call the Election for Joe Biden," *Los Angeles Times*, November 7, 2020, https://www.latimes.com

/entertainment-arts/business/story/2020-11-07/joe-biden-president-elect-television
-news-networks

18. Adam Winkler, "Trump's Wildest Claims Are Going Nowhere in Court. Thank Legal Ethics." *Washington Post*, November 20, 2020, https://www.washingtonpost.com/outlook/trump-lawyers-legal-ethics/2020/11/20/3c286710-2ac1-11eb-92b7-6ef17b3fe3b4_story.html

19. Donald J. Trump for President *et al* v. Secretary Commonwealth of Pennsylvania *et al*, United States Court of Appeals for the Third Circuit, No. 20-3371, November 27, 2020, https://www2.ca3.uscourts.gov/opinarch/203371np.pdf

20. "Joint Statement from Elections Infrastructure Government Coordinating Council & The Election Infrastructure Sector Coordinating Executive Committees," November 12, 2020, https://www.cisa.gov/news/2020/11/12/joint-statement-elections-infrastructure-government-coordinating-council-election

21. Michael Balsamo, "Disputing Trump, Barr says No Widespread Election Fraud." *AP News*, December 1, 2020, https://apnews.com/article/barr-no-widespread-election-fraud-b1f1488796c9a98c4b1a9061a6c7f49d

22. Dan Berry and Sheera Frenkel, "'Be there. Will Be Wild!': Trump All but Circled the Date," *New York Times*, January 6, 2021, https://www.nytimes.com/2021/01/06/us/politics/capitol-mob-trump-supporters.html

23. For a transcript of Trump's January 6 speech, see "What Trump Said to Supporters on Jan. 6 Before Their Capitol Riot," *Wall Street Journal*, January 12, 2021, https://www.wsj.com/articles/what-trump-said-to-supporters-on-jan-6-before-their-capitol-riot-11610498173. For his part, Vice President Pence issued a statement before the congressional proceedings stating, "[it is] my considered judgement that my oath to support defend the Constitution constrains me from claiming unilateral authority to determine which electoral votes should be counted and which should not." See "Read Pence's Full Letter Saying He Can't Claim 'Unilateral Authority' to Reject Electoral Votes," *PBS News*, January 6, 2021, https://www.pbs.org/newshour/politics/read-pences-full-letter-saying-he-cant-claim-unilateral-authority-to-reject-electoral-votes

24. For timelines of the events of January 6, 2021, see Shelly Tan, Youjin Shin, and Danielle Rindler, "How One of America's Ugliest Days Unraveled Inside and Outside the Capitol," *Washington Post*, January 9, 2021, https://www.washingtonpost.com/nation/interactive/2021/capitol-insurrection-visual-timeline/; Laurel Wamsley, "What We Know So Far: A Timeline of Security Response at the Capitol on Jan. 6," *NPR*, January 15, 2021, https://www.npr.org/2021/01/15/956842958/what-we-know-so-far-a-timeline-of-security-at-the-capitol-on-january-6

25. Timothy Bella, "After 15 Hours and Rioters Attacking the Capitol, Pence Officially Affirms Biden's Win," *Washington Post*, January 7, 2021, https://www.washingtonpost.com/politics/2021/01/06/congress-electoral-college-vote-live-updates/#link-BSNDBVLWEVGJFCQJL4K4SXYX2E

26. As noted in chapter 2, since 1972, Maine has used a system in which the statewide plurality-vote winner receives two electoral votes, and the plurality winner in each of the state's congressional districts receives that district's single electoral vote. Nebraska has used a similar system to allocate its Electoral College votes since

the 1992 election. In our previous books we have not always reported these district-level results, but we do so here because in the 2020 election Trump won one electoral vote from Maine's second congressional district and Biden won one electoral vote from Nebraska's second congressional district.

27.   For a state-by-state reporting of the official presidential election returns for 2016, see John H. Aldrich, Jamie L. Carson, Brad T. Gomez, and David W. Rohde. 2019. *Change and Continuity in the 2016 Elections.* Thousand Oaks, CA: Sage/CQPress, Table 3-1.

28.   Electors from the Electoral College officially gathered in their respective state capitals to cast ballots for president and vice president on December 14, 2020. For more on the workings of the Electoral College, visit the Office of the Federal Registrar website, https://www.archives.gov/electoral-college.

29.   For a cross-national comparison of US presidential selection rules, see Matthew Soberg Shugart, "The American Process of Selecting a President: A Comparative Perspective," *Presidential Studies Quarterly* 34 (September 2004): 632–655.

30.   The respective plurality winners of the popular vote were Andrew Jackson in 1824, Samuel J. Tilden in 1876, incumbent President Grover Cleveland in 1888, and Al Gore in 2000. In 1824, no candidate won a majority of the electoral vote, so the election was thrown to the House of Representatives, where Adams was elected. In 1824, more than a fourth of the electors were chosen by state legislatures.

31.   Jonathan Mahler and Steve Eder, "Many Call the Electoral College Outmoded. So Why Has it Endured?," *New York Times*, November 11, 2016, P8. Interestingly public support for or opposition to the Electoral College is likely biased by whether one sides with the winning or losing candidate; see Bradley Jones, "Majority of Americans Continue to Favor Moving Away from Electoral College," *Pew Research Center*, January 27, 2021, https://www.pewresearch.org/fact-tank/2021/01/27/majority-of-americans-continue-to-favor-moving-away-from-electoral-college/; see also John H. Aldrich, Jason Reifler, and Michael C. Munger, "Sophisticated *and* Myopic? Citizens Preferences for Electoral College Reform," *Public Choice* 158 (March 2014): 541–558.

32.   For a history of the Electoral College, see Alexander Keyssar, *Why Do We Still Have the Electoral College?* (Cambridge, MA: Harvard University Press, 2020).

33.   These fourteen winners were James K. Polk (Democrat) in 1844, with 49.5 percent of the popular vote; Zachary Taylor (Whig) in 1848, with 47.3 percent; James Buchanan (Democrat) in 1856, with 45.3 percent; Abraham Lincoln (Republican) in 1860 with 39.9 percent; James A. Garfield (Republican) in 1880, with 48.3 percent; Grover Cleveland (Democrat) in 1884, with 48.9 percent; Cleveland in 1892, with 46.0 percent; Woodrow Wilson (Democrat) in 1912, with 41.8 percent; Wilson in 1916, with 49.2 percent; Harry S Truman (Democrat) in 1948, with 49.5 percent; John F. Kennedy (Democrat) in 1960, with 49.7 percent; Richard M. Nixon (Republican) in 1968, with 43.4 percent; Bill Clinton (Democrat) in 1992, with 43.0 percent; and Clinton in 1996, with 49.2 percent.

34.   Maurice Duverger, *Political Parties: Their Organization and Activity in the Modern State*, trans. Barbara North and Robert North (New York: Wiley, 1963), 217.

In the original Duverger's proposition is *"le scrutin majoritaire à un seul tour tend au dualisme des partis."* Duverger, *Les partis politiques* (Paris: Armand Colin, 1958), 247. For a discussion, see William H. Riker, "The Two-party System and Duverger's Law: An Essay on the History of Political Science," *American Political Science Review* 76 (December 1982): 753–766. For a more recent statement by Duverger, see "Duverger's Law Forty Years Later," in *Electoral Laws and Their Political Consequences*, eds. Bernard Grofman and Arend Lijphart (New York: Agathan Press, 1986), 69–84. For more general discussions of the effects of electoral laws, see Rein Taagepera and Matthew Shugart, *Seats and Votes: The Effects and Determinants of Electoral Systems* (New Haven, CT: Yale University Press, 1989); and Gary W. Cox, *Making Votes Count: Strategic Coordination of the World's Electoral Systems* (Cambridge, UK: Cambridge University Press, 1997).

35.   Duverger's inclusion of "a single ballot" in his formulation is redundant because, in a plurality-vote win system, there would be no need for second ballots or runoffs unless needed to break ties. With a large electorate, ties will be extremely rare.

36.   Duverger, *Political Parties*, 218.

37.   William H. Riker, *The Art of Political Manipulation* (New Haven, CT: Yale University Press, 1986), 79.

38.   For the most extensive evidence for the 1968, 1980, and 1992 elections, see Paul R. Abramson et al., "Third-Party and Independent Candidates in American Politics: Wallace, Anderson, and Perot," *Political Science Quarterly* 110 (Fall 1997): 349–367. For the 1996 and 2000 elections, see Paul R. Abramson, John H. Aldrich, and David W. Rohde, *Change and Continuity in the 1996 and 1998 Elections* (Washington, DC: CQ Press, 1999), 118–120; and Paul R. Abramson, John H. Aldrich, and David W. Rohde, *Change and Continuity in the 2000 and 2002 Elections* (Washington, DC: CQ Press, 2003), 124–126.

39.   Britain provides an excellent example of the effects of plurality-vote win systems on third parties. In Britain, as in the United States, candidates for the national legislature run in single-member districts, and in all British parliamentary districts the plurality-vote winner is elected. In all twenty general elections since World War II ended in Europe, the liberal Democrats (and its predecessor, the Liberal Party) has received a smaller percentage of seats in the House of Commons than its percentage of the popular vote. For example, in the December 2019 election, the liberal Democrats won 11.6 percent of the popular vote but won only 1.7 percent of the seats in the House of Commons.

40.   Third-party candidates are not always underrepresented in the Electoral College. In 1948, J. Strom Thurmond, the States' Rights Democrat, won only 2.4 percent of the popular vote but won 7.3 percent of the electoral vote. Thurmond won 55 percent of the popular votes in the four states he carried (Alabama, Louisiana, Mississippi, and South Carolina), all of which had low turnout. He received no popular vote at all in thirty-one of the forty-eight states.

41.   See George C. Edwards III, *Why the Electoral College is Bad for America*, 2nd ed. (New Haven, Conn.: Yale University Press, 2011).

42.   Edwards argues that "[a] constitutional amendment is not a pipe dream," noting that a constitutional amendment to establish direct election of the president passed

the House on a bipartisan vote in 1969. The amendment, which was publicly endorsed by President Nixon, was filibustered in the Senate, however, by southern senators. See Ibid., 203.

43. For the most extensive argument in favor of this reform, see John R. Koza et al., *Every Vote Equal: A State-Based Plan for Electing the President by National Popular Vote*, 4th ed. (Los Altos, CA: National Popular Vote Press, 2013).

44. Adoption of the district system would likely increase the incentive for state legislatures to gerrymander given that presidential electors would now be at stake.

45. David Nir, "Daily Kos Elections' Presidential Results by Congressional District for 2020, 2016, and 2012," *Daily Kos*, November 19, 2020, https://www.dailykos.com/stories/2020/11/19/1163009/-Daily-Kos-Elections-presidential-results-by-congressional-district-for-2020-2016-and-2012

One should always be cautious when constructing counterfactuals such as this. Had the election taken place under these rules, the candidates most certainly would have campaigned using different strategies, and voter participation would have changed in all likelihood in response to varying levels of electoral competition across districts.

46. A.C. Thomas and colleagues offer a systematic study of alternative elector apportionment proposals using data from 1956 to 2004. They conclude that both the current Electoral College and the direct popular vote are substantially less biased than the district method. See A. C. Thomas, Andrew Gelman, Gary King, and Jonathan N. Katz, "Estimating Partisan Bias of the Electoral College Under Proposed Changes in Elector Apportionment," *Statistics, Politics, and Policy* 4 (Issue 1, 2013): 1–13.

47. Daniel Gans views much of presidential election history as what statisticians call a "random walk," meaning that party success from one election to the next is essentially random. See Daniel J. Gans, "Persistence of Party Success in American Presidential Elections," *Journal of Interdisciplinary History* 2 (Winter 1986): 221–237.

48. Walter Dean Burnham, *Critical Elections and the Mainsprings of American Politics* (New York: Norton, 1970).

49. Stanley Kelley, Jr., establishes three criteria to classify an election as a landslide: if the winning candidate wins 53 percent of the popular vote *or* wins 80 percent of the electoral vote *or* wins 80 percent of the states. This definition may be too generous, but Reagan's 1984 victory, which met all three of Kelley's criteria, was most certainly a landslide. See Stanley Kelley, Jr., *Interpreting Elections* (Princeton, NJ: Princeton University Press, 1983).

50. For a study of the Whig Party, see Michael F. Holt, *The Rise and Fall of the Whig Party: Jacksonian Politics and the Onset of the Civil War* (New York: Oxford University Press, 1999).

51. Former Whigs founded the Constitutional Union Party in 1860. Its candidate, John Bell, won 12.6 percent of the popular vote and thirty-nine of the 303 electoral votes.

52. For a discussion of agenda-setting during this period, see William H. Riker, *Liberalism against Populism: A Confrontation between the Theory of Democracy and the Theory of Social Choice* (San Francisco: W. H. Freeman, 1982), 213–232; and

John H. Aldrich, *Why Parties? A Second Look* (Chicago: University of Chicago Press, 2011), 130–162.

53.   Not all scholars agree with this assessment. The most important dissent is found in David R. Mayhew, *Electoral Realignments: A Critique of an American Genre* (New Haven, CT: Yale University Press, 2002), 43–69.

54.   The election of 1912 is the last in which a party other than the Democrats and Republicans finished among the top-two vote getters. Former Republican president Theodore Roosevelt, running as the nominee of the Progressive Party (the "Bull Moose Party"), finished second in both the popular and Electoral College votes.

55.   See David R. Mayhew, "Incumbency Advantage in U.S. Presidential Elections: The Historical Record," *Political Science Quarterly* 123 (Summer 2008): 201–228. An individual-level study of survey responses from the 1952 through 2000 American National Election Studies suggests that incumbent presidential candidates—controlling for a variety of other factors—enjoy a six percentage point advantage over their challengers in the popular vote; see Herbert F. Weisberg, "Partisanship and Incumbency in Presidential Elections," *Political Behavior* 24 (December 2002): 339–360.

56.   Cleveland is America's 22nd and 24th president. Two other former presidents have attempted to win a nonconsecutive term in office: Martin Van Buren in 1848 (previously elected as a Democrat, Van Buren was the nominee of the Free Soil Party and finished third) and Theodore Roosevelt in 1912 (previously elected as a Republican, Roosevelt was the nominee of the Progressive "Bull Moose" Party and finished second).

57.   Jodi Enda, "When Republicans Were Blue and Democrats Were Red: The Era of Color-coded Political Parties Is More Recent than You Might Think," November 1, 2012, smithsonian.com. The association of Republicans with the color red is actually a bit curious, given the color's historical association with revolution and socialism. For example, the song "The Red Flag," composed by James Connell in 1889, became the official song of the British Labour Party. As for flags specifically, the flag of the Soviet Union featured a solid red field with a gold hammer and sickle. Fear of the Soviet Union and the spread of communism in America, particularly during the 1950s, was called the "Red Scare."

58.   Since ratification of the Twenty-third Amendment in 1961, the District of Columbia has had three electoral votes, which it first cast in the 1964 election.

59.   Data are collected by Kantar/CMAD with analysis by the Wesleyan Media Project (https://mediaproject.wesleyan.edu/). The number of campaign ads aired on broadcast television (excluding national cable airings) between April 9, 2020 and October 25, 2020 are reported by media market. https://www.dropbox.com/s/ap3ms-dzenjkizuq/Release20_mapdata.xlsx?dl=0

60.   This is not to say that campaigns view larger states alone as important to their Electoral College strategy. With one Electoral College vote up for grabs, the Omaha, Nebraska media market, which broadcasts across Nebraska's 2nd congressional district, broadcast 6,150 campaign ads—more than California and Texas combined.

61.   US Department of Commerce, *Statistical Abstract of the United States*, 101st ed. (Washington, DC: Government Printing Office, 1980), 514.

62.   Edward Alden, "The Biggest Issue That Carried Trump to Victory," *Fortune*, November 10, 2016, http://fortune.com/2016 /11/10/trump-voters-free-trade-glob alization/

63.   Maxwell Tani, "Democrats Think Trump Won on Economic Issues—But Exit Polls Offer a More Complicated Story," *Business Insider*, December 24, 2016, http://www.businessinsider.com/democrats-trump-econmic-issues-polls-2016-12

64.   See Morris P. Fiorina, with Samuel J. Abrams and Jeremy C. Pope, *Culture War? The Myth of a Polarized America*, 3rd ed. (New York: Pearson/Longman, 2010); and Andrew Gelman et al., *Red State, Blue State, Rich State, Poor State: Why Americans Vote the Way They Do* (Princeton, NJ: Princeton University Press, 2008).

65.   We use the Census Bureau's definition of the Northeast, which includes Connecticut, Maine, Massachusetts, New Hampshire, New Jersey, New York, Pennsylvania, Rhode Island, and Vermont.

66.   From 1992 to 2012, the only northeastern state to cast its electoral votes for a Republican was New Hampshire in 2000, giving George W. Bush four electors. In the three elections preceding Clinton's victory in 1992, the Republicans fared quite well in the Northeast. The region was solidly pro-Reagan in 1980 (losing only Rhode Island) and 1984, and George H. W. Bush won six of the region's nine states in 1988.

67.   Although Trump won 90 percent support from self-identified Republicans in Arizona, according to a voter survey conducted by the Associated Press, Biden may also have benefited from the support of some moderate Republicans and independents in the state who may have been offended by the president's treatment of longtime Arizona senator John McCain (see "Arizona Voter Surveys: How Different Groups Voted," *New York Times*, https://www.nytimes.com/interactive/2020/11/03/us/elec tions/ap-polls-arizona.html.) Trump repeatedly expressed contempt for McCain, the 2008 Republican presidential nominee and former Navy pilot who had spent five years as a prisoner of war and was tortured by his North Vietnamese captors. In 2015, Trump told an audience, "He's not a war hero. . . . He's a war hero because he was captured. I like people that weren't captured, okay." Trump also referred to McCain as "a loser" and reportedly told his senior staff when the senator died in August 2018, "We're not going to support that loser's funeral" (see Jack Brewster, "Trump Says He Never Called McCain a 'Loser'—Here's the Evidence that He Did," *Forbes*, September 4, 2020, https://www.forbes.com/sites/jackbrewster/2020/09/04/trump -says-he-never-called-mccain-a-loser-heres-the-evidence-he-did/?sh=3c0e7eea25cc). The president was not invited to McCain's funeral, and Cindy McCain, the senator's widow, endorsed Biden during the 2020 campaign.

68.   Following the election, hand count audits of the ballots were conducted in 10 of Arizona's 15 counties, and a full statewide hand count audit of over 5 million ballots was conducted in Georgia. While no discrepancies were found in Arizona (see "Summary of Hand Count Audits—2020 General Election," *Arizona Secretary of State's Office*, November 17, 2020, https://azsos.gov/election/2020-general-election -hand-count-results), some minor discrepancies were found in 4 of Georgia's 152 counties, netting Trump an additional 1,274 votes (see "Historic First Statewide Audit of Paper Ballots Upholds Result of Presidential Race," *Georgia Secretary of State's Office*, https://sos.ga.gov/index.php/elections/historic_first_statewide_audit_of_paper

_ballots_upholds_result_of_presidential_race). Both elections were certified as Biden victories.

69. Trump won these states by an average margin of 23.5 percentage points in 2016, and Republican nominee Mitt Romney won these states by an average of 20.9 percentage points in 2012.

70. Joseph A. Schlesinger, *Political Parties and the Winning of Office* (Ann Arbor: University of Michigan Press, 1991).

71. See Schlesinger, *Political Parties and the Winning of Office,* Figure 5-1, 112. Schlesinger does not report the exact values, but he provided them to us in a personal communication. Including the District of Columbia, which has voted for president since 1964, increases the standard deviation because the district always votes more Democratic than the most Democratic state. We report Schlesinger's results for states, not for his alternative results that include DC. Likewise our updated results are for the fifty states.

72. The state-by-state deviation of 11.96 in the 1964 contest between Johnson and Goldwater is the highest deviation of any postwar election.

73. Since 1988, the last election reported by Schlesinger, state-by-state variation in party competition has increased slightly: 1988 (5.60), 1992 (5.96), 1996 (6.70), 2000 (8.51), 2004 (8.39), 2008 (9.54), 2012 (10.29), 2016 (10.35) and 2020 (10.43), with standard deviations in parentheses.

74. See Aldrich, *Why Parties? A Second Look*, Part 3.

75. "2020 Census: Apportionment of the U.S. House of Representatives," *U.S. Census Bureau*, April 26, 2021, https://www.census.gov/library/visualizations/2021/dec/2020-apportionment-map.html. Texas is set to gain two Electoral College votes, and Florida and North Carolina will each gain one elector. The only other states to gain electoral votes are Colorado, Montana, and Oregon, one each. Seven states will lose a single electoral vote: California, Illinois, Michigan, New York, Ohio, Pennsylvania, and West Virginia. If the distribution of electoral votes had been in place in 2020, Biden would have won 303 votes to 235.

76. V. O. Key, Jr., *Southern Politics in State and Nation* (New York: Knopf, 1949), 5.

77. There have been many excellent studies of the postwar South. For three recent excellent volumes examining the political transformation of the South, see Eric Schickler, *Racial Realignment: The Transformation of American Liberalism, 1932–1965* (Princeton, NJ: Princeton University Press, 2016); Robert Mickey, *Paths Out of Dixie: The Democratization of Authoritarian Enclaves in America's Deep South, 1944–1972* (Princeton, NJ: Princeton University Press, 2015); and John H. Aldrich and John D. Griffin, *Why Parties Matter: Political Competition and Democracy in the American South* (Chicago: University of Chicago Press, 2018).

78. South Carolina was the most solidly Democratic, with an average Democratic vote share of 91.4 percent; Tennessee had the lowest with 56.7 percent of the vote going to the Democrats. Estimates calculated by the authors.

79. See Nancy J. Weiss, *Farewell to the Party of Lincoln: Black Politics in the Age of FDR* (Princeton, NJ: Princeton University Press, 1983).

80. Earlier that month, southern Democrats suffered a defeat at the Democratic presidential nominating convention. Their attempts to weaken the national party's

civil rights platform were defeated. At the same time, Hubert Humphrey, then mayor of Minneapolis, argued that the platform was too weak and offered an amendment for a stronger statement. Humphrey's amendment passed by a vote of 651½–582½. That victory led the southern delegations to walk out and thus led to the States' Rights Democratic Party, better known as the Dixiecrat Party.

81. Kennedy made a symbolic gesture that may have helped him with African Americans. Three weeks before the election, Martin Luther King, Jr., was arrested in Atlanta for taking part in a sit-in demonstration. Kennedy telephoned King's wife to express his concern, and his brother Robert F. Kennedy, Jr., acting as a private citizen, made a direct appeal to a Georgia judge that led to King's release on bail. This incident received little notice in the press, but it had a great effect on the African American community. See Theodore H. White, *The Making of the President, 1960* (New York: Atheneum, 1961), 321–323.

82. Alabama, Georgia, Louisiana, Mississippi, and South Carolina are considered the five Deep South states. They are also five of the six states with the highest percentage of African Americans.

83. John B. Judis and Ruy Teixeira, *The Emerging Democratic Majority* (New York: A Lisa Drew Book/Scribner, 2002). See also Ruy Teixeira, "The Emerging Democratic Majority Turns 10," theatlantic.com, November 9, 2012.

84. Pew Hispanic Center, "An Awakened Giant: The Hispanic Electorate Is Likely to Double by 2030," November 14, 2012, http://www.pewhispanic.org/2012 /11/14/an -awakened-giant-the-hispanic-electorate-is-likely-to-double-by-2030/

85. U.S. Census Bureau, "American Community Survey," http://www.census .gov/acs/www/

86. Scholars have already noted the electoral consequences of Hispanic population growth. Alan Abramowitz argues that since 2000, increases in the Hispanic vote have transitioned New Mexico from a swing state to a safe Democratic state and caused the formerly Republican-leaning states of Colorado and Nevada to become Democratic-leaning. See Alan Abramowitz, "The Emerging Democratic Presidential Majority: Lessons of Obama's Victory," paper presented at the Annual Meeting of the American Political Science Association, Chicago, Illinois, August 31, 2013.

87. See, for instance, Paul R. Abramson, John H. Aldrich, and David W. Rohde, *Change and Continuity in the 1984 Elections*, rev. ed. (Washington, DC: CQ Press, 1987), 70–75.

88. According to Marjorie Randon Hershey, the Republicans had a "clear and continuing advantage" in presidential elections. See Marjorie Randon Hershey, "The Campaign and the Media," in *The Election of 1988: Reports and Interpretations*, ed. Gerald M. Pomper et al. (Chatham, NJ: Chatham House, 1989), 74.

89. Jens Manuel Krogstad, "Key Facts about the Latino Vote in 2016," *Pew Research Center*, October 14, 2016, http://www.pewresearch.org/fact-tank/2016/10 /14/key-facts-about -the-latino-vote-in-2016/

90. See Jens Manuel Krogstad and Antonio Flores, "Unlike Other Latinos, about Half of Cuban Voters in Florida Backed Trump," *Pew Research Center*, November 15, 2016, http://www.pewresearch.org/fact-tank/2016/11/15/unlike-other-latinos -about-half-of-cuban-voters -in-florida-backed-trump/

91.   Matt Barreto and Kevin Munoz, "Here's What We Learned about the Florida Hispanic Vote," *Tampa Bay Times*, January 19, 2021, https://www.tampabay.com/opinion/2021/01/19/heres-what-we-learned-about-the-florida-hispanic-vote-column/

92.   For a figure demonstrating the Republican dominance between 1972 and 1988, see Abramson, Aldrich, and Rohde, *Change and Continuity in the 1992 Elections,* rev. ed., 47.

93.   See Daron R. Shaw, *The Race to 270: The Electoral College and the Campaign Strategies of 2000* (Chicago: University of Chicago Press, 2006).

94.   We elected to start our measure in 1988, which reports the electoral balance following the 1972, 1976, 1980, 1984, and 1988 elections to eliminate observations that would have to use the 1968 presidential election, in which electoral votes were cast for a third-party candidate.

95.   Twenty states have voted Republican in each of the past five elections. These solidly Republican states tally 153 electoral votes. Texas with thirty-eight electoral votes is the only large state among the twenty, and four of these states have the minimum of three votes. There are sixteen states, along with the District of Columbia, that have voted Democratic in the last five elections. Although seemingly less impressive than the twenty states held comfortably by Republicans, the solidly Democratic group represents 200 electoral votes, significantly more the GOP strongholds.

An admitted weakness of this measure is that it does not account for the average vote share within a state over time. Thus a state that consistently sided with the same party by narrow margins is equivalent to a state that consistently sided with the same party by large margins—both are categorized as "uncompetitive."

Chapter 4

1.   Michael McDonald reports that the voting-eligible population in 2020 was 239,247,182. This number is calculated by subtracting from the voting-age population those who are ineligible to vote, such as noncitizens, citizens living abroad, and when state law applies, felons and those judged mentally incompetent. McDonald estimates that nearly 18.3 million voting-age people living in the United States are ineligible to vote. McDonald, "2020 General Election Turnout Rates," United States Election Project, http://www.electproject.org/2020g. Our numerator, the total number of votes cast in the presidential election, comes from the Federal Election Commission's "Official 2020 Presidential General Election Results," https://www.fec.gov/documents/2840//2020presgeresults.pdf

2.   The turnout measure for the United States divides the number of voters by the voting-age population. The International Voter Turnout Database measures turnout for the other countries by dividing the number of voters by the number of people registered. In most democracies, voter registration is the responsibility of government, which maintains the voter rolls and automatically registers all eligible citizens for voting. Registration in the United States, however, is an individual responsibility. The

US Census estimates that 72.7 percent of American adult citizens are registered to vote. See US Census Bureau, "Voting and Registration in the Election of November 2020," https://www2.census.gov/programs-surveys/cps/tables/p20/585/table01.xlsx

3. For a comprehensive discussion of turnout change in comparative perspective, see Mark N. Franklin, *Voter Turnout and the Dynamics of Electoral Competition in Established Democracies Since 1945* (New York: Cambridge University Press, 2004).

4. In Australia, nonvoters may be subject to a small fine. In Belgium, nonvoters may suffer from future disenfranchisement and may find it difficult to obtain a public-sector job. For more on the effect of compulsory voting on voter turnout, see Pippa Norris, *Election Engineering: Voting Rules and Political Behavior* (New York: Cambridge University Press, 2002); and Anthony Fowler, "Electoral and Policy Consequences of Voter Turnout: Evidence from Compulsory Voting in Australia," *Quarterly Journal of Political Science* 8 (2013): 159–182.

5. See André Blais and Kees Aarts, "Electoral Systems and Turnout," *Acta Politica*, 41 (2006): 180–196 for a review and Carlos Sanz, "The Effect of Electoral Systems on Voter Turnout: Evidence from a Natural Experiment," *Political Science Research and Methods* 5 (2017): 689–710 for more direct causal evidence in support of the relationship.

6. Of the remaining seven democracies in our sample, six have experienced no significant changes in turnout rates, and only one, Malta, has experienced a significant increase in the postwar period. Much of the increase in Maltese voter turnout was experienced after the archipelago nation achieved colonial independence from Great Britain. Elections in Malta are held via a proportional representation system using the single transferable vote.

7. This chapter focuses on one form of political participation, voting. For a major study of other forms of political participation, see Sidney Verba, Kay Lehman Schlozman, and Henry E. Brady, *Voice and Equality: Civic Voluntarism in American Politics* (Cambridge, MA: Harvard University Press, 1995). For a collection of essays on voting as well as other forms of political participation, see Russell J. Dalton and Hans-Dieter Klingemann, eds., *The Oxford Handbook of Political Behavior* (New York: Oxford University Press, 2007).

8. Alexander Keyssar, *The Right to Vote: The Contested History of Democracy in the United States*, rev. ed. (New York: Basic Books, 2000), 2. Keyssar's book is arguably the definitive account of the legal and political history of suffrage in the United States.

9. The Seventeenth Amendment to the United States Constitution, ratified in 1913, established direct election of United States senators by popular vote.

10. In 1790, ten of the thirteen states had property requirements for voting, and three of the thirteen limited suffrage to white males only. By 1820 property requirements were in effect in nine of the twenty-three states, and fourteen of the twenty-three states had race exclusions. See Keyssar, *The Right to Vote*, Table A.3 and Table A.5.

11. For a useful summary of the history of turnout in the United States, see Michael P. McDonald, "American Voter Turnout in Historical Perspective," in *The Oxford Handbook of American Elections and Political Behavior,* ed. Jan E. Leighley (New York: Oxford University Press, 2010), 125–143.

12.   It is difficult to calculate the exact number of voters who turn out for an election. It is common to use the total number of ballots cast for the presidency as a substitute for the number of voters because in most elections more people vote for president than for any other office.

13.   Women's suffrage was adopted in many of the western territories of the United States as a way of attracting female settlers. Wyoming, Utah, Washington, and Montana enfranchised women decades before they joined the union. Wyoming officially became the first state to give women the right to vote in 1890, when it obtained statehood.

14.   At the outset of the Civil War, only five states—all in New England—granted blacks the right to vote. A sixth state, New York, allowed blacks who met a property requirement to vote. The Fifteenth Amendment was ratified in 1870. See Keyssar, *The Right to Vote*, 69–83.

15.   See Martin J. Kousser, *The Shaping of Southern Politics: Suffrage Restrictions and the Establishment of the One-Party South, 1880–1910* (New Haven, CT: Yale University Press, 1974); and John H. Aldrich and John D. Griffin, *Why Parties Matter: Political Competition and Democracy in the American South* (Chicago: University of Chicago Press, 2018). For a more general discussion, see Paul Kleppner, *Who Voted? The Dynamics of Electoral Turnout, 1870–1980* (New York: Praeger, 1982), 55–82.

16.   There is disagreement about the reasons for and the consequences of registration requirements. For some of the more interesting arguments, see Walter Dean Burnham, "The Changing Shape of the American Political Universe," *American Political Science Review* 59 (March 1965): 7–28; Philip E. Converse, "Change in the American Electorate," in *The Human Meaning of Social Change,* eds. Angus Campbell and Philip E. Converse (New York: Russell Sage, 1972), 266–301; and Walter Dean Burnham, "Theory and Voting Research: Some Reflections on Converse's 'Change in the American Electorate,'" *American Political Science Review* 68 (September 1974): 1002–1023. For two other perspectives, see Frances Fox Piven and Richard A. Cloward, *Why Americans Still Don't Vote and Why Politicians Want It That Way* (Boston: Beacon Press, 2000); and Matthew A. Crenson and Benjamin Ginsberg, *Downsizing America: How America Sidelined Its Citizens and Privatized Its Public* (Baltimore, MD: Johns Hopkins University Press, 2002).

17.   This term originates from the fact that in 1856, two Australian colonies (now states) adopted a secret ballot to be printed and administered by the government.

18.   For a rich source of information on the introduction of the Australian ballot and its effects, see Jerrold G. Rusk, "The Effect of the Australian Ballot on Split-Ticket Voting, 1876–1908," *American Political Science Review* 64 (December 1970): 1220–1238.

19.   The secret ballot, like a few of the other "good government" electoral reforms of the Progressive Era, such as literacy tests, often had unintended consequences or were used in the South to disenfranchise African Americans. An analysis by Jac C. Heckelman estimates that the introduction of the secret ballot lowered voter turnout in US gubernatorial elections by seven percentage points. See Jac C. Heckelman, "The Effect of the Secret Ballot on Voter Turnout Rates," *Public Choice* 82, no. 1/2 (1995): 107–124.

20.   Keyssar, *The Right to Vote*, 115.

21.   Burnham presents estimates of turnout among the "politically-eligible population" between 1789 and 1984 in "The Turnout Problem," in *Elections American
Style*, ed. James A. Reichley (Washington, DC: Brookings, 1987), 113–114. In a
series of personal communications, Burnham provided us with estimates of turnout
among the "voting-eligible population" between 1988 and 2004: 52.7 percent in
1988, 56.9 percent in 1992, 50.8 percent in 1996, 54.9 percent in 2000, and 60.7
percent in 2004. McDonald and Popkin's estimates of turnout between 1948 and
2000 are available in Michael P. McDonald and Samuel L. Popkin, "The Myth of
the Vanishing Voter," *American Political Science Review* 95 (December 2001): 996.
McDonald's estimates for the 2004, 2008, 2012, and 2016 elections are available on
his United States Elections Project website, http://www.electproject.org/home/voter
-turnout/voter-turnout-data

22.   Only Maine, Vermont, and the District of Columbia allow prisoners to vote.
In recent decades, states, through statutes or popular initiatives, have moved to reinstate voting rights after felons complete their sentence. In twenty-one, voting rights
are restored immediately upon release. Sixteen states restore rights after incarceration
and an additional period of time (some also require payment of outstanding fines or
restitution), and eleven states include an additional step requiring gubernatorial par-
don or approval by a state commission.

23.   McDonald's estimates of the eligible population do not account for the number of permanently disenfranchised felons "since time-series statistics on recidivism,
deaths, and migration of felons are largely unavailable." See McDonald, "How Is
the Ineligible Felon Population Estimated," http://www.electproject.org/home/voter
-turnout/faq/felons

24.   McDonald, "2016 General Election Turnout Rates," http://www.electproject
.org/2016g

25.   Thomas E. Patterson, *The Vanishing Voter: Public Involvement in an
Age of Uncertainty* (New York: Knopf, 2002). See also Pippa Norris, *Democratic
Participation Worldwide* (Cambridge, UK: Cambridge University Press, 2002).

26.   See note 21.

27.   J. Kevin Corder and Christina Wolbrecht, *Counting Women's Ballots: Female
Voters from Suffrage to the New Deal*. (New York, NY: Cambridge University Press,
2016).

28.   See Glenn Firebaugh and Kevin Chen, "Vote Turnout among Nineteenth
Amendment Women: The Enduring Effects of Disfranchisement," *American Journal
of Sociology* 100 (January 1995): 972–996.

29.   For estimates of this reform on turnout, see Raymond E. Wolfinger and
Jonathan Hoffman, "Registering and Voting with Motor Voter," *PS: Political Science
and Politics* 34 (March 2001): 86–92. David Hill argues that whereas motor voter
legislation has made the election rolls more representative, it has had little effect
on turnout. See David Hill, *American Voter Turnout: An Institutional Perspective*
(Boulder, CO: Westview Press, 2006), 49–52, 55.

30.   See Matt Vasilogambros and Lindsey Van Ness, "States Expanded Voting
Access for the Pandemic. The Changes Might Stick," *Pew Research*, November
6, 2020, https://www.pewtrusts.org/en/research-and-analysis/blogs/stateline/2020/11
/06/states-expanded-voting-access-for-the-pandemic-the-changes-might-stick. For

details about states' convenience voting laws, see National Conference of State Legislatures, "Early Voting Laws," https://www.ncsl.org/research/elections-and-campaigns/early-voting-in-state-elections.aspx#Early%20Voting%20Law%20Table.

31. National Conference of State Legislatures, "Absentee and Mail Voting Policies in Effect for the 2020 Election," https://www.ncsl.org/research/elections-and-campaigns/absentee-and-mail-voting-policies-in-effect-for-the-2020-election.aspx

32. The seven states are Colorado, Hawaii, Nevada, Oregon, Utah, Vermont, and Washington. National Conference of State Legislatures, "Absentee and Early Voting," https://www.ncsl.org/research/elections-and-campaigns/absentee-and-early-voting.aspx

33. The 2020 Current Population Survey (CPS) is based on more than 54,000 respondent households nationally with sizable (and representative) samples drawn for each state. The CPS's November Supplements during election years is commonly used in studies of turnout, although the Census Bureau only measures voting behavior along with demographic variables (federal law does not allow the Census Bureau to measure individual's political attitudes). The most important study to use the CPS remains Raymond E. Wolfinger and Steven J. Rosenstone, *Who Votes?* (New Haven, CT: Yale University Press, 1980).

34. Conventional political wisdom held that early voting laws would decrease the costs of voting, increase turnout, and disproportionately benefit Democratic candidates. A recent empirical study examining the effects of various state election laws on voter turnout suggests that early voting may actually benefit Republican candidates on average, although the effects are likely highly contingent on contextual factors. See Barry C. Burden, David T. Canon, Kenneth R. Mayer, and Donald P. Moynihan, "The Complicated Partisan Effects of State Election Laws," *Political Research Quarterly* 70 (2017): 564–576.

35. John H. Aldrich, Jamie L. Carson, Brad T. Gomez, and David W. Rohde, *Change and Continuity in the 2016 and 2018 Elections* (Thousand Oaks, CA: Sage/CQ Press, 2020), 269–371.

36. Alan I. Abramowitz, "Assessing the Impact of Absentee Voting on Turnout and Democratic Vote Margin in 2020," *University of Virginia Center for Politics*, February 25, 2021, https://centerforpolitics.org/crystalball/articles/assessing-the-impact-of-absentee-voting-on-turnout-and-democratic-vote-margin-in-2020/

37. Jacob Fabina, "Despite Pandemic Challenges, 2020 Election Had Largest Increase in Voting Between Presidential Elections on Record," *U.S. Census Bureau*, April 29, 2021, https://www.census.gov/library/stories/2021/04/record-high-turnout-in-2020-general-election.html

38. When appropriate we also rely on estimates from the 2020 CPS and exit poll data. The Census Bureau published a detailed report of its 2020 survey in March 2021. See US Census Bureau, "Current Population Survey, November 2020, Voting and Registration Supplement, Technical Documentation," https://www2.census.gov/programs-surveys/cps/techdocs/cpsnov20.pdf. Interested readers can access data from the 2020 CPS, November Supplement (as well as other Census Bureau studies), using the Census Bureau's application programming interface (API), https://www.census.gov/data/developers/data-sets.html

Exit polls were conducted by Edison Research of Somerville, New Jersey, for the "National Election Pool," a consortium of ABC News, CBS News, CNN, and NBC News. The exit polls are not a representative sample of the nation. Instead polls were conducted in twenty-three states. Precincts in each state were selected by a stratified-probability sample, and every *n*th voter in the precinct was given a questionnaire to complete. In states with significant early and/or absentee voting, a supplemental telephone survey was conducted.

39. Respondents to the postelection survey of the ANES are asked: In talking to people about elections, we often find that a lot of people were not able to vote because they weren't registered, they were sick, or they just didn't have time. Which of the following statements best describes you?

One, I did not vote (in the election this November).

Two, I thought about voting this time, but didn't.

Three, I usually vote, but didn't this time.

Four, I am sure I voted.

We classified respondents as voters if they were sure that they voted.

40. These studies suggest, however, that African Americans are more likely to falsely claim to have voted than whites. As a result, racial differences are always greater when turnout is measured by the vote validation studies. Unfortunately, we have no way of knowing whether this difference between the races has changed as African American turnout has increased with time. For results for the 1964, 1976, 1978, 1980, 1984, 1986, and 1988 elections, see Paul R. Abramson and William Claggett, "Racial Differences in Self-Reported and Validated Voting in the 1988 Presidential Election," *Journal of Politics* 53 (February 1991): 186–187. For a discussion of the factors that contribute to false reports of voting, see Brian D. Silver, Barbara A. Anderson, and Paul R. Abramson, "Who Overreports Voting?" *American Political Science Review* 80 (June 1986): 613–624. For an alternative study that argues that biases in reported turnout are more severe than Silver, Anderson, and Abramson claim, see Robert Bernstein, Anita Chadha, and Robert Montjoy, "Overreporting Voting: Why It Happens and Why It Matters," *Public Opinion Quarterly* 65 (Spring 2001): 22–44.

41. Barry Burden reports that the overreporting of voter turnout in the ANES increased with time. He attributes this to declining response rates for the ANES rather than question wording changes or other problems with the survey. See Barry C. Burden, "Voter Turnout and the National Election Studies," *Political Analysis* 8 (July 2000): 389–398. See Michael P. McDonald, "On the Overreport Bias of the National Election Study Turnout Rate," *Political Analysis* (May 2003): 180–186; and Michael D. Martinez, "Comment on 'Voter Turnout and the National Election Studies,'" *Political Analysis* (May 2003): 187–192 for counterarguments to Burden.

In an analysis of the 2008 vote validation study, the ANES staff and principal investigators found a surprisingly high level of accuracy in self-reported turnout when compared with official turnout records, suggesting that overreporting comes from sources other than respondents simply saying they voted when they did not. See Matthew K. Berent, Jon A. Krosnick, and Arthur Lupia, "The Quality of Government Records and 'Over-estimation' of Registration and Turnout in Surveys: Lessons from the 2008 ANES Panel Study's Registration and Turnout Validation Exercises," American National Election Studies, Working Paper no. nes012554, August 2011, http://www.electionstudies.org/resources/papers/nes012554.pdf

42. The response rate for ANES has declined significantly over the years as the number of surveys has proliferated. In 2012, the ANES response rate was a record low 38 percent.

43. Sidney Verba and Norman H. Nie, *Participation in America: Political Democracy and Social Equality* (New York: Cambridge University Press, 1972).

44. See Henry E. Brady, Sidney Verba, and Kay Lehman Schlozman, "Beyond SES: A Resource Model of Political Participation," *American Political Science Review* 89 (June 1995): 271–294; and Sidney Verba, Kay Lehman Schlozman, and Henry E. Brady, *Voice and Equality: Civic Voluntarism in American Politics* (Cambridge, Mass.: Harvard University Press, 1995).

45. Nicholas Confessore, "For Whites Sensing Decline, Donald Trump Unleashes Words of Resistance," *New York Times*, July 14, 2016, A1; and Emma Green, "It Was Cultural Anxiety that Drove White, Working-Class Voters to Trump," *The Atlantic*, May 9, 2017, https://www.theatlantic.com/politics/archive/2017/05/white-working -class-trump-cultural-anxiety/525771/. For a more general treatment of growing white discontent amid increasing racial diversity, see Ashley Jardina, *White Identity Politics* (New York, NY: Cambridge University Press, 2019).

46. "Full Text: Trump's Comments on White Supremacists, 'Alt-Left' in Charlottesville," *Politico*, August 15, 2017, https://www.politico.com/story/2017/08 /15/full-text-trump-comments-white-supremacists-alt-left-transcript-241662

47. "Map: Protests and Rallies for George Floyd Spread Across the Country," *NBS News*, June 1, 2020, https://www.nbcnews.com/news/us-news/map-protests-ral lies-george-floyd-spread-across-country-n1220976

48. Max Cohen, "Trump: Black Lives Matter is a 'Symbol of Hate.'" *Politico*, July 1, 2020, https://www.politico.com/news/2020/07/01/trump-black-lives-matter -347051

49. Leo Shane III, "Trump Argues Confederate Base Names, Battle Flags Should Stay," *Military Times*, July 20, 2020, https://www.militarytimes.com/news/penta gon-congress/2020/07/20/trump-argues-confederate-base-names-battle-flags-should -stay/

50. Russell Vought, "Memorandum for the Heads of Executive Departments and Agencies: Training in the Federal Government," *Executive Office of the President*, September 4, 2020, https://www.whitehouse.gov/wp-content/uploads/2020/09/M-20 -34.pdf

51. Respondents were classified by the interviewer into one of the following categories: white; black/African American; white and black; other race; white and another race; black and another race; and white, black, and another race. We classi fied only respondents who were white as whites; except for Asians, respondents in the other categories were classified as blacks.

52. Of course, voter turnout levels among black voters were not always close to those of whites. In 1964, the year prior to the passage of the Voting Rights Act, the CPS reported whites were 12.2 percentage points more likely to vote than blacks. In

2012, the voter turnout rate among blacks exceeded that among whites for the first and still only time in US history: black participation was 2.1 percentage points higher than that among whites. The decline in the turnout gap between whites and blacks marks a significant change in voting behavior (and American politics generally) over the last half century.

Bernard Fraga explains that the racial gap in voting is not simply a function of disparities in resources but largely attributable to the geography of political competition. When a group is perceived to drive electoral outcomes in a particular geographic area, members of that group are more likely to turn out to vote. In geographic areas that are electorally competitive, however, the turnout gap dissipates. See Bernard L. Fraga, *The Turnout Gap: Race, Ethnicity, and Political Inequality in a Diversifying America* (New York, NY: Cambridge University Press, 2018).

53.   The church has been demonstrated to be an important mobilizer of black political participation; see Frederick C. Harris, *Something Within: Religion in African-American Political Activism* (New York: Oxford University Press, 1999). In past studies we too have shown that African Americans who regularly attend church ("once a week") are more likely to vote than those who never attend. The 2020 ANES estimates that blacks who attend church regularly were 6.6 percent more likely to turn out than those who do not attend church or do so infrequently.

54.   Benjamin Highton and Arthur L. Burris, "New Perspectives on Latino Voter Turnout in the United States," *American Politics Research* 30 (May 2002): 285–306 utilize CPS data to investigate socioeconomic, ethnic, and place-of-birth differences among Latinos. These authors find that native-born Latinos are more likely to turn out. Matt Barreto, however, using data from California, finds that Latino immigrants were more likely to vote than were native-born Latinos. Clearly this warrants further investigation. See Matt A. Barreto, "Latino Immigrants at the Polls: Foreign-born Voter Turnout in the 2002 Election," *Political Research Quarterly* 58 (March 2005): 79–86.

55.   New York Congresswoman Geraldine Ferraro was the Democratic Party's vice presidential nominee in 1984, and Hillary Clinton was the Democrat's presidential nominee in 2016. Kamala Harris was the third woman, second African American, and first person of South Asian descent to be on the ticket.

56.   Abramson, Aldrich, and Rohde, *Change and Continuity in the 2008 Elections*, 98.

57.   For an early example of this work, see M. Kent Jennings, "Another Look at the Life Cycle and Political Participation," *American Journal of Political Science* 23 (November 1979): 755–771.

58.   John B. Holbein and D. Sunshine Hillygus, *Making Young Voters: Converting Civic Attitudes into Civic Action* (New York, NY: Cambridge University Press, 2020).

59.   United States Census Bureau, "Reported Voting and Registration by Race, Hispanic Origin, Sex, and Age Groups: November 1964 to 2018," https://www2.census.gov/programs-surveys/cps/tables/time-series/voting-historical-time-series/a1.xlsx

60.   Jan E. Leighley and Jonathan Nagler, "Socioeconomic Class Bias in Turnout, 1972–1988: The Voters Remain the Same," *American Political Science Review* 86 (September 1992): 725–736.

61. See Warren E. Miller, Arthur H. Miller, and Edward J. Schneider, *American National Studies Data Sourcebook, 1952–1978* (Cambridge, Mass.: Harvard University Press, 1980), Table 5.23, 317.

62. David Macdonald, "Labor Unions and White Democratic Partisanship," *Political Behavior* 43 (June): 859–879.

63. For example, Robert D. Putnam and David E. Campbell, *American Grace: How Religion Divides and Unites Us* (New York: Simon and Schuster, 2012).

64. See the Pew Religion and Public Life Project, "The Global God Divide," https://www.pewresearch.org/global/wp-content/uploads/sites/2/2020/07/PG_2020. 07.20_Global-Religion_FINAL.pdf, and "In U.S. Decline of Christianity Continues at Rapid Pace," https://www.pewforum.org/wp-content/uploads/sites/7/2019/10/ Trends-in-Religious-Identity-and-Attendance-FOR-WEB-1.pdf. When asked "How important is religion in your life?" 82 percent of Americans said it was either "very important" or "somewhat important" in 2014. The 2019 survey records a ten percentage point decline in the importance of religion. In 2014, 52 percent of Americans reported attending religious services "weekly or more" or "once or twice a month"; that number declined to 45 percent in 2019.

65. See Dietram A. Scheufele, Matthew C. Nisbet, Dominque Brossard, and Erik C. Nisbet, "Social Structure and Citizenship: Examining the Impacts of Social Setting, Network Heterogeneity, and Informational Variables on Political Participation," *Political Communication* 21 (2004): 315–338.

66. For general treatments, see Clyde Wilcox and Lee Sigelman, "Political Mobilization in the Pews: Religious Contacting and Electoral Turnout," *Social Science Quarterly* 82 (September 2001): 524–535; and David E. Campbell, "Acts of Faith: Churches and Political Engagement," *Political Behavior* 26 (June 2004): 155–180. For an examination of the mobilizing role of churches in the African American community, see Fredrick C. Harris, "Something Within: Religion as a Mobilizer of African-American Political Activism," *Journal of Politics* 56 (February 1994): 42–68.

67. Federal law prohibits the Census Bureau from measuring religious preferences on the CPS.

68. Miller, Miller, and Schneider, *American National Data Sourcebook,* Table 5.23, 317. Between 1952 and 1976 Catholics were on average 8.0 percentage points more likely to vote in presidential elections, and between 1958 and 1988 they were 10.8 points more likely to vote in midterm elections.

69. As noted earlier, exit polls were not conducted in all states but instead were used in states that were deemed most competitive. This may have affected the estimates of the religious composition of the electorate. Consider the fact that several states with the largest Catholic populations (e.g., Louisiana, Massachusetts, and Maryland) were not included in the 2016 exit polls. Nationally aggregated responses to the exit poll are also unweighted, so the exit poll results for religion may differ from those produced by a nationally representative probability sample, such as that used by the ANES.

70. For a study of Conservative Christian mobilization in a recent US election, see J. Quin Monson and J. Baxter Oliphant, "Microtargeting and the Instrumental

Mobilization of Religious Conservatives" in David E. Campbell, ed. *A Matter of Faith: Religion in the 2004 Presidential Election* (Washington, DC: Brookings Institution, 2007).

71.   Respondents were asked, "Would you call yourself a born-again Christian, that is, have you personally had a conversion experience related to Jesus Christ?"

72.   Pew Research Center, "Religious Landscape Survey," http://www.pewforum .org/religious-landscape-study/

73.   Due to data availability issues, we were unable to construct this measure in 2012. Our measure for 2016, which does not include an indicator of the respondent's frequency of prayer, differs slightly from that used in 2008 and earlier. For details regarding the construction of the religious commitment measure in earlier studies, see Abramson, Aldrich, and Rohde, *Change and Continuity in the 2008 Elections*, Chapter 4, note 49.

74.   Kenneth D. Wald, *Religion and Politics in the United States*, 4th ed. (Lanham, Md.: Rowman and Littlefield, 2003), 161.

75.   R. Stephen Warner, *New Wine in Old Wineskins: Evangelicals and Liberals in a Small-Town Church* (Berkeley: University of California Press, 1977), 173.

76.   The branching questions used to classify respondents into specific denomi-national categories were changed in 2008, and therefore it is not possible to repli-cate our analyses of the 1992, 1996, 2000, and 2004 categories. In creating these new classifications, we relied largely on the Pew Forum on Religion and Public Life, *U.S. Religious Landscape Survey: Religious Affiliation, Diverse and Dynamic* (Washington, DC: Pew Forum on Religion and Public Life, 2008), 12. In addition, we were assisted by Corwin D. Smidt. Our classification for 2016 used the following procedures. We used the variable V161248 in the 2016 ANES survey to determine the respondent's denomination. Codes 2, 3, 4, 6, 9, 13, 14, 17, and 20 for this vari-able were classified as mainline; codes 1, 8, 12, 15, 16, 18, and 19 were classified as evangelical. In 2020, ANES variable V201458x distinguishes between mainline and evangelical Protestants.

77.   Wolfinger and Rosenstone, *Who Votes?*, 102.

78.   For the effect of education on political knowledge and political awareness, see Michael X. Delli Carpini, and Scott Keeter, *What Americans Know about Politics and Why It Matters* (New Haven, CT: Yale University Press, 1996); and John R. Zaller, *The Nature and Origins of Mass Opinion* (New York: Cambridge University Press, 1992), respectively. Henry E. Brady, Sidney Verba, and Kay Lehman Schlozman, "Beyond SES: A Resource Model of Political Participation," *American Political Science Review* 89 (June 1995): 271–294, discuss how education enhances both political engagement and civic skills.

79.   Richard A. Brody, "The Puzzle of Political Participation in America," in *The New American Political System*, ed. Anthony King (Washington, DC: American Enterprise Institute, 1978), 287–324.

80.   Robert D. Putnam makes a similar argument, claiming that political disen-gagement was largely the result of the baby-boom generation and that generational succession reduced other forms of civic activity as well. Putnam writes: "The declines in church attendance, voting, political interest, campaign activities, associational

membership and social trusts are attributable almost entirely to generational succession." See Robert D. Putnam, *Bowling Along: The Collapse and Revival of American Community* (New York: Simon and Schuster, 2000), 265.

81.   Steven J. Rosenstone and John Mark Hansen, *Mobilization, Participation, and Democracy in America* (New York: Macmillan, 1993), 214–215.

82.   George I. Balch, "Multiple Indicators in Survey Research: The Concept 'Sense of Political Efficacy,'" *Political Methodology* 1 (Spring 1974): 1–43. For an extensive discussion of feelings of political efficacy, see Paul R. Abramson, *Political Attitudes in America: Formation and Change* (San Francisco: W. H. Freeman, 1983): 135–189.

83.   Our first analysis studied the decline of turnout between 1960 and 1980. See Paul R. Abramson, John H. Aldrich, and David W. Rohde, *Change and Continuity in the 1980 Elections*, rev. ed. (Washington, DC: CQ Press, 1983), 85–87. For a more detailed analysis using probability procedures, see Paul R. Abramson and John H. Aldrich, "The Decline of Electoral Participation in America," *American Political Science Review* 76 (September 1982): 502–521. For our analyses from 1984 through 2008, see Abramson, Aldrich, and Rohde, *Change and Continuity in the 2008 Elections*, 105–108 and Chapter 4, note 73.

84.   ANES respondents are asked, "Generally speaking, do you usually think of yourself as a Republican, a Democrat, an Independent, or what?" Persons who call themselves Republicans are asked, "Would you call yourself a strong Republican or a not very strong Republican?" Those who call themselves Democrats are asked, "Would you call yourself a strong Democrat or a not very strong Democrat?" Those who called themselves independents, named another party, or who had no preference were asked, "Do you think of yourself as closer to the Republican party or to the Democratic party?"

85.   The seminal work on party identification is Angus Campbell, Philip E. Converse, Warren E. Miller, and Donald E. Stokes, *The American Voter* (New York: Wiley, 1960), 120–167.

86.   See Morris P. Fiorina, "The Voting Decision: Instrumental and Expressive Aspects," *Journal of Politics* 38 (May 1976): 390–413; and John H. Aldrich, "Rational Choice and Turnout," *American Journal of Political Science* 37 (February 1993): 246–278.

87.   For a detailed discussion of party identification from 1952 to 2016, along with tables showing the distribution of party identification among whites and blacks during these years, see chapter 6 in this volume as well as the appendix.

88.   As Steven E. Finkel notes, the relationship between political efficacy and political participation is likely reciprocal. Not only do feelings of efficacy increase the likelihood of participation, participation increases individuals' feelings of efficacy. See Steven E. Finkel, "Reciprocal Effects of Participation and Political Efficacy: A Panel Analysis," *American Journal of Political Science* 29 (November 1985): 891–913.

89.   See Abramson and Aldrich, "The Decline of Electoral Participation in America," 515.

90.   The procedure uses the 1960 distribution of partisans by levels of efficacy as our base, thus assuming that levels of turnout for each subgroup (e.g., strong partisan/high efficacy and strong partisan/medium efficacy) would have remained the same if

partisanship and efficacy had not declined. We multiply the size of each subgroup (set at 1960 levels) times the proportion of the whites who reported voting in each subgroups in the 2016 election. We then sum the products and divide by the sum of the subgroup sizes. The procedure is detailed in Abramson, *Political Attitudes in America: Formation and Change*, 296.

91. For a discussion of political trust, see Abramson, *Political Attitudes in America*, 193–238. For a more recent discussion, see Marc J. Hetherington, *Why Trust Matters: Declining Political Trust and the Demise of American Liberalism* (Princeton, NJ: Princeton University Press, 2005).

Russell J. Dalton reports a decline in confidence in politicians and government in fifteen of sixteen democracies. Although many of the trends are not statistically significant, the overall decline is impressive. Dalton's report includes results from the ANES, where the trend toward declining confidence is unlikely to occur by chance on two of the three questions. See Russell J. Dalton, *Democratic Challenges, Democratic Choices: The Erosion of Political Support in Advanced Industrial Democracies* (Oxford: Oxford University Press, 2004), 28–32.

92. Respondents were asked, "How much of the time do you think you can trust the government in Washington to do what is right—just about always, most of the time, or only some of the time?"

93. This question was asked of a randomly selected half-sample in 2008.

94. See Brad T. Gomez, Thomas G. Hansford, and George A. Krause, "The Republicans Should Pray for Rain: Weather, Turnout, and Voting in U.S. Presidential Elections," *Journal of Politics* 69 (August 2007): 649–663.

95. The recent proliferation in electoral laws allowing early voting is likely to diminish the chances that bad weather on election day will reduce voter turnout. Laws that allow citizens to vote by mail, such as those found in Colorado, Oregon, and Washington, make election-day weather inconsequential.

96. W. Dana Flanders, William D. Flanders, and Michael Goodman, "The Association of Voter Turnout with County-level Coronavirus Disease 2019 Occurrence Early in the Pandemic," *Annals of Epidemiology* 49 (September): 42–49.

97. In the past half century, a handful of elections could be classified—based upon pre-election polling—as "dead heats" going into election day. Recall from chapter 3, for example, that the average of nine pre-election polls in 2012 showed a virtual tie between Obama and Romney. In contrast, in 1964, the final Gallup Poll before the election predicted a twenty-eight-point victory in the popular vote for Lyndon Johnson over Barry Goldwater.

98. See Anthony Downs, *An Economic Theory of Democracy* (New York: Harper and Row, 1957); and William H. Riker and Peter C. Ordeshook, "A Theory of the Calculus of Voting," *American Political Science Review* 72 (March 1968): 25–42.

99. These are Colorado, Florida, Iowa, Michigan, Minnesota, Nevada, New Hampshire, New Mexico, North Carolina, Ohio, Pennsylvania, Virginia, and Wisconsin.

100. The use of randomized field experiments in political science pre-dates the work of Gerber and Green, although these authors are certainly responsible for the revived interest in the research design in the discipline. In the 1920s, Harold Gosnell sent postcards to randomly assigned nonvoters emphasizing the importance of voter registration before the 1924 presidential election. Gosnell found a significant increase

in voter registration among those who received the postcard treatment compared to those in his control group who received nothing. In the 1950s Samuel Eldersveld used random assignment to test the effectiveness of mail, phone, and in-person canvassing in a local mayoral race. It would be decades before another field experiment design was published in the academic journals of political science. See Harold F. Gosnell, *Getting Out the Vote* (Chicago: University of Chicago Press, 1927); and Samuel J. Eldersveld, "Experimental Propaganda Techniques and Voting Behavior," *American Political Science Review* 50 (March 1956): 154–165.

101. See Alan S. Gerber and Donald P. Green, *Field Experiments: Design, Analysis, and Interpretation* (New York: Norton, 2012), for an introduction to field experimentation in the social sciences.

102. See Donald P. Green and Alan S. Gerber, *Get Out the Vote: How to Increase Voter Turnout*, 2nd ed. (Washington, DC: Brookings Institution Press, 2008), for a summary of findings in this research program.

103. This is not to say that it is impossible to make causal inferences from survey data. Panel designs, where survey respondents are interviewed repeatedly at multiple time periods, can establish temporal order and provide the best opportunity to establish causation.

104. Respondents were asked, "The political parties try to talk to as many people as they can to get them to vote for their candidate. Did anyone from the political parties call or come around to talk with you about the campaign this year?"

105. Lisa Desjardins and Daniel Bush, "The Trump Campaign Has a Ground-Game Problem," *PBS Newshour*, August 30, 2016, http://www.pbs.org/newshour/updates/trump-campaign-has-ground-game-problem/; Chris Cillizza, "No, Donald Trump—You Still Don't Have a Ground Game," *Washington Post*, September 2, 2016, https://www.washing tonpost.com/news/the-fix/wp/2016/09/01/donald-trump-has-1-field-office-open-in-all -of-florida-thats-a-total-disaster/?utm_term=.13b7 10ba1cc7; and Susan Milligan, "The Fight on the Ground," *US News and World Report*, October 14, 2016, https://www.usnews.com/news/the-report/articles/2016-10 -14/donald-trump-abandons-the-ground-game

106. Seymour Martin Lipset, *Political Man: The Social Bases of Politics*, exp. ed. (Baltimore: Johns Hopkins University Press, 1981), 226–229.

107. See James DeNardo, "Turnout and the Vote: The Joke's on the Democrats," *American Political Science Review* 74 (December 1980): 406–420; and Thomas G. Hansford and Brad T. Gomez, "Estimating the Electoral Effects of Voter Turnout," *American Political Science Review* 104 (May 2010): 268–288.

108. In addition to the partisan effect of high turnout, Hansford and Gomez argue that incumbents from both parties lose vote share as turnout becomes higher, suggesting that peripheral voters, that is, those who vote irregularly, are less supportive of incumbents than dedicated voters.

109. As reported by the National Conference of State Legislatures, see http://www .ncsl.org/legislatures-elections/elections/voter-id.aspx

110. In 2013 the US Supreme Court, in a 5–4 vote, struck down provisions—Sections 4(b) and 5—of the 1965 Voting Rights Act (VRA) that required several states with histories of racial discrimination in voting (mostly southern states, including North

Carolina) to obtain "preclearance" from the federal government before changing their voting laws or practices. See *Shelby County v. Holder*, 570 U.S. 2 (2013). Following this decision, several states—Alabama, Arizona, Arkansas, North Carolina, Ohio, Wisconsin, and Texas—once covered by the VRA's preclearance requirements moved swiftly to alter their election laws. All of these states are governed by Republicans.

111. Robert Barnes and Ann E. Marimow, "Appeals Court Strikes Down North Carolina's Voter-ID Law," *Washington Post*, July 29, 2016, https://www.washing-tonpost.com/local/public-safety/appeals-court-strikes-down-north-carolinas-voter-id -law/2016/07/29/810b5844-4f72-11e6-aa14-e0c1087f7583_story.html?utm_term= .0431a0552c6a

112. "Supreme Court Rejects Appeal to Reinstate North Carolina Voter ID Law," *Fox News*, May 15, 2017, http://www.foxnews.com/politics/2017/05/15/supreme -court-rejects-appeal-over-nc-voter-id-law.html

113. "Voting Laws Roundup: October 2021," *Brennan Center for Justice*, October 4, 2021, https://www.brennancenter.org/our-work/research-reports/voting -laws-roundup-october-2021

114. See Campbell, Converse, Miller, and Stokes, *The American Voter*, 96–115.

115. The kind and number of issues used varied from election to election. We used only issues on which respondents were asked to state their own positions and where they thought the major-party candidates were located. See table 7.4 for the number of issues used in each election between 1980 and 2008.

116. Our issue scale differs slightly from the one used in our 2008 analysis, which included seven items. Since 2012, the ANES no longer asks respondents' opinions regarding the role of women in society. Consequently this item has been removed from our scale.

117. In their county-level analysis of the electoral effect of voter turnout in the 1944 through 2000 presidential elections, Hansford and Gomez use simulations from their statistical model to demonstrate that a 4 percent swing in turnout (from 2 percent below to 2 percent above actual turnout) leads to an average change in Democratic vote share at the national level of just under one percentage point. However, small changes are not necessarily trivial. The authors go on to show that varying turnout from two points above and below observed values causes an average change of approximately twenty Electoral College votes per presidential election in nonsouthern states. See Hansford and Gomez, "Estimating the Electoral Effects of Voter Turnout," 284.

118. For the most influential statement of this argument, see Wolfinger and Rosenstone, *Who Votes?*, 108–114.

Chapter 5

1. For a classic treatment of the subject, see M. Kent Jennings and Richard G. Niemi, *Generations and Politics: A Panel Study of Young Adults and their Parents* (Princeton, NJ: Princeton University Press, 1981).

2. See Larry M. Bartels, "What's the Matter with *What's the Matter with Kansas?*" *Quarterly Journal of Political Science* 1 (2006): 201–226.

3. See Paul R. Abramson, John H. Aldrich, and David W. Rohde, *Change and Continuity in the 2008 and 2010 Elections* (Washington, DC: CQ Press, 2012), 116–141.

4. The social characteristics used in this chapter are the same as those used in chapter 4. The variables are described in the notes to that chapter.

5. In 2020, the National Election Pool consortium was composed of ABC News, CBS News, CNN, and NBC News.

6. As noted in chapter 4, note 37, the exit polls are not a representative sample of the nation. The exit polls were conducted separately in twenty-three states. In-person exit poll interviews of election-day voters represent 33 percent of the vote, in-person exit polls of early voters represent 24 percent, and the remainder of interviews were conducted by phone, 43 percent, a much higher percentage than other elections given the high prevalence of vote by mail in 2020. We draw on 2020 exit poll reports from CNN (https://www.cnn.com/election/2020/exit-polls/president/national-results). For a discussion of the 2016 exit polls, see Abramson, Aldrich, Gomez, and Rohde, *Change and Continuity in the 2016 Elections*. Exit polls have three main advantages: (1) they are less expensive to conduct than the multistage probability samples conducted by the American National Election Studies; (2) because of their lower cost, a large number of people can be sampled; and (3) because part of the sample are selected to be interviewed as they leave the polling stations, the vast majority of respondents have actually voted. But these surveys also have four disadvantages: (1) organizations that conduct exit polls must now take into account the growing number of voters who vote early—about 69 percent of voters in 2020; (2) the self-administered polls used for respondents leaving the polls must be relatively brief; (3) it is difficult to supervise the fieldwork to ensure that interviewers are using the proper procedures to select respondents; and (4) these studies are of relatively little use in studying turnout because persons who do not vote are not sampled. For a discussion of the procedures used to conduct exit polls and their limitations, see Albert H. Cantril, *The Opinion Connection: Polling, Politics, and the Press* (Washington, DC: CQ Press, 1991), 142–144, 216–218.

7. This brief discussion cannot do justice to the complexities of black electoral participation. For an important study based on the 1984 ANES survey of blacks, see Patricia Gurin, Shirley Hatchett, and James S. Jackson, *Hope and Independence: Blacks' Response to Electoral and Party Politics* (New York: Russell Sage Foundation, 1989). For two important studies that use this survey, see Michael C. Dawson, *Behind the Mule: Race and Class in African American Politics* (Princeton, NJ: Princeton University Press, 1994); and Katherine Tate, *From Politics to Protest: The New Black Voter in American Elections* (Cambridge, MA: Harvard University Press, 1994). For a recent examination of the black electorate, see Ismail K. White and Chryl N. Laird, *Steadfast Democrats: How Social Forces Shape Black Political Behavior* (Princeton, NJ: Princeton University Press, 2020).

8. For a review of research on Latinos as well as African Americans, see Paula McClain and John D. Garcia, "Expanding Disciplinary Boundaries: Black, Latino, and Racial Minority Groups in Political Science," in *Political Science: The State of the Discipline II*, ed. Ada W. Finifter (Washington, DC: American Political Science

Association, 1993), 247–279. For analyses of Latino voting in the 2008 and 2012 elections with an eye toward the future of Latino politics, see Matt Barreto and Gary Segura, *Latino America: How America's Most Dynamic Population Is Poised to Transform the Politics of the Nation* (New York: Public Affairs Books, 2014). For a review, see John D. Garcia, "Latinos and Political Behavior: Defining Community to Examine Critical Complexities," in *The Oxford Handbook of American Elections and Political Behavior*, ed. Jan E. Leighley (New York: Oxford University Press, 2010), 397–414.

9.   Trump's comments about Mexican immigrants came on June 16, 2015, during the announcement of his presidential candidacy. For a transcript of his full remarks, see https://www.washingtonpost.com/news/post-politics/wp/2015/06/16/full-text-donald -trump-announces-a-presidential-bid/?utm_term=.826619831a93

10.   https://www.usatoday.com/story/news/politics/2019/02/07/democrats-trump -administration-family-separation-policy-border-immigration/2794324002/ Accessed August, 17, 2021.

11.   For more discussion of the voting behavior of Asian Americans and Pacific Islanders, see Wong, Janelle S., S. Karthick Ramakrishnan, Taeku Lee, and Jane Junn, *Asian American Political Participation: Emerging Constituents and Their Political Identities* (New York, NY: Russell Sage Foundation, 2011). For additional data, see aapidata.com.

12.   For three reviews of research on women in politics, see Susan J. Carroll and Linda M. Zerelli, "Feminist Challenges to Political Science," in Finifter, *Political Science: The State of the Discipline II*, 55–76; Nancy Burns, "Gender: Public Opinion and Political Action," in Katznelson and Milner, *Political Science: The State of the Discipline*, 462–487; and Kira Sanbonmastu, "Organizing American Politics, Organizing Gender," in Leighley, *Oxford Handbook of American Elections and Political Behavior*, 415–432.

13.   The gender gap in 1980, coupled with Ronald Reagan's opposition to abortion rights and the Equal Rights Amendment, led the former president of the National Organization for Women, Eleanor Smeal, to write a report for the Democratic National Committee detailing how Democrats could take back the White House if the party placed a woman on the ticket in the next election. In 1984, Democratic Congresswoman Geraldine Ferraro became the first female vice-presidential nominee in US history. Reagan won reelection in a landslide.

14.   See Abramson, Aldrich, and Rohde, *Change and Continuity in the 1980 and 1982 Elections* (Washington, DC: CQ Press, 1983), 290.

15.   Jane Junn, "The Trump Majority: White Womanhood and the Making of Female Voters in the U.S." *Politics, Groups, and Identities* 5 (2017): 343–352, p. 345.

16.   The ANES survey reports six types of marital status: married, divorced, separated, widowed, never married, and partners who are not married.

17.   Respondents were asked, "Do you consider yourself to be heterosexual or straight, homosexual or gay (lesbian), or bisexual?"

18.   Abramson, Aldrich, and Rohde, *Change and Continuity in the 2004 and 2006 Elections* (Washington, DC: CQ Press, 2007), 124–127. For cross-national evidence, see Ronald Inglehart, *Modernization and Postmodernization: Cultural, Economic,*

and Political Change in 43 Societies (Princeton, NJ: Princeton University Press, 1997), 255; and Russell J. Dalton, *Citizen Politics: Public Opinion and Political Parties in Advanced Industrial Democracies*, 5th ed. (Washington, DC: CQ Press, 2008), 145–152.

19. Jeffrey M. Stonecash, *Class and Party in American Politics* (Boulder, CO: Westview Press, 2000), 87–121; Larry M. Bartels, *Unequal Democracy: The Political Economy of the New Gilded Age* (New York: Russell Sage Foundation, 2008), 64–126.

20. For the single best summary, see Kenneth D. Wald and Allison Calhoun-Brown, *Religion and Politics in the United States*, 6th ed. (Lanham, MD: Rowman and Littlefield, 2011). For a discussion of religion and politics in a comparative context, see Pippa Norris and Ronald Inglehart, *Sacred and Secular: Religion and Politics Worldwide* (Cambridge, UK: Cambridge University Press, 2004).

21. David E. Campbell, ed. *A Matter of Faith: Religion in the 2004 Presidential Election* (Washington, DC: The Brookings Institution), 1.

22. See Robert D. Putnam and David E. Campbell, *American Grace: How Religion Divides and Unites Us* (New York: Simon and Schuster, 2010).

23. Pew Research's Religious Landscape Study estimates that only 3 percent of American Catholics are African American. Thus Latinos are the main contributor to nonwhite support among Catholics. See http://www.pewforum.org/religious-land-scape-study/religious-tradition/catholic/

24. The question, which was asked to all Christians, was "Would you call yourself a born-again Christian; that is, have you personally had a conversion experience related to Jesus Christ?" This question was not asked in the 2004 ANES survey.

25. Lyman A. Kellstedt, "An Agenda for Future Research," in *Rediscovering the Religious Factor in American Politics*, ed. David C. Leege and Lyman A. Kellstedt (Armonk, NY: M. E. Sharpe, 1993), 293–299.

26. https://www.pewresearch.org/fact-tank/2015/05/13/a-closer-look-at-americas-rapidly-growing-religious-nones/. Accessed August 25, 2021.

27. Morris P. Fiorina and his colleagues have pointed out that ANES surveys suggest that the relationship between church attendance and the tendency to vote Republican was substantially higher in 1992 than in 1972, although the relationship leveled off or declined slightly between 1992 and 2004. See Morris P. Fiorina, with Samuel J. Abrams and Jeremy C. Pope, *Culture War? The Myth of a Polarized America*, 2nd ed. (New York: Pearson/Longman, 2006), 134.

28. Robert Axelrod, "Where the Votes Come From: An Analysis of Electoral Coalitions," *American Political Science Review* 66 (March 1972): 11–20. Axelrod updates his results through the 1984 elections. For his most recent estimate, including results from 1952 to 1980, see Robert Axelrod, "Presidential Coalitions in 1984," *American Political Science Review* 80 (March 1986): 281–284. Using Axelrod's categories, Nelson W. Polsby estimates the social composition of the Democratic and Republican presidential coalitions between 1952 and 2000. See Nelson W. Polsby and Aaron Wildavsky, *Presidential Elections: Strategies and Structures of American Politics*, 11th ed. (Lanham, MD: Rowman and Littlefield, 2004), 32. For an update through 2004, see Nelson W. Polsby, Aaron Wildavsky, with David A. Hopkins,

Presidential Elections: Strategies and Structures in American Politics, 12th ed. (Lanham, MD: Rowman and Littlefield, 2008), 28.

29.   John R. Petrocik, *Party Coalitions: Realignment and the Decline of the New Deal Party System* (Chicago: University of Chicago Press, 1981).

30.   Harold W. Stanley, William T. Bianco, and Richard G. Niemi, "Partisanship and Group Support over Time: A Multivariate Analysis," *American Political Science Review* 80 (September 1986): 969–976. Stanley and his colleagues assess the independent contribution that group membership makes toward Democratic loyalties after controls are introduced for membership in other pro-Democratic groups. For an update and an extension through 2004, see Harold W. Stanley and Richard G. Niemi, "Partisanship, Party Coalitions, and Group Support, 1952–2004," *Presidential Studies Quarterly* 36 (June 2006): 172–188. For an alternative approach, see Robert S. Erikson, Thomas D. Lancaster, and David W. Romero, "Group Components of the Presidential Vote, 1952–1984," *Journal of Politics* 51 (May 1989): 337–346. For Democratic groups in the contemporary political environment, see Douglas J. Ahler and Guarav Sood, "The Parties in our Heads: Misperceptions about Party Composition and their Consequences," *Journal of Politics* 80 (April 2018): 964–981.

31.   See Axelrod, "Where the Votes Come From."

32.   The NORC survey, based on 2,564 civilians, used a quota sample that does not follow the probability procedures used by the ANES. Following the procedures used at the time, southern blacks were not sampled. Because the NORC survey overrepresented upper-income groups and the middle and upper-middle classes, it cannot be used to estimate the contribution of social groups to the Democratic and Republican presidential coalitions.

33.   Abramson, *Generational Change in American Politics,* 65–68.

34.   As Figure 5.1 shows, Bill Clinton did win a majority of the white major-party vote in 1992 and 1996.

35.   Racial voting, as well as our other measures of social cleavage, is affected by including Wallace voters with Nixon voters in 1968, Anderson voters with Reagan voters in 1980, Perot voters with Bush voters in 1992, and Perot voters with Dole voters in 1996. For the effects of including these independent or third-party candidates, see Abramson, Aldrich, and Rohde, *Change and Continuity in the 1996 and 1998 Elections* (Washington, DC: CQ Press, 1999), 102, 104–106, 108, and 111.

36.   The statements about low turnout in 1996 are true regardless of whether one measures turnout based on the voting-age population or the voting-eligible population. Turnout among the voting-eligible population fell about 9 percentage points between 1960 and 1996. And even though black turnout fell in 1996, it was still well above its levels before the Voting Rights Act of 1965.

37.   As we explain in chapter 3, we consider the South to include the eleven states of the old Confederacy. Because the 1944 NORC survey and the 1948 University of Michigan Survey Research Center survey did not record the respondents' states of residence, we cannot include these years in our analysis of regional differences among the white electorate.

38.   See, for example, chapter 3, where we compare Kennedy's black support in the South in 1960 with Carter's in 1976.

39.   Officially known as the Labor-Management Relations Act, this legislation, passed in 1947, qualified or amended much of the National Labor Relations Act of 1935 (known as the Wagner Act). Union leaders argued that the Taft-Hartley Act placed unwarranted restrictions on organized labor. This act was passed by the Republican-controlled Eightieth Congress, vetoed by Truman, and passed over his veto.

40.   The Bureau of Labor Statistics estimates that in 2020, 10.8 percent of wage and salary workers are members of union, down from four years earlier. African American workers have a higher rate of union membership (12.7 percent) than white workers (11.5 percent). See Bureau of Labor Statistics, "Economic News Release: Union Members Summary," January 22, 2021, https://www.bls.gov/news.release/union2.nr0.htm

41.   This percentage may well be too low. According to the 2008 pool poll, Obama received 53 percent of the vote. Members of union households made up 21 percent of the electorate, and 50 percent voted for Obama. These numbers thus suggest that 23 percent of Obama's vote in 2008 came from members of union households. Even if one takes into account that not all these union voters were white, these numbers suggest that about one in five of Obama's votes in 2008 came from union households.

42.   Exit polls conducted between 1972 and 2020 show the same pattern. In all thirteen elections Jews have been more likely to vote Democratic than white Catholics, and white Catholics have been more likely to vote Democratic than white Protestants.

43.   For a discussion of the impact of religion on the 1960 election, see Philip E. Converse, "Religion and Politics: The 1960 Election," in *Elections and the Political Order*, ed. Angus Campbell et al. (New York: Wiley, 1967), 96–124.

44.   The 1976 Democratic Party Platform can be found at http://www.presidency.ucsb.edu/ws/?pid=29606

45.   In our sample, 39 percent of Latinos identify themselves as Catholic.

46.   Estimates from the Pew Forum on Religion and Public Life, *U.S. Religious Landscape Survey*, https://www.pewforum.org/2021/05/11/the-size-of-the-u-s-jewish-population/

47.   States are listed in descending order according to their estimated number of Jews.

48.   Another interesting comparison is the Catholic vote in 1960 and 2004. See J. Matthew Wilson, "The Changing Catholic Voter: Comparing Responses to John Kennedy in 1960 and John Kerry in 2004," in *A Matter of Faith*, ed., David E. Campbell (Washington, DC: Brookings Institution Press, 2007).

49.   Robert Huckfeldt and Carol Weitzel Kohfeld provide strong evidence that Democratic appeals to blacks weakened the party's support among working-class whites. See their *Race and the Decline of Class in American Politics* (Urbana: University of Illinois Press, 1989).

50.   For evidence on this point, see Paul R. Abramson, *Political Attitudes in America: Formation and Change* (San Francisco: W. H. Freeman, 1983), 65–68.

51.   Edward G. Carmines and James A. Stimson, *Issue Evolution: Race and the Transformation of American Politics* (Princeton, NJ: Princeton University Press,

1999). For a critique of their thesis, see Alan I. Abramowitz, "Issue Evolution Reconsidered: Racial Attitudes and Partisanship among the American Electorate," *American Journal of Political Science* 38 (February 1994): 1–24.

Chapter 6

1. Angus Campbell et al., *The American Voter* (New York: Wiley, 1960); Warren E. Miller, "Party Identification, Realignment, and Party Voting: Back to the Basics," *American Political Science Review* 85 (June 1991): 557–568; Warren E. Miller and J. Merrill Shanks, *The New American Voter* (Cambridge, Mass.: Harvard University Press, 1996).

2. Ibid., 121.

3. For the full wording of the party identification questions, see chapter 4, note 83. Note how simple this scientific advance was. They took a long-running question originally developed for the Gallup Poll survey and added the questions about "strength" of partisans and "party leanings" of independents. A simple measure of a rich theoretical concept can make a major difference.

4. For evidence of the relatively high level of partisan stability among individuals from 1965 to 1982, see M. Kent Jennings and Gregory B. Markus, "Partisan Orientations over the Long Haul: Results from the Three-Wave Political Socialization Panel Study," *American Political Science Review* 78 (December 1984): 1000–1018, and see Laura Stoker and M. Kent Jennings, "Of Time and the Development of Partisan Polarization," *American Journal of Political Science* 52 (July 2008): 619–635, which cover 1965 to 1997.

5. V. O. Key, Jr., *The Responsible Electorate* (Cambridge, MA: Belknap Press of Harvard University Press, 1966).

6. Morris P. Fiorina, "An Outline for a Model of Party Choice," *American Journal of Political Science* 21 (August 1977): 601–625; Morris P. Fiorina, *Retrospective Voting in American National Elections* (New Haven, CT: Yale University Press, 1981).

7. Benjamin I. Page, *Choices and Echoes in Presidential Elections: Rational Man and Electoral Democracy* (Chicago: University of Chicago Press, 1978), provides evidence of this. Anthony Downs, *An Economic Theory of Democracy* (New York: Harper and Row, 1957), develops a theoretical logic for such consistency in party stances on issues and ideology over time. For more recent theoretical and empirical developments, see John H. Aldrich, *Why Parties? A Second Look* (Chicago: University of Chicago Press, 2011).

8. See Christopher H. Achen, "Parental Socialization and Rational Party Identification," *Political Behavior* 24, no. 2 (2002): 151–170.

9. Robert S. Erikson, Michael B. MacKuen, and James A. Stimson, *The Macro Polity* (Cambridge: Cambridge University Press, 2002).

10. Donald P. Green, Bradley Palmquist, and Eric Schickler, *Partisan Hearts and Minds: Political Parties and the Social Identities of Voters* (New Haven, CT: Yale University Press, 2002).

11. See, for example, Donald P. Green, Bradley Palmquist, and Eric Schickler, "Macropartisanship: A Replication and Critique," *American Political Science Review* 92 (December 1998): 883–899; and Robert S., Erikson, Michael B. MacKuen, and James A. Stimson, "What Moves Macropartisanship: A Reply to Green, Palmquist, and Schickler," *American Political Science Review* 92 (December 1998): 901–912.

12. Douglas W. Rae and Michael Taylor, *The Analysis of Political Cleavages* (New Haven, CT: Yale University Press, 1970); Michael Taylor and Douglas Rae, "An Analysis of Crosscutting between Political Cleavages," *Comparative Politics* 1, no. 4 (July 1969): 534–547.

13. See, for example, Nicholas T. Davis, Samara Klar, and Chritopher R. Weber, "Affective Consistency and Sorting," *Social Science Quarterly* 100 (2019): 2477–2494.

14. There is some controversy about how to classify these independent leaners. Some argue that they are mainly "hidden" partisans who should be considered identifiers. For the strongest statement of this position, see Bruce E. Keith, David B. Magleby, Candice J. Nelson, Elizabeth A. Orr, and Mark C. Westlye, *The Myth of the Independent Voter* (Berkeley: University of California Press, 1992). In our view, however, the evidence on the proper classification of independent leaners is mixed. On balance, the evidence suggests that they are more partisan than independents with no partisan leanings but less partisan than weak partisans. See Paul R. Abramson, *Political Attitudes in America: Formation and Change* (San Francisco: W. H. Freeman, 1983). For an excellent discussion of this question, see Herbert B. Asher, "Voting Behavior Research in the 1980s: An Examination of Some Old and New Problem Areas," in *Political Science: The State of the Discipline*, ed. Ada W. Finifter (Washington, DC: American Political Science Association, 1983), 357–360. See also Samara Klar and Yanna Krupnikov, *Independent Politics: How American Disdain for Political Parties Leads to Political Inaction* (New York: Cambridge University Press, 2016).

15. Martin P. Wattenberg, *The Decline of American Political Parties, 1952–1996* (Cambridge, MA: Harvard University Press, 1998).

16. Gary C. Jacobson, "The 2008 Presidential and Congressional Elections: Anti-Bush Referendum and Prospects for a Democratic Majority," *Political Science Quarterly* 124 (Spring 2009): 1–20; Gary C. Jacobson, "The Effects of the George W. Bush Presidency on Partisan Attitudes," *Presidential Studies Quarterly* 39 (June 2009): 172–209.

17. For explanation on this point, see Paul R. Abramson and Charles W. Ostrom, Jr., "Macropartisanship: An Empirical Reassessment," *American Political Science Review* 86 (March 1991): 181–192; and Paul R. Abramson and Charles W. Ostrom, Jr., "Question Wording and Partisanship: Change and Continuity in Party Loyalties during the 1992 Election Campaign," *Public Opinion Quarterly* 58 (Spring 1994): 2148.

18. See Abramson, Aldrich, and Rohde, *Change and Continuity in the 2004 and 2006 Elections*, 186–192.

19. The ANES did not conduct a congressional election survey in 2006.

20. In the November 1–4, 2012 Gallup Poll, in contrast, they report 12 percent independent leaners for Republicans and 15 percent for Democrats. See http://www .gallup.com/poll/15370/party-affiliation.aspx

21.   Ismail K. White and Chryl N. Laird, *Steadfast Democrats: How Social Forces Shape Black Political Behavior* (Princeton, NJ: Princeton University Press, 2020).

22.   For evidence on the decline of Republican Party loyalties among older blacks between 1962 and 1964, see Paul R. Abramson, *Generational Change in American Politics* (Lexington, MA: D.C. Heath, 1975), 65–69. For a long-term historical perspective in the South, see John H. Aldrich and John D. Griffin, *Why Parties Matter: Political Competition and Democracy in the American South* (Chicago: University of Chicago Press, 2018).

23.   For the results of the white vote by party identification for the three leading candidates in 1968, 1980, 1992, and 1996, see Abramson, Aldrich, and Rohde, *Change and Continuity in the 1996 and 1998 Elections*, 186–187. Among blacks there is virtually no relationship between party identification and the vote. Even the small number of blacks who identify as Republicans usually either do not vote or vote for the Democratic presidential candidate.

24.   See also Larry M. Bartels, "Partisanship and Voting Behavior, 1952–1996," *American Journal of Political Science* 44 (January 2000): 35–50.

25.   Aldrich and Griffin, *Why Parties Matter*.

26.   https://www.pewresearch.org/politics/2015/04/07/a-deep-dive-into-party -affiliation/, Accessed September 12, 2021.

27.   See Matthew Levendusky, *The Partisan Sort: How Liberals Became Democrats and Conservatives Became Republicans* (Chicago: University of Chicago Press, 2009).

28.   An important illustration is that since 1952, presidents have often won reelection with landslide elections, or at least they did, such as Eisenhower in 1956, Johnson in a quasi-reelection in 1964, Nixon in 1972, and Regan in 1984. Since then, however, second elections have been losses (the senior Bush in 1992) or wins by considerably less than landslide proportions (Clinton in 1996, Bush in 2004, and Obama in 2012). That is because, like Jacobson, "2008 Presidential and Congressional Elections"; and Jacobson, "Effects of the George W. Bush Presidency," show, for presidential approval measures, presidents can no longer win support to any significant degree from out-party partisans.

29.   And with so few pure independents (with leaners voting like partisans, as we have seen), there are few truly uncommitted voters for parties and candidates to try to woo to their side.

Chapter 7

1.   This set of attitudes was first formulated and tested extensively in Angus Campbell et al., *The American Voter* (New York: Wiley, 1960), using data from what are now called the ANES surveys. The authors based their conclusions primarily on data from a survey of the 1956 presidential election, a rematch between Democrat Adlai Stevenson and Republican (and this time the incumbent) Dwight Eisenhower. Recently Michael S. Lewis-Beck, William G. Jacoby, Helmut Norpoth, and Herbert

F. Weisberg applied similar methods to data from 2000 and 2004. See their *The American Voter Revisited* (Ann Arbor: University of Michigan Press, 2008).

2.   See, for example, Wendy M. Rahn et al., "A Social-Cognitive Model of Candidate Appraisal," in *Information and Democratic Processes,* ed. John A. Ferejohn and James H. Kuklinski (Urbana: University of Illinois Press, 1990), 136–159, and sources cited therein.

3.   For the most extensive explication of the theory and tests in various electoral settings, see Gary W. Cox, *Making Votes Count: Strategic Coordination in the World's Electoral Systems* (New York: Cambridge University Press, 1997). For an examination in the American context, see Paul R. Abramson et al., "Third-Party and Independent Candidates in American Politics: Wallace, Anderson, and Perot," *Political Science Quarterly* 110 (Fall 1995): 349–367.

4.   Or, at least, that is the conventional scholarly assumption about the causal ordering of influences, rather than, say, attitudes toward Trump leading the respondent to change their policy beliefs. Obviously, the latter is a possibility that needs to be taken seriously.

5.   Ballotpedia (https://ballotpedia.org/Presidential_candidates,_2020) reports that 1,212 candidates filed a "Statement of Candidacy" with the Federal Election Commission.

6.   Such multicandidate elections are discussed in Paul R. Abramson, John H. Aldrich, and David W. Rohde, *Change and Continuity in the 1980 Elections*, rev. ed. (Washington, DC: CQ Press, 1983); Abramson, Aldrich, and Rohde, *Change and Continuity in the 1992 Elections*, rev. ed. (Washington, DC: CQ Press, 1995); Abramson, Aldrich, and Rohde, *Change and Continuity in the 1996 and 1998 Elections* (Washington, DC: CQ Press, 1999); and Abramson, Aldrich, and Rohde, *Change and Continuity in the 2000 and 2002 Elections* (Washington, DC: CQ Press, 2003).

7.   Note that this percentage lead for Biden in the ANES thermometer ratings reflects the percentage lead he won in the election exactly. A relatively smaller proportion than usual, 5 percent of respondents, rated the two candidates equally, suggesting how clearly the electorate distinguished the two candidates in 2020.

8.   For what limited comparisons are possible to earlier surveys, see Abramson, Aldrich, and Rohde, *Change and Continuity in the 2008 and 2010 Elections*, Table 6-2A, 146; and Abramson, Aldrich, and Rohde, *Change and Continuity in the 2012 and 2014 Elections*, Table 62-A, 149.

9.   For a discussion of earlier elections, see earlier editions of *Change and Continuity*.

10.   This was usually called a "pooled poll" in 2012, although typically referred to simply as an exit poll in 2016 and 2020.

11.   Concerns about foreign policy were also low in 1976, during the Cold War, although that occurred at a particularly low point of "détente" in it, and it was also the first election held after the withdrawal of the last American troops from Vietnam (and also of the defeat of our erstwhile allies there, the Republic of Vietnam).

12.   Two such scales were used for the first time in 1968, and their popularity led to the larger and more diverse set of scales used thereafter. See Richard A. Brody

and Benjamin I. Page, "Comment: The Assessment of Policy Voting," *American Political Science Review* 66, no. 2 (1972): 450–458; Benjamin I. Page and Richard A. Brody, "Policy Voting and the Electoral Process: The Vietnam War Issue," *American Political Science Review* 66, no. 3 (1972): 979–995; and John H. Aldrich, "Candidate Support Functions in the 1968 Election," *Public Choice* 22, no. 1 (1975): 1–22.

13.   See Abramson et al., *Change and Continuity in the 2008 and 2010 Elections,* for data and discussions about the 2008 data.

14.   The only consistent exception since 1972 has been a women's rights scale, for which public opinion had become so favorable to the liberal end of the issue scale that it was dropped from the survey in 2012 due to lack of variation in opinion.

15.   On government services the difference was actually 2.9 points, whereas on defense spending it was 2.2.

16.   This theme is also a major claim in Achen and Bartels, *Democracy for Realists*, which is to say that one of the great recurring concerns in studying public opinion and voter behavior is the understanding of how much (or little) people know and how accurate what they claim to know actually is.

17.   To maintain comparability with previous election surveys, for surveys from 1996 through 2012, we have excluded respondents who did not place themselves on an issue scale from columns II, III, and IV of Table 7-4. Because we do not know the preferences of these respondents on the issue, we have no way to measure the ways in which their issue preferences may have affected their votes.

18.   For details, see Abramson, Aldrich, and Rohde, *Change and Continuity in the 1980 Elections*, Table 6-3, 130; Abramson, Aldrich, and Rohde, *Change and Continuity in the 1984 Elections*, rev. ed. (Washington, DC: CQ Press, 1987), Table 6-2, 174; Abramson, Aldrich, and Rohde, *Change and Continuity in the 1988 Elections*, rev. ed. (Washington, DC: CQ Press, 1991), Table 6-2, 165; Abramson, Aldrich, and Rohde, *Change and Continuity in the 1992 Elections*, Table 6-6, 186; Abramson, Aldrich, and Rohde, *Change and Continuity in the 1996 and 1998 Elections*, Table 6-6, 135; Abramson, Aldrich, and Rohde, *Change and Continuity in the 2000 and 2002 Elections*, Table 6-4, 137; Abramson, Aldrich, and Rohde, *Change and Continuity in the 2004 and 2006 Elections*, Table 6-4, 152; and Abramson, Aldrich, and Rohde, *Change and Continuity in the 2008 and 2010 Elections*, Table 6-4, 158.

19.   Although this is evidence that most people claim to have issue preferences, it does not demonstrate that they do. For example, evidence indicates that some use the midpoint of the scale (point 4) as a means of answering the question even if they have ill-formed preferences. See John H. Aldrich et al., "The Measurement of Public Opinion about Public Policy: A Report on Some New Issue Question Formats," *American Journal of Political Science* 26 (May 1982): 391–414.

20.   We use "apparent issue voting" to emphasize several points. First, voting involves too many factors to infer that closeness to a candidate on any one issue was the cause of the voter's choice. The issue similarity may have been purely coincidental, or it may have been only one of many reasons the voter supported that candidate. Second, we use the median perception of the candidates' positions rather than the voter's own perception. Third, the relationship between issues and the vote may be caused by rationalization. Voters may have decided to support a candidate for

other reasons and also may have altered their own issue preferences or misperceived the positions of the candidates to align themselves more closely with their already favored candidate. See Richard A. Brody and Benjamin I. Page, "Comment: The Assessment of Policy Voting," *American Political Science Review* 66 (June 1972): 450–458.

21. Many individuals, of course, placed the candidates at different positions than did the public on average. Using average perceptions, however, reduces the effect of individuals rationalizing their perceptions of candidates to be consistent with their own vote rather than voting for the candidate whose views are actually closer to their own.

22. https://www.npr.org/2020/09/28/917827735/a-look-at-amy-coney-barretts -record-on-abortion-rights, Accessed September 29, 2021.

23. https://www.npr.org/2021/09/09/1035092720/progressives-want-justice-ste-phen-breyer-to-retire-his-response-not-yet. Accessed September 29, 2021.

24. Biden's position on abortion has changed over the years. He is personally opposed to abortion, but is a defender of Roe v. Wade. Trump's position has changed a great deal over the years, and it was really only in 2016 that he adopted the now-standard pro-life position of his party.

25. Bernard R. Berelson, Paul F. Lazarsfeld, and William N. McPhee, *Voting: A Study of Opinion Formation in a Presidential Campaign* (Chicago: University of Chicago Press, 1954), 215–233. The extent to which voters' perceptions were affected, however, varied from issue to issue.

26. See Brody and Page, "Comment: The Assessment of Policy Voting"; and Morris P. Fiorina "An Outline for a Model of Party Choice," *American Journal of Political Science* 21 (August 1977): 601–625.

27. Table 7.9 includes data from only the 2020 election, but earlier elections can be found in table A.7.1 in the appendix. Because this measure uses the median placement of the candidates on the issue scales in the full sample, much of the projection effect is eliminated. For the relationship between party identification and the balance-of-issues measure in 1972, see Abramson, Aldrich, and Rohde, *Change and Continuity in the 1980 and 1982 Elections*, Table 8-5, 171.

28. Matthew Levendusky, *The Partisan Sort: How Liberals Became Democrats and Conservatives Became Republicans* (Chicago: University of Chicago Press, 2009).

Chapter 8

1. Cited in Russell Dalton, *Democratic Challenges, Democratic Choices* (Oxford, UK: Oxford University Press, 2004, 126).

2. Jeffrey M. Jones, "Trump Job Approval Slides to 39%," *Gallup*, June 10, 2020, https://news.gallup.com/poll/312572/trump-job-approval-slides.aspx. For an interactive presentation of all Gallup presidential approval data going back to Harry S. Truman in 1945, visit Gallup's "Presidential Job Approval Center" website, https://news.gallup.com/interactives/185273/presidential-job-approval-center.aspx

3.   Lauren Bauer, Kristen Broady, Wendy Edelberg, and Jimmy O'Donnell, "Ten Facts about COVID-19 and the U.S. Economy," *Brookings Institution*, September 2020, https://www.brookings.edu/wp-content/uploads/2020/09/FutureShutdowns_Facts_LO_Final.pdf

4.   U.S. Bureau of Labor Statistics, "Unemployment Level," *FRED, Federal Reserve Bank of St. Louis*, October 2021, https://fred.stlouisfed.org/series/UNEMPLOY

5.   E.g., Brooke Singman, "Trump Campaign Returns to Economy with 8-Figure Ad Buy, Calls it 'Defining Issue in this Race,'" *Fox News*, September 14, 2020, https://www.foxnews.com/politics/trump-campaign-returns-to-economy-with-8-figure-ad-buy-calls-it-defining-issue-in-this-race; Maggie Haberman, "Trump, Facing Headwinds in Ohio, Talks Up Economy in Campaign Swing," *New York Times*, August 17, 2020, https://www.nytimes.com/2020/08/06/us/politics/trump-economy-ohio.html?searchResultPosition=2

6.   Here we treat retrospective evaluations as directly related to attitudes, opinions, and choices. The alternative view is that these are not directly implicated in voting. Rather, they are simply bits of evidence as people make judgments about what the candidates and parties will do in the future.

7.   Elena Moore, "Trump's and Biden's Plans for the Environment," *NPR*, October 16, 2020, https://www.npr.org/2020/10/16/920484187/trumps-and-biden-s-plans-for-the-environment

8.   Jeremy B. White, "Trump Blames California for Wildfires, Tells State 'You Gotta Clean Your Floors,'" *Politico*, August 20, 2020, https://www.politico.com/states/california/ story/2020/08/20/trump-blames-california-for-wildfires-tells-state-you-gotta-clean-your-floors-1311059

9.   V. O. Key, Jr., *Politics, Parties, and Pressure Groups*, 5th ed. (New York: Thomas Y. Crowell, 1964); V. O. Key, Jr., *The Responsible Electorate* (Cambridge, MA: Belknap Press of Harvard University Press, 1966).

10.   Recent scholarship notes have cautioned about the causal nature of the relationship between retrospective evaluations and the vote. Thomas Hansford and Brad Gomez provide evidence that individuals' economic perceptions may be clouded by their appraisals of the incumbent, interpreting the state of the economy more favorably when they like the incumbent and taking a more negative view of economic performance when they don't like the incumbent. Thomas G. Hansford and Brad T. Gomez, "Reevaluating the Sociotropic Economic Voting Hypothesis," *Electoral Studies* 39 (September): 15–25. See also Geoffrey Evans and Mark Pickup, "Reversing the Causal Arrow: The Political Conditioning of Economic Perceptions in the 2000-2004 U.S. Presidential Election Cycle," *Journal of Politics* 72 (October): 1236–1251.

11.   Anthony Downs, *An Economic Theory of Democracy* (New York: Harper and Row, 1957).

12.   Morris P. Fiorina, "An Outline for a Model of Party Choice," *American Journal of Political Science* 21 (August 1977): 601–625; Morris P. Fiorina, *Retrospective Voting in American National Elections* (New Haven, CT: Yale University Press, 1981).

13.   Angus Campbell et al., *The American Voter* (New York: Wiley, 1960).

14. Fiorina, *Retrospective Voting in American National Elections*, 83. The Downs-Fiorina version of retrospective voting is supported by the work of Christopher H. Achen and Larry M. Bartels, *Democracy for Realists: Why Elections Do Not Produce Responsive Government* (Princeton, NJ: Princeton University Press, 2016), except that Achen and Bartels show that many voters rely disproportionately on the most recent evidence they heard, and it is therefore not very "retrospective," not necessarily based on evaluations of outcomes over which the president could reasonably be said to have any influence over, nor a very sound basis for building a democracy that relies on independent assessments of voters to shape elite choices. Here, we focus on just those things that presidents often claim to have at least significant degrees of influence over, notably war and peace and economic outcomes.

15. See Benjamin I. Page, *Choices and Echoes in Presidential Elections: Rational Man and Electoral Democracy* (Chicago: University of Chicago Press, 1978). He argues that "party cleavages" distinguish the party at the candidate and mass levels. This proved to be a forecast of the partisan polarization that began in earnest only a few years later.

16. See Brad T. Gomez and J. Matthew Wilson, "Political Sophistication and Economic Voting in the American Electorate: A Theory of Heterogeneous Attribution," *American Journal of Political Science* 45 (October): 899–914.

17. See, for example, Arthur H. Miller and Martin P. Wattenberg, "Throwing the Rascals Out: Policy and Performance Evaluations of Presidential Candidates, 1952–1980," *American Political Science Review* 79, no. 2 (1985): 359–372.

18. Note that this question is quite different from the questions we analyzed in election studies prior to 2012. These were questions asking the respondent about the government's handling of the most important problems facing the country. This question does not specifically ask about the government, nor does it ask about the most important problem per se. It is more general in its coverage and only by inference is attributable to the government.

19. Each respondent assesses government performance on the problem he or she considers the most important. In the seven surveys from 1976 to 2000, respondents were asked, "How good a job is the government doing in dealing with this problem— a good job, only fair, or a poor job?" In 1972, respondents were asked a different but related question (see the note to table A.7.1 in the appendix). In 2004, respondents were asked another question (see chapter 6, note 9) and were given four options for assessing the government's performance: "very good job," "good job," "bad job," and "very bad job."

20. Questions about which direction the country is going are asked by many polling agencies to gauge the feelings of the public, and Real Clear Politics (www .realclearpolitics.com/) reports an averaging across these many polling outfits. Using their aggregated data we find that before the 2020 election, a majority of the public had viewed things as being on the wrong track since June 2009."Polls: Direction of Country," *Real Clear Politics*, https://www.realclearpolitics.com/epolls/other/direction_of_country-902.html

21. See Gerald H. Kramer, "Short-Term Fluctuations in U.S. Voting Behavior, 1896–1964," *The American Political Science Review* 65, no. 1 (1971): 131–143,

doi:10.2307/1955049; Fiorina, *Retrospective Voting in American National Elections*; M. Stephen Weatherford, "Economic Conditions and Electoral Outcomes: Class Differences in the Political Response to Recession," *American Journal of Political Science* 22 (November 1978): 917; D. Roderick Kiewiet and Douglas Rivers, "A Retrospective on Retrospective Voting," *Political Behavior* 6, no. 4 (1984): 369–393; D. Roderick Kiewiet, *Macroeconomics and Micropolitics: The Electoral Effects of Economic Issues* (Chicago: University of Chicago Press, 1983); Michael S. Lewis-Beck, *Economics and Elections: The Major Western Democracies* (Ann Arbor: University of Michigan Press, 1988); Alberto Alesina, John Londregan, and Howard Rosenthal, *A Model of the Political Economy of the United States* (Cambridge, MA: National Bureau of Economic Research, 1991); Michael B. MacKuen, Robert S. Erikson, and James A. Stimson, "Peasants or Bankers? The American Electorate and the U.S. Economy," *American Political Science Review* 86 (September 1992): 597–611; Robert S. Erikson, Michael B. MacKuen, and James A. Stimson, *The Macro Polity* (Cambridge, UK: Cambridge University Press, 2002).

22.　John Mueller, *War, Presidents and Public Opinion* (New York: Wiley, 1973).

23.　For data extending back as far as 1972 (the year this question first appeared in the ANES), see previous volumes in the *Change and Continuity* series.

24.　We assume that people respond reasonably accurately and factually when talking about their personal situations. However, we are also assuming that they perceive that presidential (or governmental) performance is one of the reasons for their personal situation, which may well be a stretch. The overall view of the economy is, of course, a belief but one that is presumed to be grounded in real conditions, which are typically easily conveyed facts ("conveyed" does not mean "believed" or even remembered). And, in this case, lots of political actors are seeking to acclaim the successes or lament the failures of the incumbent and his or her party in achieving those outcomes.

25.　For timelines of how the coronavirus disease 2019 (COVID-19) pandemic unfolded, see "A Timeline of COVID-19 Developments in 2020," *American Journal of Managed Care*, January 1, 2021, https://www.ajmc.com/view/a-timeline-of-covid19-developments-in-2020, and Derrick Bryson Taylor, "A Timeline of the Coronavirus Pandemic," *New York Times*, March 17, 2021, https://www.nytimes.com/article/coronavirus-timeline.html. For data about the number of COVID cases and deaths in the United States, see "COVID Data Tracker," *Centers for Disease Control and Prevention*, https://covid.cdc.gov/covid-data-tracker/#datatracker-home.

26.　Matthew J. Belvedere, "Trump Says He Trusts China's Xi on Coronavirus and the US has it 'Totally Under Control,'" *CNBC.com*, January 22, 2020, https://www.cnbc.com/2020/01/22/trump-on-coronavirus-from-china-we-have-it-totally-under-control.html

27.　Hannah Lang and Bryan Mena, "U.S. Coronavirus Recession Lasted Two Months, Ended in April 2020, Official Arbiter Says," *The Wall Street Journal*, July 19, 2021, https://www.wsj.com/articles/u-s-recession-lasted-two-months-ended-in-april-2020-official-arbiter-says-11626715788

28.　Julie Pace and Hannah Fingerhut, "AP-NORC Poll: Few Americans Trust Trump's Info on Pandemic." *APNews.com*, April 23, 2020, https://apnews.com/

article/virus-outbreak-donald-trump-us-news-ap-top-news-politics-87f1545cea4b5e8
c96e6e902a8d9e9bd

29.   Katherine Schaeffer, "A Look at the Americans Who Believe There is Some Truth to the Conspiracy Theory that COVID-19 was Planned," *Pew Research Center*, July 24, 2020, https://www.pewresearch.org/fact-tank/2020/07/24/a-look-at -the-americans-who-believe-there-is-some-truth-to-the-conspiracy-theory-that-covid -19-was-planned/

30.   Fiorina, *Retrospective Voting in American National Elections*.

31.   Surveys have a very high degree of external validity. That is not only the strength of the survey method, but they are almost the only means by which one can make scientifically sound inferences about the voting public. Surveys are, however, weaker on internal reliability, that is, the ability to make a causal infer- ence about "what causes what." Experiments (including perhaps the ultimate, the survey-embedded experiment) are one way to deal with the issue of causation. In a straight survey like (almost always) the ANES, it is difficult to say whether one approves of the job the president is doing because the president has done well in the respondent's eyes or whether the voter simply likes the president and therefore approves of whatever he or she does (at least up to some apparently very generous limits).

32.   In the 1984 and 1988 surveys, this question was asked in both the pre-election and the postelection waves of the survey. Because attitudes held by the public before the election are what count in influencing its choices, we use the first question. In both surveys, approval of Reagan's performance was more positive in the postelection interview: 66 percent approved of his performance in 1984, and 68 percent approved in 1988.

33.   Gary C. Jacobson, "Party Polarization in National Politics: The Electoral Connection," in *Polarized Politics: Congress and the President in a Partisan Era*, vol. 5 (Washington, DC: CQ Press, 2000), 17–18, demonstrates that evaluations of presidential performance have become much more sharply related to party identifica- tion in recent years compared to the earlier years of the ANES studies.

34.   A summary measure of retrospective evaluations could not be constructed using either the 1972 or the 2004 ANES data. We were able to construct an alterna- tive measure for 2004. See Abramson, Aldrich, and Rohde, *Change and Continuity in the 2004 and 2006 Elections*, chap. 7, Tables 7-9 and 7-10, 178–180, and 371n18. For procedures we used to construct this measure between 1976 and 2000, see Paul R. Abramson, John H. Aldrich, and David W. Rohde, *Change and Continuity in the 2000 and 2002 Elections* (Washington, DC: CQ Press, 2003), chap. 7, 328n13). A combined index of retrospective evaluations was created to allow an overall assess- ment of retrospective voting in 2020. To construct the summary measure of retrospec- tive evaluations, we used the following procedures. First, we awarded respondents four points if they approved of the president's performance, two if they had no opin- ion, and zero if they disapproved. Second, respondents received four points if they thought the country was on the right track, zero if they thought the nation was on the wrong track, and two if they had no opinion. Finally, respondents received four points if they thought the incumbent president's party would do a better job handling the

most important problem, zero points if they thought the challenger's party would do a better job, and two points if they thought there was no difference between the parties, neither party would do well, both parties would do the same, another party would do the better job, or they had no opinion. For all three questions "don't know" and "not ascertained" responses were scored as two, but respondents with more than one such response were excluded from the analysis. Scores on our measure were the sum of the individual values for the three questions and thus ranged from a low of zero (strongly against the incumbent's party) to twelve (strongly for the incumbent's party). These values were then grouped to create a seven-point scale corresponding to the seven categories in table 8.9.

35.   This measure is different in 2012, 2016, and 2020 than in prior elections due to our use of the "right track/wrong track" question. Other election years are also not always comparable, although they are more similar to each than to 2012. See Paul R. Abramson, John H. Aldrich, and David W. Rohde, *Change and Continuity in the 1996 and 1998 Elections* (Washington, DC: CQ Press, 1999), 158–159, for data on our (different) summary measure from 1972 to 1996; Abramson, Aldrich, and Rohde, *Change and Continuity in the 2000 and 2002 Elections*, 164–165; Abramson, Aldrich, and Rohde, *Change and Continuity in the 2004 and 2006 Elections*, 178–180, 187–191, for analyses of those elections, respectively, in these terms.

36.   The characterization of earlier elections is taken from Abramson, Aldrich, and David Rohde, *Change and Continuity in the 2000 and 2002 Elections*, 164.

37.   For data from the 1976 and 1980 elections, see Abramson, Aldrich, and Rohde, *Change and Continuity in the 1980 and 1982 Elections* (Washington, DC: CQ Press, 1983), Tables 7–8, 155–157; from the 1984 election, see Paul R. Abramson, John H. Aldrich, and David W. Rohde, *Change and Continuity in the 1984 Elections*, rev. ed. (Washington, DC: CQ Press, 1987), Tables 7–8, 203–204; from the 1988 election, see Paul R. Abramson and Charles W. Ostrom, Jr., "Macropartisanship: An Empirical Reassessment," *American Political Science Review* 86 (March 1991): 181–192, Table 7, 195–198; from the 1996 election, see Abramson, Aldrich, and Rohde, *Change and Continuity in the 1996 and 1998 Elections,* 159–161; from the 2000 election, see Abramson, Aldrich, and Rohde, *Change and Continuity in the 2000 and 2002 Elections*, 165–166; and from the 2004 election, see Abramson, Aldrich, and Rohde, *Change and Continuity in the 2004 and 2006 Elections,* 178–180. The 2008 election is reported in Paul R., Abramson, John H. Aldrich, and David W. Rohde, *Change and Continuity in the 2008 and 2010 Elections* (Washington, DC: CQ Press, 2011), 188–191; and for 2012, see Paul R. Abramson, John H. Aldrich, Brad T. Gomez, and David W. Rohde, *Change and Continuity in the 2012 Elections* (Washington, DC: CQ Press, 2015), 188–191. The small number of seven-point issue scales included in the ANES survey precluded performing this analysis with 1992 data.

38.   The question measuring approval of the president's handling of economic policy was not asked in ANES surveys before 1984. In our study of these earlier elections, an alternative measure of economic retrospective evaluations was created and shown to be almost as strongly related to party identification. See Paul R. Abramson, John H. Aldrich, and David W. Rohde, *Change and Continuity in the 1984 Elections*,

rev. ed. (Washington, DC: CQ Press, 1987), Table 8-6, 221. We also found nearly as strong a relationship between partisanship and perceptions of which party would better handle the economy in the data from 1972, 1976, and 1980 as from later surveys reported here. See Abramson, Aldrich, and Rohde, *Change and Continuity in the 1980 and 1982 Elections*, 170, Table 8-6, 173.

39.   Our summary measure of retrospective evaluations has changed over time due to the use of alternative component measures. Earlier measures and its relationship with partisan identification are reported in Abramson, Aldrich, and Rohde, *Change and Continuity in the 2000 and 2002 Elections*, Table 8-7, 185–186, discussed on 184–189; in Abramson, Aldrich, and Rohde, *Change and Continuity in the 2004 and 2006 Elections*, Table 8-7, 202, discussed on 201–203; and in Paul R. Abramson, John H. Aldrich, Brad Gomez, and David W. Rohde, *Change and Continuity in the 2012 and 2014 Elections* (Washington, DC: CQ Press, 2016), Table 8-8, 219, discussed on 218–221.

Chapter 9

1.   One independent was Bernard Sanders of Vermont, who was elected as an independent to the House from 1990 through 2004. Sanders had previously been elected mayor of Burlington, Vermont, running as a socialist. However, throughout his House service he caucused with the Democrats; he continued that course after his initial election to the Senate in 2006 and following his unsuccessful attempts at the Democratic nomination for president in 2016 and 2020. The second independent is Angus King of Maine. King had served as governor of Maine from 1995 to 2003, also as an independent, before being elected senator for the first time in 2012. We will count both of these senators as Democrats in all of the analyses in this chapter.

2.   *Incumbents* here is used only to indicate elected incumbents. This includes all members of the House because the only way to become a representative is by election. In the case of the Senate, however, vacancies may be filled by appointment. We do not count appointed senators as incumbents. Senator Johnny Isakson (R-GA) resigned at the end of 2019 citing his health as the primary reason and Governor Brian Kemp (R) appointed Kelly Loeffler (R) in early January 2020 as his replacement. She was not treated as the incumbent when she ran in a special election in 2020 and was ultimately defeated by Raphael Warnock (D) in the January 2021 runoff election.

3.   The classification of primary-versus general-election defeats is complicated by the atypical processes used in California, Louisiana, and Washington. In California and Washington, all candidates regardless of party affiliation compete in a single primary. The two candidates who received the highest number of votes then compete in the general election. Thus the general election may include two Democrats or two Republicans. In Louisiana all candidates appear on the general election ballot, and if no candidate receives a majority of votes, the top two vote getters proceed to a runoff in December. These types of situations seem more akin to a primary runoff than the usual idea of a general election, so we classify results that way. If two candidates of the same party face each other in the general election, we count that as a primary,

with the winner unopposed in the general election. If both are incumbents, the defeat is treated as a primary loss.

4.   Although gerrymandering cannot be the only contributing factor, it could be a part of the explanation for this modest House-Senate difference.

5.   The Republicans had won control of the House in eight consecutive elections from 1894 through 1908, far short of the Democratic series of successes.

6.   The regional breakdowns used in this chapter are as follows: *East*: Connecticut, Delaware, Maine, Massachusetts, New Hampshire, New Jersey, New York, Pennsylvania, Rhode Island, and Vermont; *Midwest*: Illinois, Indiana, Iowa, Kansas, Michigan, Minnesota, Nebraska, North Dakota, Ohio, South Dakota, and Wisconsin; *West*: Alaska, Arizona, California, Colorado, Hawaii, Idaho, Montana, Nevada, New Mexico, Oregon, Utah, Washington, and Wyoming; *South*: Alabama, Arkansas, Florida, Georgia, Louisiana, Mississippi, North Carolina, South Carolina, Tennessee, Texas, and Virginia; *Border*: Kentucky, Maryland, Missouri, Oklahoma, and West Virginia. This classification differs somewhat from the one used in earlier chapters (and in chapter 10) but is commonly used for congressional analysis.

7.   Over the years changes in the southern electorate have also made southern Democratic constituencies more like northern Democratic constituencies and less like Republican constituencies, North or South. The East also exacerbates this tendency just for the opposite party reasons. These changes also appear to have enhanced the homogeneity of preferences within the partisan delegations in Congress. This partisan congressional polarization has been the subject of a great deal of research over the last three decades. Two good overviews are offered by John H. Aldrich, *Why Parties? A Second Look* (Chicago: University of Chicago Press, 2011); and Marc J. Hetherington and Thomas J. Rudolph, *Why Washington Won't Work: Polarization, Political Trust, and the Governing Crisis* (Chicago: University of Chicago Press, 2015).

8.   The ratings were taken from various issues of *The Cook Political Report*. Competitive races are those Cook classified as only leaning to the incumbent party, toss-ups, or those tilted toward the other party.

9.   There were 35 Senate seats up for election in 2020 since Georgia had two seats in play—one held by incumbent Republican David Perdue, who had been elected in 2014, and the other held by Kelly Loeffler, who had been appointed by Governor Kemp after Senator Johnny Isakson announced his retirement in December 2019 due to health considerations.

10.   See Paul R Abramson, John H. Aldrich, and David W. Rohde, *Change and Continuity in the 1996 and 1998 Elections* (Washington, DC: CQ Press, 1999), 207–212.

11.   These polling data on Congress were taken from www.gallup.com/poll/1600 /congress -public.aspx

12.   Chris Cillizza, "Here's a Number that Should Terrify Every Republican on the Ballot this Fall," *CNN*, June 8, 2020, https://www.cnn.com/2020/06/08/politics/ generic-ballot-house-democrats-republicans/index.html

13.   For a discussion of the increased role of national party organizations in congressional elections over the last few decades, see Paul S. Herrnson, Costas

Panagopoulous, and Kendall Bailey, *Congressional Elections*, 8th ed. (Washington, DC: CQ Press, 2020), chap. 4.

14. Laura Litvan and Daniel Flatley, "Democrats Short on Recruits for Bid to Retake Senate in 2020," *Bloomberg*, May 3, 2019, https://www.bloomberg .com/news/articles/2019-05-03/democrats-short-on-recruits-for-bid-to-retake-senate -in-2020

15. Bridget Bowman, Simone Pathe, and Stephanie Akin, "The 10 Most Vulnerable Senators in 2020: Republicans Play Defense," *Roll Call*, November 4, 2019, https://www.rollcall.com/2019/11/04/the-10-most-vulnerable-senators-in-2020 -republicans-play-defense/

16. Karl Evers-Hillstrom, "Prolific Fundraising Gives Pelosi the Edge in Speaker Election," *Open Secrets*, November 16, 2020, https://www.opensecrets.org/news /2020/11/pelosifundraising-edge-in-speaker-race/

17. See *Open Secrets*, https://www.opensecrets.org/members-of-congress/nancy -pelosi/summary?cid=N00007360&cycle=2020&type=C

18. See *Open Secrets*, https://www.opensecrets.org/members-of-congress/steny -h-hoyer/summary?cid=N00001821&cycle=2020

19. See "Who's Raised the Most," *Open Secrets*, https://www.opensecrets.org/ overview/topraise.php

20. Super PACs are a new kind of political action committee that "may raise unlimited sums of money from corporations, unions, associations and individuals, then spend unlimited sums to overtly advocate for or against political candidates. . . . Unlike traditional PACs, super PACs are prohibited from donating money directly to political candidates." See "Super PACs," *Open Secrets*, http://www.opensecrets.org/ pacs/superpacs.php

21. See "2020 Outside Spending, by Race," *Open Secrets*, https://www.opense-crets.org/outsidespending/summ.php?disp=R

22. See "2016 Outside Spending, by Race," *Open Secrets*, https://www.opense-crets.org/outside spending/summ.php?cycle=2016&disp=R&pty=A&type=A

23. See "2020 Outside Spending."

24. Richard F. Fenno, Jr., *Home Style: House Members in Their Districts* (Boston: Little, Brown, 1978). For a discussion of how relationships between rep-resentatives and constituents have changed over time, see Fenno, *The Challenge of Congressional Representation* (Cambridge, MA: Harvard University Press, 2013).

25. See David W. Rohde, "Risk-Bearing and Progressive Ambition: The Case of Members of the United States House of Representatives," *American Journal of Political Science* 23 (February 1979): 1–26.

26. For example, analysis of Senate races in 1988 indicated that both the political quality of the previous office held and the challenger's political skills had an indepen-dent effect on the outcome of the race. See Peverill Squire, "Challenger Quality and Voting Behavior in U.S. Senate Elections," *Legislative Studies Quarterly* 17 (May 1992): 247–263. For systematic evidence on the impact of candidate quality in House races, see Gary C. Jacobson and Jamie L. Carson, *The Politics of Congressional Elections*, 10th ed. (Lanham, Md.: Rowman & Littlefield, 2020), chap. 3.

27. A recent analysis uses expert survey responses instead of office experience to measure candidate quality. It concludes that quality candidates do better and that

the effect increases as ideological differences decline. See Matthew K. Buttice and Walter J. Stone, "Candidates Matter: Policy and Quality Differences in Congressional Elections," *Journal of Politics* 74 (July 2012): 870–887.

28.　Data on candidate backgrounds were taken from various issues of *The Cook Political Report* and *The Green Papers* (http://www.thegreenpapers.com/G16/).

29.　Data on earlier years are taken from our studies of previous national elections.

30.　Data collected by authors. Note that the figures in this paragraph include races in which only one of the parties fielded a candidate as well as contests where both did.

31.　See Jacobson and Carson, *The Politics of Congressional Elections*; Jon R. Bond, Cary Covington; Richard Fleischer, "Explaining Challenger Quality in Congressional Elections," *Journal of Politics* 47 (May 1985): 510–529; and David W. Rohde, "Risk-Bearing and Progressive Ambition: The Case of Members of the U.S. House of Representatives," *American Journal of Political Science* 23 (February 1979): 1–26.

32.　L. Sandy Maisel and Walter J. Stone, "Determinants of Candidate Emergence in U.S. House Elections: An Exploratory Study," *Legislative Studies Quarterly* 22 (February 1997): 79–96.

33.　See Peverill Squire, "Preemptive Fund-raising and Challenger Profile in Senate Elections," *Journal of Politics* 53 (November 1991): 1150–1164; and Jay Goodliffe, "The Effect of War Chests on Challenger Entry in U.S. House Elections," *American Journal of Political Science* 45 (October 2001): 1087–1108.

34.　Jeffrey S. Banks and D. Roderick Kiewiet, "Explaining Patterns of Candidate Competition in Congressional Elections," *American Journal of Political Science* 33 (November 1989): 997–1015.

35.　Canon, *Actors, Athletes, and Astronauts.*

36.　See Thomas E. Mann and Raymond E. Wolfinger, "Candidates and Parties in Congressional Elections," *American Political Science Review* 74 (September 1980): 617–632.

37.　See David R. Mayhew, "Congressional Elections: The Case of the Vanishing Marginals," *Polity* 6 (Spring 1974): 295–317; Robert S. Erikson, "Malapportionment, Gerrymandering, and Party Fortunes in Congressional Elections," *American Political Science Review* 66 (December 1972): 1234–1245; and Warren Lee Kostroski, "Party and Incumbency in Postwar Senate Elections: Trends, Patterns, and Models," *American Political Science Review* 67 (December 1973): 1213–1234.

38.　Edward R. Tufte, "Communication," *American Political Science Review* 68 (March 1974): 211–213. The communication involved a discussion of Tufte's earlier article: "The Relationship Between Seats and Votes in Two-Party Systems," *American Political Science Review* 67 (June 1973): 540–554.

39.　See John A. Ferejohn, "On the Decline of Competition in Congressional Elections," *American Political Science Review* 71 (March 1977): 166–176; Albert D. Cover, "One Good Term Deserves Another: The Advantage of Incumbency in Congressional Elections," *American Journal of Political Science* 21 (August 1977): 523–541; and Albert D. Cover and David R. Mayhew, "Congressional Dynamics and the Decline of Competition in Congressional Elections," in *Congress Reconsidered*, 2nd ed., eds. Lawrence C. Dodd and Bruce I. Oppenheimer (Washington, DC: CQ Press, 1981), 62–82.

40. Morris P. Fiorina, *Congress: Keystone of the Washington Establishment*, 2nd ed. (New Haven, CT: Yale University Press, 1989), esp. chap. 4–6.

41. See several conflicting arguments and conclusions in the following articles published in the *American Journal of Political Science* 25 (August 1981): John R. Johannes and John C. McAdams, "The Congressional Incumbency Effect: Is It Casework, Policy Compatibility, or Something Else? An Examination of the 1978 Election" (512–542); Morris P. Fiorina, "Some Problems in Studying the Effects of Resource Allocation in Congressional Elections" (543–567); Diana Evans Yiannakis, "The Grateful Electorate: Casework and Congressional Elections" (568–580); and McAdams and Johannes, "Does Casework Matter? A Reply to Professor Fiorina" (581–604). See also Johannes, *To Serve the People: Congress and Constituency Service* (Lincoln: University of Nebraska Press, 1984), esp. chap. 8; and Albert D. Cover and Bruce S. Brumberg, "Baby Books and Ballots: The Impact of Congressional Mail on Constituent Opinion," *American Political Science Review* 76 (June 1982): 347–359. The evidence in Cover and Brumberg for a positive electoral effect is quite strong, but the result may be applicable only to limited circumstances.

42. Ferejohn, "On the Decline of Competition," 174.

43. Cover, "One Good Term," 535.

44. More recent research shows that the link between party identification and voting has strengthened again. See Larry M. Bartels, "Partisanship and Voting Behavior, 1952–1996," *American Journal of Political Science* 44 (January 2000): 35–50.

45. On this point, see Gary Jacobson, "It's Nothing Personal: The Decline of the Incumbency Advantage in U.S. House Elections," *Journal of Politics* 77(July 2015): 861–873.

46. For thorough analyses of the growth of, and reasons for, anti-Congress sentiment, see John R. Hibbing and Elizabeth Theiss-Morse, *Congress as Public Enemy* (New York: Cambridge University Press, 1995); and Thomas E. Mann and Norman J. Ornstein, *The Broken Branch: How Congress Is Failing America and How to Get It Back on Track* (Oxford: Oxford University Press, 2008).

47. It is important to note, however, that a substantial number of incumbents had already been defeated in the primaries, and many weak incumbents had retired.

48. For an analysis suggesting that the variations in incumbents' vote percentages have little implication for incumbent safety, see Jeffrey M. Stonecash, *Reassessing the Incumbency Effect* (New York: Cambridge University Press, 2008).

49. Jacobson, "It's Nothing Personal," 861–862.

50. Gary Jacobson, "The Congress: Ever More Polarized and National," In *The Elections of 2020*, ed. Michael Nelson (University of Virginia Press, 2021).

51. Gary C. Jacobson, "The Triumph of Polarized Partisanship in 2016: Trump's Improbable Victory," *Political Science Quarterly* 132 (Spring 2017): 32.

52. The body of literature on this subject has grown to be quite large. Some salient early examples, in addition to those cited later, are Gary C. Jacobson, *Money in Congressional Elections* (New Haven, CT: Yale University Press, 1980); Jacobson, "Parties and PACs in Congressional Elections," in *Congress Reconsidered*, 4th eds., eds. Lawrence C. Dodd and Bruce I. Oppenheimer (Washington, DC: CQ Press, 1989), 117–152; Jacobson and Samuel Kernell, *Strategy and Choice*

in Congressional Elections, 2nd ed. (New Haven, Conn.: Yale University Press, 1983); John A. Ferejohn and Morris P. Fiorina, "Incumbency and Realignment in Congressional Elections," in *The New Direction in American Politics*, eds. John E. Chubb and Paul E. Peterson (Washington, DC: Brookings Institution, 1985), 91–115.

53. See Jacobson, *The Electoral Origins of Divided Government,* 63–65.

54. See Gary C. Jacobson and Samuel Kernell, *Strategy and Choice in Congressional Elections*, 2nd ed. (New Haven, CT: Yale University Press, 1983).

55. Evidence indicates challenger spending strongly influences public visibility, and substantial amounts of spending can significantly reduce the recognition gap between the challenger and the incumbent. See Jacobson and Carson, *The Politics of Congressional Elections*, 10th ed., 68–73.

56. The 2020 spending data were obtained from the Federal Election Commission (www.fec.gov).

57. See Paul R. Abramson, John H. Aldrich, Brad T. Gomez, and David W. Rohde, *Change and Continuity in the 2012 and 2014 Elections* (Washington, DC: CQ Press, 2016), 245–248, and the earlier work cited there.

58. See Jacobson, *The Electoral Origins of Divided Government*, 54–55, and the work cited in note 48.

59. Donald Philip Green and Jonathan S. Krasno, "Salvation for the Spendthrift Incumbent: Reestimating the Effects of Campaign Spending in House Elections," *American Journal of Political Science* 32 (November 1988): 884–907.

60. Gary C. Jacobson, "The Effects of Campaign Spending in House Elections: New Evidence for Old Arguments," *American Journal of Political Science* 34 (May 1990): 334–362. Green and Krasno's response can be found in the same issue on pages 363–372.

61. Gary C. Jacobson, *The Politics of Congressional Elections*, 8th ed. (Boston, MA: Pearson, 2013), 156.

62. See Alan I. Abramowitz, "Explaining Senate Election Outcomes," *American Political Science Review* 82 (June 1988): 385–403; Alan Gerber, "Estimating the Effect of Campaign Spending on Senate Election Outcomes Using Instrumental Variables," *American Political Science Review* 92 (June 1998): 401–411.

63. Gary C. Jacobson, "Campaign Spending and Voter Awareness of Congressional Candidates," paper presented at the Annual Meeting of the Public Choice Society, New Orleans, Louisiana, May 11–13, 1977), 16.

64. An incumbent in a district that is tilted toward the opposite party may need to spend more to be able to distinguish his- or herself from the party's unattractive but (in recent decades) precise party reputation. See Henry A. Kim and Brad l. Leveck, "Money, Reputation, and Incumbency in U.S. House Elections, or Why Marginals Have Become More Expensive," *American Political Science Review* 107 (August 2013): 492–504.

65. Spending data are taken from www.fec.gov.

66. See "Incumbent Advantage," *Open Secrets*, https://www.opensecrets.org/elections-overview/incumbent-advantage

67. Of course, open seats tend to involve considerably greater sums of money because there is no incumbent seeking reelection.

68.   Challengers were categorized as having strong experience if they had been elected US representative, to state wide office, to the state legislature, or to county-wide or citywide office (e.g., mayor, prosecutor, etc.).

69.   Paul R. Abramson, John H. Aldrich, and David W. Rohde, *Change and Continuity in the 1980 Elections*, rev. ed. (Washington, DC: CQ Press, 1983), 202–203. See also Paul Gronke, *The Electorate, the Campaign, and the Office: A Unified Approach to Senate and House Elections* (Ann Arbor: University of Michigan Press, 2001).

70.   Other Democratic Senate winners in 2000 who spent millions of their own money included Maria Cantwell of Washington and Mark Dayton of Minnesota.

71.   See "Most Expensive Races," *Open Secrets*, https://www.opensecrets.org/elections-overview/most-expensive-races

72.   Quoted in Angela Herrin, "Big Outside Money Backfired in GOP Loss of Senate to Dems," *Washington Post*, November 6, 1986, A46.

73.   See David W. Rohde, *Parties and Leaders in the Postreform House* (Chicago: University of Chicago Press, 1991), especially chapter 3; and Rohde, "Electoral Forces, Political Agendas, and Partisanship in the House and Senate," in *The Postreform Congress*, ed. Rodger H. Davidson (New York: St. Martin's Press, 1992), 27–47.

74.   For discussions of the ideological changes in the House and Senate over the last four decades, see John H. Aldrich and David W. Rohde, "The Logic of Conditional Party Government: Revisiting the Electoral Connection," in *Congress Reconsidered*, 7th ed., eds. Lawrence Dodd and Bruce Oppenheimer (Washington, DC: CQ Press, 2001), 269–292; Gary C. Jacobson, "The Congress: The Structural Basis of Republican Success," in *The Elections of 2004*, ed. Michael Nelson (Washington, DC: CQ Press, 2005), 163–186; and Sean Theriault, *Party Polarization in Congress* (Cambridge: Cambridge University Press, 2008).

75.   Alexander Burns, *The New York Times*, "Joe Biden's Campaign Announcement Video, Annotated," April 25, 2019, https://www.nytimes.com/2019/04/25/us/politics/biden-campaign-video-announcement.html

76.   https://www.federalregister.gov/presidential-documents/executive-orders/joe-biden/2021

77.   Ibid.

78.   Tyler Pager, "Biden Unveils Commission to Study Possible Expansion of Supreme Court," *The Washington Post,* April 9, 2021, https://www.washingtonpost.com/politics/biden-to-unveil-commission-to-study-possible-expansion-of-supreme-court/2021/04/09/f644552c-9944-11eb-962b-78c1d8228819_story.html

79.   On this point, see especially William Howell, *Power without Persuasion: The Politics of Direct Presidential Action* (Princeton: Princeton University Press, 2003).

80.   Tamara Keith, "With 28 Executive Orders Signed, President Biden Is Off to a Record Start," *NPR,* February 3, 2021, https://www.npr.org/2021/02/03/963380189/with-28-executive-orders-signed-president-biden-is-off-to-a-record-start, and https://www.federalregister.gov/presidential-documents/executive-orders/joe-biden/2021

81.   See Paul R. Abramson, John H. Aldrich, and David W. Rohde, *Change and Continuity in the 1992 Elections*, rev. ed. (Washington, DC: CQ Press, 1995),

339–342; and John H. Aldrich and David W. Rohde, "The Transition to Republican Rule in the House: Implications for Theories of Congressional Politics," *Political Science Quarterly* 112 (Winter, 1997–1998): 541–567.

82. Naomi Jagoda, "Pelosi Announces Creation of Select Committee on Economic Inequality," *The Hill*, December 30, 2020. https://thehill.com/policy/finance/532099 -pelosi-announces-creation-of-select-committee-on-economic-inequality

83. Ibid.

84. Larry Buchanan, Lazaro Garnio, Christina Kelso, Dmitriy Khavin, Lauren Leatherby, Alicia Parlapiano, Scott Reinhard, Anjali Singhvi, Derek Watkins, and Karen Yourish, "How a Pro-Trump Mob Stormed the U.S. Capitol," *New York Times*, January 7, 2021, https://www.nytimes.com/interactive/2021/01/06/us/trump-mob -capitol-building.html

85. Lisa Mascaro, Mary Clare Jalonick, Jonathan Lemire, and Alan Fram, "Trump Impeached after Capitol Riot in Historic Second Charge," *AP*, January 13, 2021, https://apnews.com/article/trump-impeachment-vote-capitol-siege-0a6f2a3 48a6e43f27d5e1dc486027860

86. Lauren Lantry, "Former President Donald Trump Acquitted in 2nd Impeachment Trial." *ABC News,* February 13, 2021, https://abcnews.go.com/Politics /president-donald-trump-acquitted/story?id=75853994

87. Julia Manchester, "Senior Dem says Pelosi will be Speaker for as Long as she Wants," *The Hill*, October 1, 2018, https://thehill.com/hilltv/rising/409206-senior -dem-says-pelosi-will-be-speaker-for-as-long-as-she-wants

88. Clare Foran and Manu Raju, "Anti-Pelosi Democrats Publicly Vow Opposition in House Speaker Race: 'The Time has Come for New Leadership,'" *CNN*, November 20, 2018, https://www.cnn.com/2018/11/19/politics/anti-pelosi -democrats-letter-speakers-race/index.html

89. Mike DeBonis, Elise Viebeck, and Paul Kane, "Democrats Nominate Pelosi for Speaker, a Show of Strength to be Tested in the Next Congress," *The Washington Post*, November 28, 2018, https://www.washingtonpost.com/powerpost/house-lead ership-elections-pelosi-seeks-to-shore-up-votes-for-speaker/2018/11/28/c9b2abf0 -f30e-11e8-aeea-b85fd44449f5_story.html

90. Allan Smith, Pelosi Wins Re-election as House Speaker with Slim Majority," *NBC News*, January 3, 2021, https://www.nbcnews.com/politics/congress/pelosi -readies-speaker-vote-new-congress-sworn-n1252688

91. Zachary Hudak, Rebecca Kaplan, Caroline Linton, Melissa Quinn, Grace Segers, and Kathryn Watson, "Liz Cheney Removed from House GOP Leadership," *CBS News,* May 13, 2021, https://www.cbsnews.com/live-updates/liz-cheney -removed-gop-leadership/

92. For specific details on the bill, see https://www.congress.gov/bill/117th-con gress/house-bill/1319/text

93. Marianne Levine and Sarah Ferris, "Dems Sweat a Summer Pileup of Big Votes on Biden's Agenda," *Politico*, May 24, 2021, https://www.politico.com/news /2021/05/24/democrats-brace-for-heated-legislative-summer-490184

94. Carrie Blazina and Drew Desilver, "A Record Number of Women are Serving in the 117th Congress," *Pew Research Center*, January 15, 2021, https://

www.pewresearch.org/fact-tank/2021/01/15/a-record-number-of-women-are-serving -in-the-117th-congress/

95.   For details on the Jeffords switch, see Paul Abramson, John Aldrich, and David Rohde. 2002. *Change and Continuity in the 2000 Elections* (Washington, DC: CQ Press), 225–226.

96.   The literature on the filibuster is substantial. A good entry point is Gregory Koger, *Filibustering: A Political History of Obstruction in the House and Senate* (Chicago: University of Chicago Press: 2010).

97.   The data cited were taken from a table on "Senate Action on Cloture Motions,"   www.senate.gov/pagelayout/reference/cloture_motions/cloture-Counts.htm

98.   Sheryl Gay Stolberg, "Swing Senators Face New Test in Supreme Court Fight," *New York Times*, July 14, 2005, http://www.nytimes.com/2005/07/14/us/ swing-senators-face-new -test-in-supreme-court-fight.html

99.   See Ramsey Cox, "Reid: Senate Dems will vote to limit GOP use of filibuster," *The Hill*, November 27, 2012, 3.

100.   Jeremy Peters, "In Landmark Vote, Senate Limits Use of the Filibuster," *New York Times*, November 21, 2013, http://www.nytimes.com/2013/11/22/us/politics/ reid-sets-in-motion -steps-to-limit-use-of-filibuster.html

101.   Ibid.

102.   See Mallory Shelbourne, "Schumer Regrets Dems Triggering 'Nuclear Option,'" *The Hill*, January 3, 2017, http://thehill.com/homenews/senate/312540 -schumer-regrets-dems -triggering-nuclear-option

103.   See Burgess Everett, "McConnell Throws Down the Gauntlet: No Scalia Replacement Under Obama," *Politico*, February 13, 2016, http://www.politico.com/ story/2016/02/mitch-mcconnell-antonin-scalia-supreme-court-nomination-219248

104.   Julie Hirschfeld Davis, "Joe Biden Argued for Delaying Supreme Court Picks in 1992," *New York Times*, February 22, 2016, https://www.nytimes.com/2016/02/23/ us/politics/joe-biden-argued-for-delaying-supreme-court-picks-in-1992.html

105.   Adam Liptak and Matt Flegenheimer, "Neil Gorsuch Confirmed by Senate as Supreme Court Justice," *New York Times*, April 7, 2017, https://www.nytimes.com /2017/04/07/us/politics/neil-gorsuch-supreme-court.html

106.   Jordan Carney, "McConnell says Trump Nominee to Replace Ginsburg will get Senate Vote," *The Hill*, September 18, 2020, https://thehill.com/homenews/senate /517178-mcconnell-says-trump-nominee-to-replace-ginsburg-will-get-senate-vote

107.   Sam Gringlas, "Trump Announces Amy Coney Barrett as His Supreme Court Nominee," *NPR*, September 26, 2020, https://www.npr.org/sections/supreme-court -nomination/2020/09/26/916921211/trump-set-to-formally-announce-his-supreme -court-nominee

108.   Barbara Sprunt, "Amy Coney Barrett Confirmed to Supreme Court, Takes Constitutional Oath," *NPR,* October 26, 2020, https://www.npr.org/2020/10/26 /927640619/senate-confirms-amy-coney-barrett-to-the-supreme-court

109.   Paul Krawzak, "Parliamentarian Guidance Deals Blow to Reconciliation Strategy," *Roll Call,* June 2, 2021, https://www.rollcall.com/2021/06/02/democrats -reconciliation-strategy-dealt-blow-senate-parliamentarian/

110. Jonathan Weisman, "Manchin Vows to Block Democratic Voting Rights Bill and Preserve Filibuster." *The New York Times,* June 6, 2021, https://www.nytimes.com/2021/06/06/us/politics/joe-manchin-op-ed.html

111. Lauren Fox, "Limits of a Democratic Majority Highlighted as Key Votes Hang in the Balance," *CNN,* May 26, 2021, https://www.cnn.com/2021/05/26/politics/congress-negotiations-key-votes/index.html?utm_source=facebook&utm_medium=news_tab&utm_content=algorithm

112. Earlier research indicated that for these purposes, voters tend to regard a president whose predecessor either died or resigned from office as a continuation of the first president's administration. Therefore these data are organized by term of administration rather than term of president. See Abramson, Aldrich, and Rohde, *Change and Continuity in the 1980 Elections*, rev. ed., 252–253.

113. Edward R. Tufte, "Determinants of the Outcomes of Midterm Congressional Elections," *American Political Science Review* 69 (September 1975): 812–826; and Tufte, *Political Control of the Economy* (Princeton, NJ: Princeton University Press, 1978); and Jacobson and Kernell, *Strategy and Choice in Congressional Elections,* 2nd ed.

114. The Jacobson-Kernell hypothesis was challenged by Richard Born in "Strategic Politicians and Unresponsive Voters," *American Political Science Review* 80 (June 1986): 599–612. Born argued that economic and approval data at the time of the election were more closely related to outcomes than were parallel data from earlier in the year. Jacobson, however, offered renewed support for the hypothesis in an analysis of both district-level and aggregate data. See Gary C. Jacobson, "Strategic Politicians and the Dynamics of House Elections, 1946–86," *American Political Science Review* 83 (September 1989): 773–793.

115. Alan Abramowitz, Albert D. Cover, and Helmut Norpoth, "The President's Party in Midterm Elections: Going from Bad to Worse," *American Journal of Political Science* 30 (August 1986): 562–576.

116. Bruce Oppenheimer, James Stimson, and Richard Waterman, "Interpreting U.S. Congressional Elections: The Exposure Thesis," *Legislative Studies Quarterly* 11 (May 1986): 228.

117. https://news.gallup.com/poll/329384/presidential-approval-ratings-joe-biden.aspx

118. Mike Schneider, "Winners and Losers from First Release of 2020 Census Data," *AP*, April 26, 2021, https://apnews.com/article/electoral-college-census-2020-government-and-politics-politics-86e1a31aeeea02004a3c71abd58097ee

119. The six states are: Alaska, Delaware, North Dakota, South Dakota, Vermont, and Wyoming.

120. See https://ballotpedia.org/Redistricting_commissions

121. Grace Segers, "John Lewis Voting Rights Bill Faces Bleak Future in the Senate after McConnell Deems it 'Unnecessary,'" *CBS News*, June 10, 2021, https://www.cbsnews.com/news/john-lewis-voting-righs-bill-senate/

122. Ally Mutnick and Melanie Zanona, "Inside Republicans' Plans for a House Takeover," *Politico,* February 10, 2021, https://www.politico.com/news/2021/02/10/republicans-plan-house-takeover-468237

123. Nathan Gonzales, "2022 House Takeover Lists Should Come with Big Asterisks," *Roll Call*, April 12, 2021, https://www.rollcall.com/2021/04/12/2022 -house-takeover-lists-should-come-with-big-asterisks/

124. https://ballotpedia.org/Special_elections_to_the_117th_United_States _Congress_(2021-2022)

125. Christine Mai-Duc, "Democrats Target 7 Congressional Seats Held by California Republicans for 2018 Midterm Elections," *Los Angeles Times*, January 30, 2017, http://www.latimes.com/politics/essential/la-pol-ca-essential-politics-updates -dccc-sets-sights -on-seven-california-1485806622-htmlstory.html

126. Elise Viebeck, "Here's Where GOP Lawmakers Have Passed New Voting Restrictions Around the Country," *The Washington Post*, June 2, 2021, https://www .washingtonpost.com/politics/2021/06/02/state-voting-restrictions/

127. Ibid.

128. https://ballotpedia.org/United_States_Senate_elections,_2022

129. https://insideelections.com/ratings/senate. Accessed May 15, 2021.

130. https://ballotpedia.org/United_States_Senate_elections,_2022

Chapter 10

1.   As we saw in chapter 5, the 2020 ANES survey results slightly overreported the Democratic share of the presidential vote and underreported the Republican share of the presidential vote for Trump. In contrast, there is a somewhat larger bias in the House vote in favor of the GOP. According to the 2020 ANES survey, the Republicans received 52 percent of the major-party vote, whereas official results show that the Republicans received 49 percent of the actual national vote. To simplify the presentation of the data, we have eliminated from consideration votes for minor-party candidates in all the tables in this chapter. Furthermore, to ensure that our study of choice is meaningful, in all tables except tables 10.1 and 10.2, we include only voters who lived in congressional districts in which both major parties ran candidates.

2.   We will confine our attention in this section to voting for the House because this group of voters is more directly comparable to the presidential electorate. We employ the same definitions for social and demographic categories that were used in chapters 4 and 5.

3.   See Larry M. Bartels, "Partisanship and Voting Behavior, 1952-1996," *American Journal of Political Science* 44 (January 2000): 35–50; and Bartels, "Failure to Converge: Presidential Candidates, Core Partisans, and the Missing Middle in American Electoral Politics," *ANNALS of the American Academy of Political and Social Science 667* (2016): 143–165.

4.   ANES respondents are asked, "Generally speaking, do you usually think of yourself as a Republican, a Democrat, an Independent, or what?" Persons who call themselves Republicans are asked, "Would you call yourself a strong Republican or a not very strong Republican?" Those who call themselves Democrats are asked, "Would you call yourself a strong Democrat or a not very strong Democrat?" Those who called

themselves independents, named another party, or who had no preference were asked, "Do you think of yourself as closer to the Republican party or to the Democratic party?"

5. Because we present the percentage of major-party voters who voted Democratic, the defection rate for Democrats is the reported percentage subtracted from 100 percent.

6. Paul R. Abramson, John H. Aldrich, and David W. Rohde, *Change and Continuity in the 1980 Elections*, rev. ed. (Washington, DC: CQ Press, 1983), 213–216.

7. Alan I. Abramowitz, "Choices and Echoes in the 1978 U.S. Senate Elections: A Research Note," *American Journal of Political Science* 25 (February 1981): 112–118; and Abramowitz, "National Issues, Strategic Politicians, and Voting Behavior in the 1980 and 1982 Congressional Elections," *American Journal of Political Science* 28 (November 1984): 710–721.

8. Abramowitz's ideological clarity measures were based on pre-election descriptions of the contests from *Washington Post* and *Congressional Quarterly Weekly Report*.

9. See Michael Ensley, "Candidate Divergence, Ideology, and Vote Choice in U.S. Senate Elections," *American Politics Research* 35 (2007): 103–122.

10. Robert S. Erikson and Gerald C. Wright, "Voters, Candidates, and Issues in Congressional Elections," in *Congress Reconsidered*, 3d ed., ed. Lawrence C. Dodd and Bruce I. Oppenheimer (Washington, DC: CQ Press, 1985), 91–116.

11. Erikson and Wright, "Voters, Candidates and Issues in Congressional Elections," in *Congress Reconsidered*, 6th ed., ed. Dodd and Oppenheimer (Washington, DC: CQ Press, 1993), 148–150.

12. Erikson and. Wright, "Voters, Candidates and Issues in Congressional Elections," in *Congress Reconsidered*, 8th ed., ed. Dodd and Oppenheimer (Washington, DC: CQ Press, 2005), 93–95. See also Stephen Ansolabehere, James M. Snyder, Jr., and Charles Stewart III, "Candidate Positioning in U.S. House Elections," *American Journal of Political Science* 45 (January 2001): 136–159.

13. Albert D. Cover, "One Good Term Deserves Another: The Advantage of Incumbency in Congressional Elections," *American Journal of Political Science* 21 (August 1977): 523–541. Cover includes in his analysis not only strong and weak partisans but also independents with partisan leanings.

14. Recall that because we present the percentage of major-party voters who voted Democratic, the defection rate for Democrats is the reported percentage subtracted from 100 percent. Among Republicans the percentage reported in the table is the defection rate. By definition, independents cannot defect.

15. It should be noted that the 2020 ANES survey may contain biases that inflate the percentage who report voting for House incumbents. For a discussion of this problem in earlier years, see Robert B. Eubank and David John Gow, "The Pro-Incumbent Bias in the 1978 and 1980 Election Studies," *American Journal of Political Science* 27 (February 1983): 122–139; and David John Gow and Robert B. Eubank, "The Pro-Incumbent Bias in the 1982 Election Study," *American Journal of Political Science* 28 (February 1984): 224–230.

16. Richard F. Fenno, Jr., "If, As Ralph Nader Says, Congress Is 'The Broken Branch,' How Come We Love Our Congressmen So Much?" in *Congress in Change:*

Evolution and Reform, ed. Norman J. Ornstein (New York: Praeger, 1975), 277–287. This theme is expanded and analyzed in Richard F. Fenno, Jr., *Home Style: House Members in Their Districts* (Boston: Little, Brown, 1978).

17.   This was calculated by summing the percentages in the cells in table 10.4 and dividing by four.

18.   This was calculated by dividing the *N* in the first cell (637) by the sum of the *N*s in the first column (1,103).

19.   To calculate these percentages, we divide the total number of individuals across the three groups of party identifiers (for both incumbent types) that approve and those that disapprove by the total number of respondents for each category.

20.   Abramson, Aldrich, and Rohde, *Change and Continuity in the 1980 Elections*, 220–221.

21.   Opinion on this last point is not unanimous, however. See Richard Born, "Reassessing the Decline of Presidential Coattails: U.S. House Elections from 1952-80," *Journal of Politics* 46 (February 1984): 60–79.

22.   John A. Ferejohn and Randall L. Calvert, "Presidential Coattails in Historical Perspective," *American Journal of Political Science* 28 (February 1984): 127–146.

23.   Calvert and Ferejohn, "Coattail Voting in Recent Presidential Elections," *American Political Science Review* 77 (June 1983): 407–419.

24.   James E. Campbell and Joe A. Sumners, "Presidential Coattails in Senate Elections," *American Political Science Review* 84 (June 1990): 513–524.

25.   Franco Mattei and Joshua Glasgow, "Presidential Coattails, Incumbency Advantage, and Open Seats," *Electoral Studies* 24 (2005): 619–641.

26.   Gary C. Jacobson, "It's Nothing Personal: The Decline of the Incumbency Advantage in U.S. House Elections," *Journal of Politics* (July 2015): 861–873.

Chapter 11

1.   The ANES conducted the first true national election sample with fully randomized sampling in 1948. It included, however, a much more limited set of questions than in 1952, which therefore began the longest running series of national election studies in the world.

2.   Perhaps the biggest constitutional change affecting House and state legislative elections was the substantial redistricting that ensued in the wake of *Baker v. Carr*, 398 U.S. 186 (1962), and other Supreme Court cases that defined "one person, one vote" more clearly. See chapter 9. Note also that the fact of single-member districts is not constitutional, but was created by an act of Congress in 1842.

3.   Senators were chosen by state legislatures until ratification of the Seventeenth Amendment to the Constitution in 1913 (although some states had held a state primary election, called the "Oregon system," to instruct state legislators in who to choose for the Senate).

4.   The Twenty-second Amendment to the Constitution was ratified in 1951 which limited the president to two terms in office. As Franklin Roosevelt was the only president to serve for more than two terms, and as his opponent in 1944, Thomas Dewey, called for this amendment during the campaign, it is ironic that the

first president to be limited by the Constitution to two terms was Republican Dwight Eisenhower, the successor to Dewey in his party.

5.   The Electoral College failed to select a president in 1800 (when Thomas Jefferson and his running mate Aaron Burr tied in the Electoral College) and in 1824 (when the House selected John Quincy Adams over Andrew Jackson and Henry Clay in what Jackson supporters called [likely incorrectly] a "Corrupt Bargain"). In 1876, several slates of electors were disputed and the resolution was decided through actions in both houses of Congress, effectively selecting Rutherford B. Hayes as president over Samuel Tilden. The Electoral College vote was determinative in all other cases.

6.   The information in this paragraph comes from Markus Prior, *Post-Broadcast Democracy: How Media Choice Increases Inequality in Political Involvement and Polarizes Elections* (New York: Cambridge University Press, 2007), 1–2.

7.   *Buckley v. Valeo*, 424 U.S. 1 (1976).

8.   *Citizens United v. Federal Election Commission*, 558 U.S. 310 (2010).

9.   *McCutcheon v. Federal Election Commission*, 572 U.S. 185 (2014).

10.   As we noted earlier, Wallace was the only third-party candidate since 1952 to win electoral votes.

11.   As discussed in chapter 3, the "mechanical" effect is the way that single-member districts lead to the exaggeration of plurality votes and often translate them into majorities, and that exaggeration of the vote for the leading party comes most heavily at the expense of any third parties. The "psychological" effect is the voter reaction to the mechanical effect, such that people are not willing to "waste" their vote on a sure loser and so are likely to choose between only the two leading parties (see chapter 7). Maurice Duverger, *Political Parties: Their Organization and Activity in the Modern State* (New York: Taylor & Francis, 1964) (originally published in French in 1951).

12.   Joseph A. Schlesinger. *Ambition and Politics: Political Careers in the United States* (Chicago, IL: Rand McNally, 1966).

13.   The Vietnam War drove a second wedge in the Democratic Party in the middle to late 1960s.

14.   Boris Shor, and Nolan McCarty, "The Ideological Mapping of American Legislatures." *American Political Science Review* 105 (August 2011): 530–551; Aldrich, John H. and Danielle Thomsen, "Party, Policy, and the Ambition to Run for Higher Office." *Legislative Studies Quarterly* 42, no. 2 (2017): 321–343.

15.   See, for example, Alan I. Abramowitz, *The Disappearing Center: Engaged Citizens, Polarization, and American Democracy* (New Haven, CT: Yale University Press, 2010) in which he argues for public polarization, and Morris P. Fiorina, Samuel J. Abrams, and Jeremy Pope, *Culture War? The Myth of a Polarized America* (New York: Pearson Longman, 2010), who argue the opposite.

16.   See Matthew Levendusky, *The Partisan Sort: How Liberals Became Democrats and Conservatives Became Republicans* (Chicago: University of Chicago Press, 2009).

17.   For a detailed look at the dynamics discussed in this section, see Aldrich, John H. and John D. Griffin. 2018. *Why Parties Matter: Political Competition and Democracy in the American South* (Chicago, IL: University of Chicago Press).

18. For a recent summary, see John H. Aldrich and David W. Rohde, "Consequences of Electoral and Institutional Change: The Evolution of Conditional Party Government in the U.S. House of Representatives," in *New Directions in American Political Parties*, ed. Jeffrey M. Stonecash (New York: Routledge, 2010), 234–250.

Index

abortion issue, 198–99, 374n24

Abramowitz, Alan I., 269, 283–84, 349n86, 391n8

absentee voting, 133; by Dems., 62; states for, 64, 68–69, 105–6, 126, 341n12, 354n38

ACA. *See* Affordable Care Act

Adams, Jerome, 2

Affordable Care Act (ACA), 184, 208–9, 234, 259; candidates and backlash on, 248

age differences, in voting, *110*, 113–14

Aldrich, John H., 35, 329n50

ambition theory, 24–26

American National Election Study (ANES) Time Series Survey, 16–18, 97; COVID-19 and surveys of, 13, 331n66; nationwide surveys by, 38, *39*, 170, 187, 293, 370n19, 372n12, 392n1; overestimates by, 108, 277, *278–79* , 390n1, 391n15; on partisan alignment, 38, 164, *164*, 334n31, 360n84, 390n4; on partisan politics, 38, 334n31; on regional voting, 150; sample sizes and probabilities by, 13–15; on social groups, 108–9, *110–11* , 133–39, *134–35* , 355n39; on voter choices, 191–93, *192*, 373n17,

373n19; voting misrepresentations by, 108, 133, 355n41, 356n42

The American Voter (Campbell, et al), 12, 126

ANES. *See* American National Election Study Time Series Survey

approval ratings: on Biden, *179*, 179–81, *180*, *181*, 270; of candidates, 179, *179*, 372n7; on congressional incumbents, 286; in presidential elections, 51, 220, 225–26; on Trump, 51, 65–66, *179*, 179–81, *180*, *181*, 205, 218, *221*, 221–22

Arizona, 347nn67–68

Asian American voters: Dem. party and, 157, 174; Harris candidacy and, 47, 357n55; as increasing, 108, 112, 132–33, *134*, 136

Axelrod, Robert, 143–44

balance-of-issues measure: partisan alignment with, 199–200, *201*, 202–3, 222, 374n27; among partisan groups, *312–14* ; on voters, 197–98, *198*

Banks, Jeffrey S., 248

Barr, William (Rep. attorney general), 69

About the Authors

John H. Aldrich is Pfizer-Pratt University Professor of Political Science at Duke University. He is author of *Why Parties? A Second Look* (2011) and *Before the Convention* (1980) and coeditor of *Positive Changes in Political Science* (2007), and he has also published numerous articles, chapters, and edited collections. He is past president of the Southern Political Science Association, the Midwest Political Science Association, and the American Political Science Association.

Jamie L. Carson is UGA Athletic Association Professor of Public and International Affairs II in the Department of Political Science at the University of Georgia. His research interests include congressional politics and elections, American political development, and separation of powers. He is coauthor of *Ambition, Competition, and Electoral Reform* (2013), *Electoral Incentives in Congress* (2018), and *The Politics of Congressional Elections* (2020). He has published articles in the *American Political Science Review, American Journal of Political Science, Journal of Politics, Legislative Studies Quarterly*, and other journals.

Brad T. Gomez is associate professor and chair of political science at Florida State University. His research interests focus on voting behavior and public opinion, with a particular interest in how citizens attribute responsibility for sociopolitical events. His published work has appeared in the *American Political Science Review, American Journal of Political Science, Journal of Politics*, and other journals and edited volumes.

Jennifer L. Merolla is professor of political science at the University of California, Riverside. Her research focuses on how the political environment

417

influences public opinion, evaluations of political leaders, and voting behavior. She is coauthor of *Democracy at Risk: How Terrorist Threats Affect the Public* (2009), *Framing Immigrants: News Coverage, Public Opinion and Policy* (2016), and coeditor of *The Hillary Effect: Perspectives on Clinton's Legacy* (2020). Her published work has appeared in the *American Political Science Review*, *Journal of Politics*, *Proceedings of the National Academy of Sciences*, and other journals and edited volumes.